Haunted Liverpool 28

Tom Slemen

The Tom Slemen Press

Copyright © 2017 Tom Slemen

All rights reserved.

ISBN-10: 1977960324
ISBN-13: **978-1977960320**

For

Georgina Ward

CONTENTS

Fire is the Muse	1
Possessed by a Long-dead King	21
Limbo Ward	37
Werewolf Lover	45
Crime and the Supernatural	57
Ghosts that Persecute	96
Zarazznar	116
The Pleasure Dome Mystery	133
Three Strange Books	143
The Haunted Bachelor	170
The Nyctalope	182
Liverpool's Cursed Families	198
Take My Wife	239

The Pink Pillow	259
Devils in the Church	266
Five Sinister Warnings	270
Funnybone	288
The Little Trumpeter	303
Lady Sorrow	312
The Wardrobe Man	317
The Many Wives of Stephen	340
Some Walk by Day	349
The Coat of Narcissus Messinger	371
Slinky's Twin	391
Things Unknown	394
The Man at the Side of the Bed	418
The Minikins Are Coming	427
The Gambier Terrace Terror	435
The Satanic Archbishop of Lark Lane	459

A Vampire in Gateacre	464
Barnaby Bright	470
Timeslips Galore	474

FIRE IS THE MUSE

The Grassendale mansion of thirteen rooms still stands today, and even the most thick-skinned disbelieving sceptic will mention the sinister aura that hangs over the tall and imposing dark sandstone residence. It nestles among a constant gloom afforded by a grove of tall centenarian oaks, and at the time of my visit in September 2007, the filament of a sodium streetlamp with an automatic cadmium-sulphide electric-eye switch was merrily burning away hundreds of watts with an orange glow on a summer's day because of the localised patch of night under those gnarled overhanging trees. A local rumour has persisted locally for decades about something macabre happening at the mansion in the 1930s, but no one knows just *what* took place there. Many researchers – myself included among them – have pored over censuses, scanned miles of microfilmed newspapers and searched online archives to find anything untoward regarding the Grassendale mansion – all to no avail. A woman in her nineties could have told me a decade ago, for she had written to me care of my publishers in the Bluecoat Chambers, but her letter was sadly found too late among the bundles of other letters from readers, and all I could glean from the short letter was that the lady had wanted to tell a shocking story about the mansion. She had lived near to it as a child in Edwardian times and had been left dumb by the traumatic shock she had sustained from seeing something in the cellar of the Gothic mansion. Alas, by the time I had received the old lady's missive, she had passed away from a short illness. This story, however, is another one regarding the minatory mansion in Grassendale, and it begins in the year 1970. In early December of that year, a 21-year-old actress named Anais, a 37-year-old American playwright named Angus, and their eight-month old baby daughter May Belle moved into the Grassendale mansion. Angus wasn't keen on the dwelling, calling it 'a dreary and uninspiring place,' but Anais loved the grand house. She was a Liverpool girl, born in Woolton, and she had met Angus, who hailed from San Francisco, at the Hampstead Theatre Club down in London in 1968. They'd both gone there to see an experimental drama called *Little Boxes* by John Bowen, and after the play, Anais had fallen on top of Angus after getting up from her seat a little too quickly – and through the resulting kinetic introduction, the couple had become entangled in mind and body. The Wooltonian and the San Franciscan were as good as married, but had never legally and ritually tied the knot. Had Angus met Anais in 1965, he would have married her in order to smoothly acquire British citizenship, but after months of wading through red tape he had been granted his citizenship papers in 1966 and had relinquished his US nationality for some reason he refused to discuss with Anais. Angus wanted to be a playwright, but held a job in Liverpool as a librarian. He really had no need to work as he had been left a substantial fortune by his late uncle. Anais had obtained a few bit parts in plays and had an audition for TV commercial coming up, and although she was a pretty decent actress, she found that the acting profession was overcrowded and good parts for females were very hard to come by. The willowy Anais had wheat-coloured hair, gentian blue eyes, and she possessed a perfect nose – according to a plastic surgeon she'd had an affair with three years ago. He had traced a line with his index finger from her nostril to a point about an inch below her earlobe, and had informed a bemused Anais that she had the so-called Perfect Columellar Facial Angle, which was 106 degrees and very aesthetically pleasing. 'I think most producers and directors in the acting profession are more interested in the size of your honkers rather than the honker on your face,' Angus had told his aspiring partner in one of his typical put-downs.

On this gunmetal grey December afternoon, snow was falling beyond the parlour window where Angus was seated at a desk with his arms folded as he gazed at the keys of the Smith Corona Compact 200 typewriter. He inserted a sheet, turned the paten knob, wound the paper round, lifted the paper bail, adjusted and fidgeted with it to get the right alignment of the paper, and then he brought the white enamelled mug with the royal blue rim to his mouth and tilted in some "old thought provoker" – about ten drams of Long John Scotch whisky, and summer burned on his tongue as his eyes thinned with pleasure. Feathery flakes twirled beyond the panes and a dusting of snow was settling on the tops of the front garden wall and the mossy pineapple finials adorning the gateposts, and as the whisky warmth of his throat and chest lingered, Angus thought an open fire was needed in this fridge of a parlour. He turned around in his chair, meaning to look at the spot where the parlour's fire surround had been bricked up, and instead he saw a naked Anais with an annoyed expression standing there. She'd wanted to sneak up on him and curl her hands around his eyes, but he turned away.

'You're going to catch your death of cold,' he told her, and tapped the spacebar of the typewriter.

She didn't reply but he knew she'd be feeling upset and embarrassed. Her behaviour was predictable – there were patterns to her actions, given a certain stimulus. He expected her to storm out the parlour, but she stayed put.

'We need an open fire,' he said, and his words seemed flat and lifeless. He hated himself for feeling so guilty at his indifferent attitude towards her.

'Yes, things have become rather cold of late, haven't they?' Anais replied, and then she turned and her bare feet padded gently out of the room, and he poured some more Long John into his enamel mug. He heard May Belle crying in the bedroom and so he scraped the chair backwards from the desk and left the room, and Anais was cradling the baby, and now the infant had closed her eyes and seemed to be dropping off again.

'Put your clothes on, she'll think its feeding time if she sees those things,' said Angus, and he turned his eyes up from her small breasts and shot an insincere smile at Anais.

'Don't tell me what to do – go and write,' she said, rocking the baby and turning away from him.

He said nothing and left the room, and about ten minutes later, Anais walked into the parlour with tears in her eyes. Now she was wearing a negligee. She hugged him from behind as he sat at his machine, and she rested her head close to his head of unfashionably-short red curly hair and whispered, 'I'm sorry.'

'Ah, it's alright,' he muttered.

'Don't you love me anymore?' she asked, and her voice sounded choked.

'Oh stop fishing for compliments Anais,' he answered, and he wiped away a tear that had fallen from her eye onto the side of his face.

'I'm not fishing for compliments!' she yelled after recoiling from his remark.

'Of course I still love you,' he said, twisting towards her in his chair.

'I don't turn you on any more, do I?' she asked, and he heard her gulp.

He raised his eyebrows and his heavy-lidded eyes regarded her with a glazed look of boredom. 'I'm not one of those insecure arseholes who get the name of their partner tattooed on their arms, because I think love for someone should be action, not talk and skin banners and all that shit. I think you should know I love you.'

'I think there's something going on with that woman you work with,' Anais suddenly said, and the look of sorrow on her face evaporated immediately and she crossed her arms. 'What's her name? Tilly; yeah, that's it - Tilly.'

'Matilda,' said Angus, and he seemed puzzled by the

mention of her name.

'Yeah, but you call her Tilly for short,' Anais said, and she turned away, and then started to pace in a circle in the parlour. 'Tilly the librarian. I bet you've had her in the romance section haven't you?'

'You're like a living parody of yourself, you really are,' said Angus, and he turned his attention back to his typewriter.

'Haven't you, you dirty American swine?' she walked around the desk and stood in front of the window and pointed at his face with a slight grin, but this only irritated him.

'The best place for a cheat to hide is behind a pointed, accusing finger,' he told her, and his nostrils flared and he grabbed the bottle of Long John and muttered profanities as he filled the enamel mug to the brim this time.

'What are you trying to say?' she asked, lowering the finger she'd pointed at him in jest.

He gulped from the mug and then he smirked and shook his head.

'No, come on! Why am I a cheat?' she asked, then leaned over the desk, and her dark-blue eyes were wild and bulging.

'You – what's the word you use here? You *thespians* - you never stop acting; you're all lost! The curtains never come down – ever! Your lives are like a play inside of a play!'

She pounded her little fist on the three-page outline of an abandoned play. 'This is not acting, you self-righteous failed hack! This is real! This is really me being hurt because you have just said that I'm a cheat!'

'I'm sorry! It's writer's block!' he roared, and his

outburst made Anais jump. 'I get ratty when I get writer's block.'

May Belle started crying in the bedroom.

'Failure's block, more like!' Anais bawled, and ran out of the parlour.

On the following morning a fresh crisp blanket of snow had settled on Grassendale, and yet the shelter of the oaks had protected most of the mansion's front garden from the wintry fall. At 7.10am, Anais kissed Angus at the doorstep, and then, carrying little May Belle in a cocoon of blankets, she left for the lime-green Opel Kadett thrumming in the road beyond the gate. Judy honked the horn, ready to take her best friend and the baby down to London in this treacherous weather to the audition for the TV soap-powder commercial. Angus hadn't wanted Anais to take their baby but Anais had insisted.

Anais rang him from the film studio at Teddington that evening at 7pm and told Angus she was staying in the capital overnight. He thought he detected something in her voice – something indefinable which had cried infidelity – and she seemed in such a hurry to get off the phone, he had to ask her if she'd landed the role.

'Oh yes, sorry,' Anais replied, and sounded out of breath, 'they said I was a natural for the part. It's all so very corny. I play a housewife on the brink of a nervous breakdown because her children keep coming home covered in mud, but I'm reborn after a man in a white suit calls and gives me a box of biological powder.'

'Where are you staying?' Angus asked, and listened carefully to the cadence of her voice.

'At the house of Judy's friend, Max; he lives in Shepherd's Bush,' Anais said, and it all sounded so honest, yet something at the back of the San Franciscan's mind told him she was not telling the truth, and he paused for a moment to process his almost subliminal suspicion.

'Oh,' he uttered.

'So, see you tomorrow, Angus,' she said, and hung up.

She returned three days later, and there was something quite odd on the roof rack of Judy's car – a fireplace. When Angus opened the door, he glared at his wife standing there with May Belle in her arms. She stared into his eyes sheepishly with a painful-looking smile. She had guilt written all over her face, and he came straight out with it.

'You didn't call me for three days – how could you, Anais?'

She walked past him into the warmth of the house. 'The snow was too bad, love, and I didn't want to risk coming home in weather like that with May Belle.'

'Bullshit – you stayed with someone – the director I bet!' bellowed Angus, and he saw Judy starting to untie the ropes securing the fire surround to the roof rack of her car, and she beckoned him, but he ignored her and went after Anais. 'And what really makes it all even shittier is that you had our daughter with you!'

'You need to piss off back home and see that shrink of yours, Angus,' Anais said, going into the lounge. She rested a smiling May Belle in her bundle of blankets on the sofa.

Anais took off her snow-flecked coat and threw it over an armchair. 'Judy was there with me all the time, and she'll vouch for me – not that I have to explain myself to you!'

Angus grabbed her with both hands on her shoulders and turned her in a very rough manner to face him. 'It's common decency to call your husband – even a common-law husband – when he's worrying himself sick over you!'

'Get off me!' she gasped, 'You're hurting me!'

May Belle started to cry.

Judy entered the room. 'Calm down, Angus!' she shouted at the American. 'Anais was with me all the time – she hasn't been seeing anyone.'

Angus let go of Anais and she went to the baby and held her and kissed her till she stopped crying.

'You're being paranoid mate,' Judy told Angus, and she smiled and with great calm in her voice she explained: 'The snow's really bad down in London, and I was not taking any chances driving with Anais and the baby through snowdrifts, so blame me.'

'But you couldn't telephone? It stinks to me, Judy,' said Angus, and he went to the window and looked out at the ivory December street.

Judy came behind him and patted his back. 'My friend's not on the phone, and the nearest telephone box was streets away. We should have called – I agree it was a daft thing to do, us not calling you.'

'Always remember something, Judy,' said Anais, rocking the baby as she sat on the mustard leather sofa, 'you are under no obligation to explain yourself to any man.'

Judy smiled and said to Angus, 'Come and see what Anais got you for Christmas,' and she gave a sidelong nod towards the door and walked out the room into the hallway. 'Come on!'

Angus followed her with an annoyed expression. He went outside and saw the metal fire surround tied to the roof of the Opel Kadett. 'What is it?' he asked.

'Anais went out of her way to get this for you,' Judy told him, unwinding some of the ropes that bound the fireplace to the rack.

'That's cast iron,' said Angus, feeling the metal mantelpiece, 'where did she get it from.'

'She saw it in a shop in London, and I think she paid about fifty quid for it;' said Judy, 'let's get it unloaded, it's denting the roof.'

They carried it inside and Angus half-heartedly thanked Anais for the unusual Christmas gift but she ignored him and looked at May Belle, who was making a babbling sound. Angus dragged the heavy fireplace to the chimney breast and positioned it where the parlour's original fireplace had been bricked up in the past. He telephoned around until he found a fireplace restoration expert from Garston named James Weybridge, and when Angus asked him for a quote, Weybridge said he'd have to come to the house first to see what needed to be done. Weybridge inspected the bricked up fireplace and immediately said it was just a matter of removing the bricks, checking the chimney, and fitting the vintage cast iron fireplace – and that would cost £150.

Angus gave the renovator a tempting incentive: 'If you can do the job before Christmas, Mr Weybridge, I'll give you two ton.'

By Christmas Eve the new fireplace was installed, and Weybridge had even cleaned the chimney. Then the obsession with the fire began. A hundredweight of coal was purchased from the local coal merchant, and bundles of wood were bought from a chandler's shop on Aigburth Road, and Anais noticed that Angus hardly got any writing done because he continually sat in an armchair pulled close to the open fire and was always feeding papers into the flames. He even threw his old books into the fire; Bertolt Brecht's *The Caucasian Chalk Circle*, Arthur Miller's *Death of a Salesman*, Eugene O'Neill's *The Iceman Cometh*...

'Angus! Stop it!' Anais startled him one night as he tore the pages of *Hamlet* apart and crumpled and placed them on the coals. He was sitting there in his underpants and a string vest with chilblains on his legs and a flushed face. He turned to face her and she saw an odd vacant hollowness in his watery eyes after she had recalled his wandering mind from the hypnotic incandescence in the grate.

'Alright, alight! I'm coming to bed now!' he protested at her touching his forearm and her gentle pull – which meant she wanted him in bed.

'Why are you burning all these good books?' she asked, and seemed genuinely sad. 'The Nazi Party didn't burn as many as you.'

'Not funny, Anais,' he turned back to the flames and he threw the spine of *Hamlet* into the fire and watched it flare up and crackle because of the bookbinding glue. 'I'm getting rid of these books because I want my plays to be original – not influenced and contaminated by these pricks.'

'Shakespeare's not a prick, you firebug Philistine,' Anais told him and tutted. 'You've got corned-beef legs, love,' she observed, and stroked his shins with her small soft white hands, but he knocked her hands away.

On Christmas Day Angus and Anais had a traditional Christmas dinner and even pulled crackers and watched the *Morecambe and Wise Show*. They enjoyed a bottle of sherry and went to bed together for once, but at 4am, Anais awoke, turned in the bed, and found an empty space. She went downstairs, and in the hallway she could see the golden light from the fire producing a flickering illuminated line at the bottom of the lounge door, and she could hear the soft rumbling of fire consuming paper. She opened the door inches and peeped into the lounge. She could not believe her eyes.

'What are you doing?' she asked, and he did not even react.

He was kneeling naked on the hearthrug and he was putting her sanitary towels in the fire. The light in the lounge was out and the only illumination was from the flames of that new open fire.

'Angus, what do you think you're doing?' Anais switched on the light, walked over to her partner and grabbed the two towels that were remaining from his hand, and he made a grabbing motion for them but she backed away with them to the open door. His crazy behaviour was scaring her. He stood up, turned to her, and said, 'I'm sorry. Help me Anais.'

He seemed dizzy, and he staggered as he tried to walk towards her, and then his eyes rolled upwards and he fell onto the sofa.

She went to him and crouched to look at his face. It looked blotchy and red, and his eyeballs were pink. 'Angus, I think you've been working too hard,' she said, as she started to cry. 'I think you're close to a nervous breakdown my love; we'll have to get the doctor out to have a look at you.'

On Boxing Day, Anais begged the family physician Doctor Barron to come out to have a look at Angus, and he reluctantly paid a visit and diagnosed overwork as the cause of the pyromania exhibited by the aspiring playwright. He produced a small brown glass bottle of sedatives and gave them to Anais. In a stern voice, he told Angus: 'You must spend more time with your wife and take interest in your baby daughter – and above all you must keep well away from that fire. You have central heating installed in this house and have no need for an open fire. Do you understand?'

Angus nodded.

Doctor Barron continued: 'Whenever you feel an urge to burn things, you must be aware of your urge and question it, and you must take a sedative to dampen the compulsion.'

Anais escorted the physician to the car, and when she was sure Angus was out of earshot, she asked the family doctor why her common law husband was fixated with burning things. Dr Barron told her: 'I don't want to get all Freudian, but Angus fits the classic pyromaniac model; they are often males, and they derive intense sexual pleasure from watching fires they've started, and even get aroused by the blue flashing lights of the fire engines when they set fire to buildings. It usually starts off like this – an uncontrollable urge to burn things of value, and some have even been known to burn small pets – never their own pets though.'

'Oh my God,' Anais gasped, 'it's serious then?'

'I'm not a psychiatrist, Anais,' said Doctor Barron,

fastening his seat belt. He closed the door of his car, wound down the side window and gave a faint smile. 'Hopefully he won't give in to his compulsion to burn things, but if things do worsen, you *will* have to bring in a psychiatrist.'

Anais went back into the house, and she saw Angus sitting on the sofa, looking at his hands in his lap. He seemed to be deep in thought. This wasn't the bright witty man she knew. She looked up at the picture of Mary and the infant Jesus on the December picture of the calendar, and started to cry. She thought of May Belle – would she lose her father to mental illness?

She sat down next to Angus and put her arm around him, then placed her cheek against his and whispered, 'I love you.' She gently ran her index finger down his nose and said, 'You've got May Belle's nose.'

He smiled.

'May Belle loves you too, Angus, and you're going to be fine.'

'They used to throttle babies and give them to Moloch,' he suddenly said.

Anais went cold in the pit of her stomach when she heard this weird and callous comment. 'What?' she said, and slowly pulled away from him.

'Moloch told me,' said Angus, still gazing at his hands in his lap. 'Moloch said "Break free of your chains of morality and become like me!" That's what he said. If I do things for him, my writing will succeed.'

'Who's Moloch?' Anais asked, and stood up.

'An old god,' Angus replied, and he swivelled his eyes up to her face, and they were glistening.

'Angus, I'm going to make you a nice cup of coffee,

and then I want you to take a sedative. Dr Barron said it'll calm you down,' said Anais.

He nodded and looked at his hands again.

Anais went into the kitchen, fighting back tears, and she made the coffee strong, the way he always had it, and she sat with him, and gave him the sedative, which he took, and half an hour later he started to yawn. He talked about his writing, and seemed to return to normal, and Anais was so grateful.

The couple went to bed, and he tried to make love to her, but fell asleep beside her, and she hugged him.

She awoke at five in the morning and found the bed empty. She rose on one elbow and looked at the baby's cot.

May Belle was not there.

Panic electrified her nervous system, and she threw back the duvet and lunged out of the bed. She opened the bedroom door and almost fell as she descended those stairs with her heart kicking hard in her bare bosom. She sprinted across the hall, and saw that same golden line of light from the fire at the bottom of the lounge door. She barged into the lounge and there was Angus, kneeling naked, putting May Belle on the incandescent coals of the fire!

Anais ran to the fire and saw that the persimmon-orange coals were smoking through the blankets the baby was swathed in, and the flames were now licking around the head of May Belle and singeing her golden wispy curls.

Anais lifted the baby off the fire, and as she did she heard a deep groan from the fireplace. She turned and ran out of the lounge with her screaming baby and took her to the kitchen. May Belle was placed on the aluminium draining board and the light was switched on. Anais removed the baby's clothes and examined her back and she was relieved to see that she had sustained no burns. She cupped her hand under a steam of lukewarm water from the tap and poured it over the little child's head, and May Belle's eyes widened with surprise, and then she smiled, and that smile had such a reassuring effect on Anais, but then Angus came into the kitchen, and his arms were reaching out like a sleepwalker – and those arms were reaching for May Belle.

Anais ran across the kitchen, picked up a heavy maple wood rolling pin and she swung it hard, striking the head of Angus. He fell down onto his knees and groaned, and she hit him again, and he fell sideways onto the chequered black and yellow tiles of the kitchen floor. Anais picked up her baby and stepped over him to get to the door. She headed for the stairs, intending to dress before making her escape from her deranged partner, but she heard a loud groan from the lounge, and it was as loud as a foghorn, yet it sounded as if a person was making this unearthly sound. The door of the lounge was ajar, and she tiptoed over to the doorway and peeped in. What she saw would haunt her for the rest of her life. The fireplace was a living thing – with a mouth of fire and glowing coal, and above the mouth was the protuberance in metal of a nose, and a foot below the mantelpiece was a pair of evil-looking eyes which glowed with an uncanny white light. Those eyes were fixed upon Anais and her baby, and the fireplace mouth opened wide as the entity cried out some unintelligible word, spitting embers and red-hot lumps of coal onto the hearthrug. Anais lifted her baby over her right shoulder and closed the lounge door. She ran upstairs, put on a bathrobe and slippers, wrapped May Belle up in a blanket and a woollen shawl, and then she ran to the house of a neighbour she did not even know, and she hammered on the door until someone answered.

Angus was taken to a mental hospital, and it took almost six months for him to recover. Anais moved in with Judy, and later went to live in London with May Belle. I researched the case and discovered that the fireplace in question – which has long since been lost – had not been bought by Anais in some London shop at all that December in 1970. Anais had slept with a certain television producer – and he had repaid her by giving her the role of the housewife in that soap powder advert. The producer had lived at a prestigious town house on Upper Wimpole Street, London. The town house had been undergoing renovation at the time of the fling with the producer, and the old fireplace, which dated back to Victorian times, had been ripped out. Anais asked the producer if she could have it, and he said it was hers if she could get it to Liverpool. It so happens that the fireplace once belonged to a Colonel Robert Cook, and this man was once accused of burning a baby. The newspaper report covering this accusation is to be found in the pages of *The Times* for 31 July, 1883. The article states that on the Sunday evening of 29 July, 1883, at around 10.30pm, Colonel Robert Cook of Upper Wimpole Street, Cavendish Square, was standing on his doorstep smoking his pipe when a 50-year-old woman named Harriet Arthur, a dressmaker by trade, appeared on the scene and accused Colonel Cook of being a 'monster' who had forced her to burn a newborn baby. 'They will transport you when I tell them what you made me do, you bastard!' Harriet cried, and Cook warned her that, unless she left him alone, he would have her arrested. The dressmaker continued to make her disturbing accusations, and when a constable came down Upper Wimpole Street, Harriet Arthur called him over and asked him: 'You see that fine-looking gentleman standing there?' And she pointed at the anxious-looking Colonel, who was standing beneath the pillared portico of his white-painted mansion.

'Is this woman bothering you, sir?' asked PC Fidler 224D.

Before Cook could answer, Harriet Arthur became very emotional and she said to the policeman: 'This reprobate here made me burn a newborn baby girl! Yes, him there! He's no gentleman! I worked for his sister at a house in St John's Wood. He made me burn a baby girl in his fire, and he said I'd be killed if I didn't do it!'

'Constable, I have never set yes on this woman before in my life!' Cook countered.

'Look, move along madam, or I'll run you in,' said PC Fidler, and he placed his hand on Harriet Arthur's shoulder and shoved her.

'Get your hands off me!' The dressmaker slapped his hand away.

'Now then,' the constable was saying when Harriet talked over him.

'I can prove I worked for his sister!' she cried, 'Ask her if you want, and I can even show you the house in St John's Wood!'

'Move along – I won't warn you!' said PC Fidler, and

he noticed the curtains in the upmarket houses of Cavendish Square twitching.

'She broke my windows last week!' Colonel Cook suddenly remarked.

'I thought you said you hadn't set eyes on me before!' Harriet Arthur yelled at Cook, and laughed. She revealed more details about the alleged baby-burning: 'It was in January 1881 constable, he got three big strapping men to pick me up at King's Cross Road, and I tried to escape, but they took me back to his sister's house, and they forced me to burn the little newborn baby girl. They worship the Devil!'

'That's enough, I am arresting you for disorderly conduct and annoying this gentleman!' PC Fidler announced and he took the woman into custody. A detective then investigated Harriet Arthur's apparently far-fetched claims out of curiosity – and discovered that she had indeed been employed by Colonel Cook's sister at a well-to-do house in St John's Wood, but some person or persons unknown stepped in and hampered any further investigations, and the detective was moved to another metropolitan division. Harriet Arthur was bound over to keep the peace and was warned that she'd have to pay five pounds or go to jail if she went anywhere near Colonel Cook again. That same address in Cavendish Square comes up many times in rumours of all sorts of Satanic goings-on and orgies over the years, and that was the very house Anais had taken the Victorian cast-iron fireplace from. Angus himself mentioned "Moloch" and even said the entity had talked to him about breaking free of "moral chains". Moloch was an ancient god mentioned many times in the Old Testament. There is one piece of chilling scripture concerning Moloch that comes to mind; in Leviticus 18:21, it is written: *And thou shalt not let any of thy seed pass through the fires of Moloch. Neither shalt thou profane the name of thy God. I am the Lord.*

In an academic paper recently published by Dr Josephine Quinn of Oxford University's Faculty of Classics in the highly-respected archaeological journal *Antiquity* (Volume 87), Quinn presents convincing proof of human sacrifices to a deity at Carthage in ancient times. She says that children were sacrificed to a deity at Topheth in Jerusalem, whereas the 20th century historians had claimed that the cremated remains of hundreds of children were nothing but the remnants of a crematorium. It has been claimed for centuries that children and babies were 'put through the fire' – cruelly burned to death in specially-constructed metal and stone statues in the likeness of Moloch – who is often depicted as a man with a bull's head. Fires were lit in the statues and babies – sometimes groups of up to twenty of them – were places in the outstretched arms of the idol and jets of flame which issued from the breast of the statue slowly roasted them. In return for burning the babies, Moloch was said to award wisdom, success in all endeavours, and wealth. There are some people – usually branded as 'conspiracy nuts' by the media – who maintain that sacrifices are still being made to Moloch today...

POSSESSED BY A
LONG-DEAD KING

The following strange story took place in Liverpool in 1969. I've changed a few details for legal reasons.

Florist Edmund Canterbury had a comb-over, was five stone overweight, and had virtually no confidence when it came to talking to women, and he was in love with Rowena, the wife of his younger brother Trevor – a much-respected barrister. Bachelor Edmund had told his one good friend Hugh Stafford about his crush, and had been strongly advised to find a *single* girl.

'No other girl will do, Hugh,' Edmund told his confidant, 'and I think that if I can make the right moves in a Machiavellian sort of way, I can actually have her.' Edmund then likened the machinations leading to the acquisition of Rowena to the chess moves of those grandmasters Byrne and Fischer in that electric 1956 tournament in New York.

'Works in chess but not in real life, Edmund,' Hugh told his 26-year-old fantasy-prone friend, adding, 'and you're just an average chess-player Ed, not Mossley Hill's answer to Moriarty.'

'Trust you to throw cold water on my plans,'

Edmund sighed in a descending tone.

'That's what friends are for,' said Hugh with a tight-lipped smile, 'and I'm sure you'd bring me around to reality if I was harbouring some airy-fairy notions.'

Hugh had been a friend of Edmund Canterbury since they were in diapers, and they had attended the same schools and university, and when, at the age of 16, Hugh had informed Edmund that he was a homosexual (a big deal in 1960, when homosexuality was – believe it or not – a criminal offence) his friend told Hugh his secret would always be safe with him. Long before civil partnerships became a reality, Hugh met a slightly older man named Jacob, and he fell madly in love with him. Jacob talked Hugh into a secret marriage, and the clandestine matrimonial ceremony was actually conducted at a certain church in London in the dead of night, with Hugh and his partner being married by a young open-minded priest. Instead of wearing physical wedding bands, Hugh and Jacob had a 'ring of thorns' tattooed on the third fingers of their left hands – the thorns symbolising the torment of a love hidden away, but a permanent love and a rock-steady marriage all the same. Edmund Canterbury had been the best man at the cloak-and-dagger wedding that night, as a thick jade fog enveloped the metropolis. One drunken guest even managed to ring the bells of the church as the union of Hugh and Jacob was solemnized. Alas, life can be very cruel sometimes, and it's even worse when death is untimely, for in 1967, in the very week homosexual acts between consenting adults were decriminalised, Jacob died in his sleep from natural causes. He was only in his late twenties, and Hugh never found anyone like him again. People often asked Hugh what the strange tattoo on his wedding finger signified, and he would just say he'd had it done in memory of someone he had dearly loved - and lost. And now, Hugh was a highly-paid executive, due for promotion at any time, but unfortunately his boss, Gus Krindler, was an utter homophobe who held views about homosexuals that belonged back in the Victorian era, and some of the claims of Gus were rather outré to say the least, like his persistent claim that some of the most prominent members of Liverpool society were secret homosexuals who attended "Drag Balls" where they all dressed up as women, and what's more, the women who attended these balls were said to dress and act as men. Hugh was certain that if Gus discovered he was homosexual he'd sack him immediately, and so when his boss kept asking Hugh when he was going to marry and settle down, Hugh went along with the charade and would always say he was still searching for Miss Right. Edmund had told his friend to tell 'Ghastly Gus' the truth and be damned – but Hugh really did want that promotion and believed Gus – who was seventy years of age – was ready to fall off his perch soon anyway.

So, back to that Saturday afternoon in November 1969; Edmund was moping around, thinking constantly of Rowena, when he decided he and Hugh should drive to town and do a spot of shopping. Hugh wasn't keen on the idea, as he despised crowds, and he knew the shopping thoroughfares would be teeming with people at the weekend, but he also knew how much Edmund enjoyed a trawl through the second-hand stores and antique shops, so he reluctantly went along with the idea. The two friends got into his Edmund's Austin Westminster and drove from Mossley Hill to a little parking space unknown to most people down near Bold Place, and from there the two young men walked to Renshaw Street.

'Will you look at that, Hugh?' Edmund bent forward in front of the Georgian style bow window of Oculus Antiques Ltd on a corner of Renshaw Street and a dark cobbled alleyway. Edmund's small eyes ran over an unusual chess set. The chessmen were made of some red and black resin and they were all highly detailed statues.

Hugh yawned, and scanned the motley collection of quaint furniture in the window. These items were rather grandiosely described by ornate tags which stated things like: "Genuine Hepplewhite Secretaire Bookcase, circa 1785 - £25" and "Sheraton Parlour Chair (sat on by Rosamund Clifford, mistress of King George III) £50".

Hugh was a devil at teasing people, and out the corner of his left eye he could see the shop's proprietor, Mr Proops, a thin-faced man with a high forehead – a dead ringer for the actor Peter Cushing – as he stood peeping out the entrance of the premises, puffing on his pipe as he eyed the two prospective customers.

'Oh look at that, Edmund!' Hugh exalted, and pointed at the furniture in the window. 'A Grecian couch! By the stars! I have always wanted a Grecian couch! Oh Edmund, imagine that Grecian couch in your actual abode!'

Edmund stifled a chuckle, knowing that his friend was cruelly winding up old Proops, who suddenly told

Hugh: 'We have another Grecian couch – a Regency one too, it is, in the back, if you'd like to have a look.'

'Really?' replied Hugh, 'Splendid, but I am not sure whether I want a Grecian couch or that 16th century milking stool.'

'Stop it, Hugh!' Edmund whispered out the side of his mouth, and then he beckoned Proops with a curl of his chubby forefinger and asked: 'What are those chessmen made of? They're very unusual.'

'Oh, those?' Proops thinned his eyes at the chess set. 'I am reliably informed that they are made of a type of resin that's no longer manufactured. It has an amusing aroma very reminiscent of old Mansion Polish. They were found in the attic of a house in Corwen, in Wales. They have something of a supernatural reputation, according to the lady who sold them to us, but she didn't really expound her reasons for stating this.'

'A haunted chess set?' asked a bemused Hugh. 'I've heard of everything now. Do they move around by themselves and play against one another in the middle of the night?'

Proops returned an annoyed grimace at Hugh and told him rather haughtily: 'I'm only stating something which was related to me, sir, and I neither believe nor disbelieve in things of the supernatural sphere.'

'How much are they?' Edmund Canterbury asked, placing his cupped hand between the side of his right eye and the window pane. 'I can't see the price tag.'

Proops gave a little cough, then told him the asking price. 'Seven pounds, sir, including the brass-bordered ebony and ivory chess board. Duncan Mackintosh, the local chess champion, was looking at the item yesterday.'

'I'll take it,' said Edmund with a smile.

'Oh, splendid sir,' said Proops, and he gave a little bow and held the stem of his pipe aloft. 'Come on in, and do mind the step.' Proops then asked Hugh: 'And are you still interested in the Grecian couch, sir?'

'I think I'll sleep on it – er, not literally - I mean I'll think about it first, sorry,' a japing Hugh told him as Edmund pushed past him to get to the counter.

'That dagger accompanied this lot,' said Proops, tapping his index finger on the glass case on the counter. It contained a 9-inch-long black-handled dagger with two blood-red garnet stones set at each end of the archaic weapon's crossguard. 'An expert is of the opinion that the dagger dates back to Tudor times.'

'I might come back for that,' said Edmund, 'how much are you asking for it?'

'Three pounds – very reasonable for a Tudor dagger,' answered Proops, and he went to the window to collect the chessmen and their board.

The two men then left the antiques shop and went to enjoy some afternoon tea and cakes at a Bold Street café.

Edmund collected chessmen and various chessboards, and often journeyed down to London to buy old 18th and 19th century chess sets from Baumkotter Antiques on the Portobello Road, but he had never seen anything like the set he'd purchased from the Renshaw Street second-hand shop. The detail in the 5-inch-tall pieces was breathtaking, and the red queen actually bore a strong resemblance to Rowena – the sister-in-law he sorely longed for. Edmund was not imagining this peculiar likeness in the queen, for it was

Hugh who had first drawn his attention to the charming coincidence.

Something strange happened that evening as Edmund set the pieces up on the chessboard. The eyes in the face of the red king actually became animated – they moved. Edmund thought he was seeing things because of strained vision at first and so he placed his face in his hands and squeezed his eyes shut. He took a slow deep breath, removed his hands, opened his eyes, and took a closer look at the king. The eyes of the long-haired and bearded red king widened into a mad stare and seemed to bulge as they looked at Edmund, and the florist felt something powerful invade his mind. Somehow he sensed that the force infiltrating his mind was ancient – and violent - and it pushed at every corner of his brain until it possessed him. He got up from his chair in a panic, and his knee knocked the table, knocking over all the chessmen. He staggered to the window and saw that the moon, which was hanging over the chimney pots of Mossley Hill, was blood red. He was steadily losing his identity. It was like a dream in which the dreamer is someone else, living some other life – but why was this happening? Edmund's heart pounded in his chest, and he clutched the heavy plum-coloured curtains and almost pulled them off their pole. He looked down at his clothes – his green woollen jersey and the grey trousers and black brogues, and he grunted. He believed that his attire was not fit for that of a king. Why am I dressed like a commoner? He wondered, alarmed at being out of his kingly robes. 'What hast becometh of me?' he growled, and then vague splintered recollections told him that his soul had somehow been trapped within that chess piece by Merlin himself. His lackeys and advisers and plotters had also been encased for all time as bishops, rooks, knights and pawns! But what of my beloved Queen Rowena? She had been spared of this cruel sorcerous imprisonment! Edmund's soft cushy voice had been replaced by a harsh scalpel of a voice which ranted: 'Curse thee Merlin! Thy witchery has thrown me out of my kingdom down to this! To this!' He tore at the drab plebeian clothes and cried.

The transformation – the possession – was now complete; Edmund Canterbury's personality had been discarded, and now "King Vortigern" – some unknown monarch of yore – had taken over the body of the affable overweight florist. Edmund was still there, somewhere in the back of the brain that had once been his, and he felt like a paralysed backseat passenger watching a maniac at the wheel of a car.

The released spirit of the king chess piece went to a mirror and found himself addressing his reflection with strange words. 'Thou art King Vortigern the Warlord, and Rowena is thy queen.'

To outsiders who were not aware of the unearthly possession, Edmund seemed to have become a devious, scheming and paranoiac man who talked in a bizarre put-on voice in a lingo that bordered on nonsense. Most who knew the florist believed he had suffered a nervous breakdown – and Edmund's brother, Trevor and friend Hugh Stafford were very concerned.

'Why are you talking like this, Edmund?' Hugh asked his friend, hearing the bizarre jargon, which struck him as ribald, coarse, and even pornographic. Sometimes it sounded medieval, with touches of back slang, Welsh, and a smattering of the Shakespearean. 'You are upsetting everybody, Edmund, calling them all sorts of nasty names – what the devil has gotten into you?' Hugh looked at the tattered clothes his friend wore, torn by his own hands.

'Silence, you pie jaw!' Edmund bawled, shaking his fist at Hugh, 'You address a king here you word grubber!

'A king?' Hugh shook his head with a morose look, fearing for his friend's sanity.

'Clotpole! Edmund – or was it Vortigern – snarled.

Hugh became very upset seeing his friend acting like this. 'Edmund, I think you've had a nervous breakdown, probably because of your emotional state regarding Rowena.'

There was a pause, and then, for just a moment, Edmund – the friend Hugh knew so well – seemed to return, and this manifestation occurred in the eyes, and then in a slight smile, and the voice softened. 'Hugh, help me,' he said.

'That's more like it – welcome back,' Hugh held out welcoming arms.

Edmund slapped his hands away and Vortigern returned with a vengeance and his eyes rolled up into his forehead as he snapped: 'Get thee behind me, Edmund Canterbury!'

However, from that moment on, after what seemed like an attempt by Edmund to take control back from this ancient entity, Vortigern spoke more like a modern-day man, and was easier to understand, but unfortunately what he said next was *chillingly* understood by poor Hugh.

'You will do as I say from now on, Stafford, or I will

let slip your dark, dark secret! Yes! *That* secret, and I will lay that secret bare before Gus Krindler!'

'I don't care,' Hugh told him, stepping back in shock. He felt as if his world was about to be tipped over.

'Very well, I shall!' Vortigern went over to the green telephone, picked up the handset, and placed it against his ear, but he held it upside down so that the mouth piece was pressed against his ear and the earpiece was at his lips. His eyes thinned and his face took on a most sinister aspect with a crooked grin. With barely contained excitement he told Hugh: 'I will summon Gus, for I am privy to the number of the man,' and he tapped his forehead with his finger and said, 'what Edmund holds in his brain is in my knowledge also.'

Hugh began to perspire. 'I'm sick of hiding in the shadows; tell him what you want!'

King Vortigern smiled as he placed his fingertip in the hole of the rotary dial and quoted the number he was calling – Gus Krindler's number: 'Seven! Nought! Nine!'

Hugh looked on in horror.

'Five! Three!' Vortigern continued.

'No! Stop! Stop!' Hugh cried out.

King Vortigern continued to dial the number.

'No! Edmund, don't! Please don't!'

Vortigern's eyes widened and an almost childlike smile broke out on his bearded face as he heard a faint voice come from the earpiece, which was of course, placed against his mouth because of his technical incompetence.

'Gus Krindler,' said the tinny-sounding voice.

Vortigern gave a deep chuckle at what seemed like

some magical manifestation to him.

'Who is this? Hello?' Gus Krindler asked, then hung up.

The devious blackmailer from a bygone era stopped smiling and put the telephone down. He told Hugh that if he did not do as he was commanded, his secret would be given out to all and sundry. Hugh was instructed to go to that antiques shop where the chess set had been purchased, and he was to buy that dagger there, for it had belonged to Vortigern. The dagger was duly bought and brought to Vortigern, and then Hugh tried to get his old friend back by telling Vortigern he didn't belong in this era. The returned ruler was furious, and he lifted the dagger above his head, ready to bring its blade down into Hugh, but started to shake and foam at the mouth. He lowered the weapon, calmed down and said: 'There is only one thing on my mind now, Stafford, and that is to take Rowena for my wife. I do desire my Queen Rowena.'

'She's married, and to your brother too,' Hugh reminded the egotistical throwback.

'All is fair in love and war,' Vortigern opined through gritted teeth.

'She'll never leave Trevor for you – ' Hugh began to tell him but Vortigern lifted that dagger above his head again and cried: 'Silence! That is not a marriage they have! That is heresy! Rowena was put upon this earth for one man only – and that man is me!'

Hugh thought it would be wise to go along with his plans for now until he could talk to a doctor – or perhaps even a priest - about his friend's dangerous mental state.

'You will call Trevor on this device,' Vortigern

pointed at the telephone, 'and you will invite him and Rowena to dinner. Do it now at once!'

'What are you planning to do?' asked a worried Hugh Stafford.

'Summon them at once,' Vortigern prodded the green telephone with the tip of his dagger, and then sidled up to Hugh, and brought his lips close to his left ear and intoned, 'He that tells a secret, is another's servant, and you, Stafford told me your most darkest secret.'

Hugh swore and then he went to the telephone and he felt so confused. His mind was fogged by the strange unearthly predicament and he just felt that perhaps he could somehow warn Trevor after he arrived for dinner - *if* he decided to come at all. He telephoned Trevor Canterbury and told him that he and his wife were invited to a special dinner Edmund was having tonight over something or other. Trevor seemed very surprised at the invitation, and initially said he couldn't make it, but Hugh heard Rowena advising him to go in the background. 'Er, yes, it appears I can make it tonight, but at what time?'

'At eight,' said Hugh, close to tears, and he put the telephone down.

Nothing at all was prepared for the dinner that evening – nothing was cooked at all, and when Trevor and Rowena arrived, they saw that Edmund still looked dreadful with his long hair and that awful thick beard. Trevor asked his brother how he was feeling, and Vortigern didn't seem to hear the question, for he seemed in awe of Rowena. Realising Trevor had said something to him, Vortigern merely pointed to the decanter of red wine, and then he took hold of

Rowena's pale hand and kissed her knuckles.

'You really do need to sort your wardrobe out Edmund,' Trevor quipped, looking at the grubby and mismatched clothes of his brother.

Vortigern watched with wide eyes as Trevor poured the decanter into a glass. He was a selfish man, and instead of decanting into the glass set out for Rowena, he poured for himself – and Vortigern knew he'd do this.

'No! Don't drink it!' Hugh suddenly cried out, and he rushed forward, intending to seize the glass from Trevor, but the latter pulled the glass from his reaching hand and joked: 'Oh my liver can take it!'

Hugh slapped the glass out of his hand, and it smashed in the fireplace.

'What the devil – '

Edmund pulled out a dagger and shouted at a startled Trevor: 'God damn your blood and liver! I shall put you in an eternity box!' He threw the dagger at Trevor, and it glanced off his upper left chest – where his rather thick wallet lay in his inside jacket pocket. The dagger's blade embedded itself in the floor.

As Rowena screamed, Trevor tried to seize Edmund's hand and the brothers rolled about, onto the table, and then onto the floor. Hugh hit Edmund over the head with a wine bottle, but it had no effect on him, and now his possessed friend was throttling Trevor. Hugh went to the fireplace and grabbed the poker hanging from the andirons stand, and he brought it down on the back of Edmund's head, knocking him clean out.

'Oh! I've killed him, I've killed him!' Hugh cried,

kneeling beside Edmund, who was now slumped face down in a rug.

Trevor rolled his brother over and ascertained that he was thankfully still alive. 'Telephone an ambulance Hugh, quickly!'

Hugh dialled 999 and only told them that a friend had been accidentally concussed, and immediately the operator despatched an ambulance to the Mossley Hill address. Hugh then turned around, and he saw something which filled him with dread: Rowena was looking at that old chess set. Despite the attack on her husband and the presence of her unconscious brother-in-law on the floor, Rowena held the red queen, and was remarking upon its likeness to her. Hugh snatched it from her, for he realised now that the chessmen had been the sole cause of this whole nightmare. He threw the pieces in the fireplace and then he brought a bottle containing spirit of turpentine from the cupboard under the sink and he emptied the entire contents over the accursed pieces scattered on the grey ashes and burnt-out coal lumps. He set the chessmen alight, and the ball of ignited gas flew up and singed his eyebrows. The chessmen flared up into strange reddish flames as their faces melted into unnatural, weird contorted visages. The dagger which Vortigern was so endeared to was thrown in the bin outside by Hugh.

When Edmund regained consciousness he seemed to be his old self, and could not believe he had long hair and a beard, and he recalled virtually nothing about "Vortigern" for a while, but the memories of the awful possession returned days later. Rowena was flattered at being the object of Edmund's infatuation, and fate took a twist a year later when she divorced Trevor after he admitted having an affair with his secretary, and finding Edmund to be a loving and romantic man, she ended up marrying him after a year of courting. Hugh Stafford was the best man at the wedding.

Possession is a reality, and there is a large body of literature on this disturbing phenomenon dating back to Bible. Positive possession is when say, a person is possessed by the Holy Ghost, which some Christians regard as a very valuable experience, but there is also demonic possession, and there are many accounts in the New Testament of Jesus casting unclean spirits out of people. But could a spirit or demon be contained by a chess piece? I do not know with any certainty, but there have been cases of people being possessed by ancient artifacts unearthed during archaeological digs. I have a feeling that the thing which took over the mind of Edmund Canterbury was perhaps a "mindkin" – a term invented by the philosopher C. D. Broad to describe a sort of shell of the mind left behind after the death of a person. A mindkin – along with all of the traces of a person's memory and personality – may become absorbed by a physical object; a car, or a piece of furniture say – or even a chess piece. This is, admittedly, just a vague attempt at explaining the possession of Edmund. The King Vortigern – which the entity claimed to be – was a real historical personage. When the last Roman ship left our shores around AD 410, there was an outbreak of chaos across the land as every petty chieftain tried to become the leader of tiny localised kingdoms. This squabbling and in-fighting went on for forty years until a ruler named Vortigern decided to take control by importing soldiers to help him defeat some troublesome northern tribes. Boatloads of these soldiers landed in England. They were Jutes, Angles, Saxons, Franks and Frisians – and they never went home again. King Vortigern had unwittingly triggered the Anglo-Saxon invasion, and as a result, the real native Britons – the Celts, were driven into the outskirts of the British Isles. Vortigern's second wife, by the way, was named Rowena...

LIMBO WARD

He awoke in the hospital bed and felt as if he was being watched. He sat up and looked around him at the small brightly-lit ward of about twelve beds – and all of them except his own were empty but immaculately made. There were three long windows to his left, but they were of frosted glass and white daylight was diffused through their panes. He was a little dizzy getting out the bed and finding his legs weak, he grabbed the crutches lying across the blue padded armchair. Derek Wild found himself in a small ward in some hospital, and not a soul seemed to be about. He quickly learned to use the crutches and went out into the long corridor. 'Hello?' he yelled, stationary now. No answer came. 'Nurse!' he shouted and stumbled against the corridor wall as he coughed. 'Where is everybody?' He hollered, and his voice echoed back. He checked the men's toilets – no one there. He tried the nurse's station, and found no one there either. He rested a crutch against a counter and picked up a telephone and there was not even an active line purring from its earpiece – just silence. He went in search of an exit, but there were no ways out of the hospital, just swinging grass-green doors to other wards, all empty.

Feeling a little self-conscious, even in the absence of people, he told himself: 'My name is Derek Wild,' and he felt the fog of amnesia lifting. He voiced another unfolding recollection: 'I recently came out of prison.' He remembered it all now. He was skilful at picking locks, and had been caught on a job and sent down for eighteen months as a result. He had fallen ill in the Manchester prison – so how did he end up here? The place looked like the Royal Infirmary on Pembroke Place in his hometown of Liverpool, but he could see nothing through those windows, just that steady white light, as if a luminous fog had smothered the streets outside, and stranger still there was no sound of traffic out there.

To the ground-glass window pane he muttered: 'I may have to smash you in as a last resort if I can't find a way out.' He tapped the pane with his knuckles, and it seemed awfully thick – too thick for any normal window.

Derek heard a low rumbling noise, and to his ears it sounded just like a gas boiler igniting into life. He returned to the room he'd awakened in, and saw fish and chips and peas on a plate on a shelf. There was a glass of sarsaparilla next to the plate, and a knife and fork lying on a folded paper napkin. The food was hot. Someone was playing games with him. 'Oh thanks for that, I'm famished,' he said, and although the inexplicable appearance of the meal and drink made him quite nervous, he was very hungry, and quickly ate the fish and chips and gulped down the soft drink. He replaced the cleared plate and empty glass on the shelf where they had appeared, and then he nervously arranged the knife and fork on the plate at a twenty minutes past four position, an idiosyncrasy of his. He went back out into the corridor, and looked at the walls. The bottom half of the wall was green and other half was cream coloured. Upon the wall there were no signs, pictures or even a fire extinguisher – just an electric clock about nine feet up, and it displayed the time – three minutes past three. If the light - however artificial it looked – coming through those frosted windows was anything to go by, then it was surely 3.03pm.

'What day is it?' he asked himself, testing his memory with a slow mental calculation. 'It must be - let me see - Saturday, 25th March, 1961,' he whispered. He sniffed the air – that disinfectant smell that was commonplace in hospitals was not present here. Like a bug captured by a kid continually trying to find its way out of a jar, Derek kept looking for an exit. He began to feel a bit claustrophobic as he went into an empty storeroom and finally realised that this place simply didn't have a way in or out. 'How did I get in here if there's no way in?' he asked in a voice that sounded as if he was about to cry. He felt strong enough to walk unaided now, and threw away the crutches. He went back to the clock and saw the time was now 3.50pm. He gave a type of ultimatum to whoever was keeping him prisoner in this hospital, and he turned slowly as he issued it, shouting at the walls and even the ceiling. 'Look, I think you've taken this joke a bit too far! Now I've got a sense of humour too, but this is now beyond a joke. If you don't show yourselves, I swear I will destroy this place. I have a violent streak and you know I'm also a convicted criminal, so please don't underestimate me! If you don't show yourselves I'll burn this place down! If you don't believe me just try me!'

He heard a faint click come from the ward where he had first awakened to this nightmare, and he gingerly crept in there, regretting he had ditched the crutches because one of them would have made a useful weapon.

The plate and drinking glass were gone from that shelf – and yet no one had passed him to take them. Were they invisible? He wondered – or was there some secret hatch door in the wall that shelf was attached to? He rapped the second joint of his index finger on the wall above the shelf and plainly ascertained that there was some hollowness there.

'What's the game eh?' Derek addressed the wall he was examining. 'I know you're there!'

He had an urge to go to the toilet, and left the ward. His eyes scanned the walls and ceiling of the corridor on the way to the toilet, checking for the lenses of closed-circuit television cameras, but saw none. After he had been to the toilet he washed his hands when he suddenly saw what he thought were ghosts, reflected in the mirror, standing behind him. The semi-transparent figures were in white with weird hoods. These were no ghosts, he realised – they were hidden observers looking through that one-way mirror over the wash basin. He tapped his fingertips on the mirror and said, 'Hello! I can see you in there!'

The figures seemed to fade away, as if the hidden room they were in behind the mirror had been plunged into darkness.

He thought about going to get one of his crutches to ram through that trick mirror, but now he was a little afraid. Those suits looked like the type of thing astronauts wore, or workers at an atomic power station. This was looking serious and very scary now to Derek Wild. He walked out of the toilet and strolled about for what seemed like miles down empty corridors, until he came to a huge metal door. That ominous rumbling sound he'd heard earlier was emanating from behind that door. 'I can open you, I'm the best lock-picker in the city,' he murmured to the door. Maybe this was the way out; that would explain why it was so reinforced. Derek found a chair, and he placed it under that electric clock. He stood on the chair, ripped the electric clock from the wall, severing its thin black and red wires, and then he smashed it on the floor. He used its metal fingers as picklock rods, and went to work on that heavy door. Within a few minutes he heard the tell-tale click, and then he opened the door. It looked heavy and yet it was well balanced and its hinges were lubricated, so a single finger was able to swing it open.

He muttered the f-word when he saw the second door behind it with a glass window that was some four inches thick. Through that window he saw a grey oblong block, and on the top surface of this block there was the outline of a body – a mere shadow. All around the room were roaring jets of flame, coming out of the floor and the walls. This room was some huge incinerator, and by the looks of it, someone had recently been burnt to dust.

It hit him in an instant after the finding of this cremation room. He had some contagious disease, and this was an isolation ward, and if he didn't recover they'd incinerate him. That had to be the answer. He must have contracted something very contagious and deadly.

Derek ran off down the corridor, knowing now that he must find a way out. He was so afraid, he could hardly breathe. They came out of a doorway which slid open in the wall of the corridor, just twelve feet ahead of him. They had on their white spacesuits and before he could turn and run in the other direction, they sprayed him with what looked like white fire extinguishers – but the canisters they brandished obviously contained knockout gas aerosols. Derek lost his balance as he inhaled the sweet-smelling gas. He fell to his knees, and then slumped to the floor, and he thought the entire building had tipped over before he lost consciousness. When he awoke in a hospital in Liverpool he had a beard. They said he'd been in a coma for a month, but Derek knew otherwise. The specialist looked at him and Derek got the impression that he was waiting for his patient to mention the deserted unidentified ward and the men in the white decontamination suits, but Derek had a sharp criminal mind and was a step ahead of the specialist. He said nothing.

'You had appendicitis and some abreaction to the anaesthetic,' said the medical man. 'You went into a coma. Did you have any strange dreams?'

'No,' Derek told him, 'I can't remember a thing.'

Derek has pondered on just what had happened to him after he had fallen ill at the prison back in 1960, and even underwent hypnotic regression – which resulted in him recalling the strange detainment at the unknown hospital in great detail. A friend of Derek's said he might have been abducted by aliens, but Derek doubts this. I think Derek Wild picked up one of the so-called Doomsday Viruses that are suspected to be knocking about. There are many viruses which pose a global threat to humanity, and one in particular which keeps rearing its ugly head is the H1N1 flu virus – a living remnant of the virus that killed around 100-500 million people in a pandemic between January 1918 and December 1920. Today, we know this Biblical pandemic by a name it should never have been given – Spanish Flu. The flu was wrongfully associated with Spain by propagandists. World War One was still going on as the flu decimated the globe, and wartime censors on both sides, fearing the news of millions of deaths from the flu in their own countries would be demoralising, chose to report only on the Spanish cases of the pandemic – as Spain was neutral. The origins of the global influenza outbreak were never determined (although the first confirmed case took place at the US Army's Fort Riley in Kansas), but it was found in almost every country, and even in the Arctic. Unlike the usual influenza which attacked children and the elderly, the 1918-1920 flu mostly killed people between the ages of 20 and 40. After almost a third of the world had died from the "Spanish" Flu, the virus went into retreat – but it has not gone away completely, and there are versions of it still knocking about today in various forms of Avian Influenza – Bird Flu. Besides influenza, some other strange viruses are also in circulation throughout our world, from the human immunodeficiency virus, commonly known as HIV (which was first noted in the Congo in the 1920s) to the Zika virus (first isolated as early as 1947 in a rhesus macaque monkey in

Uganda's Zika Valley). Then there are the mutations – viruses that suddenly change their structure, making it notoriously difficult for virologists to anticipate an outbreak. These mutations could occur in the middle of New York City or London, and by the time they are identified their host is either dead or in a highly contagious condition. Containment squads are rumoured to exist in most cities in the West; these are supposedly military-operated front-line teams that whisk a person infected with some highly-dangerous virus to a secret isolation unit – where the person is either cured with a vaccine, or succumbs to the virus and is ultimately cremated to prevent the virus from spreading. This might have been the case with Derek Wild, only he might have been the lucky one who survived from the infection, with his body making antibodies that could be used as a vaccine.

Had he come down with some deadly version of H1N1 virus? Or had he been deliberately infected with some manmade virus and used as a guinea pig? Unless the truth emerges one day on WikiLeaks we'll probably never know.

WEREWOLF LOVER

I've changed a few names and minor details in this strange story, which touches on the hoary old subject of lycanthropy – the alleged ability of some humans to change into an animal, namely a werewolf.

In the late 1960s, an 18-year-old Huyton girl named Stella Winters began to develop a strange psychic ability; when she looked at a person, she would sometimes see a ghostly image of that person's true nature standing behind them. It all started one evening as Stella took her dog Sandy on a walk through Jubilee Park, just a few minutes from her home on Rupert Road. The time was almost 10pm, and being summer, it was still quite light as Stella encountered a middle-aged man she only knew as Mr Jones, a rather quiet and reserved individual who lived next door but one to Stella and her family. As Mr Jones approached, Stella thought someone was walking closely behind him, as she could distinctly see a man of an identical height and build to her neighbour just to the right of him. Jones slowed down when he saw Stella, smiled, and nodded, but then the stranger behind him also slowed down, and as Stella said, 'Good evening Mr Jones,' she saw something eerie and disturbing; the figure behind Mr Jones was his very double – only he had a most sinister, leering face, and he was staring at Stella over the right shoulder of Mr Jones. The immediate impression Stella had of this creepy lookalike of Mr Jones was that of a man who had a sexual craving he could not control; in other words, a potential rapist.

'Evening Stella,' Jones said in reply to the teenager's greeting, but he noticed that Stella seemed to be looking at someone or something behind him, and so he turned, to see what she was looking at, but he evidently saw no one else in the park.

Stella gasped as the sleazy version of Mr Jones suddenly faded away. She walked on, past Jones, and he asked her if she was alright, but the teen didn't answer, and she curtailed the usual mile walk with Sandy and went home, a little shaken by the weird incident. Stella mentioned what had happened to her mother, and was told in reply that there are no such things as ghosts. 'It's been his shadow, Stella,' Mrs Winters assured her daughter. 'It's a bit misty out there and you've probably seen a car's headlights casting a shadow of Mr Jones behind him.'

'Mum, that's rubbish,' Stella told her, shaking her head, 'it was *not* a shadow! It was a man who was the spitting image of Mr Jones only he looked really seedy, like some dirty old man.'

'Then you're seeing things Stella,' her mother told her, annoyed at her daughter's nonsensical assertion. 'You'll have to go and see the quack if this goes on.'

About a week after this, an unsettling rumour went around about Mr Jones constantly following a beautiful woman who lived in the area, and there were also claims that the quiet Mr Jones was something of a Peeping Tom who had been seen looking through binoculars into the bedrooms of several women. Stella was convinced that the apparition she had seen behind

Mr Jones in Jubilee Park was some sort of symbolic image of his true self: a sex maniac. This theory was vindicated a few days later when Stella once again witnessed the uncanny manifestation of another double – this time of a young man named Graham who was serving in the local newsagents. Stella clearly saw Graham's doppelgänger standing behind him, only it was dressed in a beret and military uniform. After a few moments the ethereal double faded. Stella was curious about the phantom replica, and so she asked Graham if he had ever thought of going in the Army. He was mentally adding up the total to the items Stella had bought when the question threw him. He looked at Stella, puzzled, then asked: 'Me? The Army? Well yes, why do you ask?'

'Oh, you just strike me as a military type,' Stella told him, thinking on her feet, 'and you walk pretty straight-backed like my Uncle David – he was in the Royal Engineers.'

'Well, it's funny you should ask,' Graham replied, 'because I tried to join but they wouldn't have me; I have a heart condition see; it's not serious but they won't have me because of it. It's a shame really because my father and grandfather had careers in the Army.

'I'm sorry about that,' Stella told him, reaching for her purse.

'I suppose they've got to be careful – I mean you've got to be A1 to be a soldier and that, but – well – ' he said, and seemed to abandon what he was going to say; his voice trailed off into silence, and then he whispered the prices of Stella's purchased items.

Stella was naturally worried; why had she started to

see these projected personifications of the inner nature of people? Was something happening in her brain? She told her mother about the latest ghostly double and Mrs Winters persuaded her daughter to go and see the family doctor. Stella, worrying that she might be going mad, visited the doctor's surgery and made an appointment to see him. The doctor decided that Stella was experiencing some form of hallucination and decided to refer her to a psychiatrist named Richard Quaylian. Minutes after Stella Winters met Dr Quaylian, she witnessed a strange form slowly coalesce behind him as he stood there. A jumble of amorphous grey shapes came together to create a terrifying being that looked half man, half animal. She was not expecting this at all, and Quaylian, noticing his patient was looking at something behind him, asked Stella what she could see. 'A werewolf!' she gasped, and found she was unable to get the rest of her words out. What she was seeing did not make any sense at all. She got up out of her chair, ready to flee, yet somehow fascinated by the lupine vision.

The psychiatrist seemed to recoil in shock when the girl gave her reply to his question. His eyebrows lifted, his eyes widened and his mouth opened, forming a small 'o' – Stella had obviously said something which struck a major chord in the mind of the psychiatrist. 'A werewolf?' he asked, and then gave a weak smile and blushed, and to the teen it was strange seeing a man in his fifties do that.

The human-animal hybrid was quite tall, because Quaylian was a six-footer and this thing towered at least a foot over him. As Stella was about to turn and run out of the room, the werewolf vanished into thin air. This was the first time she'd seen the alter ego of a person in the form of something resembling an animal, and she wondered what the significance of the werewolf was; surely that beast was not lurking somewhere in the persona of this mild-mannered psychiatrist?

'Please sit down,' said Dr Quaylian, and Stella slowly sat in the chair on the other side of the mahogany desk and took furtive glances at the space behind the doctor, who now sat down himself. 'So, you saw a werewolf Stella,' said Quaylian, 'that's very interesting. They call that zoopsia – hallucinations that take the form of animals.'

'They're not hallucinations,' Stella told him sternly, angling her head down and casting a burning stare from under her strong eyebrows. 'They are images of what a person really is – the true nature of a person – the stuff they try to hide.'

Quaylian produced an uneasy smile. 'Oh, so you're the judge of what people are really like? And these – images - as you call them, vindicate your judgement.'

'You're twisting what I'm saying Mr Quaylian, and you're going to have me committed because you and your psychology can't explain my ability.' Stella wiped a tear from her eye.

'Stella, I'm going to try a little hypnotism next time I see you, and let me assure you, no one will be getting committed to some old Victorian asylum,' Quaylian told her, and then he did something quite unprofessional. He came around the desk, took hold of her hand, and kissed her knuckles. 'Now, Stella, I'll see you here in three days. You have nothing whatsoever to worry about. I know you're not insane.

We'll try and get to the bottom of these visions you're having.'

Stella found something vaguely attractive about the psychiatrist, even though he was old enough to be her father – and what's more, she had noticed his wedding band, so he was also married. Quaylian had, just by talking to her, smoothly allayed Stella's fears. He had lifted her depression, and made her feel like a woman - not a teenager – when he had kissed her hand. Stella had only had two boyfriends in her life so far – both of them around her age, and she was still a virgin.

On the second visit to the psychiatrist, Stella noticed that Quaylian was wearing the same cologne her Uncle Gareth wore – Eau Sauvage by Christian Dior. It was a manly scent, and Stella quickly felt as if the psychiatrist intended to seduce her, which made her very nervous, even though she did find him quirkily attractive. She looked at the space behind him and saw nothing this time, but she quickly averted her gaze just in case that thing appeared again.

'Before we start, would you like some coffee or tea, or even some lemonade to calm you down, Stella?' Dr Quaylian asked, and he beamed a disarming smile at her.

Stella sat there, very stiff, and she briskly shook her head. 'No, no thanks. What are you going to do?'

'We're going on a desert island, just you and I,' Quaylian answered in a soft, seductive voice.

'A what?' Stella asked, perplexed by the statement.

'You'll have to lie down on here,' he indicated the long chesterfield sofa with his hand. 'You'll be alright, Stella, you can trust me, come on – I'm qualified,' he said, and he pointed to the diploma on the wall and smiled.

She went to the sofa and sat on it.

'Lay back, please,' Quaylian told her, and she did what he said.

With his deep rich voice, Richard Quaylian painted the relaxing scene in the teenager's mind: she was on a sleepy hot and sunny island, beneath a blue sky and waving palms, and as the psychiatrist narrated this fantasy, Stella heard the gentle rhythmic white-noise sounds of the sea lapping at the golden beach. 'Close your eyes, Stella, the sun is in them, and you can just lie back in the soft hot sand as you listen only to my voice...'

The next thing Stella knew, she was being awakened from the immensely relaxing holiday on the far side of her mind with the snap of Quaylian's fingers. She woke up and felt as if her whole body was burning from exposure to that unrelenting tropical sun, and found that her arms were actually red – a product of the psychosomatic effect of suggestion on the subcutaneous nerves of the skin. The psychiatrist was standing over Stella and he seemed very concerned about something.

'Stella, I have tried the most powerful hypnosis and it would seem that your gift – this ability to see the real inner person as an apparition – cannot be blocked or turned off. This is off the record, but I really do believe you have a psychic talent – and that's something most doctors and psychiatrists – anyone with scientific training – will never tell you, because they do not recognise the psychic sphere.'

Stella put her hand to her temple. Her head pounded, just the way it had once when she fell asleep under the blazing sun in her garden. It felt like sunstroke. 'So I don't have anything wrong with me, then?' She asked, and dragged herself off the chesterfield.

'As far as I can tell, no,' Quaylian turned his back on Stella and then went to sit at his desk.

She stood before him at the desk. 'So what now, then?'

'Stella, you must be wondering what that thing was you saw behind me...' he said, but his voice trailed off and he looked at his watch, but he wasn't checking the time – he was fidgeting, being awkward about something.

'I'm not sure what it means,' Stella told him, 'but I didn't like it, and I felt – well, I felt as if you have another side to you – a sort of animal side. I don't know what to make of it.'

'Stella, I have never told anyone this, not even my wife, but I'm going to tell you, and because I know you're a loving and thoughtful person, I am sure you will not tell anyone my secret if I ask you not to.'

'Secret?' Stella wasn't sure she wanted to hear just what this secret was.

'Do you promise me you won't tell a living soul about my secret?' he asked, and his eyes seemed so sad.

'Do you really have to tell me?' Stella asked.

'I feel I have to, somehow,' Quaylian confessed, and he looked uncertain, and became fidgety again. He looked away, as if he was scared to look the teen in the eye.

'Why?' Stella asked, 'Why me?'

'Stella, I suppose this is – well, I *know* it is – what

they call professional misconduct, but here goes. The first time I saw you – when was that? Three days ago. I was struck by your beauty, and yes, that's very shallow of me, but then I saw that you were lovely underneath all that as well.'

Stella looked stunned. She was speechless.

'And now I find I have feelings for you,' he said, and made eye contact at last. 'You're probably thinking I'm old and have nothing whatsoever that you could be attracted to, but I am telling you this because I have to.'

'You hardly know me; this is nuts,' she said, and tried to smile, but she was so nervous now, her smile was lopsided and she looked embarrassed. She wondered if he was some sex-mad fiend who could hypnotise her into bed.

He became a little incoherent. 'That might be so to you, but – well – anyway, the secret.'

Stella couldn't look him in the eye now, and she just knew he was going to say something ominous.

'I'm a werewolf.' He said this and nothing more for a while, and the ticking of the electric clock on the wall became noticeable.

'I should go,' Stella said, and she turned and walked to the door.

'No! Don't go, please!' Quaylian flew past her and reached the door. He blocked her exit with his broad frame. 'I have to tell someone Stella, and that person is you.'

'What can *I* do about it?' she asked, and she tried to reach for the door handle but his hand seized her hand and stopped her from turning the handle. She pulled her hand out of his large hand and stepped back from him.

'Stella, do you know what it's like, having a double life?' he asked, and now he had tears in his eyes. 'It's one of the clichés of modern times, but you know what? My wife really doesn't understand me, and that's just me being a human – if she knew what else I become she'd run a mile. We have no children. There's no love; it's just a marriage of convenience, and it's wearing very thin.'

'I came here hoping you'd get rid of this curse I have – and instead I meet a – ' she couldn't say the word because it scared her.

'A werewolf,' Quaylian bowed his head, and the tears came flowing down his face. He moved away from the door and walked back to his desk. He slowly lowered himself into his chair. 'You can go Stella, I must have been crazy to think I'd have a chance with you. Forgive me.'

Stella put her hand on the door handle but she could not turn it. She turned back to him. 'How did you become a werewolf?'

'Stella, never mind.' He held one hand to his sobbing face and the other one waved her away. 'I'll be alright. Just don't tell anyone, please.'

'Who'd believe me?' she said, and gave a little painful chuckle. She went to the psychiatrist and took his handkerchief out of his breast pocket, unfolded it, then gently pressed it against his eyes. Once she had wiped the tears, he looked up and gave a sort of crooked smile, as if he was holding back more tears.

'It's okay,' she told him, and then she shook her head and looked at the clock with a far away expression.

'I'll be alright,' he said, and kissed her hand.

She felt an electric jolt of pleasure course through her when he did this.

They began an affair, and one night as they made love in a field near Ormskirk, Quaylian turned into a werewolf. Stella was terrified at the transformation. Her hands felt hair sprout out of his pores and she felt his muscles bulge and then she heard him groan and swear – something he normally never did in front of her. His height and weight increased by the second and at one point she thought he'd crush her, but he got off her, and his metamorphosed face was mostly in shadow because the full moon was behind him in the sky. The transformed Quaylian ran off, but she shouted for him to come back. She stood up, naked, and he came back to her and stood there for a moment. Her heart pounded, because he growled and she thought he might attack her and kill her, but he walked in a circle around her, then went to her and made love to her again.

She continued to see him, and still he would not tell her how he had become a werewolf, and she felt that it was something traumatic in his past that was better left undiscussed. Richard took a drug - lithium carbonate - twice a month, to allegedly minimize the number of times he underwent 'the change' (as he called the metamorphosis).

One evening as Stella waited for her lover to meet her in that secluded field, a youth she knew named Bryan accosted her and asked Stella to go out with him, and she warned him that she had a very jealous and dangerous boyfriend and advised Bryan to leave at once, but the young man laughed and produced a flick knife. Stella could see a frail child-like version of Bryan behind him, and she knew he was a coward at heart, just acting tough. All of a sudden, Stella heard a rustle from the nearby bushes, and out of them flew Quaylian in his werewolf form. He slammed into the lad, knocking him twenty feet across the ground. The winded youth was so afraid, he passed out, and Stella and Quaylian fled into the moonlit evening. The affair continued for years, and when Quaylian's wife died from cancer, he married Stella Winters and it is said that they had many children. I wonder if any of the children inherited some strange abilities from their parents...

CRIME AND THE SUPERNATURAL

In the 1970s there was a two-bit crook – we'll call him Tony – forever in and out of prison for petty larceny. Tony envied a kingpin of crime who often visited the city for various nefarious reasons, and this gangster had a Rolls Royce, a Mercedes-Benz, homes in Spain, Australia and the United States, a stunning partner, and enough money in his Swiss Bank to buy Malta. By the strange force of capricious fate, Tony found himself seated at the same table as this big shot racketeer extraordinaire at a certain top-notch restaurant, and after all of the crooks had discussed business, a fawning Tony asked the virtuoso villain what the secret of his success was.

'I made a pact with the other Big Guy – down there,' was the reply, and the drunken arch-criminal whispered spine-chilling directions on how one goes about entering into a pact with the Devil. Tony hung on to every word and committed it to memory. That night he hardly slept because he was so seduced by the real possibility of the way the Devil could get him into the big time. When he did manage to sleep, Tony had strange dreams where he was walking with a tall man in black in some vast beautifully-kept garden with rainbows of flowers and exotic-looking trees. The stranger in the dream plucked a huge rosy apple from one tree and handed it to Tony. Tony bit into the giant apple and the crunch awakened him. He realised the meaning behind the symbolism of the dream and got out of bed. It was time to ask for *his* help...

Within three weeks there was a new big cheese in the Liverpool underworld. Tony tried his hand at every form of crime with astonishing success, and when a rival gangster arranged to have him beaten up, the wrong man received a hiding. Then came the rise and rise of Tony, and his newfound 'career' brought him respectability; sherries and investment advice with the bowing bank manager, and constant invitations from every prestigious gentleman's club. Three years went by, and Tony confided in a friend that he now had to honour his part of the bargain with 'you-know-who' and a shadowy man in a trilby and long coat began to visit Tony on the night streets of Liverpool whenever he was leaving a pub or a club on his own. This mysterious personage was alleged to be one of the Devil's agents, constantly reminding Tony to pay his dues. Tony's friend urged him to visit a priest and seek sanctuary. Tony got married at this time, and threw a party at a Lime Street pub (possibly The Vines) for his friends. He left the pub to visit his wife at the honeymoon suite in the nearby Adelphi Hotel – and on his way he bumped into that agent of the world's oldest trickster.

'Look, just give me one night, to spend with my wife!' Tony pleaded, but the velvet-voiced shadow replied: 'We have taken her, and we have taken back everything the Master gave you.'

And then that eerie messenger simply vanished.

Tony ran to the Adelphi – and sure enough, to his

complete horror, it transpired that no one there had heard of him or his wife. Tony ran up to the room in a panic, but found no honeymoon suite, just an elderly couple fast asleep in bed in that room. He ran to the pub where he had thrown the party, and none of his friends even knew Tony had been married, and thought he was pulling their legs. Tony looked at the carnation in his lapel and realised that the Devil had taken everything back. The bank manager said he had never set eyes on Tony in his life, and there was certainly no bulging bank account in Tony's name. Tony tried to find his wife for months but it seemed she had never existed, for there wasn't a trace of her anywhere. Tony stayed with a priest for a while, and then, after telling his weird story to anyone who would listen, he vanished into obscurity. Did he manage to obtain salvation or is he now burning in the furnaces of Hell?

This is just one incident where crime and the supernatural have mingled with disastrous results, and the two areas may overlap in many ways; a criminal may be punished by some act of supernatural revenge, or a baffling crime may have some light thrown upon it when a solution is sought via some occult means – the permutations are endless but we shall examine just a couple of these cases concerning offenders, occultists and supernatural schemers within this chapter. Sometimes a supernatural crime is not immediately recognised as being a crime because it is executed in such a subtle way, and a case in point is the following one, which unfolded in the late summer of 1922 in the heart of London's Mayfair district. The mystery was largely shielded from the public, and as far as I know the story surrounding it has never been told before in print. On the sunny Friday morning of July 28, 1922, at 72 Brook Street, Mayfair, Mignon Etrenette, the French maid of Adèle Capell, the American-born Dowager Lady Essex, knocked at the bathroom door of her 63-year-old aristocratic employer, but got no answer. The maid knocked several more times upon the door, and not hearing any movement within the bathroom, she began to worry about the Countess of Essex, and so she threw caution to the wind and defied the unwritten protocol of privacy. The maid gingerly opened the door, and saw that the large ivory bath was full to the brim, but there was no sign of the Countess. The maid inched forward, and there, at the bottom of the bath lay the motionless body of the drowned Lady Essex, turned slightly to her right side, her eyes open, and a startled look upon her pallid face. The noted beauty, renowned for her 'magnolia tinted complexion' was stretched out in that bath as if it was her coffin, and although she was sixty-three years of age, her flawless face and porcelain-skinned body looked as if they belonged to a woman barely out of her thirties. Ironically, Lady Essex had recently posed for the painting *The Lady in White*, executed by Sir Hubert von Herkomer. In those days she had been one of the so-called Lovely Five – a quincunx of famous beauties comprised of Lady Warwick, Lady Sutherland, Lady Lytton and Lady Westmoreland. And now, Adèle, Countess of Essex lay there in the bath like *Hamlet's* Ophelia, her submerged lily-white corpse clad only in a chemise. The French maid stumbled back out of the bathroom in shock, and soon her screams were echoing throughout the luxurious

London residence of the deceased Dowager. Dr Gwynne Lawrence of Green Street, a superior physician who had attended Lady Essex for ten years, was quickly summoned to the opulent town house. He noted that the head of the late Countess was at the wrong end of the bath, and that rigor mortis had set in – so life had been extinct for a considerable time. The bath mat was wet underneath, as though the water from the bath had overflowed and seeped under it, and upon each of the kneecaps of the dead Dowager there was a bruise – as if she had fallen down hard onto her knees before she died in the bath. The inquest was held at the Westminster Coroner's Court by one Ingleby Oddie, and one of the witnesses called at this inquest was Margot Asquith, wife of the former Prime Minister H. H. Asquith (who was at that time the Leader of the Liberal Party). Mrs Asquith told the court that Lady Essex had dined with her at 34 Grosvenor Street – the home of their friends the Becketts – a select address where the Prince of Wales often enjoyed dinner parties which went on into the wee small hours. Mrs Asquith told the court that she'd had dinner with Lady Essex at this address on the eve of her tragic death, and that her friend had been in high spirits and had even discussed future plans as they played Honeymoon Bridge. Mrs Asquith said that the Countess had been free of worries, had looked radiant and in the best of health, had talked continually about her intentions to go to Paris on the following Monday, and also had plans to visit Venice in September. She had also spoken of her longing to spend the winter abroad. However, there was one strange topic which arose in the course of the conversation between the two well-heeled friends, and this was about the strange gloom and melancholia which had infiltrated several of the upper rooms in the house of Lady Essex. The Countess had overheard the servants talking of the cold spots and strange impressions of something ghastly on the third floor of the Brook Street residence, and not long afterwards, Lady Essex experienced the uncanny phenomenon herself. Whenever she entered her bedroom or bathroom, she would be overcome with an intense feeling of misery and dread. This talk of supernatural phenomena was deemed to be superfluous to any valuable testimony on the part of Mrs Asquith, so it was struck from the court stenographer's records. Mrs Asquith herself and many of the more intimate visitors to the home of Lady Essex also talked of the strange wretched atmosphere on the upper floors of the house, and just before the funeral, Archie, a relative of the late Countess got in touch with a certain Reverend Hamilton in Liverpool – a clergyman who was regarded as something of an expert on black magic and the occult. The Reverend Hamilton was asked to bless the upper rooms of 74 Brook Street, but he did not do as Archie requested, for the holy man was of the opinion that the almost suffocating atmosphere of acute melancholy in the bathroom and bedroom was being 'beamed' into the dwelling from somewhere else, possibly streets away, and he set about unpacking some strange paraphernalia from his Gladstone bag. Something resembling a large magnetic military compass was placed on the floor of the bathroom where Lady Essex had been found dead, and the Reverend took out a small notebook and a stubby pencil, and he hummed and muttered to himself as he made repeated glances at the red pointer under the glass dial. That pointer rested on a pivot, and was pointing towards a wall. In the circular metallic band surrounding the pointer, there were lines marked with tiny numerals, and the clergy man turned that band twice. 'Now, I need to access to the bedroom of the late Countess,' he asked, and Hamilton was escorted into the bedroom by Archie and a butler. The curtains in the bedroom had been replaced with white drapes that had been drawn to allow little light into the room. The Reverend Hamilton placed his peculiar "compass" on a dresser in the room and again took some readings which were jotted down in his notebook. He then took a pendulum out of his bag which had a clear crystal as its bob, and Archie and the intrigued butler observed the way the crystal swayed when it was dangled at various points in the room. More notes were taken down, and then the Reverend Hamilton asked Archie if he felt low-spirited in the room. Archie said he did, and the butler was asked the same question, and he also said he had noticed the effect on the landing outside the bedroom and the bathroom, as well as something he could only describe as a 'biting coldness' in his limbs. The butler and other servants had noticed this localised zone of intense gloominess about a week before the death of Lady Essex.

The wise man of the cloth looked at his notes and told Archie: 'There is a beam, and its point of origin is west south west, and from my basic calculations, the beam's point of generation must be no more than a quarter of a mile away. It's passing through the bathroom and this bedroom at a downward angle, which would indicate that it is coming from someone's attic. Now, all I have to do is obtain more readings and plot the beam on a map, and we can hopefully identify the address of the culprit.'

'Let us leave this accursed room,' said Archie, walking to the door, 'I feel downright suicidal in here.'

'Until this matter is thoroughly resolved, I would strongly advise you to keep this room and the bathroom out of bounds,' said the Reverend, putting the pendulum and his compass-like device back in the Gladstone bag. The three men went to the drawing room and the Reverend Hamilton and Archie had a brandy, for they both felt as if they were suffering from a winter chill – even though it was summer outside.

'Why is the beam still exerting its wicked influence?' the Reverend mused, thinning his eyes as he gazed at the prismatic colours of the afternoon sunlight refracting through the crystals of the chandelier. 'It's done its dirty work, so why let it continue to shine its black light on this house?' Twenty minutes later, the man of the cloth and Archie were walking up Brook Street – to the west – to the general direction of the sinister beam's origin. The Reverend Hamilton held that compass in one hand and the little pencil in the other. Archie held a rolled up street map, and every thirty feet or so, Hamilton would nod to his companion and he would quickly unroll the map so the Reverend could mark the approximate direction of the beam. They established that the beam passed through the upper floors of a house on Grosvenor Square, and Archie said he knew the owner of that house well – he was just Horace to Archie, but his official title was the Earl Farquhar – and despite his advanced age (he was 78) and although he had undergone a serious operation several years ago – he had until recently been quite a sprightly and active man – but for the past few weeks he had been plagued with anxiety and had even talked of suicide.

'Very interesting Archie,' said the Reverend, and he halted and made a few more marks upon the map, then looked up and pointed to the treetops of Grosvenor Square Garden. He told Archie: 'The beam travels across here, almost diagonally across the garden to a point beyond that corner – to Upper Grosvenor Street if I am not mistaken.'

They walked around the vast garden and along Upper Grosvenor Street, and here, the Reverend made some six readings in different parts of the street, and then he pointed to a certain grand-looking four-storey house. Archie knew the people who lived next door to the address – the Marquess and Marchioness Camden – but he had no idea who lived at the house the Reverend Hamilton was approaching. 'Look at the drapes,' the clergyman nodded at the ground floor windows. The curtains looked mildewed and the panes were darkened with dust. This drabness lent a forlorn and rather sinister aspect to the house.

'Well, what now, Reverend?' Archie asked, and he and his companion lingered under the pillared portico. The Reverend lifted the heavy brass knocker and slammed it down three times. He and Archie waited – but no one answered. Archie pressed the white button of the electric bell, and he and the Reverend heard the distant jingle of the said bell in the house, but again, no one appeared at the door. Archie backed away from the cover of the porch until his heels were at the kerbstone. He craned back his head and studied the grimy windows – not a flicker of a curtain or any movement whatsoever. When he walked back to the Reverend Hamilton he was shocked to see his friend inserting a strange silvery key into the front door.

'What are you doing, Reverend?' Archie gasped.

'Trying out this – it's a skeleton key – and let's see – ' he slowly but firmly turned the key and a clicking sound from the lock made him smile. 'Yes, that's it.'

Hamilton looked over his right shoulder, then turned to glance left before he pushed the large brown door open. A pile of envelopes lay on the bristly mat in the vestibule area, and a faint aroma of fungus mingled with stale pipe tobacco greeted the nostrils of the two intruders.

'This is housebreaking, Reverend,' Archie told him in a half-hearted protest, but followed him into the large hallway with a chequered floor of maroon and white tiles.

'Close the door, Archie,' the Reverend instructed his companion, and as soon as he closed the front door, Hamilton switched on the hallway light. 'There doesn't seem to be anyone at home.'

'So, this is the house where Mr X lives, and you think that beam is emanating from the attic up there?' Archie's eyes turned to the darkness at the top of the stairs where a bulb was missing. He accompanied the clergyman up four flights of steps until they came to the attic door. They waited there for a moment, and then the Reverend reached into the Gladstone bag and took out a Webley Mark 6 revolver – given to the vicar by his nephew upon his return from the trenches four years ago. It was fully loaded.

Archie's eyes bulged at the sight of the pistol. 'Was it really necessary to bring – '

The Reverend Hamilton quickly placed his index finger to his lips, and then he turned the handle of the attic door, barged in, and thrust out his gun-wielding hand. Both men were hit by a terrible stench – an aroma of decomposing flesh.

There on the floor, face down in a grubby suit, was the corpse of a man with a massive head of hair and a long matted beard.

'Oh Lord!' Archie whipped the handkerchief from his breast pocket and held it over his nose and mouth, while the Reverend walked calmly to the window as he scanned the room. He opened the window and then he saw the occult apparatus in a corner upon a card table. The device was made up of two round shaving mirrors, each on a stand, and between them, was a strange black triangular object, about six inches in height and as thin as card, and in the centre of this black triangle of metal, a greenish gemstone had been mounted. This triangle was mounted on a wooden stand and the entire contraption had been placed in a white circle that had been chalked on the green baize playing surface of the card table. Strange symbols, all Thebean, and all from the so-called "Witch's Alphabet" spelled out arcane words known only to the Reverend, and they were written within the chalked circle. 'Archie, what you are seeing here is – ' the clergyman was saying when he noticed Archie had left the attic and was standing on the landing. The stench was too much for him to endure. As the Reverend spoke he saw his condensed breath billow forth, for the attic was abnormally cold because of the powers being tapped into by the malevolent machine. It was in essence, a type of Evil Eye – only it was exerting a beam of depression in a concentrated form by the alignment of the mirrors – similar to the arrangement of mirrors in a modern laser. Had obsidian mirrors been used, the range of the device would have been trebled. The Reverend dismantled the apparatus and packed it away in his Gladstone bag, and then he picked up the small black leather-bound book on the floor besides the unknown dead man, and he took that.

'Hurry Reverend, please!' Archie urged his friend, and walked to the stairs.

They left the house on Upper Grosvenor Street and returned to 74 Brook Street – and saw that the awful feelings of gloom and dread, along with the unsettling cold spots were no longer present in the upper storey of the house.

About a week after this, the Reverend Hamilton wrote to his friend Archie from Liverpool to say that he had deciphered the text in the notebook that had belonged to the unknown dead man, and it transpired that book had been the diary of an infamous dabbler in the Black Arts who had moved to London five years ago and lived as a recluse at the palatial house. In the diary he had documented the development of his despicable device for making people ill and suicidal, and if the entries in the diary were to be believed, he had killed around one hundred people of all ages and all walks of life with his satanic contraption. He had targeted Lady Essex because of a certain lady he had hired as the sole servant in his house. The young lady -

named Christina - had told the reclusive occultist that Lady Essex had had her "fitted up" for the supposed theft of her jewellery the year before when she had been a maid at the house on Brook Street. Lady Essex had claimed the £6,000 insurance on the jewellery and used Christina as the scapegoat because she was jealous of the maid's youth and beauty. The former maid's story motivated the occultist to kill the Countess with the ray from his malign machine. Archie recalled the alleged jewel theft from the bedroom of Lady Essex in the August of 1921, and the rumours of it all being a cozenage, but the maid was sentenced all the same. Archie's eye later caught a chilling statistic printed within the staid pages of *The Times* newspaper – a small article stated that the year 1922 had been an abnormally high one for suicides in the metropolis, with exactly one hundred cases of self-destruction being reported to the Central London Coroner Walter Schroder. Were those suicides attributable to that sinister hermit of Upper Grosvenor Street? Most advanced occultists know there is a power - invisible to the uninitiated – which can be used for good or bad, and there are ways to channel and focus this power to heal – or destroy. Sometimes when I hear of a spate of inexplicable suicides in the news, I wonder if someone somewhere is using a device similar to the one that was allegedly utilised in London in 1922. However, even the most accomplished occultist is aware of the danger of rebound – when a malevolent spell is cast but sometimes is reflected back onto the Black Magician with fatal results. Perhaps this was the reason the Upper Grosvenor Street occultist was found dead in his attic. A number of years ago, there was an alleged cluster of suicides in Bridgend County Borough, south Wales. The newspapers were soon calling the spate of suicides a 'cult' and the Press and media reports might have even made the situation worse. Most of the people committing suicide were aged between 13 and 17, and perhaps the unusual high concentration of suicides was a mere statistical anomaly, but sometimes I wonder...

From the London of 1922 we now come forward fifty-three years to the spring of London in 1975, and as chance would have it, we remain in the affluent district of Mayfair to pay a visit to Grantham Place, a narrow and secluded street, just a stone's throw from Hyde Park, where the first customer of the morning – a man named Percival Fontaine – is about to have a refresher driving lesson from Liverpool-born Mandy Rogers, a 30-year-old driving instructor with the Lucky Horseshoe School of Motoring – founded by Miss Rogers in 1971. Mandy's driving school charged the cheapest rates in the capital at £1.30 per hour, but for some reason the firm was sinking fast, and now the Lucky Horseshoe had only three cars. Mandy's sleeping partner in the business, her long-suffering boyfriend Simon Davis, believed the colour of the school's cars – piggy pink – as well as their twelve-inch-high silver horseshoe logo on the roof of the vehicles – were rather off-putting to the average potential customer – but Mandy refused to change the colour scheme and the high-profile logo. And so, on this sunny April morning in 1975, Mandy had driven the piggy pink Hillman Minx from the flat she shared with Simon on Abbotsbury Road, Holland Park, to Grantham Place, where Percival was about to emerge from his upmarket residence. This would be the first time Mandy had seen the customer; up to now he'd just been the lively voice on the telephone who had booked the refresher lesson two days ago. She had imagined an older, corpulent man, but this Percival was well over six feet in height, and skinny with it. He had wavy strawberry-blond hair, a pair of small sky-blue eyes and a prominent straight nose. He came out of the entrance of the flats, halted, diligently pushed the slow-closing plate-glass brass-handled door behind him, and then he shot a puzzled smile as he looked at the pink car with its silver horseshoe on the roof. He sauntered over to the kerb, leaned right up to Mandy's face at the driver side window, and in an upper-crust voice he quipped: 'Don't tell me – you must be from the Lucky Horseshoe School of Motoring what?' And then he unleashed a very strange chortling noise from the back of his adam's apple.

Mandy feigned amusement and laughed: 'You've got it in one Mr Fontaine.'

'Oh just call me Percy, please my love,' he said, in a sort of seedy manner very reminiscent of a sleazy Leslie Phillips character. From that moment, Mandy knew she'd have a hard time. He made repeated grasps at her thigh as the car thrummed in the stagnant traffic streams of Piccadilly, and he deliberately brushed his hand against her breasts as he pretended to point to people, vehicles and streets. His driving was obviously adequate, and his confidence on the road was matched by his confidence at continually trying it on with Mandy. 'You know what, Percy? I think you don't need a refresher lesson at all,' Mandy told him, taking control back of the car as they travelled down

Cromwell Road. 'I think you're *very* experienced enough as it is.'

'Mandy, I think I've taken this charade far enough – let me tell you why I really booked you,' Percy suddenly said, turning to face her, and again he put his hand on her lap – and she slapped it away.

'Mr Fontaine!'

'No! Hear me out Mandy! Call me a romantic self-delusional fool who ought to know better, but – I saw you three days ago as you were filling your car at the Bloomsbury Service Station – and well, I know this will sound so clichéd – but – it was a case of love at first sight!'

Lust at first sight, you mean Mandy thought, and she said nothing in reply, but she performed a U-turn on Cromwell Road and headed back to Grantham Place to take the lecherous Percy home.

Percy wouldn't give up. 'Mandy, it's not what you think – I am rich and could have anyone – but there's no one else like you. I had déjà vu when I first saw you at that filling station, as if I'd known you in some previous life.'

'Percy, I'm very flattered at all this, but I've got a boyfriend already and we're very much in love,' she told him, never once taking her eyes off the busy road. The strange thing was that her comment made her realise how distant she and her boyfriend Simon were becoming. She'd gone off sex with him for the past three months and he'd been putting in a lot of overtime at the office of late, and he *did* talk about that 19-year-old Dutch secretary Valerie quite a lot...

'I'm sorry I wasted your time,' Percy bowed his head, closed his eyes and pinched the top of his nose between his finger and thumb. 'I forgot romance is a dirty word today – I – I should know better by now. I'll pay you the booking fee Mandy.'

'Nah, it's alright Mr Fontaine,' Mandy sighed, and she gave a quick sidelong glance and almost smirked at him. But when they got to Grantham Place, Percy insisted on paying the booking fee, but said that he'd left his wallet in the flat. He begged Mandy to come up to his place to get the money, and he assured her he would not be so stupid as to try anything on with her. She reluctantly went up with him to the luxury penthouse apartment on the top floor, and it was every inch the archetypal hopeless-bachelor type of residence, with a real leopard-skin rug over the parquet flooring, one floor-to-ceiling mirrored wall, and the other walls featured a multicoloured wavy psychedelic design which resembled interference on a television screen. There was a chair Mandy found very distasteful, made from a realistic mannequin of a naked woman laying on her back with her legs bent so that each knee pressed into the breasts. The black leather cushion was stuck to the area running from the back of the knees to the mannequin's bottom, and Percy waved his hand in a backwards motion to this 'chair' and said, 'Please take a seat while I mix you an orgasmic drink.'

'I'll just take the booking fee, thankyou,' Mandy told him firmly, and she glanced out the window to the street below. 'I don't want to pick up a ticket. I'm parked – '

'Oh Mandy, please relax!' Percy was already behind the counter of the zebra-striped cocktail cabinet.

Mandy then noticed something glittering in the

corner of the tacky living room. It looked like a large Eccles cake painted gold, and it was in a glass display case of the type you'd see in a jewellers. The spring sunlight was shining obliquely through the window into the glass case, and Mandy was drawn to the scintillating object.

'That's a gold nugget,' came Percy's explanation from the far end of the room, along with the xylophone notes of his glass rod as it mixed the cocktails. 'Pater found that in an Aussie mine in Kalgoorlie yonks ago. He gave it to me as a reminder of the family company's humble beginnings. Pater is the president of the Fontaine Gold Mining Company; which reminds me – the annual general meeting of the company takes place in Johannesburg next month if you fancy coming along as my partner.'

Mandy was oblivious to the invitation; she had her nose a centimetre from the glass case as she studied the hypnotic nugget. 'How much is that worth?'

'Well that weighs in at about five pounds, so it's probably worth something in the region of – let me see two hundred and eighty quid an ounce, and there are hmm – eighty ounces in five pounds – so that's about twenty two grand and four hundred quid.'

Mandy pursed her lips and shook her head. 'Wowza,' was all she could say.

'Wowza indeed,' Percy brought over the cocktails to Mandy. 'And when Daddio goes to the great gold mine in the sky – heaven forbid – my brother Geoffrey and I will inherit the company.'

Mandy saw the cocktails and shook her head. 'No, Percy, I told you, I don't want to get a parking ticket and I can't drink and drive. Maybe some other time.'

'Some other time?' Percy halted and thinned his eyes as he smiled. 'Oh, so now you've met Mammon you've changed your tune eh?'

'I beg your pardon?' Mandy slowly realised that he was trying to say that she was now willing to date him because she'd found out he was loaded.

'Has anyone ever told you that you have a strong resemblance to Diana Rigg?' he asked, and he sipped his own drink and thrust out the other to a fuming Mandy.

Mandy turned and walked to the door.

'Mandy! Where are you going?'

'Keep the booking fee!' she said, and she opened the gold framed door with its orange bubble glass and headed into the hallway.

'Mandy, what have I said to offend you?' Percy almost moaned as he gave chase. All the way down the carpeted stairs he followed her, still holding the cocktails, mouthing variations and permutations of: 'Mandy, have I said something to offend you? I'm sorry if I have! Mandy, please tell me what I've said to hurt you!'

She descended five flights of stairs and finally made it out into the spring sunshine, and already she could see the parking ticket tucked under a windscreen wiper. She made a loud grunting sound, grabbed the ticket, and got into the piggy pink Hillman Minx. Soon, Percy was a receding figure in her rear view mirror. That afternoon, Mandy gave a half-hour lesson to 70-year-old Mrs Pickering, a hopeless pupil in Shepherd's Bush who just booked her lessons out of loneliness. Then at 6.15pm it was over the Thames to South Lambeth, where Mandy gave a nervous young man named Vaughan an hour lesson – and then it was home to Holland Park. Simon arrived home late from the office again – this time around 8.20pm, and said he was tired. While he showered, Mandy picked up his shirt and sniffed it – it had the smell of that 19-year-old secretary Valerie on it – a fragrance Mandy despised because of the association – "Charlie" by Revlon. She let it go. It was a waste of time challenging him about Valerie, because Simon's father had recently loaned Mandy £700 to keep the Lucky Horseshoe Driving School afloat. She couldn't afford to kill the goose that laid the golden egg. The couple had a beef curry meal and a bottle of red wine and then it was bedtime, with Simon falling asleep within minutes of getting into bed. Mandy lay there for a while, thinking of Percy and the gold nugget, and how five pounds of metal could get her out of debt and save the driving school.

The next day at noon, Mandy returned from another lesson and decided to just have beans on toast for lunch. She was feeling pretty low, thinking about the course of her life, her happy days back home in Liverpool as a college student full of crazy ambitions, and the present shortage of money, when there was a knock at the door. She wondered if Simon had decided to come home from the office for lunch, but it was an old man, rather shabbily dressed, with a bundle of rolled-up fabric – possibly curtains – under his arm. He sounded as if he was from some East European country.

'Hello young lady, I wonder if you would be interested in some hanging mats? They are from – 'he was saying, when Mandy tried to cut the sales pitch short.

'I'm sorry, but I don't have any money,' she said, 'sorry,' and she started to close the door.

'No please, I will come back for the money when you have it,' said the old man, 'so please do have a look at these mats, they are beautiful.'

'I really don't have the money for mats – every penny is spoken for; I'm extremely broke,' Mandy told him straight. She felt sorry for him because he looked so weary and he had very kind eyes. 'I'm sorry.'

'Take one, and I'll come back in two weeks and all I will ask for is two pounds,' said the old door to door salesman, and he handed Mandy a black roll of what felt like velvet. 'Have a look at that one, it's a mandala.'

Mandy unfurled the mat and saw that it was beautiful kaleidoscopic pattern of a myriad colours featuring all sorts of interlocking circles and geometric shapes. She really liked it, and when she looked back at the man – he had gone. She stepped out the hallway onto her front doorstep and expected to see him either standing behind one of the white pillars that flanked the doorway, or walking away down the street – but he was nowhere to be seen, and this vanishing act really scared Mandy, and even though this bizarre incident had taken place in broad daylight, the way the man had disappeared into thin air really frightened her all the same. She went into the flat, closed the door, and took a look in the hallway and living room, just in case he had somehow passed her and gone into the flat, but he was plainly not there. The telephone rang. It was Mike, one of the two other employees of Mandy's driving school. He said he was packing the job in as he had found work – as a bus driver. The news depressed

Mandy, and she found she couldn't motivate herself to keep her appointments with her pupils that day, so she telephoned most of them and cancelled the lessons, claiming she'd come down with a stomach bug. She sat in her lounge, and then remembered the hanging mat she'd taken from that vanishing salesman, and she went to the parcel ledge in the hallway where she had put it down in a daze after the old man had seemingly evaporated. The hanging mat measured about five foot square, and it was mounted with three drawing pins on the wall over a cabinet. It gave a bohemian feel to the lounge, and Mandy sat on the old scuffed chesterfield Simon had brought to the flat, and she looked at the centre of the mandala and suddenly realised that the shape at the centre of the design was an eye. Mandy's right hand felt something protruding from the gap between the arm of the chesterfield and the leather cushion. It was her old recorder. She'd had it since her schooldays, and she smiled ruefully as she pulled the instrument out of the sofa, tapped its head on her palm, and began to play *Twinkle Twinkle Little Star* - the very first song she'd learned on that recorder when she was twelve. She thought back to those days when she didn't have to make a living and her mother and her Nan were always there for her. Mandy played snatches of all the other pieces she'd learned over the years, and then she played the old Beatles classic *The Fool on the Hill* but had to stop because it reminded her of her late grandmother. She looked at the mandala in that black velvet mat, and then she lifted the beak of the recorder to her lips, and for some reason, she played the flute solo from *Nights in White Satin* by the Moody Blues – and something incredible but frightening took place.

As Mandy played the recorder, there was a deafening, echoing crash, as if a giant gong had been hit with a hammer – and then, two startling figures of men – one silvery blue and the other in metallic red – came flying out of the mandala in the hanging mat. Both figures were life size, about six feet in length, and they had no hair on their heads, and their eyeballs were white and radiated light. The bluish figure flew to the right and the red one to the left, and they both flew through the air with their feet together, toes pointing behind them and their arms stretched out from their bodies at right angles as if they were leaping off a diving board. The men were like mirror images of one another, both in the exact same posture as they flew through the air. They flew towards Mandy's end of the lounge and landed about six feet apart as the clash of the gong faded. Mandy was so afraid, she couldn't move.

'My name is Helios,' said the red figure, in a deep creamy baritone voice, 'I will bring you whatever you require.' His physique, like that of his blue counterpart, was perfect, and every muscle was defined.

'I am Selios,' said the silvery-blue figure, and his voice was much softer than the other one, 'I can heal you or anyone you name.'

Mandy felt faint, and the room swayed. Her heart pounded so much she saw her bosom move in spasms. She got up, and staggered with legs of jelly to the door. She went into the hall, closing the door behind her, and then she took deep, hungry breaths as shock squeezed the heart in her chest. She could not take in what she had just seen. She opened the door a few inches and looked back into the lounge and saw that the two apparitions were still there, looking at her as she peeped in at them. She closed the door again, went into the kitchen and found her car key and house keys, and then she left the house and walked briskly to her car. She intended to drive to Simon's office at Clerkenwell, but then when she was just a couple of feet from her car door she realised how unbelievable her story about the men from the mandala would seem. She halted, thought about what she had seen, and what those weird entities had told her, and she asked herself why she was running away from them. They had seemed harmless. She went back into the house and straight to the lounge – and found it empty. She picked up the recorder from the chesterfield and put it to her mouth. Once again she played that solo flute piece from the Moody Blues song – and again she heard that loud deep sonorous gong sound. It vibrated through her entire body, and the two weird men flew out of the mandala again. They landed without a sound on either side of Mandy, and this time they did not utter a word of introduction or say anything. She turned to Helios, the reddish-silvery skinned one, and asked, 'Did you say you can get me anything?'

'Yes, that is so – what do you require?' Helios answered, and he seemed to give a faint smile – but those white radiant eyes, devoid of pupils, still unnerved Mandy somewhat.

'Er, well, when I say I need something - and er, say that something belongs to someone – isn't that stealing?' Mandy wanted to know, and she felt a strange yet delicious sense of naughtiness – of doing something she shouldn't really be doing.

'Stealing is taking without the owner's consent,' Helios replied, and then he gave three slight nods, 'yes,

I steal. Helios steals, and Selios heals.'

'What are you? A ghost?' Mandy asked, starting to suspect that these two entities were something to do with the occult.

'No person on this plane of existence must know what Helios and Selios are,' was the brusque reply, and Helios straightened up when he stated this stark caveat.

'Right, so, you could get me anything I ask for within reason I suppose?' Mandy had one thing on her mind, and it was that nugget in that fragile glass case in the Mayfair home of Percival Fontaine.

'What is it that you require, Mistress?' Helios asked with an air of impatience.

'Well, there's a gold nugget, and it belongs to a man named Percival Fontaine, and he lives in Grantham Place...do you know where that is?'

Helios suddenly told Mandy what the number was on the door of Percy's flat, and she nodded, and said, 'Yes, how did you know that?'

'I will bring the nugget to you now Mistress!' Helios lifted his arms up so his hands were pointing to the ceiling like the hands of a clock at noon, and then he seemed to fall backwards, but before he could land on his back he shot off backwards, into the mandala – and he was gone. Mandy turned to ask Selios what he'd be doing while his 'brother' was away, but the unearthly being had vanished.

Mandy sat down, fidgeted with that recorder which seemed to have evoked these strange characters from somewhere, and she wondered if what she had done would have some bad repercussions. She was still wrestling with her conscience a minute later when

Helios appeared in front of her holding that nugget in his hands. He held it out to her saying: 'The gold, Mistress.'

'Oh, oh dear, thanks Helios,' Mandy took the nugget from the mysterious servant and almost dropped it because it was a bit heavier than she imagined. She placed it on the chesterfield.

'Do you require anything else Mistress?' Helios asked, and sported that ghost of a smile again.

'Er, no, no thanks Helios,' Mandy told him, and stroked the Australian nugget. 'Thank you Helios.'

He pointed his hands at the ceiling again and fell backwards. When his body was at a forty-five degree angle he flitted into mandala, and this time he did it so fast, Mandy's eyes simply couldn't follow him. She looked at the nugget which was – according to its former owner – worth in the region of £22,000. Mandy tried to get her head around the strange situation, and started to panic. Percy would tell the police that a certain female driving instructor had known about the nugget and *only yesterday* had even asked him how much it was worth. Had Percy been present when Helios stole the thing? Mandy summoned him with the recorder. 'Helios, was Percy present when you took the nugget?'

'No Mistress, there was no one about,' the supernatural skivvy told her.

Mandy picked up the nugget, intending to take it to the coffee table so she could see if it bore any identifying stamp, but she dropped the lump of gold and it landed on her foot. She was wearing tennis shoes, and she almost passed out from the pain. She just knew she'd crushed her big toe. She started to hop around in a circle, when Selios appeared, flitting down from the mandala in the hanging mat.

'I will heal you Mistress!' he announced, and he held out his palm. His hand began to give off a soft blue radiance, and he pointed the index finger of this glowing hand at Mandy's foot. Straight away the pain in her toe ceased and she felt warmth course through her foot.

'Oh thank you Selios! Thank you!' she enthused with great relief. She picked up the nugget and this time managed to convey it safely to the coffee table. It bore no stamp of any kind by which it might be registered and identified. She realised it would have made more sense simply asking Helios to go and make a few paranormal withdrawals from a few banks instead, because she could not see how she was going to cash in a nugget at a jewellers without arousing suspicions – and this one was now hot – the police would soon be notifying jewellers across London about it. This realisation made her panic. She decided it had to go back to its rightful owner, and she asked Helios to take it back, but he told her: 'I am not able to do that Mistress, I can only acquire things for you – I cannot return them.'

'Why not?' Mandy asked, and she could sense that the hyperventilation of acute anxiety was in the offing. 'What's so difficult about putting it back?'

Helios answered panicking Mandy's question. 'I can only acquire things for you, Mistress; that is what I was ordained to do.'

'I can't breathe, I'll go to prison for this – theft – oh!' she gasped, and turned to Selios. 'Help me!'

'I will calm you and heal you,' Selios raised both

palms up and they started to glow with a faint blue phosphorescence.

Mandy felt sedated all of a sudden, and then a feeling of pure tranquillity came over her.

'They are just thoughts, mere thoughts, Mistress,' Selios said in his soft velvet voice. 'Those thoughts that worry you are not even as real as a soap bubble. Just thoughts, and now they are – gone.'

'Thanks,' Mandy replied softly, and the calmness of her mind eventually lifted. She still felt worried about being in possession of a £22,000 nugget, but no longer suffered from that crippling anxiety. She took the nugget to the little cupboard-cum-cloakroom under the stairs and hid it in a dark corner till she could think of somewhere to take it. Mandy then made some Camomile tea, which she always found calming, and she sat at the table in the kitchen trying to work out how she could get shut of the accursed nugget. She went and summoned Helios, and asked him: 'Could you get me a transit van? A black one if possible with no writing on its sides.'

'Yes, Mistress,' said Helios, raising his hands, ready to fly off into the mandala.

'Oh and Helios – make sure you put the van outside *on the road* and not in here!'

'Of course, Mistress,' he said with a smile, and then he flew backwards into a vanishing point – the eye of the mandala.

Mandy opened the front door and was glad to see there was a large enough parking space outside on Abbotsbury Road. A few minutes passed, and still there was no sign of any black transit van. She closed the door, and fetched a plastic yellow bucket from the cupboard under the sink. Mandy then retrieved the troublesome nugget from the cupboard under the stairs, and put it in the bucket and covered it with an old newspaper. Then she realised her fingerprints would be on that nugget. She went back to the kitchen, put on a pair of pink rubber washing-up gloves, and found a dust cloth. She rubbed and polished the nugget, and then put it back in the bucket. She then realised her fingerprints would be on that bucket. She swore, removed the nugget and newspapers and cleaned the bucket inside and out. She went to the front door again – and there was a black mark 1 Ford Transit van parked outside. She went out onto the doorstep, looked up and down the road, then approached the van muttering: 'I hope the damned keys are in here.'

She opened the front passenger door and the keys were in the ignition. She went back into the flat, grabbed her purse and then she took the bucket and got in the van. She put the bucket on the driving seat and drove off. She then noticed that the fuel gauge was pointing at 'low' and she hissed a profanity under her breath. The plan was to park the van and the accursed nugget near Hyde Park, and then the police would find it and think that the robbers of Percival's nugget had got cold feet. This would then hopefully make the law think that she was not involved in the theft in any way. But two things happened to throw a spanner in the works. Just three quarters of a mile from Mandy's flat, the van started to shudder as it ran out of petrol, so she had to pull over close to a bus stop at Notting Hill Gate. That was bad enough, because there was a crowd of potential witnesses at the stop, but then

Mandy heard a noise behind her. She looked over her shoulder, and there, in the semi darkness, by the feeble daylight coming in through the rear door windows of the van, she saw a man getting up from what looked like a sleeping bag!

'What are you playing at?' he roared at Mandy.

She opened the driver door, hopped out onto the road, and heard the pulsating horn of a car hurtling towards her. She just drew back in time and the wind from the wake of the passing car gusted against her long hair. She ran off, and soon realised she was out of shape. Everyone at the bus stop saw her as she passed them. Mandy looked back, and although she did not see the man from the van following her, she went and hid in an opticians, where she pretended to browse the collections of spectacles on display. The receptionist threw a puzzled look at Mandy's hands – she still had the pink washing-up gloves on. Mandy took them off, and then, after a few minutes, she looked out the window of the premises, down towards the bus stop, and saw the man who had chased her; he was now behind the wheel of the van, and he had a few Good Samaritans pushing it along towards a filling station. Mandy left the opticians and flagged down a hackney cab which took her back to the Holland Park flat, and she just had enough money to pay the fare. That evening at 7pm, a detective and a policeman called at the flat, and Simon, home early for once, answered.

'Does Amanda Rogers live here?' the detective asked a startled Simon.

'Yes – yes she does – wh – why – what's wrong?' Simon had never been in trouble with the law in his life and was shocked by the visiting lawmen.

'Is Miss Rogers in at the moment?' the detective asked, and looked over Simon's shoulder down the hallway.

Mandy was in the kitchen, and she heard the detective asking for her. Her mouth was bone dry, but she told herself she had nothing to worry about. That nugget was in that van.

'Yes, come in,' Simon invited the detective and constable in, and explained who he was. 'I'm Simon, by the way, Mandy's boyfriend.'

The two visitors walked past him and Mandy decided to face the music and stepped out of the kitchen into the hallway. 'I'm Mandy,' she said. She wanted to say more but the words just wouldn't come out.

'Hello Miss Rogers, can we have a word with you in here perhaps?' the detective showed her his warrant card, and walked into the kitchen. Mandy followed them, and the detective, who said his name was Calhoun, sat at the kitchen table. Mandy sat at the table too, facing him. The constable remained standing and his eyes slowly scanned the kitchen.

Calhoun's cold blue eyes drilled into Mandy as he told her: 'A client of yours – Percival Fontaine – has been burgled, and he is missing a very valuable gold nugget, worth nearly £23,000.'

'Oh,' was all the driving instructor could conjure up.

'Now, ' the detective continued, 'Mr Fontaine says that he showed you that very same nugget the day before it was stolen, so you can understand why we are paying this visit Miss Rogers.'

'Yes, I can understand Mr Calhoun,' Mandy replied, and she felt a nervous tic flickering in her cheek, 'but I am not a thief, and I have not taken his nugget. It – it's just – well – all I can say is that I give you my word, that I am not a thief.'

Calhoun's eyebrows lifted and he nodded, keeping his dead unemotional eyes fixed on Mandy's face. 'It was taken today sometime between noon and 2pm. Can you tell me where you were at that time Miss Rogers?'

She told him she had been alone in the flat at that time, and that the only person she had seen had been a man who had been selling hanging mats.

Calhoun took out a notebook and scribbled illegible-looking squiggly lines and symbols – some sort of shorthand perhaps – or just terrible writing. 'So, you talked to a door to door salesman, and you bought a mat from him. Had he called before? Do you know his name?'

'I don't know his name. I bought a mat from him,' said Mandy, choosing to leave the part about not paying, in case it made her look desperate enough to steal. She certainly could not mention the mat-seller's vanishing act. 'And er, no, I had never seen him before, but he had a foreign accent.'

'Can I have a look at the mat?' Calhoun asked. 'Might be a label on it we can trace.'

'Yes, of course,' said Mandy, getting up from the table. 'It's in the lounge.' She almost walked into Simon; he'd been in the doorway of the kitchen, listening to everything. As she passed him his eyes caught Mandy's eyes and he said: 'A nugget?'

Mandy said nothing in return. She walked on and took the hanging mat down and handed it to the detective, and he scrutinised it. 'No, no labels,' he finally said, and handed the mat back to Mandy.

'Maybe a professional burglar, or maybe a few of them, took the nugget,' Mandy suggested. 'Maybe they just took it and then drove off. Like you see in those films.'

'Well that's the thing you see,' said Calhoun, 'there are roadworks in Grantham Place now. They've dug a whopping big hole, so no car would have access to Grantham Place. They'd have to park down in Old Park Lane, but the place was milling about with workmen at lunchtime, and they saw no one. Well, no one suspicious, that is.'

'Well I'm really sorry about the theft Mr Calhoun,' Mandy told him with faux sincerity, 'but you can search this place high and low if you want. I swear before God that I do not have any nugget. I mean, how would I even cash it in at a bank?'

'Oh, they melt it down into ingots sometimes, and there are receivers who take care of all that,' Calhoun replied, and then he smiled – but that smile never reached his shop-manikin eyes. 'Well, I'm sure we'll be back in touch Miss Rogers.'

The detective and the constable then left.

On the following day, Calhoun called again, just after Mandy had returned home on her lunch-break from an hour's lesson in Battersea. He stood on the doorstep, attended by that same constable. He told her: 'Miss Rogers, we've found the nugget. It was in a van.'

'Oh, I am so glad to hear that Mr Calhoun,' Mandy said, and she asked the detective and the policeman to come in. They did, and in the hallway, Calhoun dropped the bombshell. 'The van the nugget was in belongs to a George Bolton, from Pinner. Now, this is a strange one, because Mr Bolton is homeless, and he sleeps in his van. He had virtually no petrol in the vehicle, and yet he says he woke up in the van and found that it was in Notting Hill, about eleven miles from his home.'

'Maybe he just *said* that,' Mandy surmised.

'Oh no, we checked the tank and milometer and all that technical stuff – take it from us – he *is* telling the truth,' said Calhoun. 'But here's the funny part. He said that when he woke up, a young lady was behind the wheel, and this lady's description matches you to a tee, Miss Rogers.'

'Well it *wasn't* me, I was here,' Mandy told him, and her face blushed and her throat felt as dry as sandpaper. 'This is all very complicated isn't it Mr Calhoun? Transit vans that travel miles without any petrol – '

'I never said it was a Transit van – or did I?' Calhoun asked, and seemed to know the answer. He smiled, and this time his eyes seemed to twinkle into life as if he was relishing the way he was roasting his suspect.

Mandy froze. Then she managed to say: 'So, this Mr Bolton is the man who stole the nugget then?'

'Well, his right leg is missing below the knee,' Calhoun told her, and seemed to take delight in imparting this morsel of information. 'He uses a stick to operate the pedals, like. He shouldn't be in charge of a vehicle. He's got no criminal record either, and he also has witnesses who place him at a cafe between one and two on the day of the theft. It's a strange one.'

'I really don't understand any of this Mr Calhoun,' said Mandy, and she found she could not look the detective in the eyes. 'I might have to get in touch with a solicitor,' she said, her voice faltering and fading to almost a whisper. 'I feel as if you're trying to frame me or something.'

'Oh, I don't think there'll be any need for solicitors Miss Rogers,' Calhoun told her. 'I do hate loose ends but er, it's just one of those things I suppose; you can't win them all. Anyway, I just thought I'd let you know that your client got his gold back.'

'He's not my client,' Mandy told him, annoyed at the association, 'he couldn't keep his hands off me during the lesson.'

Calhoun smiled and left the flat with the constable. They sat in the unmarked police car outside for an unbearable minute or so as Mandy watched from behind the net curtains of the bedroom. When the car finally moved off, she went into the kitchen and made herself a strong coffee. She was now determined to get one over on the police after she'd been sadistically grilled like that. She sat and schemed. She decided she wanted thousands of pounds which could not be traced – then she had a dark idea. Years ago, Mandy's father had told her how a relative had worked in the Bank of England's printing works at Debden down in Essex, and his job had been to burn thousands upon thousands of banknotes – pound notes, fivers, tenners and so on – when they were deemed to be a bit too dirty to remain in circulation. These banknotes were not sorted by their serial numbers because they were just looked at as notes that had no future, and bundles of them were thrown in the incinerator – but what if Mr Helios took some of these bundles and saved them from a fiery death?

While Simon was at work on the following morning,

Helios made repeated trips to the bank's printing works and 'rescued' bundle after bundle of condemned banknotes from a poorly-illuminated storeroom. Mandy ended up with five suitcases packed with the notes of all sorts of denominations – and it amounted to well over a million. She couldn't wait till Simon got home, for now they'd have enough money to get married, and to go on a honeymoon cruise of a lifetime – and then she would expand the Lucky Horseshoe Driving School into a big concern. She had all sorts of plans now that she had the money. Then the telephone rang at four that afternoon, and Simon told her it was over, and he wouldn't be coming home. Valerie was pregnant, and he was sticking with her. He said he was sorry, and that he'd still be her friend, but Mandy hung up, and then she disconnected the phone. She wanted to cry, but the tears wouldn't come. There was a knock at the door. She wondered if it was Calhoun; if it was she was in big trouble now with that little mountain of money under the stairs. And yet, she was so upset at the loss of Simon's love, the prospect of prison seemed to lose its menace. She opened the door, and that old man – the one who had sold her that hanging mat – stood there with a weak smile on his face. Mandy stood there in silence for a moment, and he seemed to read her mind. She went to that hanging mat, took it from the wall, and rolled it up. She took it back to the man at the door and handed it to him. 'I don't like it,' she said.

'Selios could heal your broken heart,' the stranger said, pointing to the wound-up velvet mat in his hand.

'Thanks, but – no thanks,' Mandy told him, and a tear escaped from her right eye.

'Very well,' said the perceptive old man, and he nodded to Mandy, then turned and walked away.

She closed the door, walked into the lounge, and she sat on the chesterfield with her face in her hands, leaning forward slightly. She sobbed loudly. On the following day at 7pm, Simon came around to pick up his things, and Mandy gave him a cheque for £700.

'What's this for?' he asked, reading the inscribed amount on the paper.

'I'm paying back the loan from your father,' she said, in a nonchalant manner.

A bemused Simon said, 'You haven't got two halfpennies to rub together.'

'Oh, I have now,' she told him, 'just received quite a sum from a relative who's popped her clogs back in Liverpool.'

'Really? Who's died?' Simon asked. He seemed very suspicious.

'It's no concern of yours now,' she told him with a smile.

'So are you staying on here? You *can* still pay the rent?' he asked.

'I'm looking at a flat in Knightsbridge tomorrow.'

'Knightsbridge? You must have received quite a legacy then.'

'Come on, get a move on,' she nodded to his bulging suitcases.

'We can still remain friends you know – ' he was saying but she cut him short.

'No we can't,' she said, and had cast iron determination in her voice and eyes, 'now get yourself packed and out.'

The relationship between Simon and Valerie soured,

even before the birth of their baby, and one night at 11pm, as London was being hammered by a torrential downpour, there was a heavy knocking at the door of Mandy's Knightsbridge flat. She asked who was calling so late, and she heard Simon's voice. He was begging her to open the door. She let him in, and he fell at her bare feet and pleaded to be taken back. He was soaked, and wet rat-tails of his hair clung to his face. He admitted he must have been mad to get involved with a girl like Valerie, and said they had nothing in common; they hardly spoke to one another and Simon said he'd been having heartbreaking dreams he was back in Holland Park, back in the old life he had taken for granted.

She let him grovel like this for quite some time before she said the words he'd been longing to hear – but she said there was a condition – any late nights at the office and he was out on the street. Simon never did stay late at the office again, and the couple were married in the following year. Mandy passed away from a short illness in 1990, and Simon never remarried. He tragically died due to complications of an operation for a duodenal ulcer a few years after. Mandy never told him about the true source of her wealth. She told her best friend Izzy years later, and Izzy told me the strange story. What are we to make of Helios and Selios? The etymology of the names seems to mean Sun and Moon, but were they demons, or ghosts, or did they belong to the djinn – intelligent spiritual beings in Arabian and Muslim folklore? It is hard to say. They might have been servants created by some sorcerer of long ago, but it's fruitless to speculate, and the same goes for the old man who brought the mat featuring the mandala to Mandy's house; I feel he was not human at all, but I am at a complete loss to say just what he was. For all intents and purposes, the universe is an infinitely large place, and what do we – mere bacteria on the cosmic scale – know of the strange goings-on beyond this speck of dust that we have named Earth?

GHOSTS THAT PERSECUTE

Most ghosts I investigate stick rigidly to a place and time; they walk only at certain hours and rarely venture beyond their haunting grounds, but not Liverpool's Shroud Lady, and I wish to God I could tell you why she gets around the way she does – and I wish I knew why this ominous ghoul persecutes certain people. A flesh and blood stalker is bad enough, and he or she might at least end up arrested or put away, but just how can you report a ghostly stalker to the police? The earliest report I have of the Shroud Lady dates back to April 1976. At a certain well-known hairdressers in the city centre of Liverpool that year, on a sunny April afternoon at 2.20pm, two women in their mid-thirties, Joan Myers and Jill Dawson, were sitting in sumptuous leather-padded chairs, reading glossy magazines at the upmarket salon with their heads under the hair-drying hoods, when Jill somehow sensed that someone was behind her. She lifted her eyes from the magazine and stared at the mirror ahead and in the reflection she saw that a woman with a ghastly face, in some sort of old-fashioned burial shroud, was standing behind her and Joan. She let out a yelp and the figure vanished. Joan told her friend she'd nodded off and dreamt the ghost, but Jill said she had been wide awake, and as she recalled the eyeless dark sockets in the pallid face of the apparition, she shuddered. What did the creepy visitation mean? Was it some bad sign? She felt it had been. When Jill got home she was told her grandmother had collapsed and died, so she quickly assumed that the Shroud Lady had been an omen of death. Her grandmother had died at 2.20pm that afternoon – the very time of the visit of the shrouded ghost to the hairdressing salon. Weeks after this, on the Friday evening of May 28 at around 8.30pm, Jill was sitting in her West Derby house alone as she watched American actor Bill Bixby in a TV series called *The Magician*. Jill's husband Derek was in the pub, taking part in a competition with his darts team, and Jill's two teenage daughters Angela and Alison were playing badminton at the local sports club. During the commercial break on the telly, Jill went into the kitchen, poured a glass of Coke, and then added some ice cubes. That year – 1976 – saw a record heat wave across the country and the heat was unbearable – but then Jill suddenly sensed something very cold behind her. She just knew something of a supernatural nature was standing behind her in the kitchen, but she was too scared to turn around to see what it was. She looked at the chrome kettle, and there, clearly reflected in its mirrored convex surface, Jill saw something in unfamiliar white clothes. She turned – and came face to face with the very same ghost she had briefly seen reflected in the mirror of the hairdressing salon back in April. The apparition had on the same long white burial shroud and the face looking out of the hood of the garment looked very pale and pitted with tiny holes. The face, as before, had no eyes, just black sockets, and the entity wore a poker-faced expression. On this occasion, Jill detected a terrible odour which reminded her of the stench of fish that had gone off mingled with a sickly sweet aroma.

'What do you want?' Jill whimpered. She couldn't run out of the kitchen because the terrifying ghost was blocking the only way out.

'Doe tors,' said the ghost, its lips barely moving, and then she vanished, but the smell lingered for a while.

Jill hurried out of the kitchen, switched off the television, and went next door to her neighbours, Albert and Peggy Cook, and Jill expected them to doubt her story, but the couple could tell something had happened to her, and Peggy told her to sit down and have a hot sweet tea (a universal Liverpool remedy for shock).

'She said a word that sounded like "doe tors" – what does that mean?' Jill said in a trembling voice.

'Maybe she was saying daughters,' Albert speculated, as he sat hogging the cool hair from an electric fan. This might have been a good guess from Albert, as the word *dohtor* means 'daughter' an Old English.

'What? Do you think she was referring to my daughters?' Jill immediately became concerned about her daughters; they were playing badminton in the youth sports club about half a mile away.

'Have you been getting enough sleep, Jill?' Peggy Cook asked her, stroking the head of her neighbour in a sympathetic fashion. 'Lack of sleep can cause people to see all kinds of things.'

'I think I should go and see they're alright, Peggy!' Jill got up and headed for the door, and Albert asked where her daughters Angela and Alison where, and when he heard they were in the youth sports club, he kindly offered to drive Jill there.

'I've just made her a cup of tea,' Peggy told her husband.

'It's not going to go cold in this weather, Peggy,' Albert quipped, and he went out – in his shorts and string vest – and drove Jill to the youth club.

When Jill arrived at the club, she saw her daughters talking to a man of about fifty who was sitting in a white Mini. When the girls saw their mother they looked surprised, especially as she was with Mr Cook the next-door neighbour. It turned out that the man in the Mini, had been asking the girls if they'd like to go for a drive down to the Pier Head, as he wanted to buy them ice creams. Angela was thirteen and Alison was nearly fifteen but they were very trusting and not all worldly wise yet. When the man in the Mini saw Jill approach, he drove off.

Jill was convinced that the sinister kitchen visitor had warned her that her daughters' lives were in danger. Jill never told her girls about the Shroud Lady as she knew they were both scared stiff of ghosts.

If the Shroud Lady was using Old English words to communicate, then she is possibly a lot older than I imagined – possibly even dating back to Medieval times. For the next ten years, whenever a tragedy or death was imminent in Jill's family, she would receive a visit from the Shroud Lady, and the West Derby woman saw the ominous figure in the white hooded robe a further eleven times. She appeared to her outside her shower on the occasion when an aunt had been fatally knocked down, and on another occasions a woman who was with Jill as she shopped in a supermarket also saw the long-dead harbinger of doom in her coffin finery. A priest was asked to exorcise the haggard avant-courier, but said it would be impossible as she was not possessing anyone and not confined to one locality. The Shroud Lady was eventually sent packing by an old Nigerian man – a self-proclaimed preacher – who had heard of the ghost haunting Jill. This man had been staying at the YMCA when a Catholic priest had told him about the alleged paranormal persecutor. The Nigerian gentleman wrote to Jill and asked her if he could come to her home to rid her of the 'unwholesome spirit'. Jill was naturally a bit reluctant at first but thought she'd give the Nigerian preacher a try. Jill showed the African layman the last place she had seen the ghostly hag, and a white candle was lit, placed in an old candle holder, and put on the floor where the phantom foreteller of calamity had stood. The Nigerian then looked up at the ceiling and said: Spirit, you have lived long! Go at once into the sun and stay there! Do not return to earth to interfere with the lives of the living and do not bear us malice!'

Jill, her husband, her two daughters, and the neighbour Peggy Cook, all stood there, a bit bemused by the ranting man, who was of a small stature, but the smiles were wiped off their faces when a deep loud groan vibrated through the bedroom, followed by a wind which blew the candle out and knocked over the bedside lamp. The white candle suddenly relit itself, and the wind ceased, and a pleasant smell reminiscent of roses permeated the air. Jill just knew that she would not see that accursed woman in white again, and she thanked the Nigerian and went to get her purse to pay him, but the preacher quietly left amid all the excitement after his ritual, and she never saw him again – nor did Jill ever see that Shroud Lady again – but others did. Years before, in 1981, a couple – Linda and Eddie Marr – went to visit a friend in the Royal Liverpool Teaching Hospital one evening, and got into a lift and pressed the top floor button. No one else was in that lift. The lift halted a few floors up and opened, and there stood a tall woman in a strange white hooded robe. Her face – which looked deathly pale and pockmarked - was bordered by white satin frills. Where the eyes should have been there were just two black hollows. Linda screamed and stabbed the lift buttons, and then she and Eddie drew back into a corner and held onto one another. The figure did not come into the lift, but remained outside and said something which Eddie couldn't make out. The lift door slowly closed, and Eddie swore and asked what the thing had said. 'She said "He's dead" Eddie!' Linda told her husband, and began to shake. Minutes later they reached the ward and were told their friend, a man in his early forties, had just suffered a massive heart attack and died. The couple went back down in that lift with three other people – and they all saw the distinct reflection of that woman in white in the polished walls of the lift – a reflection of a person who was not visible *inside* the lift. There are many further reports - all apparently describing the same shrouded eyeless entity, and always concerning omens of death – and now, in this century, it would seem that the Shroud Lady is still doing the rounds, for she has been seen in a wide area ranging from Seaforth to Speke. Why she persecuted Jill Dawson is a mystery – was she was some blood relative of the West Derby woman perhaps?

We now move 178 miles south of Liverpool to a call centre near Swindon for our second case of supernatural persecution. The call centre offers an accident claims service by cold calling upon almost anyone in the local telephone book. On this particular rainy afternoon in April 2014, a 22-year-old lady named Erin telephoned a number belonging to a certain residence near Wroughton, a village just six miles from the call centre. A man answered the call. 'Hello?' he said.

'Good afternoon sir,' said Erin, cheerfully, 'have you been involved in an accident?'

'Piss off!' the man roared. 'I'm ex-directory so stop calling me, you irritating arsehole or I'll have the law on you!'

Erin was no stranger to verbal abuse – it was part and parcel of her job – but this outburst scared her. She took her coffee break a bit earlier, and then she telephoned another number, and a potential customer somewhere in Liverpool answered.

'Hello?' said the man. He had a soft, calm voice with a trace of a Liverpudlian accent.

'Oh good afternoon sir,' said Erin in a bright chirpy voice, 'have you been involved in an accident?'

'Yes, I have,' the man told her.

'Oh great, er – I don't mean it's great you were in an accident sorry,' Erin said and giggled, 'but er, could you tell me what the nature of the accident was and what the outcome was?'

There was a slight chuckle from the other end of the line, and then the man answered: 'Yes, I crashed my car, and erm, it *was* my fault – I was speeding, but well, I died as a result.'

'Sorry?' Erin thought she had either misheard the man – or – he was pulling her leg.

'I died.' He said, flatly.

'You mean you died and they brought you back sort of thing? Like resuscitation?' Erin struggled to understand what the man was trying to say.

'No, I'm still dead. I died. And I get awfully lonely sometimes.'

'Oh, um,' Erin decided the man was a crank and she hung up on him. She rang another number chosen by the computer, and this time it was the telephone number of a house somewhere near Southampton.

An elderly female voice answered Erin's call. 'Hello, two four one seven. The Banks residence.'

'Oh, good afternoon, my name's Erin, and I'm calling to ask if you've been involved in an accident – '

'I'm not interested! Buzz off! Bloody cold callers!' said the woman, and she hung up.

'And a lovely afternoon to you as well,' sighed Erin, ready to make another cold call upon someone – when she heard a voice on the line.

'Yes, so I'm dead and I do get awfully lonely – so lonely I could cry sometimes.'

It was that man again – the one who had told Erin he had died in a car accident. Erin tried to disconnect him, but whenever she made more cold calls, she could hear him talking in the background, and the people she was calling could also hear him, which complicated matters. Erin told the Draconian boss about the strange man and he had her transferred to another desk in a tiny cubicle. She called a computer-conjured number to a possible customer living in Salisbury, and a timid-sounding young man said he had been involved in a mishap with his car a few months ago, but when Erin tried to procure the details from him, that unbalanced man's voice was heard again in the background. The voice said: 'So, will you come and keep me company then? I do get awfully lonely and I would love someone who is actually alive to be my friend.'

'Sorry?' said the youth, wondering who was speaking on the line.

'I'm so sorry, please ignore that person,' Erin told the Salisbury customer.

'Oh no, please don't ignore me – I've been ignored by everyone – even my own family – since I died,' said the voice.

The young man in Salisbury, perhaps thinking he was the victim of some silly practical joker, hung up.

'How are you coming onto my line all the time?' Erin asked, seething with anger. Before she could say any more the door of the cubicle burst open and her boss told her she'd have to go home till tomorrow. The boss had just had a tip-off; a Fire Safety Inspector was due to visit the call centre – which had no adequate fire exits, no fire alarms nor even a single fire extinguisher on the premises. Within ten minutes, Erin was out on the street, waiting for the bus to take her home. By 3.30pm, Erin reached her home on Burford Avenue in Swindon, where she lived with her parents and her younger brother David. She went up to her bedroom, changed into her pyjamas – something she always did on afternoons like this when she was depressed – and she lay on her bed and checked her emails and surfed the internet on her iPad. Her mother shouted to her from downstairs. It sounded like, 'Just going the shops,' but Erin never responded. She was too busy reading a rambling email from a friend who had just broken up with her boyfriend. The skies were dark outside and rain was pattering at the bedroom window. Erin's thoughts alternated between the hatred she bore towards her job at the call centre and browsing through eBay for some vintage clothes. As she browsed, she suddenly heard a voice which came from the end of the bed, and it was crystal clear and the slight Scouse accent sounded familiar.

'You didn't let me finish earlier on...' this voice intoned, and an electric jolt of horrified surprise coursed through the young woman's abdomen which shook her to the core of her heart. She looked up and saw a man, about six feet in height, standing at the foot of her bed, and he was almost entirely made of pure black silhouette. Erin found herself leaping off the bed and throwing herself to the door. She heard the apparition shout out something unintelligible as she yanked the door open and ran along the landing. She ran downstairs and discovered to her horror that her mother was not there; she had gone shopping. Erin's brother was not at home and her father wasn't due home from work till half-past-five. The young lady therefore ran out of the house barefooted in her pyjamas and went next door to Mrs Baxter, the 75-year-old neighbour. Mrs Baxter answered the doorbell and saw a tongue-tied Erin standing on her doorstep in her pyjamas with nothing on her feet. 'What's wrong, love?' Mrs Baxter asked.

'I – I've just seen a ghost in my bedroom Mrs

Baxter,' said Erin, finally getting her words out.

'A ghost?' the neighbour asked, and seeing that Erin looked very scared of something, she stepped aside and told her: 'You'd better come in Erin, come on.'

Erin went into her neighbour house, and Mrs Baxter told her to calm down and to tell her exactly what had happened. The neighbour had a cat that was absolutely doted on by Mrs Baxter night and day, and whenever anyone visited its owner, the feline would jump at them, just to get even more attention from Mrs Baxter. This day was no exception, and as Mrs Baxter told a trembling Erin to sit on the sofa before giving her account of the ghost, the cat jumped onto Erin's back, and the young woman screamed, startled by the half-hearted attack. The cat was thrown into the hallway and Mrs Baxter came back into the living room and listened to Erin's account of the silhouetted form, and how she believed it was the ghost of a man who had talked to her on the telephone at the call centre earlier on.

'Oh dear, isn't that strange?' Mrs Baxter said, and Erin was so glad her neighbour was not sceptical about her story.

'Why has it followed me home?' Erin asked, and she shuddered as she saw the reflected green light of the spoilt cat gazing through the frosted glass of the door from the darkened hallway. 'How will I get rid of it?'

'I'm not really sure, Erin, but I'd try a priest or a vicar, and tell him what you've told me. I've never seen a ghost but I know people who have.'

Erin sat in her kind neighbour's home eating Mr Kipling cakes and drinking tea until 5.30pm, when she decided she'd venture back into her home and see if her mother was back. Mrs Baxter walked with her to the front door, which was closed. Erin had carelessly left that door open when she had fled from the house. Erin's mother was furious when she answered the door. She had returned from the shopping trip and found the door open. Any passing crook could have ransacked the house, and of course her mother had naturally wondered what had become of her daughter. The story about the ghost which had apparently come to the house after speaking to her on the telephone was not taken seriously and a row ensued. Erin's father came home a little later than normal, around a quarter to six, and as soon as he stepped into the house his wife told him about Erin leaving the house with the front door open while she had tea and cakes next door with Mrs Baxter, all because she thought she had seen a ghost. Erin went up to her room in a huff and slammed the door. She refused to have her tea, despite her mother calling her down to have the meal three times. She felt a bit unnerved lying on the bed as she looked at the spot where that shadowy ghost had appeared and yet the anger towards her parents because of their scepticism regarding her account of the entity counteracted the fear to a certain extent. At 7pm, Erin's iPhone rang and she looked at the screen and saw it was her friend Charleigh calling. Charleigh was having problems with her boyfriend Markus and Erin normally didn't want to be her friend's agony aunt, but she answered and talked to her because she thought it'd take her mind of the recent supernatural proceedings.

'Hiya,' Erin greeted her friend, and Charleigh just went straight into the meat of the matter: 'His

Facebook page says "No relationship info to show" – so I've done the same on my page as well. I don't know why he's gone all salty Erin.'

Erin was just about to speak when that familiar, eerie voice cut into the conversation.

'I get awfully lonely, and when I get like that, with people like you ignoring me, I want to cry.'

There was a pause on the line, then Charleigh asked: 'Who's that?'

'Charleigh, look, er, could you phone me back on my landline?' Erin went cold and she sounded scared.

'Why? Is someone there with you?' Charleigh asked, feeling very paranoid.

'Charleigh, please just phone the landline and I'll explain what's going on,' Erin urged. She then left the bedroom and hurried down the stairs to the hallway where the rarely used landline – and old retro Trimphone model - sat on an old half-moon table. Erin looked at the telephone and waited – and waited. 'Come on Charleigh,' she muttered. Erin's mother came into the hallway and said: 'Your tea is in the oven – if you want it, you'll have to put it out yourself.'

Erin didn't even turn to acknowledge her mum. The telephone warbled. Erin quickly picked up the handset and heard Charleigh ask: 'Why can't I call you on your mobile?'

Erin attempted an explanation. 'Because, well, did you hear that man's voice?'

'Yeah, who is he?'

'You're not going to believe this but he's a ghost.'

His voice manifested on the landline, startling Erin. 'I died, and now I'm awfully lonely,' he said.

'Stop messing about Erin and grow up for Christ's

sake,' Charleigh told her in an annoyed tone.

Erin felt her heart pound as she spoke to her friend, knowing he was listening in. 'It's not a joke, Charleigh, I swear, he really is a ghost. He appeared in my bedroom.'

'I came to your room because I get awfully lonely, and I'll visit Charleigh too,' said the entity.

'Unless you stop arsing about right now, Erin, I am going,' Charleigh warned her, 'because like, I have some serious shit going on now and I am not in the mood for all this.'

'Charleigh, I give you my word that I am not – ' Erin was saying when she heard a terrible scream from Charleigh. 'Charleigh! Charleigh, what's wrong? Charleigh?'

The line went dead.

Erin ran back upstairs to her room and tried to call Charleigh on her iPhone but kept getting the automated voice telling her that the caller was not available. She tried again and again, and then Erin's mother came up the stairs, popped her head around the bedroom door and announced: 'Well, I just thought I'd let you know you tea is frazzled! Burned! So if you want anything to eat you'll have to have cheese on toast, choc ices or cornflakes, alright?' And then she went back downstairs. Erin took no notice. She dialled again, and this time Charleigh's 15-year-old brother Finn answered her mobile phone.

'Hello? Is Charleigh there?' Erin asked.

'It's Finn, Erin – Charleigh's fainted. She saw a ghost, and I saw it too, in her room.'

Erin experienced a sensation akin to an ice cube being rubbed about in her abdomen, at the mention of the ghost. 'A ghost?' was all she could say.

'Like a man all in black,' Finn told her, and Erin could hear the fear in his voice. 'He appeared by the window in her room, and he touched Charleigh on the shoulder and she fainted and then he just disappeared. Dad's phoned an ambulance 'cos we can't wake her up.'

'Oh my God,' Erin had a strong impression of someone – or something – standing behind her in her bedroom, and she walked straight to the door with a tingling sensation in the nape of her neck. She never looked back, and she walked along the landing, when she heard Finn say: 'We'll call you back when she wakes up.'

And then he hung up.

About twenty minutes later, Charleigh's mother called Erin and said her daughter had awakened and had said a black shadow in the shape of a man had appeared and had touched her on the shoulder. She had felt a stinging sensation in her neck, and had blacked out.

'It's a ghost, I saw him too,' Erin told her friend's mum, 'he appeared in my room. It all started this afternoon when he spoke to me on the phone when I was at work.'

'You and Charleigh haven't been messing with one of those weejie boards have you?' the mother asked.

'A Ouija? No, I wouldn't dare mess with one of those,' Erin assured her, 'As I was saying it all started – '

'She's calling for me, Erin, I'd better go. I'll get her to call you when she's better.'

'I visited her because I get awfully lonely you see,'

said the ghost, butting into the conversation.

'Sorry? Who's that?' Charleigh's mother asked.

'It's him!' Erin told her, 'That's the ghost!'

Charleigh's mum hung up.

'Piss off and leave me alone!' Erin yelled at her mobile.

'Hey, what's going on?' Erin's mother shouted to her daughter, who was now halfway down the stairs.

'It's that ghost, mum!' Erin said, and she ended the call. 'The ghost appeared to Charleigh, and it touched her, and she fainted!'

Erin's mother gave a lopsided smirk, and angled her head so her left eye favoured her daughter. 'And this all happened since you *mentioned* seeing a ghost?'

'Mum, she's not making it up, it's the same ghost!' Erin told her. She was so offended at her mother's sceptical attitude. 'I think I should go and see a priest.'

'Oh Erin, stop it will you? You know that Charleigh's a drama queen. She told you she was pregnant not so long ago and it was a stomach bug.'

Charleigh later called Erin and gave a blow-by-blow account of how the ghost had appeared, how it had touched her, and she described how she had thrown up when she regained consciousness and she even maintained that she must have died at one point because her mother discovered her unconscious daughter had no pulse. The two friends talked for over an hour, and Erin kept expecting to hear the ghost join the conversation, but for some reason, it didn't. Erin told her parents that evening that she was chucking in her job at the call centre. She believed the weird haunting had only happened because she had dialled the number of that ghost. Her father said she was being silly and that she needed the money to pay off her credit card debt but Erin said she'd find another job and that was that.

At exactly 3am, Erin was fast asleep in bed. She'd fallen asleep with her bedside lamp on because she was still naturally afraid of the ghost materialising again. The iPhone rang. Erin felt as if her eyes were superglued shut, but she managed to open one eye and saw that the caller was unknown. She gingerly reached for the mobile and answered the call.

'I am feeling so awfully alone now,' said the ghost.

Erin felt a wave of coldness pass from the top of her head down to her stomach. 'Leave me alone,' she said. She could hardly speak because her throat was so dry.

'I wouldn't be alone if you died and joined me though,' the entity chillingly suggested.

Erin ended the call. She buried her head under the duvet, and expected him to appear in the bedroom. She eventually had to come up for air. She took a quick glance towards the bottom of the bed. By the light of the bedside lamp she could see there was no one there. She turned her eyes to the drawn blinds with their soft orange light from the street lamp diffusing through them. There was no one there. And yet she somehow knew he was coming. She told herself he wasn't coming, that she'd be okay, and that she should try and get back to sleep. She lifted the top of the duvet so it covered the right side of her head, just above her ear.

She listened. In the distance, a motorbike was travelling through the night. And then, as the noise faded, Erin just knew that he was in the room. She went cold inside and she was literally paralysed with fear. She wanted to spring from her bed and get out of the room, but she thought he might grab her and knock her unconscious the way he did with Charleigh. Then the rational part of her mind told her she was being stupid – that Charleigh was indeed a drama queen who had fainted because she had imagined the ghost.

Black fingers – pure black silhouetted fingers – emerged over the top of the duvet, inches from her face. A hand grabbed the duvet, and Erin screamed and bolted from the bed. She threw open the door and ran to the room of her parents. She barged in and saw her father, naked, on top of her mother. They were making love. She heard her father shout something harsh at her as she quickly left the room and went downstairs. Erin turned on the lights and looked up to the top of the stairs. She expected the menacing silhouette to appear, but instead, her mother came down the stairs in a nightdress, and her face was red with embarrassment. 'This can't go on, love.' She told her daughter, 'it's not normal.'

'You think I'm seeing things,' Erin told her mother with a look of utter disbelief. 'Mum, I am not seeing things! It even attacked Charleigh – '

'Don't start all that again!' her mother shouted, and she went to get her inhaler from a drawer in the kitchen. 'If you don't pipe down, you'll have to go to the doctor and get something for your nerves!'

'What was that?' came a voice from upstairs. Erin's father was on the landing in just his boxer shorts, and he was looking to his left – towards Erin's bedroom. 'Someone just peeped round the door,' he said, 'in Erin's bedroom.'

'Dad! Don't go in there! That's the ghost!' Erin ran up the stairs and grabbed her father's hand. She gently led him down the stairs, and she could see that he was a bit afraid of what he had just seen.

'Oh, don't you start!' Erin's mother trotted up the stairs despite the loud protestations from her daughter not to, and she went in to Erin's room.

'Mum! Don't go in there!' yelled Erin.

Erin's dad went up the stairs and with some hesitation he ventured into Erin's bedroom, where he saw his wife looking back at him with a concerned look. 'Is she having a breakdown, love?' she asked.

'No, she is not – I've just seen something peeping out from this doorway, and I didn't imagine it.' Erin's father looked around the bedroom, and then he and his wife went downstairs. Erin made coffee and said she was staying up, and first thing in the morning she was going to see a priest about the whole weird affair. Her father sat at the kitchen table with her and had a coffee. His wife shook her head and said, 'Well, it's nearly half-past three in the morning and I've got to be up for work at eight. I'm going to bed.'

'Love, I saw it – ' Erin's father said to the back of his wife as she marched away in a huff towards the stairs.

Erin went to see a local reverend about the ghost, and although he seemed very sympathetic to her predicament, he said he had never carried out an exorcism and really didn't believe in blessing houses. Erin got the impression that the reverend didn't even believe in God! The vicar suggested visiting a medium of all things, and then he apologised, saying he was sorry he couldn't be of any further help. Erin's father had an idea. He said that if Erin could get hold of the telephone number she had first called – the one that had apparently 'kicked the ghost off' – it might lead to a certain address and then perhaps they could research the history behind the ghost. All Erin knew was that the number she had called that afternoon had been a Liverpool one. She contacted her former boss at the call centre and asked if she could possibly have the number of that Liverpool telephone, but he swore at her and hung up. The ghost continued to jump in on conversations Erin had on her mobile, but she never saw it in person again, and she believes that's because she took to sleeping with several Bibles in her bedroom. For nearly six months, the ghost interrupted telephonic conversations between Erin and many friends, relatives and people the young lady had called when she was job hunting, and then the ghost remained silent, and has not been heard from since. Its identity remains a mystery, but Erin still lives in fear of hearing from the entity about its 'awful' loneliness.

ZARAZZNAR

There is a belief in the world of the occult that a medium – a true medium – must never use their gift to make money, or they will suffer dire consequences. Most stage mediums are charlatans; they can supply people with the *first* names of an alleged spirit they've contacted but rarely give a surname. If I stood before an audience on a stage and said "I have a woman here named Margaret who has a message,' I would see a sizeable number of people raising their hands, thinking the message was for some Margaret they have lost, as Margaret is quite a common name to the older generation. That's all most so-called mediums do. They will never say 'I have a message for David Walker who lived on Belvidere Road.' The mentalist Derren Brown has proved that anyone with a basic knowledge of psychology can give the impression they are psychic, and Derren is despised by a lot of showbiz 'psychics' who hate the gullible public being warned against the fraudsters who pretend to be clairvoyant.

I have had dealings with genuine mediums who have come from all walks of life, and none of them have made any money or a stage career out of their gift; in fact a lot of them are actually afraid of their unearthly talent as they often see future tragedies involving close friends and members of their own family, so they try to block out their eerie faculty.

In the late 1950s there was an amateur comedian in Liverpool named Paul Pessel. He bore an uncanny resemblance to the comedic actor Benny Hill, but sadly he did not possess even a fraction of Hill's talent. Pessel appeared at various clubs in the city and died onstage on all of them with his hackneyed, dated jokes, fluffed delivery and awful timing. He said that Liverpool – like Glasgow - had the most savagely critical audiences in the country, and also blamed his joke supplier. Falling behind on his rent, Pessel needed work badly and his long-suffering agent gave him a nightmare ultimatum – he could starve, or he could get fifty quid for an half-hour act at the Glasgow Empire – known in showbiz circles as the Graveyard of Comedians because the Scottish audiences were so hostile up there. Pessel was forced to take the booking, but he refused to appear alone, so he persuaded an old accordionist he knew named Billy Pickles to join him. The idea was for Billy to go on first to do an instrumental solo with his accordion, and then Pessel would come on and do his entire act in mime. This way the audience would not know he wasn't Scottish, and they'd hopefully let him live. Billy Pickles came onstage on the night, sat on a stool, and began to play an instrumental version of the traditional Scottish song *D'ye ken John Peel*. A few minutes into the instrumental solo piece, Paul Pessel made his stage entrance dressed in a huge tam-o'-shanter that was flopped over an orange spiky wig. Pessel wore a string vest, a kilt, a pair of pink tights, and a pair of oversized Army boots.

Someone in the audience shouted out, 'Fack! There's two of them!'

The crowd then became rowdy, and they were reminiscent of a raucous cup final crowd to Pessel, who started to kick his legs high in the air and do a number of silly walks that had obviously been lifted from a Max Wall routine. Unabashed by the tumultuous audience, he continued to dance to the accordion music, when an empty whiskey bottle sailed through the air, and with the precision of an intercontinental ballistic missile, it struck Billy Pickles on the forehead. The old accordionist fell backwards off the stool and an awful wheezing cacophony of notes oozed from his crumpled accordion. 'There was no need for that!' Pessel shouted at the demonic audience, and now, hearing his accent, they knew he was not a Scot. 'Get back over the border you bastard Sassenach!' someone bellowed, and as Pessel dragged the unconscious accordionist off the stage, an army of hecklers came out with funnier lines than any Pessel's joke-writer could ever come up with. Someone hurled a cigarette lighter onto the stage and it glanced off the head of the failed comedian as he sought sanctuary in the wings. Pessel had suffered some Near Death Experiences on the stages of the big theatres throughout the land, and he thought he'd never experience anything worse than the soul-destroying "Clapham Silence" from the cruel mute audience at the Clapham Grand, when he'd walked off the stage to the echo of his own footsteps. He'd even had a shipyard rivet thrown at him up at the Sunderland Empire – but this place was a theatre in Hell! Pessel saw the longed-for fifty pounds evaporate before his eyes. When he returned to Liverpool he severed his ties with his agent and decided he should either hang himself – or reinvent himself with a new act – or better still, an entirely new persona. Whenever Pessel needed ideas, he would visit the Legs of Man public house on the corner of Lime Street, next door to the Liverpool Empire Theatre. Pessel found that a few glasses of Calvert Whiskey (brought to the pub from America by the Merchant seamen) seemed to act as an idea-generator. Pessel sat in a corner of the pub, nursing a glass of Calvert as he exhaled rings from the Embassy Emperor, a large corona cigar, when Freddy, an old stagehand from the Empire walked in. Pessel immediately called him over, told him to sit down and went and bought the old man a packet of fags and a dimpled glass tankard containing a pint of the pub's finest bitter.

'Have you won the Pools Paul?' the stagehand asked, smiling at the cigarettes.

'I wish, Fred,' Paul replied, 'I just want to pick your brains about something.'

'Pick *my* brains? Ha, you'd starve mate,' Paul told him, and he sipped the bitter.

'What it is Fred, is this: I can't cut it as a comic – just haven't got a funny bone in my body, and I'm thinking of starting out again as some other act with a new name.'

'Go on,' Fred egged him on.

'Well, you've seen all the acts – what's big at the moment?' Paul asked him.

'Singers, but I take it you can't sing?' Fred asked.

'Couldn't sing to save my life,' Paul admitted.

'You can't juggle either,' Fred recalled, 'remember

that accident at the Shakespeare?'

Paul slowly closed his eyes and grimaced as if he was having an angina attack. 'Don't remind me, go on.'

Fred opened his cigarette pack and continued. 'Well, there's the magicians sawing their assistants in half and levitating, and er, the mediums and mind-reading acts – they're always popular.'

'Mind-reading act,' said Paul, and Fred could see that a light bulb had gone on in his brain the way he gave a lopsided grin. 'How do they do that?'

'Trade secret mate,' was Fred's reply. The unlit cigarette in his mouth levered up and down as he spoke.

'No, seriously, Fred, how do they do it? Do they have confederates in the audience?'

'Takes years of practice, Paul,' Fred told him, lighting the jemmying ciggie. 'You can't just bill yourself as a mind-reader; they all know you round here as the comedian.'

'I'd wear a mask,' said Paul, 'or heavy make-up, a wig, and adopt a French accent maybe.'

Fred brought him back down to earth. 'You still need the skill, Paul.'

'Fred, I heard that the mind readers and mediums use codes – is that true?'

'Yeah, of course,' said Fred, 'none of them are really psychic. A basic code could be like this: you are the mind reader, blind-folded on stage and your assistant goes in the audience and asks a random person to hold a personal item – which you have to identify. The assistant will say things like, "Let's *watch him* and see he's not peeping under that blindfold," and the word 'watch' will mean the man in the audience has chosen his wristwatch for example, or the assistant may even say, "Take your *time* Paul," emphasising the word time – a code for a timepiece. The rest is just to stick as many plants in the audience as possible. Extras from plays will willingly help out for a few bob, and stun the audience when you appear to reveal their secrets and the details of their lives.'

'I think I could do all that,' said Paul, confidently, 'there's no skill needed, just the memorising of codes and the use of people planted in the audience.'

'What name would you go under?' Fred asked with a wide grin. He really did think that Paul was just building castles in the air with his proposed mind-reading act.

'Something mysterious with an occult flavour like Mr Zodiac, I reckon,' Paul told him, and seemed to be looking into mid air in a brown study state of mind.

Well, Paul Pessel created the Zodiac character. He wore pale make-up, eyeliner to affect a penetrating stare, and he had a suit made of midnight blue velvet which featured stars and moons upon the front, and these symbols were embroidered with sparkling sequins. The gimmick was the Tie with the All-Seeing Eye – a broad scarlet silk tie that was tied in a Balthus knot, and upon the front of this tie there was an image of an open eye with lines radiating from it, embroidered in gold thread. Zodiac would claim that this tie had been given to him by a Mandarin magician he had saved from drowning in Yangtze River whilst on a pilgrimage to a Manchurian Occultist. The tie boosted the telepathic powers of Zodiac.

Pessel had to borrow from a notorious loan shark to finance his mind-reading act, and he started on the smaller clubs and theatres, and the act was quite well-received at first – until an observant member of the audience noticed that Zodiac was using the same supposedly randomly-chosen people in the audience at different venues. Paul Pessel tried to bribe the vigilant man to remain silent but he told everyone that Zodiac was a fake, and word of mouth destroyed the mind-reading act. Pessel was back to square one. He not only ended up owing back rent, he also owed money to the loan shark, and so he went to bed one night in his tiny bedsit with a bottle of whiskey and a bottle of sleeping pills, intending to end his pitiful life. He took two pills, and began to rant and shake his fist as he looked at the ceiling. He was having cross words with God. 'Why can't you just give me one break, eh? Just give me one little break – or am I asking the wrong one? Perhaps I should ask the other fellah down below, eh?'

He knocked back shot after shot of whiskey, and fell asleep before he could take the other sleeping pills. Paul Pessel had the strangest dream that night as he lay there, sedated by the barbiturates and the whiskey. He heard *Entry of the Gladiators* - that piece of music that is always played at the circus, and it was echoing, as if it was being performed in a large hall. Then he was dazzled by the glare of a light switched on above him in the darkness. He was on some old-fashioned stage in what seemed to be a Victorian or Edwardian Theatre. The footlights were not electric – they were small jets of gas, and the audience was made up of men with handlebar moustaches and women in huge flowery bonnets. Paul Pessel somehow knew that he was a magician who went by the stage name

"Zarazznar". He also felt that his real name was something like Quentin Black, or perhaps Blake, he could not be sure, but he found himself performing some very unusual acts of magic in the realistic dream. He stood there in the pale green disc of limelight, and all eyes in the theatre were upon him. He went to a small card table on the stage and reached with both hands into a bucket of what looked like sawdust, and then he clutched two fistfuls of the fine particles of wood, and proclaimed: 'Behold! The Dancing Sawdust Man!'

He threw the sawdust into the air as gasps of awe filled the theatre, and the falling clouds of dust drifted down in the limelight and began to coalesce into two pillars made up of thousands of specks of light. The pillars spun around and merged into what looked like the figure of a man. Paul looked to his left, towards the wings – and he saw two Pierrot clowns – their white painted faces looking on in awe at the spectacle, and standing on either side of the spellbound clowns were other performers looking on in amazement.

The weird faceless figure of a man made up of the vaporous sawdust danced about the stage, twirling about on one toe as the orchestra in the pit began to play a vaguely familiar tune. Zarazznar started to sing the old Grossmith song *You Should See Me Dance the Polka*. Seconds into the song, the magician produced a large wooden hoop and held it out as the Sawdust Man suddenly dived through it, and through some mind-boggling act of stage trickery, a skeleton emerged through the other side of that hoop. There were sharp intakes of breath, screams and loud cheers in the audience. Zarazznar kicked his legs high into the air in time to the music, and then he jumped higher than his own height, and he spun like a top with coat tails whipping the air before he came down to thunderous applause.

'Phantazmorama!' he shouted, and pointed to an upright coffin upstage. The door of the coffin swung open to reveal a skeleton in some white bridal dress, and it was plain to see that this thing was not some marionette – not some puppet operated by wires from the overhead rigging by stagehands – so how on earth was this done? The bride skeleton joined up with the newly-created skeleton who had emerged from the hoop, and they waltzed about on the stage as Zarazznar danced like a man possessed whilst singing the Grossmith song. Some of the people in the audience looked afraid of him, because he seemed to be a real magician and he was acting like a madman now, screaming with laughter as he performed multiple back-flips in the air. The orchestra slowed the Polka song, and the audience became a Babel of discordant voices. The skeletons fell to the ground and remained there lifeless, and Zarazznar suddenly pointed to people in the audience and cried out. 'Sinners! All of you are sinners, and I Zarazznar will look into your minds and drag your awful secrets into the light!'

A military man dressed in his Venetian red coat stood up and booed the outlandish magician, but Zarazznar gave a signal to the lighting operator and a ring of illumination swept across the boards and fell off the edge of the stage till it settled on the hissing soldier. The red-coated man froze in the spotlight, and Zarazznar suddenly produced a judge's wig from his sleeve, and quickly put it on. He addressed the soldier with a booming voice: 'Your name is Jonathan Brown, and you're a pillar of the community! Attending church every Sunday! Butter wouldn't melt in your mouth! But your fiancée, your friends and your regiment, don't know what you did to that girl in India do they Mr Brown?'

'How dare you!' the soldier said, sounding as if he was so shocked he could hardly get his words out. 'That sir, is defamation!' he warned the strange magician.

But Zarazznar folded his arms and seemed fearless as he told the fuming sergeant: 'You outraged her and you mutilated her with your bayonet! You're a veritable Jack the Ripper when you're posted abroad, aren't you Sergeant Brown?'

'I will see you in court, sir!' Sergeant Brown growled, and he tried to link his arm into the arm of the lady standing beside him, but she backed away with her hand to her mouth, as if she had realised something very unsavoury about her fiancé. She stumbled backwards, and when the sergeant went to help her up she screamed at him and told him to get away from her. A ripple of "ooh!" radiated through the audience as some of the theatregoers realised that Zarazznar had somehow read the mind of the dashing sergeant and uncovered a welt of scandalous blood-soaked secrets from his past.

The sergeant stormed off, pushing people out of his way as Zarazznar's echoing laughter bounced off the walls of the auditorium. 'Phantazmorama!' Zarazznar cried as he pointed to other members of the audience. He unmasked reverends, policemen, bank managers, and people from the lowliest walks of life to the very crème de la crème of society as child molesters, murderers, poison pen letter-writers, arsonists, adulterers, embezzlers, rapists and thieves. At one point, a gentleman Zarazznar accused of being a forger jumped on the stage and aimed a pistol at him. He fired, and at that point in the dream, Paul Pessel awoke with a start and sat bolt upright. He was drenched in sweat and it was still dark outside, but he later learned that he had been asleep for almost 24 hours.

'Zarazznar,' he muttered, recalling fragments of the dream, 'what was that all about?' And he went to his shaving mirror to look at his ghastly bloated face. For a brief second, he saw the face of a stranger looking back at him in that mirror, and the face was superimposed over his face. It was the face of a man with a pointed widow's peak, a long straight nose, a pointed chin, and a pair of dark penetrating eyes. Pessel just knew it had been the face of that long-dead magician from the Victorian era – Zarazznar. He stayed up all night, and at eight in the morning he sneaked out of the bedsit so that the landlady wouldn't hear him. She'd only pester him for rent money he didn't possess. Pessel went to a shabby café where they served breakfast cheaply, and that strange dream was still resonating in his mind. Paul Pessel had a feeling that the spirit of that mysterious mind-reading magician was slowly possessing him. Eventually, over the course of a week, Paul Pessel discovered that he could read minds – and the newfound ability scared him at first. He read the mind of his landlady and discovered that her husband Terence had left her ten years ago, and then he had been tragically knocked down and killed by a bus, which ruled out any hopes of reconciliation with his wife. Paul felt great sympathy for the landlady when he delved into her mind and discovered that she spent most nights alone in her room upstairs close to tears because she was so lonely. He also learned that the landlady's late husband had affectionately called her by her nickname, which was "Flissy" – as her name was Felicity. Then Paul read the mind of a middle-aged lodger at the house named Mr Winters, and discovered that this bachelor fancied the landlady but was too shy to ask her out. Paul played Cupid, and one evening he went and knocked on his landlady's door, and she thought for a moment that he had come to pay the back rent. Paul told her he *would* get the money to her soon, but he hadn't called to settle any account – he had come with a message from beyond the grave. At first the landlady thought it was either some joke or a confidence trick to distract her from the rent she was owed, but Paul managed to make her believe his story. He said he had attended a séance at a friend's house, and a spirit named Terence had come through and told him that he was the deceased husband of the landlady, and that he had lovingly called her Flissy when he was alive. Now Terence wanted his wife on earth to love again - with a man named Mr Winters. The landlady seemed very tearful, and after confirming that her husband had indeed been called Terence, and that he *had* called her Flissy, and that he *had* died in a road accident ten years before, she asked Paul: 'I wonder if he means Mr Winters who lives on the ground floor facing you, Mr Pessel?'

'I think that's exactly who he meant,' Paul told her.

The landlady invited him into her room and over tea

and biscuits she showed her lodger her old photograph album and the pictures of her with Terence. The little tête-à-tête between the landlady and Paul ended at 9pm, and she told him that he could pay the rent when he had the money – there was no rush. Paul assured her that he'd have the money soon. "Flissy" the landlady said she'd like to go on a date with Mr Winters but thought she was a bit too old for him. Paul assured the landlady she was a "young fifty-nine" and said she should consider getting her hair styled to get noticed by Mr Winters as her hair was undoubtedly her crowning glory. He then went downstairs and gently rapped on the door of Mr Winters, and after a minute the latter answered the door in his pyjamas. Paul said he'd like to talk to him in confidence.

'What about?' Mr Winters asked, bewildered by the late visit. 'It's gone nine o'clock Mr Pessel, can't it wait till the morning?'

'Well, let's just say that what I am about to tell you is to your advantage Mr Winters.'

Winters let his neighbour in and straight away Pessel told him that he had just been having a lovely chat with the landlady and she had, in the course of the conversation, mentioned how much she liked Winters.

Mr Winters blushed and seemed lost for words.

'She'd like you to take her out Mr Winters,' Paul told him, and then he raised his eyebrows and appeared to add an afterthought to his words: 'Unless of course, there is a Mrs Winters.'

'No, no, there isn't – er, I'm a confirmed bachelor you see,' Winters explained, 'always worked all my life and never really had time for socialising, which I now regret in my twilight years.'

'She said she hasn't been to the cinema for years; maybe you could take her to the Odeon or something,' said Paul.

'Why has she told *you* all this?' Winters asked with a trace of suspicion in his eyes. 'I've often heard her knocking at your door and demanding the rent.'

Paul smiled and slowly nodded. 'Yes, I know, but I went up to tell her I'd have the money soon and she seemed very lonely, and she brought me in and we went through a few pots of tea and a lot of biscuits, and well, she just opened up.'

'Thanks for telling me, anyway, Mr Pessel,' said Winters.

'Call me Paul. So, you'll give it a try?'

'Well,' replied Mr Winters, 'I *have* been out of action for a long time, and we bachelors get set in our ways, but I'll think about it.'

'I have a feeling we'll be hearing wedding bells soon Mr Winters,' said Paul, and he chuckled.

A few days later, Paul saw the landlady and Mr Winters going out together. He read their minds and sensed the great joy in them. It was as if they had both found their soulmates.

Paul had to keep his mindreading under control. When he was on a bus, it was like listening to a hundred radios playing different stations. The worst broadcasters were the ones with the butterfly brains who had no order to their thoughts – their attention spans were short and they flitted from one thing to another. The man sitting behind Paul had this sort of brain, and Paul heard his surreal train of transmitted thoughts which ran like this: 'Match kicks off at three...legs on her...need to get the Oxo cubes...would love to have a car like that...wonder if she's flirting with me? She is a bit young. Bet she's got a fellah and she's just teasing. Feel like a Guinness. Still got that bag of jelly babies in the cupboard. That greedy wife might have spotted them. She's getting a double chin. Dying to fart. That cold sore's still there.'

Paul had to get off a stop early because of all of the annoying telepathic chatter in his head. He went down backstreets till he reached a little run-down theatre and he asked the young girl in the box office if the manager Mr Graves was in. She said he was. 'Can you tell him Paul Pessel has a lucrative idea he'd like to share with him?'

The girl spoke on the telephone with Graves and gave Paul directions to the manager's office. Paul told Graves he had an amazing mind-reading act he wanted to perform at the theatre, and the manager sighed and said he'd seen such acts before and that they 'belonged to yesterday' – people had long seen through the hackneyed old mind-reading routines and the modern audience wanted something more exciting. Paul then read the mind of the manager and he told Mr Graves intimate and embarrassing details about his life which even Mrs Graves didn't know about. This personal demonstration of the mind-reading act persuaded Mr Graves to let Paul hire the theatre without paying the fee up front – he'd pay the manager from the takings. The first show featuring the great Zarazznar was poorly attended, but when those who did turn up witnessed the incredible telepathic abilities of Zarazznar, they told their friends and family members about the show, and within a few weeks, Paul Pessel was performing to full houses, and the managers of other, much bigger theatres, were asking Paul to put on his show at their venues. Just before Paul was due to have talks with the management of the London Palladium, he performed his finale at the small theatre in Liverpool. He started the sell-out show by telling an old lady in the front row that her budgerigar Obadiah was still with her in spirit, and as everyone laughed, the old lady cried and thanked Zarazznar, who then turned his attention to a refined-looking man. 'Mr Hamilton, you should return to your wife at once; she's about to give birth to your third child!' he said, and the man seemed ruffled as he told the concerned-looking lady beside him: 'He's talking absolute bloody rubbish!'

Zarazznar then told the man some of the other dark secrets he was hiding from his lady and the man concerned ran straight out of the theatre. Zarazznar continued to probe the nervous audience. Zarazznar told a young man the full name of the wife he had lost and assured him she was in Heaven now and missed him terribly. The audience was a sea of waving arms, all wanting readings from this genuine psychic, but Zarazznar singled out a sharp-suited man and told him: 'Your sins will find you out! Murderer! You have no conscience! The people you have killed!'

The man he was addressing rose from his seat, and before he calmly left, he told the medium: 'I'll see you soon.'

The audience became uncontrollable and Mr Graves, the manager of the theatre, had to come on stage to stop the act. They brought on a comedian called Charlie Tripe and he was instantly booed.

'How do you do it Mr Bessel? What's the gimmick?' the manager asked Paul in the dressing room, but he was at a loss to explain his amazing 'act'. The man he had accused of killing people paid Paul Pessel a visit at the hotel he was staying at - and gave him a beating so severe, he had to be hospitalised. Around this time, Pessel had a nervous breakdown because he couldn't stop reading minds. He came very close to being committed to an asylum, and had to drink pints of neat vodka and take sedatives to block out the incessant chattering of voices in his head. At 3am, as he lay in his bed at the Adelphi Hotel, Paul was visited by a caped man in black. He had seen this ghost before when he lay in the hospital bed but it had vanished when the night nurse had checked on him. The ghost stood at the foot of Paul's bed and in a rich low voice it said: 'I am the real Zarazznar, a magician of long ago. I gave you my powers as a warning! The psychic world is not for entertainment! If you continue to misuse your powers, you will be killed by a murderer you have unmasked. At this moment he is planning *your* murder. You must leave this city and live in obscurity if you wish to live.' The ghost then vanished, and Pessel's mind-reading abilities also vanished over the next few days. Paul Pessel changed his name, went to live in Nantwich, and he never went on stage again.

THE PLEASURE DOME MYSTERY

One Saturday evening around 9.30pm in the early summer of 1980 Susan and Robert, a couple in their forties, were watching an American soap opera called *Knot's Landing* on TV at their semidetached home in Whiston when they both saw a bright blue light shine through the window. The source of the steady light was something in next door's back garden, and it was reflecting off trees and filtering through the hedges. Robert went to the window and tried to see what it was. It was just out of sight, so he went into the kitchen and looked out the window – to see the upper part of what looked like a translucent dome lit up by the blue light he and his wife had seen seconds ago. The dome was protruding over the high fence at the side of the garden, so it had to be tall. 'Seen this?' Robert shouted to his wife. Susan was a big fan of *Knot's Landing* and so, with a groan she reluctantly left the living room and went to the kitchen to see what her husband was talking about. 'What is it?' she asked, thinning her eyes with puzzlement at the lit-up dome.

'I'm going to find out,' he said, and he went upstairs to the spare room, where he would have a clear view of the strange structure. When he got up there, Robert couldn't believe his eyes. In his neighbour's back garden, he could see a dome, about twenty feet in diameter and about twelve feet in height. It was lit up by a blue diffused light, and silhouetted against this light, Robert could see about ten people – and they all looked *naked*. They were jumping about in the dome as if they were on a trampoline, and some were holding hands as they jumped up and down, while others somersaulted through the air. 'Sue! Come and have a look at this!' Robert yelled down the stairs, and he heard his wife swear. When she came upstairs, he pointed out the strange spectacle to her. 'Not one of them has a stitch of clothes on!' Robert told her.

'I can see that,' Susan told him, 'but it is Saturday night. They're probably all drunk.'

'That's disgusting!' said Robert, 'those fellahs are all kissing, and those two girls, look!'

'It's like an orgy of some sort,' Susan said with a smile, and then she walked to the doorway. 'Anyway, I'm going back downstairs to watch *Knot's Landing*,' she told him, 'leave them to it and come downstairs.'

'I'm calling the police,' Robert told her sternly as he remained at the window of the unlit room. 'Bloody disgusting.'

'Robert, they all look old enough to be consenting adults – you'd get done for wasting police time,' said Susan, halting at the doorway. 'Get away from that window love – they'll think you're a Peeping Tom.'

Robert returned a perplexed look at his wife. 'Susan, can't you see that this is indecent? There might be kids looking at this round here. I'm calling the police. Bloody perverts!'

'Robert, do what you want then – I'm going to watch *Knot's Landing*!' Susan told him in a huff, piqued at what she saw as his puritanical overreaction to a group of young people having harmless fun.

She sat watching her soap opera with the volume turned up a bit, and Robert came rushing in and turned the TV's volume down, which really annoyed Susan. 'You're not going to believe this!' Robert said in an excited state. 'You know who has just gone into that dome in the nude?'

'I'm not bleedin' interested – turn that sound up!' Susan was inflamed at him having the audacity to mute her favourite television show.

'Charlie from number 22!' Robert told her. 'He stripped off in the garden then went into that thing and he's cavorting round with two women young enough to be his daughters!'

'Robert, will you please just sit down and watch the telly!' Susan lunged to the TV set and turned the volume back up.

Robert shook his head as he looked at his wife, and he turned and went into the hallway. He halted at the telephone on the half-moon table, and turned to close over the living room door to minimise the noise from the TV set as he made his call to the police.

Susan dashed to the living room door, yanked it open, and glared at her husband as he was poised to make the call in the hallway. She was fuming at his prudish behaviour. 'Robert, you can't do anything about people having a good time in the privacy of their own homes – it's perfectly legal – and yes, believe it or not, there *are* men who fancy other men and there *are* women who go with other women! We are in the 20th century now, you see? Times have moved on a bit from the days of Oliver Cromwell!'

'Charlie is *my* age!' Robert growled, picking up the telephone handset. 'I think he's actually older than me in fact – and he's carrying on with two girls barely out of their teens! Doesn't that strike you as morally wrong?'

'They are *not* children, Robert, they are over eighteen!' said Susan, and she tried to take the handset from him but he pushed her back with so much force she stumbled, so she swore at him, went back into the living room, and slammed the door hard.

'Police please,' Robert told the emergency services operator. 'Hello? Yes, I want to report an orgy in progress; yes – an orgy - and it involves a man my age – I'm er, forty-three – and he's with young girls.'

The living room door opened slowly, and Susan shook her head as she saw Robert making the report on the phone. He looked at her, but then quickly averted his gaze as he gave the rest of the details.

'Yes, that's Charlie's surname, not mine,' he told the policewoman. 'Yes, that's his address – number 22. We're at number 34. Yes, the girls look quite young. How young? I'm not sure, because of the lighting but they look very young.'

'They're over eighteen!' Susan shouted, then walked back into the living room.

'Yes, the tent is shaped like a dome, and it's in the back garden of number 32,' Robert told the police dispatcher. Then there was a pause, after which, Robert asked: 'When will you be sending someone round? Oh okay. Thanks. Bye.'

He went sheepishly into the living room to be greeted by a stony-faced Susan. He told her what the policewoman said but she didn't react. She never once turned to face him. She looked at the television screen constantly, and never gave a word of reply, so he stormed out of the living room and went upstairs. Before he even went into the spare room, he noticed the absence of that blue light that had radiated from the dome, and he went to the window – and saw the dome had gone. He opened the window to get a better look. Where the dome had stood in the garden next door, there was just a lawn. Not a trace of the domed tent was visible to Robert, not even any holes from tent pegs, and he began to panic. The police would think he was a nut. He rushed downstairs and again he turned down the volume of the television set, but this time Susan screamed at him, hurling insult after insult, and she even threatened to leave him.

'Oh my God will you please just shut up and listen? The dome has gone! It's gone!' he told her, oblivious to her revilements.

Not long after, there was a heavy knocking at the door, and Robert answered it to see two policemen standing on his doorstep. 'You reported some orgy in a tent,' said one of the policemen, and when Robert told him that the dome was now gone, the poker-faced constable informed him that he had called next door and the couple there had told him that they had only just come home from a family visit and had no knowledge of any sexual high jinks going on in their back garden. The couple had even invited the policemen into their back garden to see for themselves. Robert called Susan to the door and she backed up his story.

'I swear before God I am not a time-waster, nor is my wife,' Robert told the policeman, 'and if you go and call on Charlie at number 22 he could certainly help you with your enquiries because he was getting his oats in that dome!'

The policemen left without saying a word.

Robert and Susan watched the police car move off down the road into the night.

Three weeks after this at around 9pm on a warm June evening, Robert was working on an Airfix model of the *Golden Hind* at the kitchen table when Susan shouted to him from upstairs. 'Rob! It's back! That dome thing!'

Robert left the model on the kitchen table and hurried to the window. He saw the upper part of that blue illuminated dome again. He was upstairs in seconds, where Susan was at the open window, looking at the people milling about in the dome. This time there seemed to be more revellers in the dome, and on this occasion, Susan told her husband to fetch his old binoculars. Robert ran down to a cupboard in the kitchen and threw boxes of old football programs and various items of junk aside until he found the 10x25 binoculars in their brown leather case. He removed the binoculars from the case as he went up the stairs, and by the time he was entering the spare room he had pulled off the lens caps. Susan's left hand grabbed the binoculars and she trained them on the weird convex 'tent'. She smiled, then said, 'Oh Lord, they *are* in their birthday suits. Oh my, that is depraved - ew! I've never seen any of these people before.'

'Is Charlie from number 22 there?' Robert reached for the binoculars but Susan didn't hand them back.

'No, just young people – and I don't recognise any of them,' Susan replied, and then she handed the binoculars to her husband.

Robert took a look through them and he could not

believe his eyes for two reasons. 'Firstly these young people – not one of them looked over the age of twenty-five – were completely nude, and most of them were engaged in some sexual act – but some of them seemed to be either hovering about – or suspended from some very fine wires!

'How are they doing that?' Susan asked, noticing the weird acts of levitation. Four or five of the naked merrymakers were floating about and twirling through the air in slow motion.

'There's something very weird about all this,' Robert said, and then he took the binoculars from his eyes and announced: 'I'm going down to have a closer look.'

'Don't, they'll see you,' Susan told him, but seeing that her husband was already leaving the room she went with him. They went into their back garden and both stood on a bench so they could peer over the fence. They saw that quite a few of the naked people in that dome were indeed defying gravity somehow, and the spectacle really freaked Susan out. She saw that the dome looked as if it was made of some partially transparent plastic, and the whole hemisphere was made up of an interlocking lattice of thin triangles. Such a structure is known as a geodesic dome. Susan also noticed that the people in the structure were opening their mouths, as if they were shouting at one another, and yet she could not hear a word, nor any other noise, as if the dome was soundproof.

'I feel like some seedy voyeur watching all this,' said Susan, and she stepped down from the bench and headed back into the house via the kitchen door. Robert followed her in and said, 'Perhaps we should call next door and ask them why they are allowing such a disgraceful act in their back garden.'

'It's nothing to do with us, Robert,' Susan replied, and then she shot a knowing look at her husband and added, 'And don't go and call the police out again.'

Less than a minute later, Robert noticed that the dome had vanished into thin air. He stood on the bench and looked over the back garden fence, and saw only his neighbour's well-kept lawn. This sudden vanishing act convinced him that the dome had been some supernatural manifestation. Susan thought the same, and she said that they should get a camera loaded with film so they could take a picture of the thing next time it appeared. Some four month later, on a cold autumnal night, this time at around 11.15pm, Robert left his bed to go to the toilet, and immediately noticed the blue light shining through the bathroom windows. He rushed into his bedroom to tell his wife, and then he telephoned his friend Ian, who lived just around the corner, and told him to look out his window, because he would be able to see the dome himself. Ian had been told about the mysterious dome full of naked pleasure-seekers, and had believed it had all been some trick of the light. Ian rushed to his window and saw the blue glowing dome in the back garden of his friend's neighbours, and he could even see the figures moving about in it, but they were a bit too far to see in any detail. Susan spent nearly ten minutes trying to locate the little instamatic camera she'd bought in the hope of snapping the dome, and she went into the back garden, stood on the bench, and took two pictures of the dome from a distance of about twenty feet. Then suddenly, as she wound the film on, she saw, at close quarters, the spectacular vanishing act of the dome. She noticed that everyone in the structure suddenly froze, and then the dome vanished, as quick as a light being switched off, but it left behind a faint green after-image for a few seconds, and this vestige of the dome then faded away. The film was rushed to the chemist that day, and developed a few days later. Susan and Robert opened the little folder containing the prints and negatives, and saw that Susan had only captured the dome as a bright greenish light with silhouettes of people in it which were very blurred. The man in the chemist was shown the prints and said that Susan had obviously moved the camera as she had pressed the shutter release button – a common mistake most amateur photographers made. He asked what she had been trying to photograph and Susan told him, 'You'd never believe me.' Susan later told her husband that she thought the dome was some type of UFO and that the people in it were possibly from another planet.

It's possible that the dome was some glimpse of a party of the future being held in that garden in Whiston, and perhaps the man Robert mistook for Charlie was actually Charlie's grandson – which means the whole strange affair was down to a timeslip. Perhaps such orgiastic parties in the future will have a device which allows the revellers to entertain themselves in some localised zero-gravity environment – and perhaps such a 'pleasure dome' would also be soundproof to contain any pounding party music and thus comply with any sound pollution acts of that day and age; Susan said she had noticed that no sound came from the interior of that dome. I certainly don't think it was a landed UFO, which Susan has suggested. I will be looking at more local timeslips later on in this book.

THREE STRANGE BOOKS

Until the miracles started, 13-year-old Jimmy was called an ornament, a useless article and a dead loss by his Mam and Nan. His father never forgave him for failing the Eleven Plus exam and for supporting "the other team" – but then Jimmy's eccentric Uncle Rod died and Jimmy claimed his big black leather-bound Bible. He withdrew into his bedroom one rainy afternoon in that April of 1965, and with dogged determination he resolved – albeit unrealistically - to read that twelve-hundred-page book in a few days. It took Jimmy long enough getting through a copy of the *Beano* but the lad persevered. They all thought that Jimmy had succumbed to religious mania when he stayed in his bedroom reading the Bible, but three days after he started reading the work, he came out to play with his friends one late afternoon and some very odd things took place. Jimmy was playing football in the field at the back of Kensington Library when he leaped to head the ball – and he shot twenty-odd feet into the air. His mates all asked him how he did it, and he cryptically answered: 'Because I *believe* I can do it!'

Then they noticed what looked like a luminous halo around his head and a tongue of flame above the strange nimbus.

'Jimmy, what's wrong with yer head?' a girl asked, and Jimmy was at a loss to explain. He went and had a look at his reflection in the wing mirror of a car on Jubilee Drive and saw the halo. By then there was a small crowd around him, and one lad kept calling Jimmy Simon Templar – the name of the character (played by Roger Moore) on the television show, *The Saint* - because Templar was always shown to have a halo at the beginning of each show. As Jimmy headed home, the mysterious halo and the candle-size flame above it faded and vanished.

That evening, Jimmy's mum had toothache and her son placed his hand on her jaw and somehow the pain immediately ceased. She looked in the mirror and saw that the hole in her molar had vanished. 'I don't believe it,' she remarked, and Jimmy said: 'Doubt is a disease, Mam – try believing for a change.'

The news of "Spring-Heeled Jimmy" spread through the neighbourhood, and most believed the strange stories were pure exaggeration – until Jimmy broke a world record. It is exactly a mile from the junction of Jubilee Drive and Farnworth Street to the Lime Street end of London Road, yet Jimmy covered this distance on a Sunday morning with no traffic about in 3 minutes and thirty seconds, beating the records of Roger Bannister and Jim Ryun. Jimmy also won arm-wrestling competitions against the brawniest men in Kensington, but that was nothing compared to the day he apparently brought a friend's recently deceased grandmother back to life during a wake. As a result of this alleged resurrection, Jimmy was visited by an Irish priest who suspected him of being in league with the

Devil, and Jimmy's mum said: 'No Father, he's in league with Jesus; he's always got his nose in his late uncle's Bible.'

'And what Bible is this? May I see it?' the priest asked.

Jimmy's mother went up to her son's bedroom and brought the book down to the priest, who looked at the strange golden symbol on the front of the book; it looked more like a swastika than a Christian cross. The priest put on a pair of spectacles and read the pages. He gasped, and all of the colour drained from his face. 'Mary Mother of God! That's no Bible, woman!' he said, and began to cough and wheeze, more from shock rather than his asthmatic condition. 'Where did he get this work?' the priest asked.

'It was his uncle's, why Father?' Jimmy mum asked – she looked afraid because she could see that the priest was holding it as if it was an unexploded bomb.

'This – this is a copy of Lucifer's Book of Forbidden Knowledge, woman!' the priest cried, 'The most dangerous book in the world! Forget *Mein Kampf* and *The Last Temptation of Christ* - this book is the top of the banned books of the *Index*!'

He was referring to the Vatican's *Index Librorum Prohibitorum* – a list of heretical banned books dating back centuries.

'Oh! I didn't know, Father! I thought it was the Bible!' Jimmy's mum leaned on the mantelpiece, weak at the knees at the revelation.

'Didn't *know*, you say?' the priest asked, his tone questioning the veracity of her reply. 'You never thought to see what Jimmy had his nose in, woman?'

'I thought it was the Holy Book, before the Seven

Sacraments, I did!' she replied, on the verge of bursting into tears.

'You'll be needing confession tomorrow, you will!' the priest gravely informed her, and he took off his glasses, put the book under his arm, and left.

Jimmy received a slap to the side of his head when he came in.

'You told me that book you were reading was the Bible you liar!' his mother roared at him.

'It is! It said the Bible of Loofisser!' Jimmy replied, mispronouncing Lucifer's name.

'Lying to your mum is worst than a sin!' his mother yelled at him, and her face turned red and her eyes bulged. The outburst scared Jimmy.

'What have I done wrong?' he asked, truly baffled at his mother's harsh words.

'I'd rather have a liar than a thief any day – you can get to the bottom of a thief but not a liar!' she told him, bent over with her face close to his, and tiny drops of her spit hit his eyebrow.

'How am I a liar?' Jimmy asked, stepping back from his ranting mum.

'That book you took from Uncle Rod's house! It's an evil book and you knew!' she told him at last.

'How's it evil if I did good deeds with the lessons in it?' Jimmy asked, and a split second later the slap from his mother knocked him off balance and he fell on the old chair by the fireplace.

'You are going to confession with me tomorrow afternoon at St Anne's!' she screeched. 'I wouldn't be surprised if the statues walked out of that church in disgust Jimmy!'

Jimmy got to his feet and he ran up to his room in

tears, still in the dark regarding the strange accusations from his hysterical mother. Later that day his coalman father came home from work, and when he heard about Jimmy being in possession of the infamous book, he came up and reprimanded his son, but he also listened to what Jimmy had to say. His son assured him he had no idea that Lucifer was the fallen angel we now know as the Devil, and if he had known that, he would never have even touched the book. He asked his father what his Uncle Rod had been doing with the book in the first place but his dad was at a loss to answer. Jimmy was grounded until he had attended confession, and only then was he allowed to play football – but only in the street outside his house. A little girl who had come all the way from Boaler Street to ask Jimmy to cure her old dying cat had to be turned away, as the lad's powers to heal had now deserted him, and the gang he knocked around with laughed when they saw "Jimmy Miracle" trying, in quite a pathetic manner, to jump high into the air on Kensington Fields. He could no longer defy gravity. Doubt infected his life, and his faith in higher powers became as weak as a cobweb. He eventually believed in nothing. I asked him if he could recall the information contained in that supposed book of the Devil, and Jimmy said it had chapters on how to speak to most animals, how to make crops grow, and how to live on vegetables. There was a chapter on overcoming gravity – which Jimmy had read first, but he could no longer remember just what the secrets were. According to Jimmy, there was no mention of any evil-doing, and only one part really stuck out in his memory – something to do with man being the only evil thing on the planet. The most powerful part of the book Jimmy can vaguely recall was a section about the terrifying inner nature of the human psyche, and how to descend into its conflicting maelstroms to channel some immense atomic-like power. Jimmy didn't attempt the exercises cited to gain this inner power because he kept reading warnings from the author of the book about the disciple becoming insane if the exercises were not carried out as directed. Was the mysterious book written by Lucifer, or was it merely the work of an occultist? I simply do not know, but I have a feeling it was written by someone human and well-versed in the occult sciences. I have two more peculiar stories concerning strange books; take the case of the rare French book, *Histoires pour les Jours pluvieux* - "Stories for Rainy Days" – published in Napoleonic times. This slim scarlet book was among the vast collection of a bibliomaniac named Dustin Upton at his home in West Derby, and one night in August 1971, after Upton had retired to his bed, his 13-year-old daughter Libby silently entered the library – two rooms knocked into one and lined with books from the floor to the ceiling. Libby could have entered the out-of-bounds library with her torch, but being a romantic girl, she mooched about with a candle, and a naked flame among so much paper could have been catastrophic. She had a single aim in her mind: to obtain *that* book – the one she had overheard her father talking about to his friend Eric a week ago – the French one with the ghost. Libby could read French books, and she clearly recalled the title - *Histoires pour les Jours pluvieux*. Her father had told Eric he had placed the book on the top shelf – out of Libby's reach – as he knew his daughter was becoming obsessed with the supernatural. Her father spoke rather loud even when he thought he was whispering, and Libby had heard everything from her bedroom. She climbed the ladder. Nine shelves up, fifteen feet in the air, she saw the thin scarlet book and tilted her head right to read the tiny faded-gold title embossed on the spine. She smiled, placed candle on the ledge of the shelf, and put her pointing finger on the book. She slowly pulled it out, being careful not to break another spine – as she did so often on these crumbly old tomes. She took hold of the candle, and descended the ladder with the haunted book tucked into the armpit of her night gown. She hurried out of the library and straight back to her bed. She sat cross-legged on the duvet and by the soft lemon illumination of her bedside lamp, she opened the book. She read the title, and the smaller words below it told her that it had been published by Gide in 1822. The pages had a rather sweet but acidic smell reminiscent of the scent of pear drops, and there were little blemishes and spots of mildew on the paper, or "foxing" as her father called such imperfections. Then Libby saw something curious. The previous (female) owner of the book had written her name in ink that had long turned brown, and that name seemed to be Talia Leveque but it was smudged, and someone had drawn an arrow in pencil pointing to the blurred name with the word: 'tears'.

The first story was entitled Le Soldat de L'étain Perdu – "The Lost Tin Soldier" and there was a drawing of the toy tin soldier on the facing page as a hand-coloured lithograph plate. Quite boring, Libby thought, so she flipped through the other stories concerning "The Blue Mermaid", "The King's Cake", and "The Crooked Man" – and this latter title, and the strange drawing opposite the page – of a weird crooked skinny man in black with a very sinister face, caught Libby's eyes and her imagination, and she placed her hand on the page and settled back to read the story, which began: "Once upon a time, before this country was even named France, and even further back before it was called Gaul, there lived a crooked old wizard known as Tordu Batard...'

Libby stopped reading in shock. She was not allowed to swear. Tordu Batard meant "Twisted Bastard" in French. The use of a profanity in this book which seemed to have been written for children seemed very odd – and wrong. She continued to read the old book by the light of the bedside lamp, and after just a page she was very upset, because this evil wizard Tordu was sticking long pins in the heads of babies, blinding people while they slept with long needles thrust in their eyes, and so many other wicked things. But the biggest shock was to come. Libby turned the page. Something black and spidery had been pressed into the book, and it stood our starkly against the pale page. The teen shrieked and threw the book towards the end of the bed, and the thing fell out and landed on the duvet. Just as people press flowers and petals in books, this creature all in black, with black gloves and pointed black shoes, known as poulaines – had been pressed flat, and seemed almost as thin as tracing paper. The face was hideous and corn-yellow in colour with dark rings around its shut eyes. The long nose had been pressed into the face so the tip touched the chin.

Libby switched on the ceiling light and opened the bedroom door. She stood in the doorway, gazing at the ghastly two-dimensional figure. He looked as if he had been ironed. She decided the thing had to go back in that old book, and then she'd put it back in her father's library. Libby couldn't bring herself to touch the little pressed man in black with her fingers, so she tiptoed downstairs to get a spatula hanging on the wall of the kitchen. She then returned to her room – and saw that the compressed black figure was not on the duvet. With a mounting sense of terror, Libby quickly bent down and looked under her old bed. She couldn't see the flattened figure anywhere, so she returned the old French book to her dad's library and then came back into the bedroom and searched again for the weird paper-thin entity without success. On the following day, Libby's mother noticed her daughter was not her usual self; she looked worried, and so she asked the girl what the matter was. At this time Libby's father was at work, so the teenager decided to tell her mother what she had done.

'Oh Libby, your father's told you you're not allowed in his library – you know what he's like over his books; he won't even let me Hoover about in there.'

'I know, I know mum, but he got me intrigued saying the book was haunted; I overheard him telling Eric about it.'

The eyes of Libby's mother widened at the mention of the book being haunted. 'Oh - *that* one.' She then seemed lost for words for a moment.

'Yeah, why mum? What's up?' Libby asked, sensing her mother knew something about the book in question. 'Is it haunted? How can a book be haunted?'

'That book is hundreds of years old,' her mother replied, 'and he'll go spare if he finds out you've been reading it.'

'What was the thing that was pressed in it?' Libby asked. 'It looked like a man about eight inches long, and his face looked horrible. He was all in black.'

'We'd better have a proper look for it Libby, come on,' the girl's mum told her and headed out of the lounge.

'Mum I have looked all over my room; it isn't there!'

Mother and daughter searched every inch of the bedroom. There were screams as a disturbed spider ran from under the bed during the hunt for the pressed man. Libby put a glass over it, then slid a card under the glass and evicted the arachnid by throwing it out of the window. The search resumed, but that weird flat oddity could not be found and they had to give up the quest.

'Just don't mention this, Libby, and hopefully your father will never miss the thing – whatever it was.'

Libby's father returned home from his antiquarian bookshop in Liverpool city centre at 6pm and after tea, he went into his beloved library. Libby watched TV and kept expecting him to come out of the library after perhaps noticing something had been disturbed, but he never did. The girl called on her friend Melanie, and returned home about 9pm. She watched more television, and then, before bed, she talked with her mother in the kitchen about a boy she liked named Stuart – then went to bed around half-past ten. She sat up in bed in her tee shirt and shorts because it was such a warm August night. The radio was tuned to Radio 1 and she listened to *Late Night Extra* on low volume as she read *Look-In* magazine. Libby began to feel drowsy by midnight, and she dozed off. A stinging sensation in her left eye woke her up. Something cold was on her face and the pain in her eye was excruciating. She couldn't open her left eye and reflexively batted whatever was on her face with her hand, and then she almost fell out the bed, and with her right open eye she saw what looked like some doll at first on the bed – and then she realised it was that pressed black-clad man! He was no longer flat and two-dimensional – he was like a real living person but about as small as an Action Man doll. He held a knitting needle in his left gloved hand, and Libby realised he had stabbed her in the eye because she opened the injured left eye and everything was red and pink – from blood. She saw the blood on the fingers of her left hand, and she screamed. As she ran out the bedroom, she saw the little man in black roll off the other side of the bed, and he still had that knitting needle.

Libby ran into the bedroom of her parents but they weren't there. She ran down the stairs and bumped into her mother who was coming up the stairs to see why her daughter had screamed.

'It stabbed my eye! He stabbed me in the eye mum!' Libby told her, and became hysterical, thinking she'd been blinded in her left eye.

'Who stabbed you? Who?' her father kept saying as Libby's mother took her daughter to the kitchen to dab her eye with a towel. An ambulance was called for and within fifteen minutes the ambulance man was examining the girl's eye as she cried. 'It's alright Libby, the eyeball looks fine – it hasn't been punctured, but the eyelid has a bad graze,' he said examining the fine wound with a penlight torch.

'Will she have to go into hospital?' Mrs Upton asked, and the ambulance man said he'd take her in just so a specialist could make sure she was fine, and this answer almost caused Libby to faint. At the hospital, the ophthalmologist asked Libby how the 'accident' had happened, and she gave her unbelievable answer. The eye specialist gave a quizzical smirk and told Libby's parents: 'A nightmare, eh? Did she fall asleep knitting or was there a sharp object on the bed?'

'Er, I don't really know,' said Mr Upton, 'Can she go home?'

'Yes, but she'll need to use an ointment on her eyelid,' the ophthalmologist replied, 'and she'll be right as rain.'

When Libby Upton went home, she refused to sleep in her own bed, and so she slept with her mother and her father slept on the sofa. On the following morning, Libby asked him about the haunted book, as he now knew she'd had a look at it and had lost that pressed man in black from it. Mr Upton had said the pressed figure had just been some old cut-out of some sort, but Libby knew he was not telling the truth. Her father eventually admitted (when he'd had a few drinks later that evening) that the man who had sold him the old French book had told him the volume had something of a supernatural reputation – but that was all Libby's dad would admit. He sold the allegedly haunted book not long afterwards. The family moved out of the house in West Derby a year later when Mr Upton's brother died and left a huge mansion in Sussex to him in his will. The family moved into this mansion, but in the twelve months before they relocated, the Uptons, as well as many visitors to the house, saw what seems to have been that weird little man in black, darting about the house, mostly of a night. The figure was allegedly even seen in the house next door to the Uptons – in the bathroom of a 60-year-old widow. She saw it clearly as she was having a bath, and described it as wizened and crooked entity with beady black eyes. She hurled a back brush at the thing and let out a scream as the miniature menacing man somehow fled by squeezing through the inch-tall gap under the bathroom door. Libby wondered if that unearthly sinister little prowler was the wizard called Tordo Batard in the strange book which detailed his sadistic activities about putting pins in the heads of babies and piercing the eyeballs of sleeping people with long *needles*. Is that evil little man still at large in West Derby I wonder...

Another incident concerning a mysterious book took place at Chequers Gardens in Aigburth in July 1969. The year before, the Jones family moved into the 170 yard-long cul-de-sac of semis, and now the head of the family of four – Arthur Jones – decided to go and clear out the garage. There was a rusty old petrol-driven lawn mower that needed to be shifted as well as a mountain of musky old books, and most of these were about gardening – but Hayley, the 13-year-old daughter of Mr and Mrs Jones – discovered an old yellowed sketchbook among the books. It contained all sorts of drawings made in pencil and ink of strange-looking people with exaggerated features – like caricatures almost – and these people all wore strange items of clothing such as polka dot suits and a number of men in extravagant robes wearing tall three-tiered crowns on their heads that looked very similar to the papal tiaras worn by Popes. Arthur Jones showed the 14-page book to a friend named Alan Goodrich, who ran a second hand bookshop, and was told that the sketchbook was a Derwent brand of drawing book from the late 1920s, and that it was worth nothing except to the person who had made the sketches. The book was given back to Hayley, and the girl went into the large back garden with it on the following sunny morning. Hayley also brought her own drawing book into the garden and a tin of coloured pencils, and she sat on the lawn and looked in the old drawing book for inspiration. She flipped through the pages and her eyes kept returning to the ink drawing of a man in a suit with a strange pattern reminiscent of the pattern on a giraffe's skin. This man had a round smiling boyish face and his black hair was parted in the middle and combed up into horn shapes on each side of his head. Around noon, Hayley's father came out of the house and set up a deckchair near to her on the lawn and asked his daughter if she objected to him listening to the cricket on the radio. She said it was okay, and Arthur Jones switched on the transistor radio and tuned in to the coverage of the semi finals of the Gillette Cup on BBC Radio 2. He relaxed back into the candy-striped deck chair and smiled as he closed his eyes and soaked up the sun, but then his wife Marjorie came storming out of the house and began to nag him about getting the garden into shape.

'This garden's like a bloody jungle Arthur and you're content to leave it that way!' she told him, blocking out the sun as she stood there, hands on her hips. 'The neighbours must think we're a bunch of lazy good-for-nothing – '

'Oh will you give me some peace, woman?' Arthur snarled back. 'I haven't got a lawn mower yet and that old one in the garage doesn't work!'

'You've got a pair of shears though, and you could do with the exercise!' she told him, and pointed at his spherical abdomen bulging over his belt. 'You're turning into Billy Bunter. It'll kill you Arthur, it'll kill you all this lazing about!'

'No, you'll kill me with your nagging!' he said, and he turned the volume up on the radio.

Hayley buried her face in her palms. All the arguing was killing her inspiration to draw.

'Look at it! Look!' Marjorie Jones walked along the garden path, and then twenty feet later she was up to her waist in tall grass, purple-headed weeds, and all around her was a blizzard of dandelion seeds twirling about in the air. The weeds became so thick, Marjorie could not wade any further and she yelled something at her husband but he couldn't make out what it was because of the din from an excited cricket commentator on the radio. Mrs Jones then went back into her house and slammed the kitchen door behind her.

'Take no notice of her, Hayley,' said Arthur, 'get on with your drawing girl. Your mum isn't happy unless she's nagging me about something. The lawn's okay – just needs a few inches trimming off it, but that down there,' he nodded at the overgrown mess at the end of the path, 'that needs a JCB to level it. I think your mother just thinks I could clear that in half an hour.'

Hayley looked back at the drawing of the man with the peculiar hairstyle and the strange suit and received quite a shock, because he had moved since she had last set eyes on him. Now the drawing of him was much larger on the page – creating the eerie illusion that he had moved nearer to Hayley. Now she could see more details in the sketch of this man; she could see his teeth, his striped tie, and the fob watch chain in his waistcoat. It was really odd how the drawn image of the figure had enlarged. Hayley flipped through the pages, just in case the smaller image of the man had been a separate drawing on another page – but no, this was the only drawing of the figure, and on such a hot day a cold shiver ran through her at the impossibility of an image moving within a book.

'Do me a favour love,' said Arthur, looking at his daughter with his hand shielding his eyes from that pounding sun, 'get me a glass of orange juice and see if there are any of those Gold King choc ices left. Get one for yourself too if you like.'

'Okay...yes,' Hayley reluctantly left her drawing pad and the old sketch book on the lawn and went to the kitchen. She returned a few minutes later with two tall tumblers of orange juice and a choc ice balanced across the rim of each glass. 'Mum's talking about you to the neighbour – that Mrs Pascoe.'

'Oh is she now?' Arthur asked his daughter. He took his orange juice and choc ice and placed the cold tumbler against his forehead.

'Yes,' continued Hayley, her eyes surveying the picture of that strangely attired man. She had left the sketchbook open at the page he was featured upon. 'Mrs Pascoe's sitting in the lounge with Mum, and she said her husband's a lazy sod as well.'

'Pair of janglers,' Arthur replied, and grumbled something else as he put the tumbler down carefully on the lawn. He tore the gold-foil wrapper at the end of the choc ice and then hesitated as he listened to the uproar of the crowds on the radio.

It was broad daylight, her father was six feet away, and yet Hayley felt a mounting sense of insecurity as she looked at that man in the sketchbook because his eyes seemed real and she felt as if he was something real and that he was watching her. She looked at the goosepimples rising on her forearms as fear slowly gripped her. She closed the old dog-eared Derwent sketchbook and then she drank the orange juice, but decided to go indoors to eat the choc ice.

That evening at around 10pm Hayley went to her bedroom and changed into her nightie. It was a warm night, so she opened the window and looked out at the waning gibbous moon. Two men – Neil Armstrong and Buzz Aldrin – had recently visited that ancient orb, and Hayley's 10-year-old brother Philip, had posters of these astronauts and their spaceship on his bedroom wall. Philip was convinced he'd go to the moon himself one day, and Hayley wondered on this tranquil night in the cul-de-sac whether people from some other worlds were visiting earth now without anyone even knowing. And with this cosmological thought echoing in Hayley's mind, the girl lay on her bed and fell fast asleep. She had a vivid dream of that man in the giraffe skin suit coming into her room and taking her by the hand out of the room, down the stairs, and into the back garden. In the lucid dream, Hayley asked the man: 'Where are you taking me?'

'Up the garden path, princess,' the man answered in a strange, almost melodic voice.

'Leave me alone or I'll scream!' Hayley warned him.

'No one would hear you anyway, princess!' the stranger pulling her along told her with a chuckle in his voice.

'Why do you want me? What's all this for?' Hayley asked, ready to cry. She felt as if she was walking in slow motion along the moonlit path. She was headed for that jungle of overgrown weeds her mother had complained about today.

Her weird escort told her: 'You are to be married to my son, his name is': and he said a name that sounded like "Crabeen".

Hayley then saw about a dozen or more pale, creepy looking faces emerge from the tall weeds on either side of the path. She recognised some of these ghastly faces – they were in that old sketchbook. The girl felt as if something terrible was about to happen to her, and she screamed for her mother, and then her father, and after quite a struggle she managed to free her hand from the man's fist. That man with the hair combed up on either side of his head like horns then gritted his teeth and his face became contorted, twisted with an expression of absolute evil. 'Shut up or I'll cut your body up and hang the parts on the trees for the crows to devour!'

Hayley tried to run but fell over. She landed face down in nettles, and she felt a hand on her shoulder, but when she turned, she saw it was her father standing over her. She looked to her right and there stood her mother and her little brother Philip, his pale moonlit face full of concern.

'Are you alright, love?' Mr Jones asked, and he bent down, gently grasped his daughter's hands with his hands and lifted her to her feet.

'Where are they?' Hayley asked, her eyes darted about and then she looked at the weed jungle and thought she saw someone there but it was just shadows in the moonlight playing tricks on her frightened mind.

'You walked in your sleep, Hayley,' her mother told her, moving in to embrace her disoriented daughter. Mrs Jones smoothed her daughter's hair back from her face with her hand and told Hayley: 'Philip heard you walking down the stairs but he thought you were just going to get a drink of water.'

'Mum, it wasn't a dream!' Hayley said in a choked-up voice, 'A man from that old sketchbook tried to drag me down the path to get married to his son, and because I screamed for you and my dad he said he'd cut me up into bits and put them in the trees for the birds to eat!'

Philip's eyes widened at the shocking outburst from his sister, and he looked at his dad as if to ask: 'Did this really happen?'

'Just a nightmare love,' Arthur Jones assured his frightened daughter, and they all walked down the path, back towards the house, but as they did, Philip distinctly heard a faint voice nearby say something enigmatic. The words as he recalled them were: 'He really tilted the axis then.'

Philip turned in a heartbeat and looked towards the source of this strange utterance – the rough end of the garden where the weeds were growing rampant.

'Come on, get in!' Arthur's huge hand gently pressed against his son's back.

'Dad! Did you hear that?' Philip asked, 'Someone's in the garden!'

'It was a cat – that's all son, come on,' said Mr Jones in an impatient tone, 'Get in.'

Mrs Jones locked the door in the kitchen which gave access to the back garden and she also put the front door's mortice lock on in case her daughter slept-walk again. Mrs Jones then went and sat with Philip, who had been spooked by the sleepwalking incident and that voice he had heard coming from the impenetrable copse of weeds. His mother eventually calmed him down with jokes and a glass of ice-cold lemonade, but in the bedroom next door, Hayley was finally finding the nerve to look in that old book of sketches again. She turned the page to that man in the bizarre suit with the outré hairstyle – and she was soon sorry that she had looked at him, because now his face had changed from that smiling boyish face to an expression of intense hatred. She could see crooked teeth and a nose turned up by his snarl and the eyes radiated detestation. Hayley closed the book and held it as if she had a trapped poisonous spider between the pages. She went downstairs and looked for somewhere to hide it. She put it in the cupboard under the stairs, then turned – and screamed. Her father was standing there. He had crept down the stairs, thinking Hayley was sleepwalking again, and not wishing to wake her if she was – because that, his wife had told him, could be fatal – he had been panicking as he wondered how Hayley would react at being unable to get out of a locked house.

'You okay?' he asked her, and looked so worried. 'You *are* awake aren't you?'

'Dad! You really scared me!' Hayley placed her hands on her chest and inhaled sharply. 'Yes, I'm fine, I put the old sketchbook with that man in – the one who caused the nightmare – in the cubby hole under the stairs.'

'Come on love, get back to bed,' Arthur Jones softly told his daughter, and he followed her up the stairs and escorted her back to her bedroom. 'I hope I don't dream of *him* again,' Hayley said, and she got back into bed.

'You won't love,' her father confidently told her with a smile, 'it was just a nightmare. Have a good sleep and I'll make you a full English breakfast in the morning.' This was an in-joke in the family because Arthur could not cook to save his life. Hayley laughed, said good night to her father, then managed to fall asleep. She did not dream of that weird man, and when she awoke, sunlight was blazing into her room.

That was not the end of this strange matter, though. Philip came into his sister's bedroom that morning and seeing she was awake, he asked her about the man in the sketchbook and if it really had been just a nightmare. Hayley never lied to her brother, and she told him: 'Philip, please just forget about the whole thing – pretty please.'

'But I heard a man at the bottom of the back garden,' Philip told her excitedly, and he said: "He really tilted the axis then." That's what he said, and Dad heard it as well but told me it was a cat.'

Hayley wondered about those words her brother had heard – what *did* they mean?

'Can I see that old book with the sketches in Hayley? Can I? Please? Where is it?' Philip walked around the cluttered room, lifting up discarded underwear, folded pop posters, crumpled tee shirts, LPs, a beanbag...

163

'Philip it's not in here, I hid it – now stop talking about this subject, please,' Hayley told him, and she got up and ushered him out of the room as she went downstairs to have breakfast. That evening, something very strange took place. Philip went to bed at 9.45pm and his mother called in on him at 10.30pm to see that he was sleeping soundly. At 11.20pm, Hayley was sitting up in her bed, reading a Mills and Boon romance novel called *Dearly Beloved* when she heard what sounded like a man's voice coming from her brother's room next door. She put the book down on the duvet, then got out the bed and went to the door of the bedroom. She opened the door slowly and she crept along the landing to the door of Philip's room, just twelve feet away. She listened. She heard a familiar voice – the voice of that bogeyman from the sketchbook – calling her name. It was coming from Philip's room. Hayley was scared to go into her brother's room, but she loved Philips so dearly, she put her fear aside and opened the door. Only the nightlight was on in there, and she could see Philip lying on his back. He seemed to be asleep. His mouth moved, and the voice that came out was not the 10-year-old's voice – it was the honeyed voice of that man in the giraffe-print suit! He was talking through her brother's mouth. 'Hello princess,' he said. 'You need to come into the garden, or we would surely kill your brother, and they will be finding parts of his body in the neighbourhood in ten years time.'

Hayley's legs felt as if they had no power; they felt the way limbs do when the circulation has been cut off for a while – there was no power in them – just weakness. The girl slowly turned and walked out of the bedroom, and hearing the television on downstairs, she went down to the lounge to tell her mother and father what was happening. Her mum and dad bounded up the stairs and barged into Philip's room, and they too witnessed what struck them as some type of possession.

'If you try and wake Philip up his little heart won't take the shock and he'll die – and we will have him then!' said that menacing melodious voice.

Mr Jones lunged forward anyway, intending to wake his son up, but his wife screamed and got in the way, and she pulled him back, saying: 'Arthur! No! You heard what it said – he'll die of the shock!'

Despite the warning of sudden death from the menacing voice, Philip suddenly opened his eyes, and then he recoiled in fright as he saw his parents and sister standing there in his room. 'What are you all in here for?' the boy asked.

'Philip! Are you alright?' a relieved Hayley asked, and she sat on the edge of his bed and smiled, despite the tears in her eyes.

'You feeling okay son?' Mr Jones asked the baffled boy, and before Philip could answer, Mrs Jones and her daughter almost threw themselves on the boy.

'Come on, Philip,' said Mrs Jones, simultaneously hugging her son and dragging him from his bed, 'you're sleeping with me and your father!'

'Why?' Philip groaned in a tired voice. He was led out of the room by his mother as Hayley made a chilling discovery. On the floor next to Philip's bed lay *that* accursed Derwent sketchbook from the 1920s – the one featuring those strange drawings – including the one of the sinister man who had tried to abduct

Hayley. Philip had obviously found the book in the cupboard under the stairs. Hayley was too scared to pick the book up for a moment, and she pointed it out to her father. Arthur Jones picked the book up, and went to open it but Hayley cried: 'No! Dad, don't! You'll stir them up again! Just throw it away, or burn it!'

'Okay, okay, stop acting hysterical will you?' a startled Mr Jones told his daughter, and he left the bedroom and went downstairs.

Hayley went to see how her brother was in her parents' room and the lad said he felt embarrassed sleeping in the bed of his mum and dad but Hayley told him what had happened – that the voice of hat horrible man in the drawing book had spoke through him as he slept. This really scared Philip and Hayley's mother berated her daughter for telling her younger brother what had happened. Philip and his parents hardly got a wink of sleep that night, and Hayley kept waking up and expecting to see that creepy man in her room.

Over breakfast, Hayley asked her father if he had thrown the book out, and he nodded and assured her that it was gone.

'Where did you put it?' Mrs Jones asked as she had her cornflakes.

'In the bin outside, stop worrying,' he said, eating his mandatory egg and bacon on toast.

The entity who seemed to have had his origins in that old drawing book was seen no more at the house on Chequers Gardens, but eight years later, at the age of twenty-one, Hayley Jones became engaged to a 29-year-old man named Patrick, who lived on Barkhill

Road; this road runs parallel to the cul-de-sac where Hayley lived, and when she told her father where Patrick lived, he reacted rather strangely, and asked his daughter what number Patrick lived at in that road. When Hayley told him, Arthur's eyes widened, and he asked her, 'Do you remember old Mr Glynn?'

'Yeah, why?' a curious Hayley replied.

'Well, he was an old friend of the family,' Mr Jones replied, 'a very religious churchgoing man, and well, I told him about that drawing book; do you remember all that?'

'Drawing book?' Hayley couldn't recall what her father was referring to at first, and then with a shudder, the details of the whole weird affair came rushing back into the front of her mind. 'Oh yes – what about it?'

Mr Jones revealed something very unsavoury which made his daughter's flesh creep. 'Hayley, I gave that book to Mr Glynn, and he put it in his loft, and he put a Bible on top of the book and bound the books up.'

'You told me that you had thrown the book out – that you'd thrown it in the bin,' said Hayley, and she felt a little scared now, and also disappointed that her father had lied to her all those years ago.

Arthur Jones looked down at the floor, averting his gaze. 'I know, it was just a little white lie to stop you and your mother and Philip from worrying. I thought if I threw the book out that thing might come back. I was going to burn it, but thought that might make things worse too, so I went to Mr Glynn and he said – well, I can't really remember what he said exactly, but he told me the family would be safer if he had it.'

'Dad, tell me the truth – just this once – ' Hayley

started saying, and her father closed his eyes and screwed up his face as if he was in pain.

'Don't say things like that, Hayley, I'm not a liar; I was just trying to shield you and the family to stop all of you from worrying.'

'Then tell me exactly what Mr Glynn said, Dad,' asked Hayley, and she gave a laserlike stare which unnerved Arthur.

Arthur's reply frightened his daughter. 'He reckoned there were evil spirits in that book, and he didn't explain how, but he said the artist was a wicked woman.'

'The artist was a *woman*?' Hayley seemed shocked.

'That's all he told me love, I can't remember, and that's the truth; I was scared to you know?'

And sure enough, when Patrick was told about the haunted drawing book, he thought his fiancé was just pulling his leg at first, but when she almost started to cry, he realised she was deadly serious. He told Hayley that a Mr Glynn had indeed once owned the house he had bought, and that the old man's sister had put the house on the market after Mr Glynn was put into a care home. Patrick said he'd look in the loft, and see if that book was still there, and Hayley seemed very nervous at the suggestion. Patrick said that the book was not haunted – that no book could be haunted, and that the whole thing had been down to childish imagination and nightmares. He went into the loft that day, and when he descended the ladder, Hayley felt her heart pound with an irregular beat as she saw Patrick carrying that drawing book in his right hand. The book was bound by twine with a black leather book – which turned out to be an old copy of the Bible. Patrick cut the twine and offered the Derwent drawing book to Hayley, but she backed away and asked Patrick to open it. Her fiancée gingerly opened the book and an expression of disgust, mingled with curiosity formed on his smooth face. Hayley could not see what he was looking at in those old yellowed, mildewed pages yet. 'Skeletons and disintegrating people,' Patrick quipped, and he turned the book so Hayley could see its contents.

That man who had come out of the book and dragged her up the back garden path to some unearthly wedding ritual was only identifiable by that strange suit he wore with the pattern that looked like a giraffe's skin, but his head was a skull now. Hayley stood there in shock. Patrick turned the pages. The other weird people in the book were all in varying states of decomposition, with skeletal faces and hands and tattered clothing.

'I've seen enough! Get rid of it Patrick!' Hayley cried, and she ran along the landing into the toilet and she was sick in the wash basin.

Patrick had doubted the story of the haunted sketch book, but now, holding the old drawing book, he sensed there was something very uncanny about it, and the odour of decay it was giving off was unbearable. He took the book into the back garden and he put it on the rockery, then fetched a can of paraffin from the shed and dowsed the purple liquid onto the book. He struck three matches and threw each of them onto the soaked book until it started to burn, and he turned to see Hayley watching the cremation of God knows what from the doorway of the kitchen.

THE HAUNTED BACHELOR

His name was Paul Perrick, a 44-year-old Liverpool University lecturer in educational psychology, and the nub of his problem was this: he was being haunted by a very strange ghost – that of a woman in a pink wedding gown. Only Paul could see the ghost, and when he first saw her, he mistook her for a real person until he noticed the orange aura about her and the way she glided along without any leg movement beneath that bell-shaped ball gown of soft white satin charmeuse. She made her debut on the sunny morning of Saturday 24 May, 1969, on Myrtle Street, just outside the Children's Hospital, where Paul had been to see his post-tonsillectomy nephew. As he crossed the road from the hospital, he noticed the young lady in the out-of-place trousseau and wondered where she was going, as the nearest church was St Philip Neri on Catharine Street, but he soon realised the bride in carnation-pink was following him, and so he stopped and turned to confront her, when he saw she was hovering, and a faint amber glow surrounded her. She said something, but a bus with screeching brakes passed and drowned out the words, and Paul ran home in fright to his flat on Canning Street. The supernatural encounter ruined his weekend, and when Paul's younger brother Alec visited at noon, Paul told him what he had seen. Alec chortled: 'You of all people – a psychologist – know very well there are no such things as ghosts!'

'I *know* what I saw Alec,' Paul replied, 'but why is she haunting me?'

'Look, Paul, have you been overworking of late?' Alec bluntly asked, 'Only it's well known –'

Paul rolled his eyes and butted in before his brother could end the sentence. 'Oh for heaven's sake, Alec, this had nothing to do with stress! I actually saw something I can't explain, and it's made a mockery of all those books on psychology which classify ghosts as hallucinations – the products of an unhinged mind – but my mind is certainly not unhinged!'

'Paul, relax, please; just have a drink and calm down,' Alec almost pushed his brother onto the sofa, then went to the drinks cabinet in the corner, whistling in a manic manner. He carefully poured Emva Cream sherry into a slim-stemmed copita – that was Paul's tipple. Alec then awarded himself a few drams of neat whiskey. 'Now, brother of mine, when did you last lose yourself in a good book or submerge yourself in an LP of Handel's *Water Music* eh?' Alec handed Paul the sherry, and then he sat facing him in a comfy tartan wing back chair.

'You can be so bloody patronising Alec,' Paul told him forthrightly, and then he sipped the sherry.

'Don't you think it's telling that the ghost haunting you happens to be a bride?' Alec asked, gulped some of the whiskey down, then smacked his lips and smiled.

'I don't follow,' admitted a perplexed Paul, 'what are you driving at?'

'You being a bachelor, Paul, and a bachelor who has been avoiding marriage for years,' Alec told him, 'that's what I'm driving at.'

'Oh poppycock, Alec, you're not Sigmund Freud for God's sake, and as for marriage, I've always said that wedlock is a padlock; I prefer my freedom!'

Alec slowly closed his eyes, smiled and shook his head at his brother's retort. 'There's an old proverb Aunt Lottie used to quote about people dodging marriage till they're old: "Single long, shame at length" – does that strike a chord in your psyche, Paul?'

'There are other proverbs about the risks of marriage too, Alec: "Marriage is a lottery" for example, and then there's that classic one that should be inscribed on the door of the church: "Marry in haste and repent at leisure".'

Alec threw his head back, gulped down the rest of the scotch and went back to the drinks cabinet to pour himself another one.

'Help yourself, Mr Freud,' said Paul.

'When you do take the plunge, Paul, I'll be the best man,' Alec informed his brother as he clinked the bottle neck to the rim of the glass. He was trying to nettle Paul, but the latter was well-accustomed to Alec's little tricks and paid no heed.

Paul sipped his sweet sherry and enjoyed its Christmas cake flavour. 'In some states in America, couple's intending to marry take mandatory blood tests to see if they are biologically compatible,' Paul told his brother, all matter-of-factly.

'Bit totalitarian isn't it?' Alec mildly recoiled.

'No, practical, my boy, that's what it is. Most couples take the plunge because they are under the mistaken belief that they know the other one intimately, but they don't. The blood tests are conducted to see if either of the candidates for marriage has venereal disease, TB, sickle-cell anaemia...'

'Okay, okay, I get the picture Paul,' Alec grimaced, and returned to the wing back chair with the refill. 'You're *so* bitter old chap; is that how cruddy we become in our forties? I'm dreading the big four-oh.'

'I'm not bitter, Alec, just realistic. The blood test is to establish whether a couple are biologically compatible but I think there should be a psychological compatibility test as well; I mean, you have two people thrown together who are going to be getting on one another's nerves for the rest of their natural lives.'

'They have a thing called divorce remember,' Alec told him, and he examined his Russian wedding ring; 18 carat gold, and featuring three interlinking hoops of yellow, white and red gold. 'But I tell you what, marrying Heidi was the best thing that ever happened to me. She was all I ever wanted in life, and now I have her, and she has me, and well, it's just – great.'

'Ha! That's like something straight out of a bloody Mills and Boon book, Alec,' Paul waved his hand at him as he relaxed back into the leather sofa. 'What about Roland Coney, your old mate back in your university days? Have you forgotten what he said?'

'I *knew* you'd bring him up,' Paul replied, and thinned his eyes from some inward conflict.

'Married at twenty-one, and tried to talk us all into following suit – wanted a multiple wedding I seem to recall, and three-and a half years later came the most bitter, acrimonious divorce since the one that started the Reformation! Mrs Coney gained custody of the twins, and they eventually granted poor old Roland "reasonable access" to them. Roland had to fork out for the court costs and his ex claimed maintenance – '

'Alright, So you're anti-marriage Paul, no need to go to extremes!' Alec interposed.

Paul continued: 'And you know what Roland Coney later said to me on his seventh gin and tonic one night in a pub downtown? I remember it clearly; he said "Matrimony is a school in which one learns too late." Those were his actual words.'

'Well, on that cheerful note, Paul, 'said Alec, rising from the chair, 'I am off home to my loving wife who will at this moment be preparing a scrumptious lunch for me.' He clunked the empty glass on the mantelpiece and walked to the door. 'Don't get up – I'll let myself out!' he told Paul, and left.

Paul, feeling the triumphant one in the latest argument with his brother, remained seated, but as soon as he heard his Alec's footsteps fade on the street outside, he went to the window – and there she was. The lecturer stumbled backwards in shock as he saw the eerie bride on the pavement. She was looking up at his ground floor window, which was set about seven feet up from the pavement. Paul backed away, wondering what to do. He considered leaving the flat and running after Alec to tell him about the ghost, but by then his brother, who was a fast walker, was streets away. As Paul was deciding what to do, he saw the pink apparition glide along the pavement as if she was on castors. She went in the direction of Bedford Street

South, and when Paul finally had the guts to open the door, he saw that the ghost had gone. Paul was so scared to be alone in his flat with that uncanny bride knocking about, he went to have a drink in the Blackburne Arms, less than two hundred yards away. He felt as if the old adage about safety in numbers was true, that he would be safe from that supernatural stalker in the pub. He struck up a conversation with an old man named Alf and bought him a pint of mild. The old man was talking about his days in the army when Paul thought he heard a faint echoing female voice calling him.

'Paul... Paul – listen to me...'

Paul looked around and saw no one – just people drinking and chatting among themselves. He turned his attention back to Alf when he clearly heard the same voice as before say, 'Paul, go to Amaryllis.' Paul turned, and saw to his horror that the bride from beyond had entered the pub! He knocked people out the way as he fled from the Blackburne Arms. He ran around the first corner he saw, which led him onto Falkner Street, and after covering about thirty yards he slowed and looked over his right shoulder, and he saw the woman in the pink bridal dress coming towards him as she hovered a foot off the ground. She seemed to lean forward slightly as she drifted after the terrified university lecturer. Paul ran on to the end of the street, and was almost knocked down by a hackney cab on Hope Street. To the rattled cabby, Paul smiled and apologised, and asked to be taken to Clarence Street, where a fellow lecturer named Robert Bollinger would hopefully be in. Paul was scared and confused and just had to tell someone about his unearthly ordeal, as his own brother had been of no use whatsoever.

Bollinger, a lecturer on metaphysics, was now also a Professor of Moral Philosophy, and he was currently attempting to write a book with the provisional title of *The History of Philosophy in English Literature*. Bollinger had been a pillar of the Scottish church in Liverpool until the writing of an essay on his theory that God and the Devil were simply two sides of the same coin. The church fathers deemed the essay a heresy and Bollinger was virtually excommunicated. The church considered inviting Bollinger back into their fold until they learned that the metaphysician was writing a treatise on a new religion of the future that would be based on natural psychedelic drugs that would make beatific visions immediately accessible to members of the flock.

Robert Bollinger answered the door to Paul Perrick with a curious dreamy smile upon his chubby Robert Morley face. It transpired he'd been eating hash biscuits. Bollinger was most welcoming, and not just because of the empathy-boosting effects of the cannabis-impregnated bourbon biscuits – he really did enjoy Paul's company. When Paul entered his friend's flat it was like stepping into Victorian times. The living room was decorated with William Morris wallpaper, plush velvet drapes and muslin sub-curtains that softened the daylight, rug-covered divans and a floral-patterned carpet. The original gas brackets from the 1930s were still in use here in 1967, and in the corner, an original wind-up gramophone with a huge horn was playing an LP recording of *The Mikado*. Bollinger carefully halted the gramophone and then issued an apology. 'Paul, I am so sorry for the state of the floor –

all false starts to my magnum opus,' he said, nodding to the crumpled paper roses littering the carpet, and then he stooped and his bird's beak of a nose almost touched the keys of his typewriter as he squinted (because of his farsightedness) at the few lines he'd hammered out on a sheet protruding from the machine. 'Oh dear, I've typed "the the" – I need an editor,' he mumbled.

After hesitating to tell his friend why he had paid him a visit, Paul finally came out with it. 'Robert, I have come to you because I am being haunted, and I'd like to know why it's happening to me and how I can get rid of the damned ghost.'

'Ah, very interesting,' Bollinger sat on an antique-looking scrolled and carved cabriole-leg chair and pointed to the silver tray of biscuits on a small table with a chessboard design. 'They're psychoactive. I'm just about to make a fresh pot of flowering tea if you'd like a cup.'

'No, I'm alright thanks Robert – what do you think then?' said an impatient Paul.

'Tell me about this ghost that is haunting you,' said Bollinger, and he went to the kitchenette and filled a tin kettle at the tap.

Paul followed his friend to the sink. 'It's the ghost of a woman in a wedding gown – a pink wedding gown – and I first saw her on Myrtle Street after I'd been to visit my nephew in the Children's Hospital. She's following me about.'

Bollinger lit the gas ring and placed the filled kettle on the blue flames, and then he stood there for a while in contemplative silence, apparently sifting Paul's statement through the fine gauze of his mind. Then out of that faint hiss of the gas jets and the dampened hubbub of the street traffic filtering through the window, Bollinger's voice breathed into existence. 'I've heard of something like this before, Paul,' he said, then added: 'She's trying to impart a message to you or perhaps steer you towards someone.'

'So you don't think I'm seeing things – and hearing things?' Paul asked. 'She has spoken to me too you see. She called my name, and then she said "go to Amaryllis" – but I don't think anyone else in the pub heard her – or saw her – just me.'

'In the *pub*?' Bollinger asked with a trace of suspicion in his watery pinkish eyes.

Paul was a little annoyed by his friend's suspicion. 'Not what you think Robert. I went to the pub – the Blackburne Arms – to get *away* from her, and I had only just taken a few sips of ale when she followed me in there. I swear this is not alcohol-induced Robert. When I first saw her I was stone cold sober.'

'Amaryllis – is that a name or a place?' Bollinger mused on the words as the kettle boiled its heart out. Over tea, before Robert gave his opinion of the strange matter, he asked: 'Have you ever wondered why ghosts don't appear all of the time, and why they seem to haunt for short periods?'

'Well no, because I never believed in ghosts before all of this started,' Paul told him, 'I just assumed that all supernatural phenomena could be explained away as psychoses and overactive imagination.'

'No, they exist alright, Paul, and I have studied the subject at length. I have come to the conclusion that there is some censor at work in the next world.'

'I don't quite follow you,' Paul confessed.

'Look, when you study most hauntings you will find that the ghost may walk, but not every night. It might appear tonight and then not show itself for a year or a century, and when brave investigators have posed questions to ghosts and spirits, they seem to give garbled information or partial information. A common question asked in séances – or through the Ouija board – is: what is it like over there? And more than often the spirit remains tight-lipped on the matter. I think a censor – maybe more than one censor, I don't know – prevents these beings of deceased people from revealing the truth about the world beyond. You see if most people knew there was an afterlife where their late lamented loved ones were alive and well, they'd happily commit suicide to be with them.'

'What's all this got to do with me?' Paul asked and produced an agonised smile. He looked apologetic for interrupting the Professor's take on ghosts.

'Well, I think the ghost of that woman in the pink wedding dress is being rather persistent – as if she just has to get her message across. The "Amaryllis" she mentioned might just be a person. Now, considering the fact that you are a confirmed card-carrying chartered member of the Bachelor Club, it would seem that our ghost is trying to set you up with someone, and she must be pretty determined, following you home and even into a busy pub. Do you see where I'm coming from, Paul?'

Paul nodded. 'Yes I do, but I still find it rather sinister – the idea of a ghost matchmaking. And when I think of it, Robert, and this is just something I've only just realised – but over the course of about a week before I had even set eyes on the pink lady, I have had the strangest feelings of being watched when I've been home, especially in the evenings. It gives me a shudder just thinking about it. The idea of something - well, something not living, watching me.'

'Try and find out who or what this Amaryllis is, Paul, and let me know how this intriguing matter pans out.'

A few days later, Paul visited his nephew at the Children's Hospital again, as there had been minor complications due to the tonsillectomy and he was being kept in for a few days. As Paul was walking down the corridor in the hospital towards the exit, he happened to overhear a nurse addressing a colleague by the name of *Amaryllis* – the very name the ghost had uttered.

'You have a very unusual name,' Paul told Amaryllis.

The nurse smiled at Paul and that spelt the end of his bachelorhood. He fell for Amaryllis there and then, and he engaged in some small talk about his nephew, and then he did something he had never done before with any woman – he asked Amaryllis if she'd like to go out for a meal some night.

The nurse seemed a bit taken back by the proposal, but she smiled and nodded. 'When I get some time off,' she laughed, and then added: 'yes, that would be lovely.'

He never saw that ghostly bride after that. Within a year, Paul had married the nurse, and eventually told her how that mysterious lady in the pink wedding dress had advised him to go to her. Amaryllis told Paul that in the 1950s her aunt had been jilted at the altar and had literally died of a broken heart not long after. She had worn a pink bridal gown. She showed Paul a photograph of her late auntie, and it was quite a jarring experience when he set eyes on the little monochrome picture, because it was plain to see that the woman in it was, without a doubt, the woman who had haunted him into a married life.

THE NYCTALOPE

In 1963, 38-year-old Liverpool-born private inquiry agent Mike McNeil was walking from his office in a narrow London alleyway off Fleet Street when a woman in shades and a headscarf approached from the direction of St Bride's Church with an unlit cigarette in her hand. She asked Mike for a light, and as the private eye delved into his jacket pockets to search for his lighter, the woman produced a cylinder from behind her back and threw its contents into his face. Half a pint of bleach splashed into Mike's face and as he stumbled back against the wall, his burning eyes unable to see, the woman hurried away. She was never identified but McNeil suspected it was an act of revenge from the very woman he'd proved to be an adulterer in a messy divorce case some months back. McNeil was temporarily blinded by the bleach, and moved back to Liverpool to recuperate, and when his sight started to return, he discovered he could see weird phantom images no one else could see; shadowy figures and luminous outlines of people who were not there. He visited his doctor and was told he was a "nyctalope" – a person who could see better in the dark because of the sensitising effects of the bleach's sodium hypochlorite on his retina. The condition was sometimes permanent. The phantoms were mostly hallucinations, McNeil was told, mere products of a damaged retina. And then the PI started to see the spaceships over Liverpool – some were classic flying saucers, but every now and then a gigantic cigar-shaped craft which looked miles in length would appear above the city, and out of it flew files of those lens-shaped saucers. One afternoon in August 1963, McNeil was gazing in awe at the titanic gun-metal-coloured fusiform craft hanging ominously over the city centre as he bought a copy of the *Liverpool Echo* from a newspaper-seller who startlingly lifted his eyes to the thing in the sky and remarked, 'Thank God they're friendly, eh?'

McNeil realised the newspaper man could see the gargantuan visitor too and gasped: 'You can see them? Thank heavens; I'm not losing my mind then. You *can* see them can't you? Tell me what you see, please!'

'The Big Cigar I call it. Keep your voice down though. They've been coming here since those atom-bombings of Japan in 1945,' said the vendor, 'but a word of advice friend, keep it to yourself and don't keep looking up at them, or they'll take you away.'

'Who'll take me away?' the intrigued private eye asked, and the newspaper-seller's reply shocked him.

'They have agents disguised as people just like us, and they are always watching the masses. They watch us in case someone starts seeing them. They're not very good at imitating humans though; they stand out a mile. They don't look right; they seem to have make-up on, and their lips are too red – and they have obvious wigs on as well. Their dress sense is way out as well; the clobber they wear looks as if it belongs to the early 1950s; very square-looking. I call them squares.'

McNeil nodded, and he couldn't help himself – he had to take a quick glance at that massive ship hanging in the sky.

'They all look the same – the squares do,' said the vendor, 'like carbon copies.'

McNeil was still looking skyward. 'Jesus, that plane's gonna hit that thing!' he said in an unguarded manner, raising his voice. The light aircraft he was referring to flew into the colossal cylindrical UFO via a rectangular hatch.

'Stop looking up, they'll see you!' The vendor warned, and then he told McNeil: 'They do that now and then – just take our planes for some reason. Anyway, keep your eyes at street-level. Bye friend.'

A week later, McNeil realised he was being followed everywhere by one of the 'squares' the vendor had told him about, so he figured they must have noticed him looking up at things not meant to be seen by human eyes. McNeil walked down every alleyway in the city centre in a vain attempt to evade the sinister pursuer, until he realised that there were actually three of them, all like clones of one another. They seemed very robotic in their movements. McNeil made a frantic dash to his Hanover Street office to get a camera to snap the unearthly trinity – and the UFOs whizzing through the skies. He decided the time had come to tell the sleepwalking population that the planet was being invaded by an alien intelligence, and the private eye was prepared to risk being killed to get the story to the Press. He slammed the door on Hanover Street behind him and bounded up the stairs two steps at a time until he reached his office. He heard footfalls on the steps below. How had they gained access to the building? He opened the door to his office and locked it behind him, and then he went to a locker and found the old loaded Browning automatic he kept for emergencies and pushed the safety catch off. He cocked the hammer and looked at the door, expecting to see the knob turn.

'Mister McNeil,' said a deep voice behind the private investigator.

McNeil swung around, ready to fire the Browning, and saw his three pursuers standing there in a row. He was not sure which one had called his name, and now, at this close range he could see that their faces looked artificial – plastic even. 'How did you get in?' he asked the sinister trio, and then he saw the intruders go out of focus and McNeil felt as if he was on a ship in rough seas; the entire room tilted forty-five degrees and he passed out.

McNeil awoke in the Royal Infirmary, heavily sedated, and a nurse bent over him told the investigator he'd had a heart attack. McNeil later discovered his eyesight had returned to normal, for he could not see the UFOs or their 'mothership' – and he never saw them again – but are they still here? For years, McNeil told no one about the UFOs he'd seen over the city, because he feared ridicule, but he later met people who had told him how they too had caught glimpses of strange giant craft over Liverpool in the 1960s. There are an estimated 700 million trillion rocky worlds orbiting the stars of the universe, and even if only a fraction of these planets harbour intelligent life, it still means there are millions of civilizations out there – and statistically, many of them will be decades and centuries ahead of our civilization. These intelligent beings will have long mastered long-distance travel across light years and parsecs of interstellar and intergalactic space, and it is highly likely that they will know there is life on this planet Earth. Ever since the dawn of radio in the late 1890s with Marconi's experiments in wireless telegraphy, we have inadvertently been announcing our presence to other worlds in space with broadcasts of electromagnetic waves. The megawatt radar beams of World War Two, and later the television and radio output of the Earth are now still moving out into space across many tens of light years in an ever expanding shell of energy – and some aliens will have longed picked these emanations up. We have even deliberately sent broadcasts to other worlds via our radio telescopes, and one such message that comes to mind was the one broadcast from the colossal 1,000-foot diameter Arecibo radio telescope on 16 November 1974. The message was aimed at the globular star cluster M13, at a target 25,000 light years away. The message consisted of a binary code which, when decoded in the right frame (73 rows by 23 columns), would show aliens receiving it where we are, what we basically look like, as well as a diagram of the DNA we are made from. Is it wise to announce our presence - along with our address – to intelligences we know nothing about? The aliens who receive the message might be intelligent people of the peace-loving kind who might have all sorts of cures for our diseases – but they could also be ruthless military-minded psychopaths or even a race that would regard humans as we regard certain animals – as a food source. Some scientists therefore think that we should not be broadcasting our presence to strangers out there; we should be spying on whatever is out there in the galactic neighbourhood first to see if they are hostile or not. Ever since the modern UFO era began (circa 1947), there have been reports of beings and machines from unearthly craft (some even disguised as mundane vehicles such as cars) abducting people and animals, and I have quite a few local reports of alleged abductions of this type, as well as attempted ones in my files. Here are just a few of them.

People vanish all the time; some make themselves scarce for criminal reasons, such as the late MP John Stonehouse, who, in 1974, faked his own death by leaving his clothes on a Miami beach – Reginald Perrin style - so he could start a new life with a new wife in Australia, far away from his fraudulent business activities as the Department of Trade and Industry started to look into his dodgy affairs. Like a twist out of a *Tales of the Unexpected* episode, Mr Stonehouse – or Joseph Markham as he had renamed himself – was arrested by the police as he entered Australia because they suspected the debonair Englishman of being another man who had just mysteriously vanished – Lord Lucan.

Some people vanish because they are murdered and their bodies are never found, such as the case of Suzy Lamplugh and, more locally, Bootle-born Helen McCourt in 1988. But there have also been cases of attempted abductions in very mysterious and paranormal circumstances, and many of these have taken place within Knowsley. In early August 1961, four children – two boys aged 7 and two girls aged 5 and 6 – were playing on Kirkby's Bewley Drive one sunny morning around half-past nine during the school summer holidays. The boys – Alan and Ken, had befriended a stray dog – possibly a Border collie breed – which they nicknamed Shep, when the dog started to act very strange. It hid behind the low garden wall of a house and kept looking up into the clear blue sky, terrified of something it could see. Besides the blinding sun, the only thing hanging in that azure sky that Alan and Ken could see was a morning moon in its last quarter, so the lads assumed Shep was scared of some wasp flying about, but about a minute later, a 6-year-old girl named Joan came out of a nearby house with her 5-year-old cousin Sue – who was peddling along on her little tricycle. It was Joan who noticed the strange orange "balloon" as she described it, hovering about over Bewley Drive at rooftop level. All four children – and Shep - looked up at the stationary globe, which now seemed about as tall as a double-decker bus. The children were too young to know about UFOs, and innocently thought it really was some giant balloon suspended in the still morning air – but then they all saw what looked like a huge grey "eye" open in the surface of the sphere, and a light shone down at the young observers. Shep turned and ran off as a loud buzzing emanated from the orange orb, and a circular opening appeared in the giant ball. The children watched in amazement as a long thin tube of the same orange colour as the spherule came quickly out of the hole and unfolded in length as if it was made of telescopic segments. This tube protruded for about twenty feet, then halted for a moment and a disc formed at its end. From this disc, another long tube shot out, down towards the kids, and at the end of the tube a C-shaped mechanical claw appeared. Sensing that the thing was about to make a grab at them, the older children ran off, leaving little Sue, who tried to pedal away from the menacing levitating object on her three-wheeler. A family were moving into the area that morning, and a van carrying their furniture came up Bewley Drive – and when the driver saw the massive orange ball and its sinister long arm making a grabbing motion at the little girl, he pulled up and bravely went to Sue's aid. As he did, the arm was quickly withdrawn into the globe and that object flew up into the sky within seconds. Not long after this there were further sightings of UFOs over Knowsley, and one "Flying Saucer" - seen hovering over Westvale primary school by scores of teachers, pupils and parents - was even reported in the local and national press. Just as our probes are now exploring the outer planets of the Solar System, I am convinced that in the 1960s, some extraterrestrial civilization (perhaps several of them) was exploring our world – and I shudder to think what might have happened to little Sue if she had been taken as a specimen.

One of the most bizarre attempted abduction cases took place in Huyton on Stanley Road, less than fifty yards from St Michael's Church, one Saturday afternoon in 1971. Brian and Barry, both aged 10, lived next door to each other on nearby Rupert Road, and they were going to call on friends to make up a five-a-side "footy" team, when Brian noticed an odd old-fashioned-looking car parked at the end of the road. What attracted Brian's attention was the driver of this car, because he didn't look real; he looked like a Supermarionation puppet out of the popular

Thunderbirds television series, but this puppet was life-size. Brian drew Barry's attention to the life-size doll in the black vintage-looking car and the boys went over to get a close look. The head of the mannequin-like driver turned to face them, and a chirpy voice from the vehicle said: 'Get in boys and I'll give you a free ride!' This voice sounded as if it was coming from a radio speaker and had a metallic quality to it. Barry gingerly opened the back door of the car and saw there was only that 'dummy driver' in it. Brian told Barry not to get in, but Barry did and eventually persuaded his friend to join him. The car engine started and the boys tried to get out the vehicle – but the doors were locked. The car moved off, turned right onto Bluebell Lane, and then onto Archway Road. For three miles that car drove all by itself, stopping at red lights and adhering impeccably to the Highway Code until it came to a juddering halt near Eccleston Park. The lively amplified voice that had invited the children into the car then warned them: 'Don't try and get out! The doors are electrified!'

The hysterical boys kicked frantically at the doors and managed to open one, and they ran to passers-by to tell them of their strange ordeal, but the car suddenly moved off into traffic and got away. I have other reports of this car across Huyton and beyond; was it some remote-controlled vehicle invented by a clever but warped child-snatcher? Was it some sort of four-wheeled drone to capture unsuspecting children? It's possible – and yet I feel that this four-wheeled trap was not of this earth – that it was possibly something extraterrestrial in origin, out to capture live specimens of humans who are in the vulnerable stage of preadolescence. It might even be the same vehicle seen in the same area of Knowsley – Huyton – twenty-two years later. James is 37 now, but the following strange story, which took place in 1993 when he was thirteen, remains fresh in his mind. It all started on the Saturday evening of October 30, 1993 at around 6.40pm. *Gladiators* – a TV show which involved contestants battling against a gladiator in various arduous events – had just ended, and before Cilla Black and *Blind Date* came on the screen after the adverts, James sneaked out of his terraced home on Huyton's Gentwood Road and made the 500-yard journey north to his friend's Nick's house on Cartmel Road. A full moon hung in the clear night sky, just above treetop level, and there was an autumnal chill also hanging in the air on this Halloween Eve. James was not a bad lad, but when he was in the company of Nick - who was something of a vandal – his mischievous side came out, and tonight was no exception to this change in his behaviour. Nick had a powerful slingshot catapult which he used to fire ball bearings at lamp post lighting elements, windows, and even the odd passerby. Nick reckoned he could hit a plane with a "bolly" (a ball bearing) if he really tried, and when a light aircraft passed overhead, James called his bluff. Nick fired the ball bearing into the night sky from his "catty" (slang for catapult), and thankfully it came nowhere near the fuselage of the Cessna, but still the projectile did inflict some damage. It fell back to earth in an arc – and put in the windscreen of an old Morris Minor parked on Barkbeth Road – and the two teenagers thought this was so funny. An old man came out of his house and held a palm on each side of his shocked face as he looked at his damaged car. Nick took another ball bearing out of his pocket, placed it in the catapult's leather pocket patch, and took aim. James laughed as the stainless steel sphere zipped through the night air and took out the vintage car's nearside window. The man screamed at the laughing teens and shook a fist at them as they ran off down Woolfall Heath Avenue. The lads wandered down Page Moss Avenue where Nick took a glance at the moon and reckoned it would be possible to hit it with a ball bearing if there was a catapult with a "lazzy" (slang for a length of elastic band) about half a mile long. James disagreed and said no catapult could send a ball bearing to the moon and as the teens argued, they suddenly heard a car approaching at quite a speed. It was a Morris Minor, just like the one Nick had vandalised a few minutes ago, and James thought that this was a coincidence. This one was speeding from Huyton House Road, and its headlamps were very faint; just two dim orange discs. The vehicle suddenly swerved and came onto the pavement. It was heading straight for James and Nick! The teens jumped over the low wall surrounding a garden and the car scraped its sides along this wall, emitting a shower of sparks. When James and Nick got up off the grass of someone's front lawn, they saw the red tail lights of the Morris Minor as it careered towards Woolfall Crescent. James told his friend: 'There was no one driving it!'

'There must have been,' Nick reasoned, slightly spooked by his friend's weird assertion.

'Nick, there wasn't,' James assured him, 'and it looked exactly like that same car you fired the catty at before!'

'Shut up!' Nick dismissed his friend's claims with a narrowing of the eyes and a fake smirk.

But then the two lads heard a screech at the end of the road, and they saw that the Morris Minor had turned around – and it was heading back towards them. They fled across the road and into a crescent known as Green Way, and half way along this curved road the terror-stricken teens were forced to run onto an expanse of green field to get out of the way of the Morris Minor – and now Nick saw that his friend had been telling the truth: there was no one in the car. The boys covered a hundred yards and hid in bushes at the edge of the field as they watched the green Morris Minor halt at the top of Aylton Road. 'I told you there was no one in it!' said James, and Nick panted as he wondered if he could risk making a run for home. Then they saw the driverless car slowly crawl along Green Way, and Nick decided to make a run for it, but as he did, the Morris Minor's engine revved into life and the empty vehicle peeled rubber as it rocketed after the teenagers. James and Nick screamed for help to two policemen on their beat on Huyton House Road, and the car with the invisible driver stopped and reversed as James pointed it out to the bemused policemen. Nick hid his catapult and the policemen advised the lads to get home. The teens took the advice and split up – James ran as fast as his legs could carry him to his house on Gentwood Road, while Nick jogged north to his home on Cartmel Road. Each boy told his parents what had happened but no one believed their crazy stories. On the following night – Halloween - around 8pm, James and Nick were trying to chat up two girls on the semi-circular green on

Fairclough Road, when they were all startled by the screech of car tyres in the direction of Woolfall Heath Avenue. James and Nick could plainly see the green Morris Minor accelerating towards them up the road, and the lads ran off, leaving the startled girls standing. James did a goalkeeper dive over the low garden wall of a nearby house, and Nick simply took a running jump and cleared the wall. Once again the Morris Minor scraped against the wall as it tried to run the teens over, and this time the householder came out and asked what all the noise was. Nick told him about the car with no one at the wheel and the man swore and told him to get out of his garden, but then the Morris Minor reversed and came around the corner at high speed. It backed into the gate of the man's garden, then drove off at about 60 mph up Fairclough Road. The teens and the man saw the vehicle cross the central reservation on Liverpool Road, and then its lights went out. Nick and James were joined by the girls – who found the whole thing exciting. The four teenagers went looking for the unearthly car, and discovered it was laying in wait on Cotsford Road. It chased them down Twig Lane and they all took refuge in Jubilee Park. The girls had now seen that no one was in the car, and they asked Nick and James to accompany them to their homes, which the lads did. After that Halloween night, the 'haunted' Morris Minor was seen no more. Given that it was Halloween, the boys regarded the driverless car as something to do with witchcraft – but perhaps the car was the very same one which had almost captured the two boys back in 1971.

In July 2016, a Kirkby man named Steve took his

dog out in broad daylight for its daily five-mile walk at around 7 pm. He usually took the dog out at 10am but was late on this occasion because he'd had to look after a sick relative. Steve walked from his home in Simonswood with his pet and went up Stopgate Lane and onto Sineacre Lane, and he had just passed a secluded semi on this rustic route when the dog began to act strange. It made yelping sounds and kept looking at the low hedge which forms a border between the road and a vast expanse of farmland. 'What's wrong with you, eh, lad?' Steve asked the pooch and bent down to give him a reassuring pat on the head, when he heard a rhythmical thumping sound like distant industrial machinery. Steve straightened up, and there, coming across the field towards him was the metallic nightmare of a figure – a robot of some sort, and Steve estimates that its height must have been about seven to eight feet at least. It had a bucket-shaped head and a greyish body that resembled a suit of armour with circular joints at the shoulders, elbows and knees. The dog was so scared it bolted off back down the lane – and its leash slipped out of Steve's hand. Steve, by his own admission, is overweight, and as he ran off, he soon found himself out of breath and was even unable to shout after the frightened dog as it fled down the road. Steve looked back and saw the gigantic robot standing there, with one foot over the hedge and the other in the field, and it was watching him as he now trotted away. Steve then noticed that about a quarter of a mile away in the field the thing was standing in, there was a craft which resembled two deep bowls with their open rims stuck together. It must have been about a hundred feet across and Steve thinks he saw two tiny figures standing next to this unearthly craft. He kept looking back at the robot and the unidentified structure on the farmland until he found his dog cowering under a hedge at the junction of Stopgate Lane and Sidling Lane. He then looked back and saw that the craft – perhaps a landed UFO – and the gigantic robot – had gone.

Weeks before this, I had received an unusual amount of UFO reports from people across Kirkby, Melling, Ormskirk, Prescot, Huyton and Halewood. I told Steve that he may have seen the so-called "Kirkby Spaceman" that made headline news on January 4 1978. A group of people saw this strange humanoid during a UFO flap, and I showed Steve the Press cuttings I had of the incident. He went pale when he saw a sketch made by a witness of the so-called "Monster of the North" published in the *Daily Express* and other newspapers across the land. The figure looked very similar to the thing he had seen off Sineacre Lane. That January in 1978, four Kirkby men were travelling down a lane in Kirkby when they saw the seven-foot-tall square-headed figure walking in a robotic fashion as it came towards them. The men were so scared by the encounter, the driver later suffered an asthma attack. One of the four witnesses said the colossal faceless robotic entity was: "horrible – a square head and no features – and dressed in a sort of white asbestos suit. It had white boots, dark hands, and red and white flashing lights on its chest. It was just like something from a science fiction film."

Merseyside Police took the testimony of the four Kirkby men – and a few other reports from people in nearby Bickerstaffe – very seriously, and a spokesman for the force told the press: "We are treating the incident seriously. We established that the men were not intoxicated. It is an unexplained occurrence which could have been an elaborate practical joke – or something more sinister."

Are these entities, such as the mechanical-looking giant encountered in 1978 and the one seen on Sineacre Lane extraterrestrial in origin – or could they be time travellers – or even the product of a timeslip? It is possible that the thing Steve saw a week ago and the so-called Kirkby Robot seen back in 1978 are a type of premonition of some future era when robots will be used routinely, perhaps for agriculture. The craft Steve saw in the field when he saw the robot might have even been some sleek combine harvester of the future – as Steve did not actually see the thing take off – but of course, it is equally possible that it might have been a landed spacecraft from any of the millions of inhabited worlds in our part of the galaxy.

LIVERPOOL'S CURSED FAMILIES

We've all had those days when nothing seems to go right, and statistically we *must* have days when we feel as if we are plagued with bad luck – but I have met people who tell me that they have an inordinate amount of such days, and many of them believe they are not only cursed, but are cursed via their bloodline; in other words: a family curse is to blame. In the world of the occult, such a jinx on a specific family is known as a generational curse because it remains active across many generations. I have studied these alleged long-lasting curses in some depth over the years and I was surprised to find them mentioned several times in the Bible. In the Book of Genesis, we read that God put a mark (i.e. a curse) upon Cain for murdering his brother Abel, and all of the descendants of Cain later perished in the Flood. In the Book of Exodus (20:5) it is written: "You shall not bow down to idols or worship them; for I, the Lord your God, am a jealous God, punishing the children for the sin of the fathers *to the third and fourth generation* of those who hate me."

Some Christians believe that because of Adam and Eve's rebellion in the Garden of Eden, every person born since them will be tinged with the Original Sin – an ancestral sin, and a hereditary 'stain' that all descendants of Adam must carry. This doctrine sounds as if it is describing an extreme version of the generational curse whereby a certain family inflicted by a curse carries it through its newborn members over several generations. Not only is a generational curse transmitted through the offspring, the anathema seems to be passed on through marriage as well, so a man or woman marrying into the cursed family will be infected and afflicted by the long-lasting curse too. Many of the world's famous families are said to be cursed, from the Kennedys to the Rockefellers, but a great number of everyday local people in Liverpool and the rest of Merseyside have written to me over the years to tell me that their family is cursed. How does a family become cursed? Well, there are many ways; a person may lay the curse upon a person and their descendants whilst in a rage, or they may formulate the curse in a very composed and premeditated manner. What follows is just a small selection of accounts of generational curses I have looked into over the years.

In 1895 a certain old lady named Rowena, who is said to have been a Gypsy with the gift of second sight and the ability to foretell the future, was often consulted at her humble home – a dank and dingy basement in a house off Scotland Road. Her reputation had spread to all quarters, and she was often visited by people from all stations in life. One day in the winter of 1895, old Rowena was visited by a Mrs McDermott, the pretty young wife of a wealthy businessman who dealt in the international cotton trade. Mrs McDermott told Rowena that she suspected her husband of seeing another woman. She had overheard him on several occasions telling a friend that he was going to visit 'the Dark Lady' – and on these occasions Mr McDermott would always tell his wife he had to visit a warehouse or a business acquaintance – and more than often he would come home in the early hours of the morning with the distinctive perfume of the Dark Lady upon him. Only two nights ago Mr McDermott had returned home in a drunken state at four in the morning, and, according to the gossip of the servants, he had not been away on business, but at some dance ball out of town. Mrs McDermott asked Rowena if she could identify the woman her husband was having an affair with, and the elderly gypsy woman nodded and told her: 'Perhaps, my dear.' Mrs McDermott then offered her quite a large sum of money. Rowena clutched a bundle of black cloth and unwrapped it to reveal a crystal ball with a green cast to it. She placed the ball in the middle of a small round table, placed the small stub of a lighted candle next to the ball, then drew the curtains. Rowena then reached out and held Mrs McDermott's small soft porcelain hand. The women from different ends of society sat together at the table and then the old woman stared at the crystal ball and started to take long deep breaths. After a few minutes, the gypsy squeezed her client's hand and the old lady's eyes widened – Mrs McDermott wondered if it was all play-acting or whether the woman could actually see something in the ball. The gypsy's eyes remained fixed on the mysterious sphere, and then she smiled, and turned to Mrs McDermott. 'The other woman is of Royal blood my dear – now isn't that something? She's as fair as a lily and very tall, and her name is Blanche Robinson.'

'Oh!' Mrs McDermott recoiled as if a great pain had jolted through her heart and her left hand pressed against her bosom. 'I know her – she is indeed very beautiful,' Mrs McDermott gasped, and a tear rolled from her eye. 'Tell me more, please, even if it will break my heart.'

The seeress began to take long deep breaths again and this time her eyes, which had been fixed on the nucleus of that all-seeing crystal ball, now rolled backwards, turning white, and this alarmed Mrs McDermott. After a long tense pause, the gypsy said: 'I beseech you, Lamassu, to tell me that which I long to know.' And then she seemed to repeat the last three words until they became too faint to hear: 'Long to know...long to know...'

What happened next was both terrifying and mystifying. Mrs McDermott had been in Gibraltar on her honeymoon several years ago and she recalled the vibrations that coursed through her bones when a huge Indian elephant from Calcutta was lowered onto the quayside from a crane. The gargantuan elephant – a gift from Queen Victoria to the Sultan of Morocco – had been in transit to his palace – and when the goliath of the animal world was lifted by crane from a steamship and clumsily deposited on the ground thirty feet from the McDermotts, the ground had shaken as if an earthquake had struck – and now, here in this hovel of a basement, something thumped against the foundations which felt like a herd of elephants crashing to earth! The tremor was so powerful, it closed the jaws of Mrs McDermott's mouth and her teeth grazed the side of her tongue. Rowena then spoke in a very strange voice – a low male voice – and it sounded unearthly. This voice said: 'William McDermott had sexual intercourse with Blanche Robinson after they attended the dance ball at Blackburn. That same night, William McDermott also had intercourse with the servant girls...'

'Oh! Enough! Enough!' Mrs McDermott cried, and she tried to wrestle her hand from the old woman's grip but Rowena held her like a vice. The gypsy seemed to be as immovable as a statue in this trance. The eerie unnerving voice rambled on about Mr McDermott outraging many other women – and men – over the years, and according to the mysterious entity, which Rowena had named Lamassu, the cotton merchant had even been involved in an infamous rape case in Australia nine years ago where several youths were hanged after being found guilty of the outrage on a servant girl. According to the spirit voice, Mr McDermott had been spared the gallows by the intervention of very influential people in high places and had been put on a ship to England.

'Stop! Please stop! Please!' Mrs McDermott screamed, and her cries seemed to break the trance. Rowena's eyes rolled down, and she let go of her client's hand and clutched her chest.

'I thank thee Lamassu...' Rowena seemed out of breath, and she got up unsteadily from the table and opened the curtains. Mrs McDermott placed a column of gold sovereigns on the table, and then she burst into tears. The revelations from the unknown entity had been too much for her to take in, and she felt shattered by them; her husband was much more than an adulterer – he was a rapist too.

When Mrs McDermott returned to her palatial home, she refused to talk to her abomination of a husband, and he repeatedly asked her why she was snubbing him. She told him she wanted a divorce.

'On what grounds?' he asked her, feigning such innocence. 'I have treated you like a queen!'

She told him about the consultation with Rowena, and he grinned at the mention of a gypsy crystal-gazer, but then his wife told him the things that had been revealed by Lamassu – and the smile was immediately wiped off William's face. He seemed confused, and then the confusion turned to anger. He picked up a brass poker from the andirons on the hearthstone and he pressed its point into the neck of his wife, who was now lying back on the chaise longue, ready to swoon.

'I'll scream and the servants will come,' she warned him in a trembling voice, 'and I will tell them things; things that could send you to the scaffold William.'

Never before had Mrs McDermott seen such a drastic change come over a person within such a short span of time; her husband had gone from a bemused and baffled smiling man to a monster with eyes like burning coals. He gritted his teeth and dug the poker's tip further into her neck and in a calm, chilling voice he said: 'The black cap can wait! By the time a servant steps foot into this room you'll be nothing more than a battered mess of blood and brains!'

Time seemed to come to an abrupt halt, and Mrs McDermott believed she really was about to meet her Maker.

Her husband withdrew the poker's tip from her delicate swan-like neck, and then he lifted his left hand, and swung it hard at her face. The back of that hand knocked Mrs McDermott of the chaise longue and she landed unconscious on the floor. A doctor was summoned, and he sedated Mr McDermott's wife with opium and chloral hydrate so when she awakened, she was in a very confused state. William McDermott told his wife she had fallen down the stairs, and yet she had a fragmentary recollection of him striking her, and she told the doctor of the attack, but the family physician assured her that she had indeed fallen downstairs after experiencing a dizzy spell. Mrs McDermott realised that the doctor and her husband had conspired to cover up the brutal assault upon her and she pretended to accept their version of events, but a month later, while William McDermott was out of the house, his wife paid a visit George W. Edwards, a Lord Street solicitor, and somehow persuaded him to go with her to the old gypsy woman Rowena at her humble basement room off Scotland Road. Mrs McDermott hoped to gather more damning information on her evil husband from the gypsy crystal-scryer, for then she could build a cast iron case against him, obtain a divorce – and possibly even see him condemned to death for all of the terrible crimes he had committed over the years. The solicitor Edwards did, however, warn his client that no court in the land would accept evidence from a soothsayer.

When Mrs McDermott called at Rowena's dwelling, her grandson answered, and said his grandmother could no longer tell fortunes because she had been blinded by a man, three weeks ago. Mrs McDermott felt faint when she heard this, fearing that her wicked husband had been responsible, and she begged the grandson to admit her and offered him money, but old Rowena herself came to the door. Her eyes were two black holes, ringed with red crusts. 'Oh! What happened?' Mrs McDermott was unsteady on her feet at the sight of the eyeless gypsy, and Mr Edwards the solicitor had to hold her upright. Rowena told her visitors to come in. She told how, three weeks ago, a well-dressed man had called on her one evening and urged her to visit his aunt, who was on her sick bed, for she longed to know if she would survive her illness. Rowena had gone in a hansom cab with the man to a location in the Aigburth district of the town, and shortly after she had entered a large house, she had been held down by two men, and then the man who had brought her to the house had taken a poker from the fire and had plunged its glowing orange tip into her left eye. Rowena had passed out from the intense pain as her eyeball had burst before cauterization – and then, when she had come to, she had realised with horror that the other eye had also been burned in its socket in the same way. A doctor at the workhouse had told her she would most likely die from the blood poisoning that follows from such deep burns and advised her to turn away from fortune telling and allow a priest to administer the Last Rites, but somehow – perhaps because of the swelling anger the old woman felt towards the monster who had blinded her and the wish to exact revenge upon him – Rowena battled the septicaemia and survived. A sobbing Mrs McDermott then told Rowena how she suspected her husband of being the wicked fiend who had blinded her – just to ensure she could no longer *gaze* into that crystal ball and see the shocking crimes he had committed.

Rowena pounded her fist on the table and cried: 'Then if that is the case, the Devil repay him! I curse the McDermott family and all of their descendants! They too shall lose their eyes! I blind them all until the end of reckoning!'

Three days after Rowena had uttered this curse, William McDermott was at his club one evening, arguing vehemently that the United States should abolish Lincoln's Emancipation Proclamation and bring back slavery, when he suddenly halted in mid-sentence and threw his hands up to his eyes, covering them. He stood up, cried out as if in immense pain, and blood was seen to trickle from under his hands.

'William! What is the matter?' a concerned friend asked the cotton broker, and when McDermott lowered his hands from his face, everyone present saw that he now had a pair of deep scarlet bloodshot eyes, and blood was streaming from them, down his face and dripping from his chin onto the front of his coat and shirt.

'I can't see!' McDermott cried out, and he walked forward and fell onto the table – as if he couldn't see it. 'I'm blind! I'm blind!' he shrieked. The blood continued to pour out of his eye sockets, and a Dr Forshaw, a member of the club who was a renowned surgeon, tried to treat the haemorrhaging eyes, but it took almost a quarter of an hour before the bleeding stopped. William McDermott was blind, and the surgeon said he had never seen a condition like it. Glaucoma of both eyes was unlikely in a man who had previously had excellent vision, and why had so much blood flown from the eyeballs when no wounds were even evident? Mrs McDermott knew the real reason for the unexplained blindness, and as the years went by, she saw how blindness also struck down the son of William – a child from a previous marriage. The brothers and even the cousins of William McDermott are said to have been afflicted by a mysterious blindness which blights the lives of those in their forties – perhaps around the age William McDermott was struck blind by the curse of a gypsy he had blinded, and I know McDermott's today who firmly believe they have inherited the generational curse, a century on.

Other families seem to believe they are being visited by the sins of their forefathers in the form of a curse; families such as the Fagans. Fagan means "little eager man" or "little trier" in Gaelic and the family may have sprung from one Patrick Fagan of Count Meath in Ireland, a man who was in fact of French descent. In the 1840s a branch of the Fagans settled in Liverpool in the Bevington Bush area and a 22-year-old member of this family – a John Fagan – was known for his get-rich-quick plans which always misfired without fail. Everything John turned his hand to fell through, and he eventually decided to opt for a life of crime, as he was illiterate and could not do any job besides labouring – and to John Fagan, work was an unmentionable four-lettered word – something to avoid at all cost. In 1842, John Fagan decided to break into the house of an Everton merchant who distrusted banks and stored his money and gold in a strong box in a certain room. John Fagan waited until nightfall and climbed a ladder to reach the room concerned. It was the wrong room. Fagan had entered the bedroom, and he scared the merchant's heavily pregnant wife who lost her baby as a result. Fagan then tried to leave the room but the accomplice below had removed the ladder after seeing a night-watchman approach. Fagan imagined the ladder was still there and after trying to place his foot on a non-existent rung he plummeted to the ground and almost broke his ankles. The merchant's wife gave birth to a stillborn boy that night, and Fagan was soon arrested for the break-in. At the trial, the sister of the merchant's wife pointed at Fagan and in front of the judge and jury at the crown court she screamed at the bumbling housebreaker: 'No boys shall be born to you or your descendants, and all of your seed shall never be rich!'

It is thought the woman laid this curse upon Fagan because he caused the death of a baby that would have been the merchant's son, and also because Fagan had wanted money – so the curse denied him having any male issue or wealth. Fagan was transported to Australia, where he would remain in chains for fifteen years. Fagan returned to Liverpool after the fifteen years were up, aged 37, and he met a woman named Anne. They had a daughter a year after being married – and then another daughter, and Fagan told his wife about the supposed curse and she laughed and dismissed it, but then a few years later, John and Anne had another daughter. The couple went to a fortune teller in Kirkdale and asked her if they would ever have a boy. The wise old woman told the Fagans: 'You will have three more children, but you will never paint a cot blue, and you will never have riches, because there is a shadow over your name, and I see a small skeleton in that shadow.'

John Fagan became nervous when the fortune teller mentioned the little skeleton because he believed she was referring to the baby boy he had caused the merchant's wife to miscarry – and he had not told his wife about that. Sure enough, Anne Fagan had three more children – all of them girls. Riches also had a habit of eluding the couple. John found a bundle of bank notes one day on the pavement, and he picked them up and ran home to show his wife his lucky find. 'So much for the curse about us being forever poor!' he laughed, and he went to get a bottle of ale out the kitchen. Anne went to get a pie from the larder, and when the couple returned to the table in the living room, the bank notes were gone. The youngest daughter had thrown the money into the fire and was chortling to herself as it burned. John's brother had six daughters, and ended up going to church to pray for a son, and a year later he was elated when his wife gave birth to a boy, but that boy in turn had only one son and many daughters, and all the males of the Fagan line never knew wealth – and I know of Fagans today who tell me that they have had incredible runs of bad luck concerning money, and they also have one son and many daughters!

Curses, like chickens, come home to roost, say the occultists, if they are not cast in a confident manner – and one must be exceedingly careful when issuing a curse. A case in point is the old miser in Old Swan, back in the days when the place was a picture postcard village. The skinflint had a magnificent apple tree in his garden, and he would religiously count each apple hanging from it. When the picking time arrived in the autumn, he counted the apples collected by his three servants and if an apple was missing the cheapskate would often whip one of these servants. On one occasion a 12-year-old boy was caught stealing an apple red-handed by the penny-pinching old man and the lad was sent to the workhouse where he was punished by being committed to the tread-mill. On this occasion the miserly curmudgeon had been keeping an eye on a huge rosy apple dangling from a branch of the tree overhanging the garden gate, and he had promised his young pregnant wife Anne that he would have a special apple pie made from this prize specimen of the fruit, as he knew Anne loved such pies with custard for dessert. The old pinchpenny went away one morning on business and when he returned in the evening he immediately noticed that the big apple over the gate was missing. He asked the servants if they'd seen the apple being pinched and they said they had seen a man pluck the apple and run off at some speed. The miser immediately laid a curse on the apple thief. He said, 'By the Devil below I curse the one who stole this apple! The one who robbed my apple shall find their bowels as lax as a dead cow's tongue! And may the children of the thief have a withered hand!'

Not long after the solemn utterance of this curse, Anne, the wife of the maledicting miser, defecated as she sat in a rocking chair in front of the fire. Her face became pale, and she got up and headed to the bucket in the yard, but her bowels were so loose she left a trail of faeces as she hurried through the cottage. At first, the old miser thought his wife had miscarried. A doctor was sent for and he diagnosed acute diarrhoea. Anne later told her husband that she had developed a strong craving for apple pie and custard while he was away on business, and she had plucked that big apple over the gate. She had then asked one of the servants to make her an apple pie, and it had taken almost four hours to prepare it. She had taken just a slice of it and had could not understand how it had disagreed with her bowels so soon.

The miser realised with mounting horror that he had laid a curse upon his own wife, and when their baby was born, it had a small withered hand – and all descendants of that male had a baby with the same sad affliction. The surname of the family is quite an unusual one and they have descendants in this city today. A similar curse – today interpreted as a medical condition – is said to affect a certain family living in the Heswall district. The story goes that a teenaged beggar was turned away from the grand dwelling of a certain family in Heswall many centuries ago, when the town was called Hesselwelle. A priest tried to help the beggar, but the ragged youth refused because he said he was the illegitimate son of the wealthy man in the mansion and it was his father's duty to give him alms. The beggar called at the stately house again and this time the master of the house had dogs set upon the young man, and in a rage the rejected son, as he was being bitten by the dogs, cursed the family. 'Father, thy cold heart shall be the death of you and all of your sons till the Day of Judgement!' he cried at the face of the bemused head of the household as he looked down from an open window in the mansion. All of the sons of the beggar's father died from ailments of the heart, and the dark influence of the beggar's curse seems to have reached down to our century, for it is a fact that all of the descendants of the man who rejected his bastard son are suffering from aortic stenosis – the narrowing of the exit of the heart's left ventricle. Everyone with the distinguished surname – and there are still many living today in Heswall – are affected with this potentially fatal condition – and the common explanation is that it must be transmitted through the genes – and yet it has only affected the *males* of this particular family.

A Liverpool man with the surname Flaherty told me that he and several members of his family have many crashes and near-fatal accidents whilst travelling along a certain stretch of the A57 as they travel to Warrington, and on some occasions relatives have seen a girl in a white dress jump out in front of their vehicles, and this has been reported at night and even in broad daylight. Mr Flaherty spent a small fortune researching his family tree and discovered a distant female relative in Wales who told him that in the 1850s, a Flaherty raped and stabbed a young woman near Bold Heath – a hamlet where so many accidents have almost claimed the lives of the Flahertys on that accursed stretch of highway. Mr Flaherty's newly-discovered relation told him that when she was a girl, she had heard a tale about a curse on the family, uttered by the raped girl with her dying breath, and many of the Flaherty clan died from sudden inexplicable illnesses, so they moved to north Liverpool and avoided the area around Bold Heath and Warrington like the plague. Since then, Mr Flaherty has done likewise; he takes the long way round when he has to visit relatives in Knutsford.

Knowing who has laid a curse upon your bloodline

is bad enough, but what if the curser up the family tree is unknown? This has been the case with a certain branch of the Fitzgerald family on Merseyside for over a century, and it is a strange curse indeed, because it always strikes around Christmas. On Christmas Eve 1917, a teenaged Patrick Fitzgerald was accidentally scalded in the kitchen of his Toxteth home when someone knocked a copper pot of boiling water onto him, and he almost died from septicaemia. The boy's grandmother immediately mentioned the Fitzgerald curse – that someone in the previous century had laid a curse upon the family after she was pushed into a fire during an altercation. The clothes of the woman caught fire and her face was disfigured by the flames. The grandmother said she couldn't remember the name of the woman but some thought she knew the curser's name but was too afraid to mention it for some superstitious reason. Without fail every year after that 1917 incident, a Fitzgerald was harmed by heat – either from boiling water or fire, and on one occasion a family member was burned to death in a house fire which broke out on a Boxing Day. At the end of this chapter I will tell you the alleged methods for lifting and breaking these curses, so I hope the afflicted branch of the Fitzgerald family will consider trying them.

In the 1970s a woman in her late forties named Elsie Lovely worked as a cleaner in several large buildings owned by Liverpool City Council, and the woman was very lonely indeed. She was pretty, and yet she had no partner, and when her best friend Joan asked her why she had never married as they mopped a hall together one morning, Elsie gave a very honest and sad reply:

'Because no one ever asked me to.'

Joan stopped mopping and said: 'Ah, you mean no fellah ever proposed to you Else?'

'I came close to being wed once,' Elsie replied, placing the mop head in the wringer basket, 'but he was in the merchant navy, and he never came back from Canada. His name was Dan, and he was nice. Took my ring measurement. Said he was going to get an engagement ring from H Samuel.'

'Maybe he died abroad,' a sympathetic Joan suggested, and started mopping again.

'Nah, he probably just lost interest; they do that,' Elsie mused with a dreamy far-away look.

'You'll find someone, Else – there's someone for everyone. All these fellahs out there don't know what they're missing.' Joan dropped the mop and hugged her friend.

'Oh go on, you soft thing,' Elsie smiled and pushed her workmate from her, and then she smiled, but her eyes seemed to be glistened with unshed tears. 'They'd also be marrying into a few bob if they went with me,' Elsie announced.

'How do you mean?' Joan asked and picked up the mop handle.

'Well, one of the benefits from being single and having no one to splash out on is that you can save up,' Elsie explained with a lopsided smile. 'Been putting a few bob away for years so I can enjoy my retirement one day - *and* get myself a decent send off when I kick the bucket.'

Joan seemed to flinch. 'Oh, don't be morbid Else, talking like that.'

'Well it's going to happen to us all one day, isn't it?

They're not burying me in a corpy coffin and that.'

'Have you really got savings Else?' Joan seemed intrigued.

'Yeah, about two thousand odd quid now,' Elsie replied, and then she shot a worried look at her friend and said: 'and don't you go repeating all this Joan. I know what you're like when you've had a few gins – you can't help yourself.'

'Oh as if I'm going to tell anyone about your savings you divvy mare,' Joan protested and seemed hurt by Elsie's suggestion. 'That's terrible that Else, making out I'm a gossip.'

'I'm sorry Joan,' Elsie told her friend with great sincerity in her eyes, 'and I hope you don't think I'm boasting about having a few bob. I know you've had money troubles yourself, and you only have to ask me, girl, and I'll give you whatever you want and you don't even have to give me it back.'

Joan smiled and nodded. 'I know, Else, but I'd never do that. Neither a borrower nor lender be, my Nan used to say. But on the other hand, seeing as you're loaded, you can buy the sausage rolls and tea at Sayers later!'

Elsie grinned but then the smile quickly evaporated as she noticed an open window in the hallway, and she tiptoed up to it and looked out. To Joan she asked: 'Hey, you don't think anyone's been out there listening to us, do you?'

'*Is* there anyone out there?' Joan sighed, placing the underside of her chin on the tip of the mop pole.

'No, not now, but you know they way people can earwig in this town – ' Elsie said as she closed the window. 'I should have put me savings in the bank.'

'Elsie, you're away with the mixer, girl! You mean you've got – ' and then she proceeded to whisper: 'two thousand nicker under the mattress?'

Elsie shook her head and answered: 'In the airing cupboard in the lobby in biscuit tins.'

Joan recoiled in shock. 'Elsie Lovely you stupid bee! Oh, what are you? Put those bloody savings in a bank or a post office savings account. God, don't you ever watch that programme *Police Five*? Some 'arl one had her life savings in this belt thingy around her knickers and these fellahs came into her house in broad daylight and took it off her.'

'In her knickers? She couldn't have had that much in her life savings!' Elsie remarked, picturing the robbery.

'Elsie, promise me you'll put the money in a bank – I'll go with you if you want.'

'Alright, alright...' Elsie mumbled and continued mopping the floor.

Three days after this, the two cleaners were at Bert's Café on Lord Street during their lunch break, enjoying the view from their window seats. Elsie sat on a long padded seat just below the window sill, and a young art student in his twenties named Simon sat next to her. He had cadged a cigarette off Elsie and he was droning on about his girlfriend of two months giving him an ultimatum; he had to get a steady job or she'd give him the "Big E" – the elbow. Elsie was hardly listening to the depressing student, and Joan, who was sitting on a chair at the side of the table opposite to Simon, was very sympathetic to the lad's plight. She actually fancied Simon but felt too old to take it further. And so with Simon's grumbling as a constant background noise, the cleaners sat there, looking out at the never-ending stream of human traffic passing up and down the thoroughfare, when they both noticed a distinguished tall debonair man approaching from the direction of the Millets store. He wore a dark green velvet smoking jacket, white crisp shirt and a royal blue bowtie. He also had on black razor-pleated trousers and a pair of highly polished slip-on shoes. A mass of white crêpe hair crowned the head of this gentleman, who seemed to be in his fifties or early sixties. Joan thought he looked like the actor Jon Pertwee. As soon as this handsome well-groomed man entered the café, he looked directly at Elsie and his eyebrows shot up. He smiled and nodded, and Elsie nodded back. As the man then walked to the counter, Joan asked her friend: 'Do you know him?'

'No,' replied Elsie. 'He was just letting on, being civil like.'

'He never let on to me. He looked at you as if he knew you, Else,' said, Joan and then she verbalised the intrigue welling up in her mind with an 'Oooh...'

'Hasn't he got a look of that fellah who plays Dr Kildare?' Elsie opined.

'Doctor Who - not Dr Kildare!' Joan corrected her friend. 'You're thinking of Neville Chamberlain.'

'Richard Chamberlain,' Elsie corrected Joan, and the two women laughed at the mix-up.

Simon left the café in a huff, for he felt as if Elsie and Joan were not interested in his miserable life, and Joan called for the art student to come back but he ran off into the crowds of Lord Street and was soon lost to sight.

The urbane stranger meanwhile was asking – in a well-spoken voice - about croissants and the uncouth man behind the counter was shaking his head. The annoyed voice of the café proprietor came through the multicoloured plastic strips hanging from the doorway at the rear of the premises, designed to keep out the flies. He shouted: 'It's Bert's Café, not the Savoy! Croissants!'

The well-dressed punter smiled at the array of pies, scones and cakes in the glass case and whispered: 'So, what little ski resort delicacies do we have here?'

The greasy-haired man behind the counter glared at him. A gang of seven workmen then entered the café. Four took the seats at the only vacant table and the other three formed a queue behind the silver-haired stranger, who decided on: 'Just a coffee, no sugar, with double cream - please.'

He was duly handed a mug of black coffee and a tiny plastic pot of cream with a peel-back lid.

'Sixteen pence,' said the grubby grouch behind the counter.

The stranger to Bert's Café paid up and went in search for a place to sit.

'Sit here if you like,' Joan told the togged-up man. She rose quickly from her chair and sat next to Elsie on the padded bench.

'Are you sure? I don't want to obtrude – ' he said, but Joan nodded and told him, 'Yes, of course, sit yourself down.'

'That's awfully kind of you,' the man replied, and he sat at the table smiled at Elsie and said: 'My name's Roland, by the way.'

'I'm Joan, and this is Elsie,' Joan turned to her friend and told Roland: 'She thought you were Jon Pertwee!'

'Pleased to meet you, Elsie and Joan. Yes, I get that

all the time;' said Roland, opening the pot of cream, 'people ask me where I've parked the Tardis.' Roland then explained that he ran an antiques shop in Chester and had just been looking at vacant premises on Whitechapel and Church Street because he was thinking of opening a second shop in Liverpool. In the course of the conversation it became clear that Roland had the eye for Elsie, and when she told him she was a cleaner he seemed surprised and he said that when he had first set eyes upon her as he entered the café he had mistaken her for an old flame named Miranda. He had broken up with her almost ten years ago. Elsie now realised why he had let on to her upon entering the café. Roland arranged to meet Elsie and Joan at a quiet pub after the ladies had finished work, and that afternoon before the meet-up, Joan told Elsie that there was something 'not quite right' about Roland; she felt as if he was something of a conman in fact. Elsie thought her friend was acting as if she was jealous, and she disagreed with her. She thought Roland was a romantic and genuine man – the sort of man who had eluded her for years. They all met up in a pub, and Joan began to hurl questions at Roland. Was he married? He said he had divorced twenty years ago after a short unhappy marriage to a woman down in London. Joan quizzed him about his business, asking how much he made from it on average. 'Oh, it has its moments, and sometimes it actually pays the rates,' Roland had replied, and looked a tad annoyed at the over-inquisitive Joan. Elsie kept glaring at her friend, but Joan made it clear that she was suspicious of Roland's intentions towards her friend. That evening, Roland asked Elsie if he could take her out to the theatre, and then on to a meal at a restaurant in Cheshire – and Joan's jaw dropped. 'Yes, I'd like that,' Elsie replied, 'I haven't had a decent night out in a long time. I don't know much about dinner etiquette and how to pass the port though!' She laughed and her eyes sparkled, and then Roland took her hand and kissed her knuckles. 'Fabulous, Elsie,' he said, then gave a slight quizzical look as he asked. 'Oh, by the way, I just realised something; I don't even know your surname.'

'Lovely,' Elsie giggled, 'Elsie Lovely.'

'Ah, names and nature often agree,' said Roland, 'a very fitting name. So, how about next Friday? Say – eight?'

'What's *your* surname, Roland?' Joan asked, as her friend was still nodding to the antique dealer's proposal.

'How silly of me – I should have mentioned that immediately,' said Roland, and he turned to look into Elsie's eyes. 'My surname's Archmayne – I believe it's Norman.'

'Oh, that's French isn't it?' Elsie asked, and hiccupped.

Roland nodded and replied: 'Yes, and the Archmayne family motto is typically Gallic; it's *Amor omnia vincit* - "Love conquers all"'

Joan killed the romantic moment with yet another probing question. 'Roland, who are you staying with in Liverpool? Just wondered; is it family?'

'I'm wearing out my welcome with a former business partner named John,' Roland told her, 'I've been staying with him for a few days while I scout for new premises, but I'll be returning home in the morning.

Can't trust my nephew with the running of the shop in Chester – he's very lazy.'

'Does John live locally?' asked Joan.

'Joan! You're like the Spanish Inquis-,' Elsie slurred her words because of all the wine she'd bibbed, 'I can't even say it. Joan, you're like a barrister in court – stop asking Roland all of these questions. It's rude.'

On the following Friday at a quarter to seven, Roland Archmayne's maroon Jaguar rolled to a halt outside Elsie little terraced home in Everton, and before Roland could get out the car to knock, the door opened and out came Elsie in a dark brown mid-thigh length coat with brass buttons and a pair of suede-finish boots that almost went to her knees. She'd had her hair done and in the eyes of Roland she looked beautiful. She locked the door, then tottered towards the Jaguar clutching her handbag. Roland quickly got out of the vehicle and gallantly opened the near-side door for Elsie, and her sweet perfume wafted his face. Twenty-eight miles and fifty minutes later the Jaguar was parking on Hamilton Place outside the Gateway Theatre. During the journey from Liverpool Roland had learned that Elsie had always wanted to be a chef, and he had told her she still wasn't too old to pursue her dream and said he had an open-minded friend running a restaurant down in London who was looking for a cordon bleu chef. The couple held hands like schoolkids on a first date throughout the production of *So Long Eden* - a comic musical about Adam and Eve set to country and western music. Elsie felt electrified just sitting there with an actual partner – someone to love – and someone who loved her – after all those years of being alone. At some times she didn't know if she should laugh or cry, and she became so afraid of losing Roland, now that she had found him.

After the musical the couple went to a cosy little bistro on Northgate Street, and as they waited for the waiter to bring the wine list to the candlelit table, Roland suddenly dropped a bombshell. 'Elsie,' he said, and looked so serious as he reached out and grasped her hand. 'I am going to lay my cards on the table because – well, if I don't, I will feel as if I am being dishonest with you – cheating on you in fact.'

Elsie braced herself.

'Elsie, I told you I had been staying with a friend in Liverpool recently – '

Elsie nodded. 'John.'

'Well, John is actually Jane – my ex wife. I have been staying at her home for the past week because I loaned money from her, but please, please believe me Elsie, I stayed in her spare room. She's with someone else, and I have no feelings towards her.'

'I don't know what to say – I – I – ' Elsie struggled, and already a tear glistened in her eye by the candlelight.

'Elsie - I know it's early days – but I'm old enough to know that I love you. I do.'

She squeezed his hand.

'And from tonight, I will have no further dealings with Jane, because it wouldn't be right – and if you were seeing some old flame and telling me it was all Platonic, I'd go through the roof. I am telling you all this because I think a relationship must be based on honesty and trust.'

'Well, I'm glad you told me, and yes, I agree people in love should always be truthful to one another,' Elsie said, and she sounded a little choked up as sorrow constricted her throat. 'Why have you got to borrow money from her? Is business that bad?'

Roland nodded and placed his other hand onto her hand. 'I'm afraid so. I had the shop refitted and had a new facade made, and I overspent a little. But please believe me, Elsie, Jane is nothing to me, and I was silly going to her for a loan in the first place. I didn't know you then, you see.'

'Oh, well, at least I know you love me Roland,' Elsie, said with a damaged smile, 'and yes, it is early days yet, but I really like you – an awful lot.'

The waiter handed the wine lists to the couple and Elsie couldn't make head or tale of her listing.

Roland put on a pair of wireframe reading glasses then looked over the top of the list and said: 'Elsie?'

'Ooh, I don't know,' she said, and blushed, 'QC Wine's all I know. Maybe we should decide on the wine after we've decided what we're eating? Doesn't the wine sort of compliment the food?'

Roland looked up at the waiter and said, 'She *has* got a point. May we see the menu please?'

The meal was superb and the wine – chosen by Elsie with a little guidance from Roland – was the best Elsie had ever had in her life. She described it as 'toasty'. Roland limited his intake because he was driving back. Before he paid the bill, Roland took out a silver cigarette case, opened it and offered it to Elsie but she said she didn't smoke. Roland produced a very unusual lighter – a small globular golden elephant with an upturned trunk. A flame issued from this trunk when he pressed down the elephant's coiled tail. Elsie got the giggles when she saw the way this lighter operated.

'I think I'm drunk,' she said.

'It's allowed, love,' Roland assured her, and after he paid the bill and gave a huge tip to the waiter, he escorted Elsie to the door, and the waiter shouted something. The couple stopped and turned. The waiter gave Elsie a red rose and said to Roland, 'Your wife is beautiful.'

'Thankyou,' Roland replied, then looked at Elsie and added: 'She *is* beautiful.'

The couple went to the car and Roland drove her to his antiques shop on Eastgate Street, not far from the Eastgate Clock. The sign above the beautiful Jacobean windows said: 'Archmayne Antiques – founded 1960'.

'Come in and have a look,' Roland suggested, and got out of the Jag. Elsie followed him and he unlocked the door and went inside, switching on lights. It was a beautiful shop, tastefully decorated with dark oak panelling and real oil paintings in old gold frames. The low beamed ceiling added to the olde world atmosphere, and of course, the place was crammed with antique furniture and curios of every kind. In the midst of all this, Elsie thought of something, and it bothered her.

'Roland, are you staying in Liverpool tonight or are you dropping me off and coming back here?'

'Coming back here, of course,' he replied, and then he thought he detected doubt in her eyes. 'I'm not staying with Jane.'

'Well, you see, you *have* been drinking a little wine tonight, and well, I just thought It'd make more sense if we stayed here.'

'I'd be perfectly alright driving – I did limit my intake,' Roland replied.

'I know Roland. But, I'd feel better if we stayed together tonight – and I'm not that type of girl who does this on a first date, but well, I don't want you being breathalysed.'

Roland nodded, and seemed lost for words for a moment before he told Elsie: 'Oh well, in that case, just let me tidy my bachelor bedroom up. It's a tip. I'll be back in a jiffy.' And he rushed to a door at the end of the room.

'You don't have to tidy up, Roland,' Elsie shouted after him, and he halted, then went out to park his car in the usual space. When he returned, he and Elsie went into a kitchenette. 'Fancy some coffee – or Ovaltine?' asked Roland.

Elsie laughed and tugged at his arm. 'No, I'm stuffed. Let's hit the flock.'

The room was littered with betting slips, and Roland came clean and admitted he did have 'a minor gambling addiction'. Elsie yawned insouciantly, undressed, and got into the bed. Roland switched off the light and turned on his bedside lamp before he got undressed, and then he got into the bed and embraced Elsie. 'Switch that lamp off,' she told him, and he did. Moonlight was filtering through the stained-glass windows of the bedroom. 'It's been a long time since I did this,' Roland told Elsie, and kissed her. *Are you sure?* she was thinking. They talked for a while, and kissed, then Elsie dozed off feeling so secure in Roland's arms.

On the following morning, Roland drove Elsie home, arriving at her home just after ten. It was a Saturday and she was not working today. Elsie changed into something more casual and then she and

Roland went to Bert's Café. Joan was there, and she was chatting to the angst-ridden art student Simon and another young man with long red hair and a thick ginger beard. He was scruffily dressed.

'Where did you get to last night?' Joan asked Elsie, all wide-eyed and obviously feigning surprise. 'I called at yours at eleven and got no answer – did you stay over in Chester?'

'Yeah, Roland had been drinking a lot of wine and I didn't want him getting pulled by the coppers driving me back home,' Elsie told her, and Roland smiled and asked everyone if they'd like tea or coffee. Simon grunted 'Tea, ta,' and his friend said something that sounded like 'coffee,' but Joan shook her head. As Roland went to the counter to get the refreshments, Joan leaned in close to her friend and remarked, 'You're a dark horse you are; did you sleep with him?'

'Joan! There are young people here,' Elsie whispered with bulging eyes, 'and mind your own business.'

When Roland came back with the tray of cups of coffee and tea, Simon's scruffy friend decided to get up and walked straight into him. The tray overturned and splashed Joan and Simon with hot tea and coffee.

'Sorry mate!' said the clumsy bearded teen, and he grabbed a napkin from a neighbouring table and dabbed at Roland's velvet jacket.

'Accidents will happen,' said a stoical Roland, and he told the teenager who had caused the little deluge: 'It's okay, sonny, it's due to go to the dry cleaners anyway.'

Simon and his friend left soon afterwards, and then, around 2.30pm, Roland said he'd better be making tracks back to Chester to avoid the Saturday rush hour, and after making a further arrangement to meet Elsie on Monday evening at her place, he kissed her in the doorway of the café and said, 'I love you Elsie.'

'I love you too, Roland,' she replied, and he kissed her again, then walked away.

When Elsie returned to Joan at the table, she reluctantly told her about Roland getting a loan from his ex-wife, and how he'd stayed with her at her place in Liverpool, and before she could tell her friend the rest – how he'd sworn he'd have nothing more to do with his ex, Joan told her: 'I *said* there was something about him, didn't I? Didn't I tell you? He's just too good to be true Elsie. He's a romancer! All that sugary talk at the pub that evening and that rubbish about him being of French descent and family mottos – and you fell for it all!'

'No, but listen, Joan he said – ' Elsie tried to get a word in edgeways.

'That's why I was giving him the third degree and asking him questions, and you were getting a cob on. I've seen these silver-tongued conmen before Elsie – you're very naive – all he's wanted is to get his leg over.'

'Joan, you're a terrible listener. He promised me – '

'You can't see it, Elsie because he's blinded you with love – taking you to the theatre and wining and dining you – and you even slept with him on the first night!'

'Oh I'm going!' Elsie rose from the table, then paused and asked, 'Will you just shut up for a minute and let me tell you what he said before you start being the judge and jury?'

'Go on,' Joan smiled and shook her head. 'Let's hear the rest of it.'

Elsie sat down again, and then looked around to see

if anyone was listening in; they weren't. 'Listen, I pulled him up about him having dealings with his ex and he promised me he would never go near her again, and listen Joan, he didn't have to tell me he'd got a loan off his ex-wife or any of it but he said he was laying his cards on the table.'

'Laying a trap, more like,' Joan replied. 'Elsie look, you're a lovely looking girl when you've had your hair done, when you've got some lippy on and nice clobber on and that, but you need to wake up.'

'Well, I'm over 21 Joan, so just let me do what I want to do. If I think he isn't being straight or something suspicious is going on, I'll call it a day, believe me.'

Elsie and Joan then went to do a bit of shopping round the city centre, then rode the bus to Everton. They split up, and Elsie went home. At 4.40pm she put the key in the lock – but it wouldn't turn – as if someone had put the catch on the Yale lock *on the other side of the door*. She took the key out and inserted it again but the door was definitely locked from inside. She called on her neighbour, a burly widowed woman named Chrissy, and she called her youngest child, 9-year-old Carl, and took him round the back of the house via the entry. Elsie watched as he climbed over the wall. He opened the backyard door – which had been bolted, then went up the yard to the kitchen door. The pane in the door had been smashed, and Carl told his mother about it. 'Look mam, Elsie's been broken into!'

'No! Oh no!' Elsie turned the handle of the kitchen door and it opened.

'Don't go in, Else! They might still be in there!'

Chrissy warned, but Elsie went in, and she walked over broken glass. Chrissy sent Carl to the other neighbour's house, where he was to tell Mr Yates, a giant of a man, that Elsie's house had been broken into.

Not much had been disturbed in the house – but the biscuit tins containing two thousand pounds of her savings were missing from the shelves in the airing cupboard. Elsie felt unsteady with the shock, and she muttered to herself, 'No, they can't have; my whole life savings. No one knew. Oh God! Joan knew, though because I told her! Big-mouthed Joan!'

'What's that on the floor, Else?' Chrissy pointed to something on the floor of the hallway. It was a golden elephant. It was Roland's lighter. That was the second big shock which nudged Elsie over the edge, and she began to cry.

Elsie walked in a daze to a public telephone box at the end of the street, and she had told Chrissy she was going to call the police, but thinking that Roland might be guilty of the housebreaking because his lighter had been in the hall, she decided she'd have to put her mind at rest first and see if it really had been him who had done this. She dialled 192 and Directory Enquiries gave her the number of Archmayne Antiques. Roland answered it in his professional voice. 'Hello, Archmayne Antiques,' he said.

Elsie could hardly get her words out because she was so choked up. 'Roland? It's me, Elsie.'

There was a pause, and then he said: 'Hello love, what's wrong?'

'I've been broken into – they took my life savings and – and – ' Elsie tried to say more but she burst into tears. She could hear Roland's faint voice coming from the earpiece.

'Elsie! Elsie, are you alright? I'll come over! Where are you?'

'I'll be at my house Roland,' Elsie told him, and she found herself hanging up. She left the red telephone box and then went back to get her purse on the shelf. She felt as if reality was moving in slow motion. As she walked along, she delved into her pocket and took out the gold elephant lighter.

Almost an hour later, Elsie looked out the bay window and saw Roland pulling up in his Jaguar. Chrissy came in from the kitchen with some more tea. She'd told Elsie over and over to report the break-in and theft to the police, and Elsie had told her that the lighter they'd found on the hallway floor belonged to her boyfriend and that it could incriminate him. Chrissy had told her to face reality – that the presence of that lighter could only mean one thing: that Roland was behind the burglary.

Elsie hurried to the front door and opened it and Roland came in and hugged her. 'When did it happen?' he asked her.

'I thought I heard a sound like a window being smashed about half-three, but I never thought any more of it,' Chrissy said coldly, looking Roland up and down. She wanted to mention his lighter being found at the scene of the crime but thought it would be better if Elsie mentioned it.

'Bastards!' Roland snarled, then turned to Elsie and asked: 'How much did they take, love?'

'Over two thousand pounds,' she replied, and she took a handkerchief from her coat pocket and dabbed her eyes.

'Tell Roland what you found in the hallway, Else,' Chrissy said. She just had to mention what she saw as damning evidence.

'Oh yes, Roland, I found your lighter,' Elsie told him in a very sheepish manner, and she slowly took the lighter from her coat pocket and placed it in his palm.

Roland gazed at it, and seemed stunned and somewhat confused. 'But – how did that get here?'

'Well, you came here this morning at ten when you brought me back,' Elsie reminded him, 'so perhaps – '

Roland shook his head of curly white hair. 'No, Elsie, I didn't smoke while I was here and I think I'd have heard something like that fall to the floor from my pocket. It's been bloody *planted* by someone.'

'Planted?' Chrissy asked, with a slight smirk. She didn't believe Roland's suggestion.

'Elsie, you've got to go to the police,' Roland advised her. 'Someone has not only taken your life savings, they are also trying to sabotage our relationship.' Roland took the silk handkerchief from his breast pocket and put the lighter in it. 'We shouldn't have touched it; our prints will be on it now.'

'I don't want you to get into trouble Roland!' Elsie admitted, and started to cry again.

Roland hugged her and tried to reassure her he had nothing to be scared of. 'Elsie, I have been serving in an antiques shop for most of the afternoon, and at half-past three, when this lady heard the window smash, I was arriving home in Chester. People saw me – there are dozens of witnesses.'

'I'll go to the police for you, Else,' Chrissy told her, and walked to the door of the living room.

Elsie tore herself away from Roland's embrace. 'No!' Chrissy, let me have a think first. I - I don't know what to do.'

'Tell the police, Elsie,' Roland urged her, 'I have nothing to hide, and the sooner they look into this the better, before the trail goes cold.'

The police investigated, and after dusting the place for fingerprints and taking the prints of Elsie, Roland and Chrissy for elimination purposes, they found no other prints – not even on the lighter. Roland's account of his whereabouts was checked out and verified, and then the investigation came to an abrupt end. A detective advised Elsie to put her money in the bank in future.

Elsie descended into a depression that was so severe, she even refused to go into work. Roland took her to his flat over the shop and nursed her back to health. Elsie remained baffled by the robbery, and Roland's sister Elspeth – a practising witch – suggested a very unusual way to find out who was behind the robbery. 'I will lay a curse upon the guilty person,' she said confidently.

Roland rolled his eyes. 'Elspeth, I don't think that's necessary – I mean, how will we know who it is just from you putting a curse on them? The thief is probably someone Elsie has never met.'

'Oh I believe Elsie – and you – *have* met the burglar,' Elspeth said, in a very cryptic manner.

'I don't follow you,' Roland told her with a faint grin. 'You're not Sherlock Holmes, Elspeth, so don't start accusing people – and certainly don't curse them either.'

Elspeth smiled at her brother. 'Roland, you told me

the other day that you hadn't worn that ridiculous velvet jacket of yours since – when?'

'Since the accident at that – that greasy spoon café – what about it?' Roland replied, still in the dark.

Elspeth nodded and said: 'Yes, and why did you have your beloved jacket dry-cleaned?'

Roland still didn't get it. 'Because that dozy young chap walked straight into the tray I was carrying.'

'Of course,' said Elsie, narrowing her eyes, 'that boy with Simon. He dabbed you with the napkin, Roland.'

'Yes, but – ' Roland was saying, when he paused and realised what Elspeth and Elsie were thinking. 'You think he took the lighter then? He'd have to be a member of the Magic Circle. Surely I'd have noticed him taking it?'

Elspeth shook her head. 'Happens every day Roland. Pickpockets distract their victim and *voila!* They have your wallet or if they're unlucky, your back pocket comb.'

Elsie nodded slowly, then said: 'And that teenaged pickpocket would have known about my savings from Joan. She *must* have told Simon. She can't help herself – she does it all the time; tells everyone other people's business. She fancies Simon too, so maybe she just told him about my money as a conversation piece - not out of any deliberate evil intent.'

'I think we should tell the police, Elsie,' Roland told his girlfriend. 'They'd raid that chap's house and probably find the money there somewhere.'

'Ah, but the problem lies in proving it, Roland,' Elspeth said, bringing her brother back down to earth. 'They won't get a search warrant for something like that, and say we are wrong? That boy might be innocent. You need proof.'

'Well why put it in our minds then throw cold water all over it?' Roland barked at his sister.

'Because I am going to curse him, that's why,' Elspeth retorted, just as loud as her sibling. 'The perpetrator can't be punished by the laws of this world so I am going to punish him with the ancient laws of the occult.'

'Oh stop this silly – and dangerous – business, Elspeth,' Roland advised, and then he went to the drinks cabinet and asked if anyone fancied a sherry.

'Could you really curse whoever was responsible?' Elsie asked Elspeth; she seemed darkly intrigued by the idea.

'Yes,' Elspeth replied, 'I've done it before. A person who killed a friend's cat in a deliberate hit and run – '

'Elspeth! Let it go now, please,' said Roland, 'now, anyone for sherry? I won't ask again.'

'Then do it then, Elspeth – you have my permission,' said Elsie, 'but don't kill him – just – well, I don't know – humiliate him perhaps.'

'Elsie, please don't encourage her,' said Roland, 'you don't know what she's like. She'll have you in her coven next.'

To Elsie, Elspeth said: 'My brother doesn't realise that the most powerful curse is not to be found in any witch's book of shadows, but in the Bible itself. And you know what that curse is called?'

A captivated Elsie shook her head.

'Psalm 109,' said Elspeth,' the so-called Cursing Psalm. The Church itself has used it to kill people, and after the Dissolution of the Monasteries by Henry VIII, the monks used the Psalm to kill members of

Henry's court and his knights – they even say Henry himself was cursed to death by them. Henry himself said as much on his deathbed. He cried out: "The monks! The monks!" and died with a look of utter horror on his face.'

'It sounds a bit lethal, Elspeth,' Elsie told her – and smiled. She turned to a horrified Roland with a twinkle in her eye. 'I think I *will* have that sherry, love.'

A week after this, Elsie and Roland paid a visit to Bert's Café and Joan was sitting there with Simon. Joan hugged Elsie and asked her how she was, and Roland asked Simon the art student how his friend was.

'What friend?' Simon asked, with an air of annoyance.

'The red-haired chap with the beard,' said Roland, 'the one who knocked the tray out my hand.'

'Why do you want to know?' Simon said, screwing up his face and looking out the window.

'Just wondered,' Roland replied, 'can I get you a coffee?'

Simon ignored him.

'His mate's in a terrible way,' Joan told Roland.

'Really?' said Roland, and he threw a knowing look at Elsie.

'Why, what's up with him?' Elsie asked her friend.

'He's covered in boils,' said Joan, moving her hands in a circular motion across her chest, 'covered in them, even on his scalp, and they took him in – to the hospital you know – and it was that bad they thought it was leprosy. His face is disfigured by them.'

'Ah, I wonder what he's got?' Elsie asked.

'I don't know,' replied Joan, 'and they don't know in

the hospital either, but I believe some of the boils are full of pus. Oh, you'd have to see it Elsie, it's like something out a horror film.'

Simon got up and walked to the café door.

'Where you going, Sime?' Joan asked.

'I'm cutting,' he said, 'I might go and see Simmo.'

'Is that the lad's name – Simmo?' Elsie asked, 'the lad with the boils?'

'Yeah,' Joan told her, 'Johnny Simpson. He was just going to go on holiday to America as well.'

Roland went out of the café and shouted after Simon. 'Simon, can I have a quick word with you?'

'About what?' the teenager said, slowing down, but he didn't turn around.

Roland ran up to him and said. 'Did you hear about Elsie getting broken into?'

The boy looked stunned. 'Yeah, what about it?'

'Do you smoke?' Roland took the golden elephant lighter out of his pocket along with his elegant cigarette case.

Simon's face went red when he saw that quirky lighter. 'No, ta.'

'Did your friend screw Elsie's house?' Roland asked in a nonchalant manner as he lit his cigarette.

'No, why would he?' Simon replied, and a nervous tic pulsed in his cheek.

'Well tell your friend from me that he has been cursed, and unless he returns the money he has stolen, his condition will get steadily worse,' said Roland, and he blew smoke into Simon's face. 'Don't forget to tell him now!' Roland turned and walked away.

'Divvy!' Simon shouted as Roland walked back towards Bert's Café, where Elsie and Joan were waiting in the doorway of the premises.

'What did you say to him?' Elsie asked.

'I just told him to pass on a *get well* message from us love,' said Roland.

Joan looked perplexed at Roland's reply.

And sure enough, Joan rang Archmayne Antiques on the following day and asked to speak to Elsie. She told her friend that Johnny "Simmo" Simpson had confessed to robbing her life savings and he had given her a brown paper parcel with seventeen-hundred pounds in with a note asking her to pass it on to its rightful owner. He said he'd somehow repay the rest of the money that he'd spent.

Elsie asked Elspeth to lift the curse, but Roland's sister said that was impossible, and to make matters worse, the curse had been laid on Johnny Simpson and his descendants. The dreadful skin disease continued to cover Johnny's body, and then it would clear up for months, sometimes for a year, only to break out again, and medical science could not explain the recurring dermatological disease. I imagine that, if Johnny Simpson had any children, they too might be suffering from that dreadful disease – even today. I certainly hope not.

So, how do you rid yourself of a generational curse – or any type of curse for that matter? I have seen people try various 'curse-breaking' spells over the years – many of them of dubious origins – and none of them seem to work. In my honest opinion, the only method which seems to work is the following. You find somewhere quiet – if possible, go to a place of worship – but otherwise a quiet corner of a bedroom will do. Kneel down, and say these words: 'I cut off all curses towards me, slander towards me, and all hatred directed towards me in the name of Jesus Christ. May Jesus be my shield. I place Jesus between me and the curser, and I ask God to protect me from all harm. In the name of Jesus I cut off the one who is cursing me and my family and loved ones. Jesus is my shield.'

Say this anti-curse prayer every night and every morning for a week, and it will firstly cause the curse to rebound back onto the person sending it, and then the curser will find that their curse has no power.

TAKE MY WIFE

Fleecy taupe-grey clouds hung motionless in a platinum sky one March afternoon in 1982, as 52-year-old company director Ned Shallet and his friend of twenty years, a 47-year-old doctor named Nigel Beresford, headed for a meet-up at an Indian restaurant called the Maharaja on Liverpool's Renshaw Street. Shallet parked his vintage 1936 Mercedes-Benz Cabriolet just around the corner from the restaurant on Oldham Street, and as he locked the vehicle, he noticed the burgundy Mini Cooper pulling up about 120 yards further up the street. That car had been following Shallet since he left his baronial home up in Crosby, and he knew why; there was a private enquiry agent in it, and he'd been hired by his wife – Moira Shallet. Ned scowled at the pallid face of the private eye just visible through the reflected sky of the Mini's windscreen. He went to the restaurant around the corner, and once he got inside the place, he noticed Nigel sitting in the far corner, looking at the menu.

'Nigel! You old leech lover!' Ned bellowed, startling some of the customers, and Nigel looked up and smiled. He was curious about the motive his friend had for this meeting. Nigel had known Ned Shallet since he was thirty and he knew just how self-oriented the company director could be.

'Why here?' Nigel asked his friend straight away before Ned could even sit.

'Huh?' Ned gave a puzzled look, and sat down.

'You usually go to that restaurant in Cheshire – so why here?' Nigel persisted. 'What's the name of that place? You always tell me it's the best little Indian restaurant this side of Hyderabad – '

'Well, yes, it is doctor,' Ned cut in, 'but I thought this place would make a nice change – and – well, Moira has eyes and ears everywhere, and so I thought this restaurant might be a little outside her surveillance network.'

'You're very paranoid Ned,' Nigel said with an off-beam grin, 'does she really have people spying on you?'

'Oh yes, Dr Beresford, she does, and she even has a private eye on my tail right now,' Ned told his friend, and put on his reading glasses.

'Oh come off it, Ned,' Nigel said in a dismissive tone with a sceptical sidelong glance. 'Whatever for? What does she think you are going to get up to in middle age?'

'She believes I'm having an affair,' Ned told him as he scanned the menu with a put-on vacuous face.

'Ha! At your age?' Nigel remarked, 'Silly woman.'

'Oh, I am,' Ned suddenly said, in a deep flat voice, and he did not lift his spectacled eyes from the laminated menu.

Nigel Beresford was dumbfounded by the off-the-cuff confession, and he attempted to chuckle. 'What?'

'I think I'll try that Pomfret,' said Ned, avoiding the question, 'it's an Indian Ocean fish that's starting to find favour among the European cooks, but then again, I've been told that there's an unusual Indian dish that incorporates the meat of the hare – you know, those things like rabbits with the big floppy ears? Apparently, hare meat is the only type of meat that can be truly heavily spiced. But then again, I might try the batair masala...'

'Ned – are you *really* having an affair?' a serious-faced Nigel asked him, reaching out to grasp his friend's menu. That got Ned's attention.

'Yes, I am,' Ned replied, and he looked past his friend, as if he was too ashamed to make eye contact. 'She's twenty.'

'Twenty?' Nigel asked, letting go of Ned's menu. His eyes thinned as a painful expression formed on his face. 'She's barely out of her teens.'

Ned took off his glasses and tucked them into his jacket's breast pocket. 'I *know* she's young Nigel, but I – I don't feel like a cradle-snatcher. I feel as if I have met the girl I've been looking for – well, for so long! I'm not a dirty old man, Nigel – stop looking at me like that.'

'Twenty...' Nigel gasped, and he shook his head and decided on what he was going to have.

'Her name's Sarah – you'd like her, Nigel,' Ned said with a warm smile. 'She wants to be a doctor. She's at college. We're going to get married.'

'You're already married, Ned,' Nigel told him, and then he paused and his eyes swivelled left as a thought struck him. 'You *have* told her you're married haven't you?'

'Of course I've told her, Nigel – what do you take me for?' Ned replied in a raised voice, 'I've been very upfront and honest with her. But I did tell her I was going to divorce Moira soon.'

'On what grounds, Ned?' Nigel asked, his face half way between astonishment and amusement.

'I'll think of something. Anyway, I want a bit of

advice from you, Nigel, and I don't want you to overreact, okay?'

'What type of advice?' a suspicious Nigel asked, and his nostrils flared with inquisitiveness – a trait that always amused Ned.

'Well, remember that conversation we had in Spain that time when we were on a bachelor holiday? We had a lot of Rioja wine sloshing about in us at the time, and er, I don't know how it came about but we talked about foolproof ways to kill a person, and you said there were certain pills and natural poisons that a coroner couldn't detect – do you remember? It was a long time ago.'

'Jesus Christ, Ned, are you suggesting what I think you are?' Nigel asked, and he felt a volcano of anger ready to erupt inside his heart.

'Well, not to put too fine a point on it Nigel, I was wondering if it would be possible to bump Moira off and make it look like natural causes – '

'No! I will not be an accomplice in the murder of your wife!' snarled Nigel, and he got up.

'Nigel, sit down – I was pulling your leg, you idiot!' said Ned, seizing the doctor's arm. 'As if I'd kill my own wife for heaven's sake!'

The prying eyes and inquiring ears of customers in the place homed in on the source of all the noise at the corner table and a ruffled waiter slowly headed for Ned and Nigel.

Nigel reluctantly sat down, pinched the top of his nose with his finger and thumb, and exhaled. 'You are bloody unbelievable sometimes, Ned. You've become like some lecherous Machiavelli since your fiftieth birthday! And I know you were not pulling my leg –

you really were serious! I – I can't believe it!'

'Nigel, I'm sorry. I'm under a lot of pressure – the company's not doing so well and Moira's also making my life a living Hell. Sarah keeps asking me when I'm getting divorced on top of all this – '

Nigel interrupted all the self-pity with a raised hand and in a low voice that was more of a hiss than a whisper he said: 'Ned, none of that is any excuse to consider murdering someone!' The doctor looked about in case someone was listening in to the bizarre conversation. 'So let's just drop the whole thing. My appetite is shot through now with all this. I should really leave.'

Ned lunged across the table and with both hands he grasped Nigel's clenched fist and squeezed it. 'Nigel old friend, you are staying and we are going to talk about old times and I give you my word – I will not mention Moira again.'

'I still can't get over it though,' Nigel said through gritted teeth, 'the audacity of it! You must have a low opinion of me!'

'Nigel, Nigel, please calm down before you give yourself a bloody aneurysm. I was thinking out loud, and it was silly talk. I must have been out of my mind, talking like that,' Ned raised his eyebrows and smiled at the doctor. 'Now, let us eat and talk of sport – anything – except this bloody subject.'

The waiter contrived a cough and Ned suddenly noticed him standing to his left. He had not noted his presence through the red haze of passion he had for ridding himself of his harridan of a wife.

The meals were ordered and some normality seeped back into the meet-up for a while.

Halfway through Nigel's meal, Ned started to talk about Sarah and Moira again, and how he needed to divorce his "totalitarian wife".

A weary Nigel sighed: 'Ned, no court in this land will grant you a decree nisi. You've accepted that Moira won't agree to a divorce, so you'll have to explain that to Sarah.'

'You used to like Moira, didn't you?' Ned suddenly asked his friend. 'She still fancies you – did you know that?'

Nigel saw right through his plans, and he shook his head. 'No, Ned, I am not having an affair with Moira so you can try and divorce her. Forget it. God, I thought you said you weren't going to talk about this anymore?'

'You're right,' Ned conceded, and he ordered a non-alcoholic drink, seeing as he was driving. 'So, Nigel, how are things going in your life?' Ned asked, but it was obvious that he was not in the least interested in the question he'd posed out of a mere nicety.

'Well,' Nigel replied, 'a friend and I - Tony Hillgrove - are thinking of approaching the National Enterprise Board for funding towards the establishment of a research company which will use genetic engineering for industrial purposes. We think we can harness molecules in human DNA to make an endless supply of a new type of antibiotic.'

'Oh, sounds interesting,' said Ned, 'maybe something I could fund?'

'No, we are looking for millions Ned,' Nigel told him and sipped his mineral water. 'The scope of this thing is huge. We might ask the Midland Bank for help as well – and that company – Technical Development

Capital.'

Ned was distracted by an Indian man in an orange turban who had just sat at the next table. He was doing all sorts of conjuring tricks and the two women at his table were clapping and cheering to the impressive magic.

'Anyway,' said Nigel, a little annoyed at the way Ned was being distracted, 'that's what I'm doing.'

'Sorry Nigel, but look at that,' Ned nodded towards the Indian magician. 'He just made that plate vanish.'

'It's all sleight of hand,' Nigel said with a grin, and tucked into his meal again.

'And for my next trick, I will produce a white dove out of thin air!' the conjurer said, and the young ladies at the table giggled as he took a large royal blue silk handkerchief from his sleeve and held it with his two hands by opposite corners. He uttered unintelligible words and then made a fanning motion with the cloth – and suddenly, a white dove fluttered from under it and flew into the face of one of the mesmerised women. She screamed and batted the bird away with the back of her hand and the other young woman screamed with laughter.

A member of the restaurant staff came over to the table and told the magician to go and get the dove and leave at once as it was against the law to bring live animals into the Maharaja.

The turbaned man clicked his fingers – and that white dove, which had been flying about at the other end of the room – suddenly vanished.

'That's absolutely amazing!' Ned Shallet said, and he clapped. He shouted over to the man in the turban: 'How did you do that?'

'Magic – that's how!' was the man's reply.

'Rubbish, ' said Nigel, 'all sleight of hand and distraction. He's a bloody conjurer - a night club magician. Tommy Cooper could do that.'

'That dove vanished, Nigel – how is that sleight of hand?' Ned asked.

'The management are probably in on it,' Nigel speculated, 'and that bird is probably trained to fly through some hatch. There's no such thing as magic.'

'Sir, you are very wrong about that! Very wrong!' the Indian magician shouted over to a startled Nigel. He rose from his seat and went over to Nigel, and a member of staff told the man to leave. The magician ignored him and went to the doctor.

'My name is Sanjeev, and I am a practitioner of Indian magic – magic that I leaned from an old yogi, and I do not take kindly to being branded as a conjurer.' Sanjeev had mad, bulging eyes, and looked unbalanced, and this scared Nigel a little.

'I did not intend to offend you Sanjeev,' said Nigel, 'but I was just expressing my personal opinion. I'm a doctor, and I only believe in science, not jiggery-pokery. You're very good, but you're just an illusionist and you shouldn't really say its magic at all but I accept that you're an entertainer I suppose.'

'This is not jiggery-pokery or illusion, it is real magic!' yelled Sanjeev. 'It is not the bloody Indian Rope Trick or that Growing Mango Tree rubbish! This is real magic, taught to me by the great Maluka!'

'Stop bothering these customers and get out of here!' cried the waiter, and he touched Sanjeev's arm. Sanjeev cried out three words in an unknown language, and there was a swishing sound – and then - that waiter vanished into thin air. The two ladies who had been seated with the magician at the table gasped in awe at the vanishing act, and many other customers in the restaurant also saw the waiter disappear.

'Do you *still* think its all sleight of hand, eh Nigel?' Ned asked his friend. He felt a little scared and intrigued seeing a person vanish like that from such close quarters.

Sanjeez clapped his hands and cried: 'Joolay!'

The waiter who had vanished seconds before reappeared in the exact same posture he'd been in when he dematerialised – with his hand reaching out for Sanjeev's arm. He seemed surprised that the magician was now standing a few feet away.

The apparently genuine magic powers being demonstrated by Sanjeez caused quite a commotion among the customers and so the manager of the restaurant warned the turbaned man to leave the premises at once or he would call the police, and he picked up the handset of the telephone on the counter to underline his threat. Sanjeez threw his hands in the air and stormed out, and the two young women who had been seated at the table with him ran after him.

'I won't be a minute – ' Ned told Nigel, and he got up and hurried after Sanjeev.

'What the – ' Nigel watched his friend blunder into other diners as he went after the magician. And then it dawned on the doctor – Ned would ask Sanjeev to spirit away Moira! Nigel left the table and headed for the door but a waiter intercepted him and said: 'Where are you going? You haven't paid your bill yet.'

'Ah, yes,' Nigel said, realising how his intentions to go after Ned (who had already left the place) looked as if he was doing a runner. 'I've left my coat on the back of my chair and my wallet's in it; I'm just trying to stop my friend from doing something stupid.'

'He'll be back soon, surely?' the waiter said, barring Nigel's exit.

Outside, Ned was pleading with Sanjeev on Renshaw Street. 'Look, I'll give you a thousand pounds if you make her vanish. I'll give you even more if that's not enough.'

'You are a very funny man,' Sanjeev told Ned, and halted with his two female friends on the corner of Oldham Street. 'I could have all the money and riches in the world with my magic. What is a thousand English pounds to me? I am only doing what I do for fun. I get my pleasure from toying with you mortals.'

'Please, Sanjeev, I know you are a true magician, and I believe you have some sort of amazing power – ' Ned told him, and he was at a loss at what to offer this man if what he said was true – that he could not be tempted by mere money.

'Why do you want your wife to take a powder?' Sanjeev asked with a smile, and his two friends giggled at the euphemism.

Ned told him the reason. 'She is making my life an utter misery, and she doesn't even love me, and I don't love her – and I have found another woman but she won't let me marry her. She won't agree to a divorce you see.'

'Do you have a photograph of this wife upon you?' Sanjeev asked.

'No, I do not,' replied Ned, 'why? Does this mean you will help me?'

'Then you must picture her in your mind right now;

do you understand what I am saying?' said Sanjeev. He walked towards Ned.

'Yes, think of her – er, just her face or all of her?' Ned asked, sensing something of great magnitude was going to happen in his life.

'Just her face, and please be careful not to think of the woman you love – the other woman – because that would be a disaster – because *she* would disappear instead!' Sanjeev warned.

Ned panicked, because the mental picture of Moira's face was replaced by the beautiful face of Sarah for a moment, so he had to concentrate hard to keep the mental image of Moira's face in his mind's eye.

Sanjeev lifted his hands and brought them together – with Ned's head in-between, so that he in effect slapped him simultaneously from both sides, and the two girls thought this double strike was hilarious.

'It is done,' announced Sanjeev, 'your ogre of a wife has vanished – gayab! Gayab!'

'Thankyou, sir, thankyou,' Ned was almost in tears – but they were tears of joy.

To the two women standing nearby, Sanjeev said: 'See how this man believes in my acts? What faith this man has.' He then pointed to the vintage Bentley and said to Ned: 'Is that your car?'

'Yes – yes it is, why?' Ned replied.

'I'd like to take these girls for a spin around the town in it,' Sanjeev said in a very nonchalant manner.

'Yes, of course, you can have it!' Ned enthused, and took the vehicle's keys out of his trouser pocket. 'Here! These are the keys. You've earned it! It's got a full tank.'

There was a faint cry behind Ned. 'Hey!'

It was Nigel, and he was hurrying from the restaurant with a very angry look. 'Ned! You didn't do what I think – '

'Yes! Yes I did!' Ned roared back, 'And all he wanted in return was the Bentley. I'm free of her, Nigel.'

'You're insane!' Nigel told him, 'You gave him a car worth thousands because of some hocus-pocus crap. I really do think you should see a psychiatrist, Ned! I'm going, anyway – I settled the bill!'

'What? No, Nigel, don't go, please, I need you!' Ned grabbed his arm and smiled. 'You'll be my best man soon. Come back with me and see if she really has gone. Please, Nigel, I know you'd never desert me in my hour of – '

'Oh for God's sake Ned! Cut the crap!' Nigel yelled. 'You really *do* believe that we'll go back to your place and Moira will have vanished into thin air don't you?'

Ned nodded. 'Yes, I do, and you think I've just been conned out of my old Bentley by some Indian charlatan don't you?'

'I do!' Nigel snapped. 'There's one born every minute of the day!'

'Well you're in for a big shock Dr Beresford!' Ned yelled back at him.

Nigel was inflamed by the challenge. He marched off to his car, which was parked off Bold Street, and as Ned tried to keep up with him, the doctor whistled cheerily, for he looked forward to seeing his friend's face when Moira answered the door of his Crosby home.

The two friends never spoke to one another once during the journey to Ned's eight-bedroom house, set in five acres of land. Upon reaching the mansion, Ned got out and pressed a code on the hidden keypad to open the gates, and Nigel drove up the long gravel drive to the front door. Ned walked along after him. He had a set of keys but he knocked at the door, hoping to prove a point – that no one would be at home.

After about ten tense seconds, the two men heard the faint tap of heels on the teak parquet tiles of the hallway, and a female face came to the frosted window in the upper half of the door. It looked like Moira.

'Looks like she's still here, then,' said Nigel all haughty.

The door opened. It was not Moira – it was her older sister Amanda Murray. She looked past Ned and Nigel at the latter's car, as if she expected to see someone there, and then she asked Ned: 'Where's Moira?'

'Why? Isn't she at home?' Ned asked, and he had the ghost of a smile on his lips as he made a quick glance sideways at Nigel.

'I wouldn't be asking you where she was if she was home!' was Amanda annoyed reply.

Ned and Nigel walked into the spacious echoing hallway, and the two of them were lost for words for a moment.

'She was er, she was here when I left about one this afternoon,' Ned told his worried-looking sister-in-law. 'She never told me she was going out.'

'Could she be in one of the rooms here?' Nigel asked, feeling very unnerved by the eeriness of the unfolding situation. 'I mean, it *is* a big place – it's just a suggestion.'

Amanda slowly shook her head. 'I have looked

everywhere, and my sister is nowhere to be seen. Perhaps I should call the police.'

'No, don't do that yet,' said Ned, 'she'll turn up. She's probably just paid a visit to one of her friends.'

'I've called all of her friends, Ned,' Amanda informed him, 'and none of them have seen her. I just know something *bad* has happened to her. I know this may sound silly but I've always had this bond with Moira, ever since we were children; it's like a telepathic link – and well, I just feel there's something very strange about her vanishing act.'

Seeing how distressed Amanda was, Nigel led her into the lounge. 'Come on Amanda, sit down. I'll make you a drink. I'm certain Moira will turn up soon.'

Amanda started to sniffle, and she asked the doctor: 'But Nigel, why would she go off like this and not leave a note or telephone someone first?'

'Sometimes we all feel like going off for a walk, or a long drive, just to escape from a bit of stress,' Nigel assured her, and then he went to the drinks cabinet. 'A medicinal measure of gin and tonic will calm you down a little,' he said, and smiled broadly.

Amanda started to take deep gulps of air and she held her hand to her bosom. 'It's not like her – she doesn't just go off like this. I have a feeling she's been taken – kidnapped!'

'Oh don't be ridiculous Amanda,' said Ned, 'you read too many Agatha Christie novels! No one has kidnapped Moira – she's probably swanning around on the high street buying cosmetics and more clothes.'

When Moira had not returned home by 7pm, Amanda telephoned the police and as the days went by, the name of Moira Shallet was put on the missing persons files. Close friends and family were quizzed by detectives, and of course that included Nigel Beresford and Ned Shallet himself. Detectives asked Ned if his wife had ever left him before and if she had ever had an affair with anyone. Ned said Moira had been very loyal but added, 'She might have met someone else during those long absences when I was away on business all over Europe. They say that the husband is always the last to know about an affair – so maybe my unintentional neglect drove her into the arms of another man.'

'But why wouldn't she write or telephone to at least let you know she was alright?' asked a detective. 'Why would she put her own sister through the trauma of not knowing what had happened to her? It doesn't make sense Mr Shallet. There's something odd about this disappearance, sir.'

Neighbours in Crosby gossiped, and sinister rumours about Ned Shallet seeing a much younger woman began to do the rounds. Many weird theories about the woman's disappearance abounded too; Ned had killed his wife in a rage, and then he had put her body on his speedboat and dumped it in the middle of Liverpool Bay with barbells tied to it. Ned's young lover Sarah also heard the strange rumours about the man who promised marriage once his wife was divorced, and she wondered - *was* he a cold-blooded murderer? When Sarah told her mother she was seeing an older man and that he was none other than Ned Shallet, she was given an ultimatum – stop seeing him or stay out of the family home. Sarah decided she loved Ned enough to believe in his innocence and she moved in with him. Nigel, on the other hand, went in search for that

Indian magician Sanjeev – but no one at the Indian restaurant knew anything about him. He had been in the restaurant three times before and had always caused a commotion, but no one knew where he was from. Nigel asked a waiter to call him should Sanjeev ever turn up at the establishment.

And then, one rainy afternoon, the private enquiry agent Moira had hired to keep tabs on her husband telephoned Ned. Ned heard the pips at the other end of the line, which meant that the caller was in a public telephone box. 'Hello? Mr Shallet? I have seen your name mentioned in many articles in the newspapers concerning the disappearance of your wife. Now, I am not saying you were responsible for her disappearance, but your wife *did* hire me to keep an eye on you just before she disappeared because she suspected you of having an affair. Yes, that's right, it's me John Walker. You'll find my card amongst your wife's personal belongings. I did notice you giving that beautiful Bentley away to that Indian man on Renshaw Street that afternoon. Did you tell the police about your moving act of kindness, sir?'

'Alright you bastard – how much do you want?' Ned seethed.

'I was thinking of a reasonable one-off contribution from you Mr Shallet – no instalments or anything – just a lump sum in the region of fifty grand?'

Ned's hand shook with anger as he held the handset. 'Look, I have nothing to hide – go to the police – and tell them about the Indian man – it means nothing! And while you're at it tell the police how you tried to blackmail me – because that's an imprisonable offence!' Ned then slammed down the telephone and he heard no more from the crooked private eye.

The locals in Crosby thought it suspicious that Sarah was moving in with Ned a mere month after the strange disappearance of Moira, and when the couple went shopping in the town or just popped into the pub for a drink, they found backs turned upon them. People were sure that the rich company director had disposed of his wife to make way for his outrageously young fiancée. Tongues also wagged about the supposed ghost of Moira which had reportedly been seen roaming the grounds of her mansion all hours in the morning. Around this time, Ned and Sarah would sometimes hear the toilet flush or the shower start to run by itself up in the bathroom. The couple also noticed that something was taking food from the pantry, leaving bite-marks in the loaves and even drinking the spirits in the drinks cabinet. Ned tried to explain all of the supernatural activity away by saying that imagination was getting the better of himself and Sarah.

Then, one night at Ned's mansion, the couple were lying in bed, embracing as a storm blew in from the Irish Sea. The wind shook the windows and doors of the sprawling residence and Sarah seemed very scared. She said she thought she had heard a woman's voice shouting for help. The wind howled like a banshee around the mansion, and at two in the morning, Ned got up to go to the toilet, and while he was gone, Sarah felt the bed shake – as if something – or *someone* - had climbed onto the mattress. The girl drew the duvet up, almost over her head, and wished Ned would return from the toilet. Close to the girl's left ear, she heard a mature female voice say: 'You trollop – get out of my bed!'

Sarah screamed, and ducked under the duvet, but then she felt hands seize her hair, and something dragged her out the bed by her long hair and shook her violently. The young woman was naked, and she kicked about and took swipes at the invisible thing shaking her. Sarah felt cloth against her face at one point in the paranormal assault, as if the thing she couldn't see was wearing clothes. The wind blasted the front of the house and a window was blown open for a moment. The gust of air parted the curtains, admitting a blaze of light from the full moon – and in that silvery beam of light, Sarah saw the semi-transparent face of a woman who looked as if she was in her fifties, and she had wild bulging eyes and a head of curly dark hair with grey locks. Sarah then recalled the photograph of Mrs Shallet that had been seen on the missing person posters around the town as well as the front pages of the local newspapers. This was obviously her ghost!

Sarah wrestled herself from the entity's hands and she ran out of the bedroom and descended the stairs screaming. Ned left the toilet and went downstairs to investigate the pandemonium. Sarah told him that Mrs Shallet's ghost had attacked her and that she wanted to go home. Ned said she had imagined the ghost but Sarah got herself into such a hysterical state, Ned had to take the girl home. Sarah later told Ned that she no longer wanted to see him as she now believed that he had killed his wife.

On the following morning, Ned was surprised to see his old vintage Bentley parked on the drive outside his house – especially because the gates to the grounds were still locked. He telephoned Nigel and told him what had been happening. Nigel came over at once and he and Ned saw the semi-transparent form of Moira moving about in the hallway and lounge. Ned seemed terrified but Nigel bravely stood his ground and when the 'ghost' was going into the kitchen, he shouted: 'Moira! I can see you! Can you see me?'

'Yes, just about! Is that you, Nigel?' came the faint echoing voice.

'Give me your hand Moira!' Nigel shouted, and he held out his hand to the spectral figure.

He felt a warm soft female hand in his hand, and he held it tight. 'Moira, how did you get like this?' Nigel asked.

'Leave her alone Nigel!' cried Ned, backing away from the lounge into the hallway.

Moira started to cry. She told the doctor: 'I just faded away and went to sleep, but then I woke up and found that no one could see or hear me – or feel me! I want to come back!'

'Keep hold of my hand, Moira!' Nigel told her, 'You seem to be getting more and more solid!'

'I tried to eat and drink but it's very difficult,' Moira sobbed, 'I feel like a ghost. Water and food go through me sometimes.'

And then suddenly, she was there – completely solid now – and no longer transparent. Her nails were long and her face looked a little different without make-up. 'Oh Nigel!' she cried out, and fainted, and Nigel caught her and took her to the sofa.

'You interfering do-gooder!' Ned shouted at his friend.

'Get that first-aid box from the kitchen you selfish bastard!' Nigel snarled at Ned. 'Go and get it!'

Ned grumbled incoherently as he rushed into the kitchen and he returned with the white tin emblazoned with a red Swiss cross. Nigel opened it and administered the smelling salts to Moira. She eventually recovered, but of course, no one believed her when she said that she had been present when everyone was looking for her, and Nigel had to say that Moira had apparently experienced some sort of nervous breakdown and had wandered off in what is known as a 'fugue' in the world of psychiatry. Moira soon returned to her normal self, and she asked Ned why he had brought that girl to his house so soon after her disappearance. Again, he asked for a divorce so he could marry Sarah and with a look of great satisfaction, Moira told her husband she would never consent to divorce. Moira outlived her husband, who died in the 1990s and she herself passed away a few years ago. It's ironic, but they say the ghosts of Ned and Moira are still heard having heated arguments in their former grand home...

THE PINK PILLOW

Suzy Lockhart and her friend Marie – both aged 19 - were skint that Sunday morning in the August of 1963, so they had to walk four-and-a-half miles home from the Cavern club to Marie's house on Muirhead Avenue East, but what a Saturday night to remember, for the girls had seen the Beatles play their final gig at the Mathew Street venue. Over a few cups of Mantunna tea, ciggies and some cheese on toast, Suzy and Marie talked about the latter's forthcoming wedding and Suzy was told again and again of her duties as a bridesmaid. Marie was tying the knot with Dennis in a fortnight, and the engaged girl almost cried when she reflected on how lucky she was to have such a lovely, selfless fiancé. Around 3.45 am, Marie went up to bed and left Suzy to sleep on the sofa. Suzy took an old tartan blanket and pink pillow from a tall wingback fireside chair where Marie's Nan always sat, and soon Suzy was in the land of nod. Suzy was one of those people who rarely experienced dreams, and yet, on this morning she had a very strange, disturbing and lucid dream. She dreamt she saw a smiling Marie in her white wedding dress, and Dennis was standing next to her in a very smart tuxedo. A church organ was playing Mendelssohn's *Wedding March*. Suzy felt so elated to see her best friend being married, but then the organ music slowed to a dirge and seemed to go backwards, and then Dennis began to hit and punch Marie. The dream was so vivid, Suzy could hear the sickening thud of the groom's fists hitting Marie's face. Suzy cried for Dennis to stop but he began to throttle the bride, and now the organ music grew louder and more discordant. 'You whore! You bloody whore!' Dennis was saying as he shook Marie with both hands clamped around her slender neck. He shook her so hard, her wedding headdress fell off and Marie began to make an awful choking sound. Suzy started to bring her fist down on Dennis's back, but he didn't seem to feel the blows, and as a horrified Suzy looked on, she saw Marie's floppy tongue hanging out of her mouth as she lost consciousness.

Marie's mother Ada shook Suzy awake and asked her if she was okay. Suzy shot up from the sofa and almost butted Ada, and then she gasped for air – and burst into tears. The girl's mascara fell in black rivulets down her cheeks.

'Suzy calm down! It's okay, it's okay love,' Ada held the girl with each of her hands gripping Suzy's upper arms. 'I heard you crying from upstairs.'

'He was strangling Suzy!' Suzy recalled the terrifying scene in the dream. 'He was choking her and her tongue – ' Suzy couldn't speak as the sorrow overwhelmed her, and a flood of tears fell from her eyes.

'Ah, it's been a nightmare, love, that's all,' Ada told her, adding: 'If you sleep with your head to the north, all the iron in your blood goes to the brain and you have nightmares; it's well known; the north pole's a magnet, see. Always sleep with your head to the south. Ah, come here you daft thing – it's just a nightmare.'

Ada hugged the crying girl, and then she went and brought a box of handkerchiefs and a packet of cigarettes and lit two of them. 'Here, blow your nose and wipe your eyes and have a smoke and calm down,' she told Suzy.

'It was so real,' Suzy told Ada, 'and I was helpless – I couldn't do anything.'

'It's just a nightmare Suzy – ' she was saying, and then she noticed the crusts of the toast with the remnants of red cheese on them on the coffee table. 'Did you have cheese on toast before you went asleep?'

Suzy nodded.

Ada smiled and rolled her eyes. 'Oh well that's why you've had a nightmare then, Suzy – eating cheese before you go to bed always causes bad dreams.'

'I don't know, it – ' Suzy decided not to finish the sentence and exhaled a jet of blue smoke.

'Dennis wouldn't harm a hair on our Marie's head – he worships the ground she walks on,' said Ada, 'and anyway, they say dreams work in reverse; if you dream someone's going to die for example, it means long life for them, and if you dream you're fighting someone, it means the opposite, that you're best friends with them. Dreams go by contraries you see.'

'Oh,' was all Suzy could manage with that graphic strangling scene still fresh in her mind.

'They say if you dream of a funeral, you'll hear of a wedding – that's another old saying,' Ada recalled, and puffed on her Embassy cigarette.

'I don't know why the mind comes up with these horrible dreams,' Suzy mused, 'I was having a real nice sleep and that nightmare shattered it.'

'They'll never get to the bottom of the human mind,'

Ada declared, and then she got up and asked Suzy if she wanted a cup of tea.

'Ah, no thanks, honest – I'll get back to sleep after I've had this,' the girl replied, glancing at the cigarette between her fingers.

'I'll get in then,' said Ada. 'Don't you fall asleep with that ciggy now Suzy.'

'No, I'll put it out now, look,' she said, and crushed the filtered cigarette in the ashtray. 'I'm dead beat meself.'

'Well sleep with your head at the other end of the sofa this time and see the difference,' Ada advised, and she left the room, switching off the light as she did but leaving the door ajar. The light was on in the hallway and it filtered into the living room. Suzy decided to sleep in the wing back armchair instead and she put her stockinged feet on a cushion from the sofa that she'd placed on the floor. She slept soundly and had no more nightmares. She awoke to the sound of Marie's father singing in the kitchen as he and Ada cooked breakfast. The ghastly nightmare now seemed so ridiculous, so Suzy asked Ada to say nothing about it to Marie as she was superstitious and it would only worry her.

Weeks after Marie's wedding, Dennis showed his true nature one night when he hit his new wife for coming home late. Suzy was with her and threatened Dennis with a poker. He went to bed in a huff. Marie stayed at her mum's that night, and Suzy went with her. Once again, Suzy slept on the sofa, and this time she had a dream that Dennis was passionately kissing a girl she knew named Frances, and she reluctantly told Marie about it. A worried Marie told Suzy that Frances now worked for the same firm as Dennis, and she later discovered he was having affair with her. Suzy naturally started to think some psychic ability was blossoming in her with this second premonition, and she asked her mother if anyone in the family had possessed the gift of second sight and such. Suzy's mum said she was not aware of anyone on her side of the family having such an unearthly talent. Suzy's father was a God-fearing man and he wouldn't even consider the question and said no good could come of dabbling with the supernatural.

Not long after this, Marie confronted Dennis when she found a condom in his jacket pocket. She asked him if he had been with Frances and he exploded into a rage. He grabbed Marie by her throat and started to shake her as he throttled her. As the life began to drain from Marie, she recalled how Suzy had tackled Dennis with the poker when he had last attacked her, and she reached out for the poker as she fell to her knees on the rug in front of the fire. Marie rammed the handle of the black cast-iron poker into her husband's mouth and broke one of his front teeth. He threw her to the floor and howled in agony. Marie then regained her breath and she began to scream, and her cries brought the neighbours to her door. 'Murder!' Marie screamed, and she ran down the stairs and opened the door. Jack Rogers, the next door neighbour asked Marie if she was alright, and when she told him that Dennis had tried to strangle her, Mr Rogers charged up the stairs and gave the violent husband a hiding.

Suzy's premonition had come to pass, and there were more of them – but Suzy realised something strange about these glimpses of the future; she only had them when she stayed over at Marie's and slept on her sofa.

Marie's Nan hinted that the pink pillow Suzy had laid her head on during the sleepovers had given her the premonitions, and warned that the pillow could reveal when someone would die.

'Oh don't talk so daft Mam,' Ada – Marie's mum – told the old lady. 'How can a pillow do *that?*'

'That pillow was made by my aunt, years ago, and she was a witch,' said Marie's Nan, gazing at the pillow in question. 'She put something in it – I don't know what she put in but my mother said she put something in it. She was a very strange one, she was, my auntie. She told me that if I put five bay leaves in my pillow case the night before Valentine's Day, I'd dream of my future husband – and as true as we're all sitting here, I did. Saw him clearly in a dream, and that was five years before I'd even met him.'

'Oh, rubbish!' Ada said, and grinned at Suzy and Marie – but they weren't smiling; they were engrossed by the old woman's account.

'Can we look inside the pillow and see what she put in it?' Marie asked her grandmother.

'No,' said Nan firmly, and she picked up the pink pillow with its white petal border, and she gazed at it pensively for a moment, and then she walked for the door of the living room. 'The time to come is no more ours than the time past,' she said as she went, and then she halted in the doorway, looked over her left shoulder at Suzy, Ada and Marie and added: 'The future's not ours to see.' She hid that pink pillow well, for no one ever found it again, even after Nan passed away. Suzy Lockhart never had any more warning dreams when she slept over at her friend's house. Marie and Dennis later divorced, and three years afterwards Marie married again and had many children. She's still married to the same man today.

DEVILS IN THE CHURCH

When I was ten, I became – by choice - an altar boy, and not only did I find the rites of the Catholic Church fascinating, I also listened to the intriguing stories of the older priests, and I am convinced an old visiting American priest who conducted a service at my old church was the very priest Father Merrin was based on in *The Exorcist* film and novel, because that story of possession really did take place in the United States in the late 1940s, only the victim was a boy – and the priest knew every detail of that disturbing case. Another priest – we shall call him Father Jones – told me how, during one of the worst snowstorms in living memory – back in the winter of 1962-63 – he expected no one to turn up for morning Mass at his church in snowbound Knowsley – but he climbed up into the pulpit all the same, just in case a handful of the faithful arrived. Ten minutes later the heavy oak door of the church burst open, and with the whirling snowflakes and howling winter wind, there entered a steady stream of people of all ages and classes, and soon the church was at full capacity. Father Jones was astounded and moved by the attendance, and after everyone had settled down, he thanked the churchgoers for braving the glacial arctic weather. Father Jones then began the Mass with a reading from the Acts of the Apostles, but he was greeted with loud laughter – it sounded like the type of canned laughter you'd hear watching a sitcom on the TV, and this outburst naturally startled him. He looked up from the Bible and saw that every single person sitting in the church had horns and the face of a devil. For a moment the priest thought he was dreaming because the sight – although it was frightening – was also very surreal, but then he slowly realised that the snowstorms outside really had kept even the most ardent worshippers away, and these beings who had filled the church were demons. Father Jones bravely carried on the readings from the Bible and he was met with echoing cries of "Liar!" and "Never happened!" along with some very offensive and indecent remarks which I cannot put into print or I would surely face prosecution under the Obscene Publications Act. The horned demons left the benches and closed in on the pulpit and encircled it, and they all began to spit up at Father Jones, who discontinued the mass and began to carry out the Rites of Exorcism.

'You don't believe in God yourself you damned hypocrite!' screeched one of the evil entities and gave the priest the two-fingered gesture, and another one shouted: 'We know all your dirty secrets, Father! Every one of them ha!' During this time, Father Jones saw the statues in the church and some of the religious friezes depicting the Stations of the Cross become animated and one statue began to make rude gestures. Some of the demonic beings grabbed candles and told the priest they were going to burn the church down, and Father Jones looked up at the arched ceiling of the House of God and shouted, 'Lord! Please rid your house of these unclean spirits!'

Seconds later, the door of the church flew open, and in came an old priest, his black cassock flecked with snowflakes. The elderly priest had only recently retired on the grounds of ill health, and he was due to retire to a care home over in Ireland. In his out-thrust hand he held a large crucifix. His voice sounded incredibly loud, as if he was speaking through an amplifier, and Father Jones recognised the words. They were the old Rites of Exorcism in Latin, and they were being uttered with an incredible conviction. The devils screamed in strange harmonies and they split into two groups and snaked along the aisles on either side of the church, some of them brushing past the old priest, who took swipes at them with the crucifix. Once the last demonic entity had left the church, the old priest slammed the door shut, and then he turned, and seemed exhausted as he came down the aisle towards the pulpit. Father Jones ran to the old man's aid, and caught him before he could fall.

'Oh Father, thank you for driving them out of here. If only I had a quarter of your faith,' he told the elderly priest, who was smiling now. He explained how he had been at his window, looking out of his quarters in the priest's house, contemplating his retirement, when he had seen the 'abominations' gathering near farmland some distance away. They had all been assembled around a tall figure, and the old priest stopped short of stating that this had been Lucifer. He then told Father Jones: 'Be on guard – be vigilant – all the time. Not only can the Devil cite Scripture, he can even enter the House of God, as you have seen this morning. Take this, and remember the power behind it,' the old priest said, handing his crucifix to Father Jones. He then said he would have to go back to his quarters because he was drained, and before he went he said, 'This decade will see the return of Devil worship and unspeakable horrors instigated by him below, and they are even watching us now – so be ready Father Jones.'

'Let me escort you back to your room Father,' Father Jones said, full of concern, but the priest waved him away and said, 'Lock this door after I have gone and prepare for the battle to come.'

Weeks after this, Father Jones was involved in one of the most terrifying exorcisms in the history of the Church, and this took place in Huyton, with a 12-year-old girl apparently possessed by something which originally convinced a doctor that the child was pregnant. The girl's stomach was swollen and the doctor and parents even felt the 'baby' kicking. Voices and strange noises then seemed to emanate from the girl's abdomen, which eventually returned to normal, and poltergeist activity erupted in the house and garden. In one version of this incident it was claimed that a terrifying face had appeared on the girl's back which had sworn at the priest, but thankfully Father Jones eventually exorcised the entity and the girl and her parents moved to St Helens, and as far as I know, they were not troubled by any further demonic intrusions. Just why a 12-year-old girl had become possessed was never ascertained, as the girl had not dabbled with a Ouija board nor had she shown any interest in the supernatural whatsoever, but then again, many victims of possession *are* often clean-living God-fearing people.

FIVE SINISTER WARNINGS

Days before Christmas in 1971, a 50-year-old newly-divorced plumber named Henry lost his job through alcoholism, and decided to go self-employed. He obtained very cheap accommodation from a kind old Chinese landlord – a basement flat on Nelson Street in the Chinatown area of Liverpool. Henry's landlord allowed him to use the communal hall telephone in the lodging house as a work number, and Henry put that phone number on a card detailing his services and stuck it in the window of the local post office. A few days later, a man named Phil in Childwall telephoned Henry to get a quote for a busted hot water boiler, and Henry made Phil a very good offer. Having no car, Henry had to get the bus to Childwall Valley Road in thick fog, and he soon fixed the boiler, which merely had a faulty thermostat. Phil, his wife, and an older woman, watched Henry fix the boiler, and with it being Christmas, Phil insisted on Henry having a festive drink – and then another and so on. Being wary of his alcoholism, Henry said he'd had enough on the fifth drink, but Phil said: 'Oh come on, it *is* the season to be jolly after all.'

Phil was soon very intoxicated, and when his wife and the other woman left the room, he winked at Henry and said, 'Here, my missus fancies the pants off you. Straight up, honest.'

'Oh,' was all Henry could say, and Phil explained that he was seeing someone and that his wife knew this and was okay with it. Phil said he was only staying with her for the sake of his daughters, Becky and Lilly. 'I'll send her in to you in a minute, and you can take it from there, Henry boy.'

Henry felt a bit uncomfortable about Phil's matchmaking intentions to say the least, and he said he'd better be going, but Phil, who was a very tall and muscular man - aggressively grabbed Henry's upper arm and through gritted teeth he said: 'You are *not* going anywhere; you will stay put, pal.' Phil then left the room. A woman who looked about 25 came in and smiled at Henry and asked the plumber if he'd like another drink, and Henry nodded, and said: 'Yes please. So, has the fire gone out of your marriage?'

'Why? Who told you?' replied the girl, 'have they been talking about me?'

Henry just smiled and said nothing.

'How did you know my marriage was in trouble?' she asked again.

Tipsy Henry suddenly slammed the drink down on the mantelpiece, grabbed the shapely young lady and began to kiss her, and she pushed him away, but then she had a change of heart. She grabbed his tie and yanked him towards her.

'You're lovely,' Henry told her, and his groping hands slid all over her.

'It's been ages since I did this,' she said, and she kissed him hard and then her tongue probed the inside of his mouth.

The door of the living room then opened, and there stood Phil, framed in the doorway. He looked at his 26-year-old daughter Becky in the arms of Henry and in a flash he was separating them. 'I'm going to have to mangle you now, pal!' Phil growled, but Henry said: 'You told me she fancies me and sent her in!'

'She's not my wife – she's my bleedin' daughter!' Phil yelled, and he threw a punch at Henry but in his drunken state he missed the confused plumber by a few inches, and he fell to the floor and rolled until he hit the table the TV set was resting on. The impact knocked the television set to the floor and its cathode ray tube broke with a bang. Henry ran out of the house and Becky dashed after him and told him she was about to leave her husband, and that they should have an affair, but Henry left her, climbed over the jammed garden gate, and walked on through the heavy damp fog. Phil came staggering out of the house brandishing a hatchet and tried to run after Henry but Becky stopped her drunken father and as she tried to wrestle the hatchet from his hand he lost his balance and fell into a neighbour's hedge of holly.

'Henry! Come back, it's alright!' Becky shouted, getting to her feet. 'He's just drunk!'

'What a bleedin' family!' gasped Henry, looking back. Visibility was bad because of the fog, and in blind panic, the plumber almost walked into a lamp post. He took a last look back at the ghostly image of Becky hurrying towards him in the fog, and then he ran off up the gentle incline of Childwall Valley Road. He soon lost his young ardent admirer but in the fog, Henry also lost his bearings for a while.

Nearly two hours and 5 miles later, Henry was on Upper Duke Street, within minutes of his home, and he found himself reconsidering Becky's offer. She *was* half his age but she was beautiful, and the notion of having children with her and making a new start and a new life with her took hold of Henry's intoxicated mind. He had the urge to relieve himself, and went into an alleyway, where he argued with himself because he couldn't pee immediately. After a long minute, he shook himself, zipped up, and he was about to walk homeward when he heard a woman's voice behind him. She said 'Hey, you!'

For a moment, Henry thought one of the family from Childwall had caught up with him. He turned, startled to see the bright red glowing apparition of a woman's head floating there, about five feet off the ground.

'Don't wreck families! I did and I'm in Hell for it!' the head shrieked, then turned into a skull-like face as it vanished. Henry stood there in shock for a moment and he detected a burning smell hanging in the fog-laden atmosphere.

Henry ran all the way to his flat, and he didn't sleep that morning, for he kept thinking about the words that terrifying apparition of the disembodied head had spoken. Henry believed those words had been a chilling warning from Hell. He knew beyond a shadow of a doubt that he had not hallucinated the ghastly manifestation, and later that morning he told his landlord about the encounter, and asked him what he thought it meant. 'What do we mortals know about anything?' said the landlord, posing a solid philosophical question. 'There is more that is unknown than is known,' added the old Chinaman, 'and before telescopes were invented, no one knew for certain what other worlds looked like out in space. Perhaps there really is a Hell, but I cannot think what that woman must have done to be cast down into such a place; perhaps she broke up a lot of families with some bad consequences, I don't know – but perhaps you should take heed of her warning.'

Henry did indeed take heed, and dropped the idea of seeing Becky. He couldn't see how he would be breaking up a family if Becky was getting divorced anyway – unless the girl had been lying about that. Henry met a woman in her forties named Paula in the following year and eventually married her. Paula was instrumental in supporting Henry when he went teetotal, and he slowly but surely rebuilt his life. The plumber never had any further encounters with ghosts and often talked about the alarming apparition he saw that foggy December morning in 1971 and the weird warning it gave to him. We now move forward nine years to a quiet street in the south of Liverpool for another incident regarding a sinister warning...

It was 22 November 1980, around 9pm, and the streets of Liverpool were noticeably quiet, despite it being a Saturday night. Soon, the episode of *Dallas* watched by 350 million people in 57 countries was going to unmask the culprit who had shot JR Ewing, and a family in a little terraced house on Dingle Grove was glued to the telly – except for Alan, the father of the family. He hated all soaps, especially the American soap-opera *Dallas*, and so he went to smoke a ciggy on the doorstep on this evening. It was already dark, and there wasn't a soul to be seen outside on the street of thirty houses. Alan took a few drags on his Woodbine and looked up at the stars when he happened to notice some dark object approach out the tail of his right eye. It was something which made his flesh creep. An old woman with a bushy head of wild white hair and a grotesque long pointed face was creeping up the street. She was dressed in a long black robe and was hunched over, and as she moved along, she made a very strange giggling sound. Alan was so spooked by the entity he stepped back into the hallway in shock, and she turned to face him. Her right eyeball was just white with ho iris in it, but her left eye was a glowing green disc with a black centre, and a bone-chilling coldness came over Alan when he saw this eye. The unearthly old hag suddenly hurried down the street and vanished into a dark entry. Alan went back inside and bolted the door. He tried to tell his wife Lily what he'd just seen but she was too wrapped up in *Dallas* so he put his coat on and went the pub. As soon as Alan's best friend Frank came into the pub, he bought him a drink, and then he told him what he'd just seen and Frank, in reply, said: 'Ah, that's very interesting, mate.' He then nodded to an old man in the corner and said to Alan, 'Do me a favour; tell him what you just told me. He saw her last week.'

'I hope you're not having me on, Frank,' Alan said, full of suspicion.

'Alan, I'm serious,' Frank gently clutched Alan's elbow and steered him in the direction of the old man. 'Tell him what you just told me.'

Alan went over to the elderly drinker and in an awkward way he asked, 'Er, did you see a strange old woman in black? Frank said you did, and er – '

The old man, whose name was George Godwin, nodded with fear in his eyes. 'Yes, I did,' he answered, 'why do you ask?'

'Well,' Alan, told him, 'I might have seen the same woman tonight.'

'You'll need a priest if you did, lad,' George told him in solemn tone, 'or you'll have no luck. Did you see her eye?'

Alan recalled the green radiant eye with a shudder and nodded. 'We've definitely seen the same thing then.'

'That's the Evil Eye,' George told him in a low grave-sounding voice. 'She follows families around; she's like a banshee. She's been seen for years I'm told.'

'Why will I need a priest?' Alan asked suddenly realising the seriousness of the old man's earlier assertion, 'You've got me worried now.'

'She's unlucky – very unlucky, and you'll need protection now,' said George, all matter-of-fact. 'Do you go to church?'

'Not since my last kid was christened,' Alan replied, and asked George what he was having. The old man shook his head and said, 'Never mind that. Listen lad, you need to get a priest in. I'm not trying to scare you, and this isn't ale talking – but you'll have the worst luck in the world now she's cast that eye on you.'

Frank came over and listened in to the conversation. He asked: 'You two sure someone hasn't hoodwinked you? There was a fellah years ago on Windsor Street who used to dress up as a woman and chase the kids.'

'This is no barmpot dressing up, Frank,' said an annoyed George, 'Me and this gentleman have seen her as clearly as we're seeing you, and I don't think she's of this world.'

Frank raised his eyebrows and there was a glimmer of a smile on his lips. 'People get up to all kinds of tricks when they're bored,' he said, and sipped his gin and tonic to hide a smile.

'I hope you don't bump into her, Frank,' George said, glaring at him because of his scepticism, 'you only live round the corner from Dingle Grove. You'll know it if you see her.'

Alan turned to Frank and told him: 'It's *not* someone playing a prank, mate. You should have seen her eye – it was the most unnerving thing I've ever seen; it was luminous – all lit up - and I went cold when I saw it. It was like that tingly feeling you get – you know, when you say someone's just walked over your grave type of thing.'

'So,' Frank looked into his glass, '*are* you going to get in touch with a priest then?'

'Yes, but I'm not saying anything to the wife yet,' Alan replied, 'Lily is terrified of this subject – the supernatural.'

Alan and his family were indeed plagued with bad luck after that night. Lily's sister, who was heavily pregnant, miscarried on the day after Alan had seen the weird old hag, and something quite bizarre happened that same morning – he opened a bottle of milk – and saw that there was blood in it. Lily said there was also blood in one of the eggs she had cracked on the pan as she made the breakfast. Then one of the kids was plagued with agonising toothache. Three days later, Alan's favourite uncle was about to get in a bath when he suffered a stroke and fell into the bath face down. Unable to move because the stroke left him paralysed, he drowned in eight inches of water.

Alan said nothing to his wife about the weird-looking hag with the glowing eye, but he went cold when she remarked, 'All this bad luck; someone's got the Evil Eye on us I'm telling you.'

Alan then received a visit from the priest he had contacted, and the holy man seemed to know something about the creepy woman, and he blessed the house and sprinkled holy water on the doorstep. The bad luck eventually ceased, but a year afterwards Alan heard that the same old hag with her Evil Eye had been encountered on Peel Street, just a stone's throw from his house. At the time of writing, a very similar entity as the old hag – with the same glowing green eye, hunched back, head of wild white hair and long black robe – has been seen in parts of Wavertree. From that sinister harbinger of bad news we go back to the Liverpool of 1965 to visit the most chilling personification of approaching death – a Grim Reaper – and this mordant being issued some very sinister warnings to a hard-boiled practised doctor. Perfectly sane people can occasionally have hallucinations, even in the absence of drink and certain drugs. We can hear ringing in the ears and even phantasmal voices if we're overtired or suffering from high blood pressure – and in recent years it has been reported that more and more people are experiencing phantom mobile phone vibrations; the phone is felt to vibrate but there is no text or voicemail message to be had. Then we have the 'hallucination' which seems to have some basis in reality, but defies a rational explanation. This was definitely the case back in 1965 on a hot June afternoon at 1.50pm, when 39-year-old Dr Robert Kroger was sitting in his surgery in Liverpool, reviewing the medical notes on one Philip Denham, a 65-year-old patient with hypertension and asthma. Dr

Kroger suddenly heard eerie echoing notes being whistled by someone. It sounded distant and he recognised the melody as *Westminster Quarter* – the ding-dong tune Big Ben chimes every hour. Dr Kroger recoiled in shock as a man with a ghastly chalk-white face and mad, staring eyes appeared at the other side of his desk. The apparition wore a black hood and robe made from a material which had a satin-like sheen. His black lips were pursed as he whistled that easily-recognisable tune the doctor had heard earlier. 'I'm taking Philip today,' the sinister vision said in a plummy voice, and he gave a broad smile.

'What – what are you?' Kroger asked, rising slowly from his chair and backing away.

'I'm a Jolly Reaper, not a grim one,' replied the entity, and then he vanished into thin air. After Kroger somehow composed himself, and after taking a deep breath to calm himself down, he asked the secretary to bring in Philip Denham – but there was no answer, so the doctor buzzed the secretary's intercom again, and in an alarmed voice she replied: 'Oh Doctor! Mr Denham has collapsed and I think he's dead!'

Philip Denham had dropped dead of heart failure in the waiting room, just before he had been due to go into the surgery to see Dr Kroger. The doctor naturally thought about the words of the apparition: 'I'm taking Philip today,' it had said – had it been referring to Philip Denham?

Dr Kroger had been warned by older doctors about the hazards of overwork – how some medical men turned to drink or even considered suicide when they stretched themselves too much and put in too many extra hours. He wondered if the reaper had been some figment of his overworked mind, and the possibility really shook him. The figure had seemed real enough, but Dr Kroger started to question his own senses – and his own sanity. He decided to slow down and to cut his hours at the surgery. He also stopped bringing his work home with him and stopped reading *The Lancet* journal in bed when he should have been getting some precious sleep.

Despite these changes to his lifestyle, the "Jolly Reaper" would make an appearance in the surgery every few weeks, and sometimes he'd say nothing; he'd just smile, and, without fail, each time he put in an appearance, one of the patients of Kroger would pass away. When the apparition did speak, its words were very cryptic to Kroger, and he could not make head or tail of one of these phrases, which went: 'Late children, early orphans.'

The 'reaper' always left a cold spot behind when he departed, and the wall thermometer registered this drop in temperature – which indicated that the visitor was not imaginary. During his fifth visit, the uncanny smiling visitant told the doctor that his name was Roger, and that he'd be calling for a certain child in three days. Dr Kroger visited the parents of this child and told them to take their young boy – who was suffering from Post-Polio Syndrome – to another surgery. The parents complained about the doctor's refusal to treat their son, but Kroger still adamantly declined to have the child at his surgery. The boy continued to live unharmed after the three-day period had elapsed, and Kroger's wife convinced him to take a holiday, believing that he was seeing things because of overwork. Dr Kroger knew he was not seeing things but took the holiday anyway. Jolly Roger was never seen by the doctor after his vacation, but then years later, a retired physician who had worked at the same surgery as Kroger in the 1930s bumped into the latter at a country club one afternoon, and during the course of the ensuing conversation, the former doctor looked about to see if anyone was within earshot, and seeing that no one was near, he leaned forward and whispered to Kroger: 'This might seem like a queer question Robert, but tell me - did you ever see the ghost in a sort of black hooded cowl in that surgery of yours by any chance?'

Kroger was lost for words for a moment, because he had told no one about the "Jolly Reaper" visits – not even his own wife; he *had* told her he thought he'd started to see things, but he never mentioned exactly what he'd seen. He nodded to the retired doctor and said: 'Talk about a bolt out of the blue; yes, I did see him – did you?'

The old doctor just gave a knowing smile and said nothing more on the matter, even though Doctor Kroger tried his utmost to get more information out of him.

Just what the reaper-like being was remains a mystery – unless we accept the claim of the weird apparition itself – that it was a jovial collector of those whose time has come; I do hope *you* won't meet him anytime soon.

Warnings from an apparently paranormal source come in all forms, from messages in dreams, tealeaves – and even through the mundane telephone. I have reported cases over the years where spoken messages and even text messages from the dead or persons unknown have warned the living of some coming calamity, and the following story is a prime example of this phenomenon. I've had to change a few minor details for legal reasons but the rest is exactly as it was reported to me. A Liverpool Professor of Mathematics, Duncan Cavendish, received the first strange telephone call one night in August 1972. A metallic, hissing female voice told him not to travel on the Breda-Rotterdam motorway on August 25 or he would be horribly disfigured by fire in a pile-up. Duncan told his separated wife Susanna about the strange call and she told him to heed it – although Susanna was a superstitious woman and she couldn't say why she believed the telephone message was some warning. Professor Cavendish reluctantly heeded the warning and travelled to his destination in Holland by way of a more long-winded route, and in doing so he avoided being a casualty in one of the most horrific pile-ups in the history of the Netherlands. Dozens of motorists were killed and seriously injured when a tanker full of inflammable liquid ran into the back of a lorry and exploded. Who had warned the professor about this tragic accident? Duncan pondered this question for years. He was a mathematician and in his brain there was no room for airy fairy notions of premonitions and voices from beyond the grave – just cold logic – and so the professor decided the warning had been made by some crank and the dreadful accident in Holland had been a mere coincidence; traffic accidents happened every day after all. Twelve years later, in 1984, Professor Cavendish was planning to take part in an anti-nuclear CND demonstration in Brighton, where, where the Conservative Party was holding a conference. This trip necessitated staying at the Grand Hotel – but he received a very strange telephone call at 10:10pm on Wednesday 10 October. That same metallic, female voice he'd heard twelve years back said: 'The Grand Hotel in Brighton will be bombed on Friday. Don't stay there.'

Mindful of the anonymous caller's last accurate warning, Duncan stayed at the Metropole Hotel in Brighton instead as a precaution, but he didn't dare tell anyone that he was heeding the warning of an anonymous caller, as he had a reputation to think of. Sure enough though, when Friday came, a bomb planted at the Grand Hotel by the IRA in an effort to assassinate Prime Minister Margaret Thatcher exploded, killing 5 people and injuring 31. The bomb went off at 3:56 am that morning, and Duncan Cavendish heard the blast and the terrible screams because he was only in the nearby Metropole Hotel down the road from the explosion. He knew at once that another prediction had come to pass, and he lay there in bed, frozen by shock. The professor told a close friend about the chilling anonymous warnings, and he was advised to hook his telephone up to a tape recorder to capture the telephonic prophet's voice. Over two years there were four more mysterious calls to the professor, all recorded, and each message issued a warning of imminent death or danger which was later fulfilled. During the fourth call, Professor Cavendish asked: 'Who in God's name are you? Why are you warning *me* of all people?'

'We are related,' the voice replied, 'my name is India [followed by garbled interference]' - then the line went dead. This baffled the professor, and he told no one except his close friend about "India". Then, in 1998, Duncan Cavendish's son became a father when his wife gave birth to a daughter. They named her India, a popular first name for girls in the late 1990s. India seems to have inherited her grandfather's talent for working with numbers, for she is a first-rate mathematician. At the time of writing India is at university – and is studying Particle Physics amongst other subjects, with a view to working at the Large Hadron Collider on the French-Swiss border. One of the particles India may experiment with one day is the tachyon – which travels faster than light and *goes backwards in time*. Now, I may be wide of the mark, but if a stream of tachyons could be modulated to carry a message into the past, they could be used to ring a telephone in a bygone decade and warn a person about a future event; why, India could even talk to her grandfather...

And finally, we close this chapter with the tale of a fifth sinister warning - a warning that seems to have come too late. In the 1960s a handsome 32-year-old bank clerk named John Bradford decided to pop the question to 22-year-old Aveline, the daughter of a wealthy businessman who owned a huge Lancashire haulage firm. John had only been dating Aveline for three months (after meeting her at a friend's cocktail party), and everyone close to Bradford knew that his true love was Marie Johnson, a girl he had been courting for six years, but her parents were poor, and rumours had it that John wanted to tie the knot with Aveline just to marry into money. John proposed to Aveline at the Steble fountain on William Brown Street on a scorching summer's day, and after accepting the offer of marriage, Aveline's controlling father jumped in and financed the wedding, sorting out the logistics of it all, hiring the limousines, booking the church and organist, hiring a dressmaker to create his daughter's gown, commissioning a top-class tailor to design Bradford's wedding suit, and he even offered to pay for the honeymoon, something the groom's family were traditionally supposed to do. On the morning of the wedding, the church in Liverpool was packed with over four hundred guests, and when the priest got to the part of the marriage liturgy which states: 'If anyone can show just cause why this couple cannot be lawfully joined together in matrimony, let them speak now or forever hold their peace",' someone at the back of the church roared: 'John Bradford is in love with Marie Johnson! He does not love Aveline - only her money! This marriage is a sham! Shame on you, John!'

It was an old voice, and it sounded just like John Bradford's father. John Bradford senior had declined to attend the wedding because he wanted his son to marry his true love – Marie Johnson. He had seen how loyal Marie was towards John and how she doted on him.

John Bradford and all of the four hundred guests turned to see a shabbily-dressed white-haired heckler hurrying out of the church with his back turned to everyone and his head bowed. A furious John Bradford loped down the aisle after the old man, but Aveline lifted the skirt of the wedding gown and ran after him. 'John! Leave him!' she cried, and the unknown objector left the church.

The commotion died down and the service continued, and after the marriage, John never spoke to his father again because he was certain that the old man had tried to wreck the big day with that outrageous outburst from the back of the church.

The first years of marriage were fine, but then John got stuck in a lift with Marie Johnson of all people one day at a department store in Liverpool, and ended up passionately kissing her. He embarked on a long affair with his old love, and one evening, when John was supposedly working late at the bank, he was in a basement club in the city centre with Marie when his wife came in – with a young stranger. Aveline didn't notice John and Marie and she began to kiss the youth. John and Marie sneaked out of the club, and John later told his wife he'd seen her with her lover going into a club, and a bitter court case ensued. Aveline's topnotch lawyers proved that John had been unfaithful first and he didn't get a penny when he was divorced, and two years after the dissolution of the marriage, John bought an engagement ring and was about to propose to Marie Johnson when she suddenly died in his arms one day from a brain haemorrhage. John Bradford turned to alcohol after the tragic loss of his beloved Marie and eventually the drinking cost him his job. He became a virtual vagrant who even resorted to begging and shoplifting to finance his drinking. He lost his handsome looks, slept rough on the streets, forever in a drunken stupor, and the years flew by. When John was sixty, he was staggering along a street one sunny day when he suddenly had an overwhelming impulse to go and visit the church where he'd been married, and he realised the date was the anniversary of his marriage all those years back. John entered the church and saw a wedding in progress. 'History repeating itself,' he muttered, but then he suddenly recognised the guests – and that couple being married looked very familiar. John realised he was somehow witnessing a ghostly re-enactment of his wedding from decades back. When the priest asked if anyone objected to the marriage, John yelled: 'John Bradford loves Marie Johnson! This marriage is a sham! Shame on you, John!'

As his words echoed throughout the church, John Bradford realised who the heckler had been all those years ago, and ran out of the church. To his dying day, John Bradford believed he had somehow gate-crashed his own wedding, decades after it had taken place, but just how this occurred remains a mystery.

FUNNYBONE

Two policemen – Fred Cartwright, 54, and Billy Greenleaf, just turned 21, were on the beat on Ranelagh Street that humid Saturday night in September 1964. 'There they go, Billy, like seagulls to the council tip,' said Fred, watching the cars rolling from Hanover Street into dimly-lit School Lane and the pitch-black L-shaped Brooks Alley (which runs behind the Old Post Office pub) – both well-known lovers' lanes in that era. Billy nodded his helmeted head and replied, 'Lucky sods – I can't seem to get a Judy.'

'It's your baby face, Billy,' explained Fred, 'grow a muzzy lad. A lot of birds don't like fellahs with faces as hairless as theirs. Grow a muzzy and you'll get a bit of how's your father I'm telling yer.'

The constables halted by the Grecian facade of the Midland Bank and surveyed the milling midnight crowds of people. Some of them were going home from the pubs and others were no doubt leaving the pubs to go on to the many clubs in the city centre.

The policemen continued on their beat up Bold Street, and they were just passing Clarks shoe shop when two young men came running up to them from behind, crying blue murder. 'Police! Oi! Police!' yelled one of the men.

Fred and Billy halted and turned to face the excited

lads.

'Some fellah dressed up as a clown's just pulled this woman out of a car on School Lane! He's got a big knife!' cried a wide-eyed frightened-looking youth.

'A clown?' Fred thinned his eyes at the youth who had made the bizarre report. 'If you're acting the goat lad, I'll do you for wasting police time!'

'I'm serious!' the youth cried back at him, 'come and see for yourself! He might have done her in by now! Come on!' He ran off with his friend and Billy bolted after the lads. Fred wheezed as he tried to keep up with the young men and he thought about the outlandish description of the attacker. It had to be a prankster at work, PC Cartwright decided.

In the stygian gloom of School Lane the policemen came upon a scene of pandemonium; hysterical girls screaming, drunken lads laughing and jeering, and eventually Fred found the alleged victim: a small slim girl of 17 with a pageboy cut named Norma, and she was surrounded by a gaggle of mostly sympathetic juveniles. In a well-spoken voice she said a man dressed like a circus clown had pulled her through the door window of her boyfriend's Ford Anglia and he had run off with her slung over his shoulder but two lads had stopped him. He had thrown Norma down onto the pavement during the confrontation with the dauntless duo before producing a long knife, and he started laughing as he took swipes at the gallant boys with the blade. He then ran off without making a sound and quickly vanished into the shadows of Church Alley. As PCs Cartwright and Greenleaf considered the testimony of Norma with dubious looks, a lad who identified himself as Joe - who looked no older than seventeen - assured the constables that a clown *had* indeed tried to abduct the girl. 'Honest a god, officers, he had on the clobber of a clown – on me mam's life!'

'Alright, alright Joe, I believe you. You lot shouldn't be carrying on down here in the dark anyway,' said Fred, and he asked Joe: 'Does your mam and dad know you carry on like this, eh?'

'Me arl fellah's in the nick and me arl lady's on the game officer,' said Joe, all tongue in cheek, and his friends sniggered at his audacious reply.

'Beat it before I burst your pimples with me knuckles,' said Fred Cartwright, pulling his fist back as if he was going to punch Joe.

'You lot can't even catch Jack the Stripper!' said Joe, eliciting more laughter from his peers. He was referring to a mysterious serial murderer who was killing prostitutes and leaving them in a state of undress down in London.

'You better get home to bed young Joe,' said Fred, 'you've got your Eleven Plus exams on Monday morning haven't yer?'

This attempted abduction of the young woman on School Lane was probably the first attack by "Funnybone" as they came to call the outré-attired assailant, and no one knows where that nickname originated. A fortnight later, a couple of teens embracing passionately in Brooks Alley behind the Old Post Office public house were separated by the white gloved hands of the eerie clown. His face was coated with white make-up, and he had thick black exaggerated sorrowful-looking eyebrows painted over his eyes, a smiling red crescent of a mouth drawn around his lips, and a huge globular red nose – but there was nothing funny about the sword he lifted high above his head as he attempted to kill the lad. The girl ran away screaming onto School Lane while her boyfriend tried desperately to get the sword from the clown's gloved hand. He was knocked clean out by Funnybone, and the clown then chased the screaming girl as far as Paradise Street, where a policeman on his beat responded to the screams. The clown escaped via College Lane, laughing hysterically this time as he ran off. The policeman put his height at about six feet, and noted that he had a one-piece purple suit on. From the athletic way the demented costumed man ran off, jumping onto the bonnet of a car at one point during his escape, the constable believed the knife-wielding crank was in his twenties – perhaps even a teenager.

Extra police were drafted into the city centre to apprehend the unbalanced 'clown' and PC Fred Cartwright was determined to catch the weirdly-attired attacker because he was striking on his beat. Most of the police engaged in the hunt for Funnybone seemed to think the whole affair was just down to the tomfoolery of some young man, and the extra coppers were soon withdrawn from the hunt.

On the Friday night of 9 October that year, Billy Greenleaf had a night off and went to see the legendary American blues singer John Lee Hooker at the Cavern with a Tuebrook girl named Trish, but by midnight she was flirting with a lad from the Bullring tenements named Tony – and he looked a tough nut with his buzz cut and stocky frame. Trish danced with Tony, and then the latter walked over to Billy and gave a little wave as he said, 'Ta ra mate – she's going with me now. Adios la.'

'I don't brush off so easily,' Billy replied, and Tony leaned forward with his hand cupped around his right ear as if he couldn't hear him with the thumping music of the band on stage and hubbub of the Cavern's crowd. Billy repeated what he'd said a little nearer to Tony's ear and received a punch that sent him flying backwards against a brick wall. Billy was helped up by a beautiful girl with a blonde beehive. He looked around for the cowardly Tony but he'd vanished into the crowds. The blonde girl who had helped Billy to his feet pulled him into an archway and asked him if he was alright. Billy said he was, and then he went off in a huff and climbed the stairs from the Cavern onto Mathew Street. The girl followed him, and as Billy walked down the street he heard her footfalls behind him. He turned, and realising she was a very attractive girl with something about her he just couldn't put his finger on, he asked her if she fancied going with him to a club on Berry Street. The girl just smiled and said she needed to get some fresh air after being cooped up in the Cavern for the past two hours. Billy offered her a cigarette but she said she didn't smoke. The girl's name was Bonnie, an 18-year-old college student studying journalism, and she was from Knotty Ash. She'd been on a blind date tonight but her date never turned up. Billy and Bonnie decided to go to a coffee bar, and walked up Church Street – where they saw a huge crowd of excited people at the Hanover Street junction. Billy wasn't sure whether a fight was in progress or if there had been some road accident, and Bonnie, wondering if it was a newsworthy event she could incorporate into her college journalism course, said, 'Let's see what's going on. Looks like a hell of a hullaballoo.'

The couple hurried to the scrum of some fifty or more people, mostly youths around their own age, and in the centre of the throng, there was a very strange sight to behold. Four young men had a strange-looking man pinned down. He was dressed like a circus clown, and Bonnie gasped in shock when she saw the clown's ghastly-looking face. He had a large round red nose and that would normally evoke a smile, but the rest of the clown's face was contorted with an expression of intense hate. He was growling and spitting and swearing with a young man kneeling on each of his shoulders, and another lad was holding his kicking reddish boots, and the fourth juvenile was trying to wrest the huge sword from his gloved hand.

'Help us will ya?' the latter youth said to the onlookers, and he seemed to cut his hand on the blade of the sword.

The body of the clown started to undulate and writhe like a snake, and it was a very sinister and bloodcurdling sight to behold.

'He's got no spine – he's like a bleedin' rat!' shouted one horrified bystander.

Billy lunged through the crowd encircling the bizarre spectacle and to one of the lads restraining the clown he announced: 'I'll help you mucker! I'm a policeman!'

The clown made a loud growling sound, and he kicked the heels of his boots into the face of the youth who had been trying to restrain him by his feet, and then he somehow got up and lashed out with a gloved fist to the young man who had been kneeling on his right shoulder. Billy saw blood issue from this punch to the youth's nose in a violent squirt. Within a heartbeat the clown was standing up and a choir of screaming voices erupted from the crowds as everyone drew back. Billy knew that this grotesque figure was Funnybone, and he tried to confront him, but the clown turned and ran, and bystanders threw themselves aside, forming an instant escape route to the terrifying figure.

Billy, Bonnie and about half a dozen young men chased the clown into the shadows of Brooks Alley, where one of the men running just ahead of Billy tripped over the kerb – and Billy fell over him. Funnybone flew down the alleyway, and his silhouette was seen darting round the corner on the left. He ran out onto School Lane and escaped once again. As the lad who had tripped got up rubbing his knee and yowling with pain, a heavy hand landed on Billy's shoulder as Bonnie helped him up. The young off-duty copper turned, startled, and then a smile broke out on his face.

It was his colleague Fred Cartwright.

'Fred!' Billy's voice echoed in the alleyway and then the lad turned to Bonnie and explained: 'This is my hoppo – did I tell you I was a copper?'

'No, no, you didn't – oh,' was a startled Bonnie's reply.

'He got away again I see, Billy,' said Fred, and he shone his torch at the young man who had tripped over the kerb. 'You alright son?'

The lad nodded, then grouchily told PC Cartwright: 'If you would have been around a few minutes ago you could have nicked him.'

'We can't be everywhere sonny, especially on a

Saturday night with all the young idiots about who can't hold their ale,' Cartwright replied, and then he turned to Billy. 'Did you get a good look at him?'

Billy nodded, 'Yeah, but he had make-up on, and I doubt I'd recognise him without it.'

'How did he get away anyway?' Cartwright asked. 'He had people pinning him down didn't he? They must have been weak as kittens!'

'He's very strong Fred and I think he's double-jointed,' Billy replied. 'You should have seen him squirm about like a worm – like he had rubber bones or something, it was dead weird.'

That morning, Billy asked Bonnie if he could see her again, and she answered in the affirmative. Thus began a relationship which would lead to marriage two years later.

Three nights later, Funnybone was seen prowling around Wood Street at around 1.40am again carrying his lethal-looking sword, and this time a policeman saw him and bravely gave chase. The clown turned right at the end of Wood Street into Berry Street, and seemed to vanish off the face of the earth at that point.

PC Cartwright had a sneaking suspicion that Funnybone was the warped alter ego of an eccentric junkshop owner on Berry Street, and one night when he was on the beat with Billy, he told his friend of his suspicions. The policemen went into an all-night café in Chinatown that night for a quick coffee and a smoke, and here, Fred elaborated on his theory by sketching a rough diagram of the surrounding streets on a napkin. He showed Billy the routes the clown had been seen to take whenever he fled from scene of his attacks, and Fred extended these routes by drawing lines – and most of the lines converged at the same point – and that was the location of a second hand shop run by a 30-year-old man named Martin Smarte – and this same fellah had been cautioned two years ago when he put on a horror mask on Duck Apple Night (now known as Halloween) and assaulted a number of girls. Smarte said he'd been drunk and that the stunt was all down to high jinks – but Fred believed that the junk store owner had some split personality.

That very morning, a fog infiltrated the North West and Liverpool became a city of shadows and rolling mists with the groans of the fog horns of the ships on the river as an eerie background noise. 'What a night for this headcase to go on the prowl eh, Billy?' said Fred, as they left the café. 'You know as you get older on this job, you develop a sixth sense towards criminals, and sometimes you know they are just going to strike. I feel as if Funnybone is out there now on the streets.'

No sooner had Fred Cartwright said these words when the coppers heard the faint screams of two women. The screams sounded as if they were coming from the direction of Duke Street, so the policemen ran off in that direction, and this time they had their truncheons with them. On the corner of Kent Street and Duke Street, Billy saw the misted silhouettes of two women huddled together about fifty yards away. The visibility was abysmal, but Billy could not see Funnybone near the figures. Fred shone his torch at the women to let them know someone was responding to their screams. The women – both prostitutes in their twenties known to Fred Cartwright – spoke at the same time in excited gibbering voices, and as Fred was telling them to calm down, Billy spotted the clown's pale face, peeping at him from the corner of Kent Street and Henry Street. He pretended not to see it, and went to his colleague, who was listening to a very disturbing account from one of the prostitutes. 'He got the handle of the sword and tried to stick it up Josie,' said Christine, a small red-haired girl of 23 years of age.

'Er, Fred,' Billy cut in.

'What,' Fred asked.

'He's behind me now. He's looking at us from the corner. See him?' Billy smiled as he saw Fred narrow his eyes and look into the night vapours.

Christine heard what Billy said and when she saw that the clown was peeping round the corner she let out a shriek, and the painted face vanished. The policemen made a dash to the corner with the sprightly Billy leading the way as usual, and the young policeman lifted his truncheon, expecting the costumed freak to lash out at him with that sword, but by the time he got to Henry Street, Funnybone had vanished into the depths of the ever-worsening fog. Fred guessed that the clown was heading back to Berry Street, but to do that he'd have to go up Suffolk Street and on to either Lydia Ann Street or Gilbert Street, so he and Billy headed back to Kent Street and hid at the corner of Lydia Ann Street – and sure enough, the clown came running silently past them.

'Hey Bollocks!' Fred roared as the clown passed him and Billy, and the clown slowed down and turned to face the two coppers. It swung the sword at them in a frenzy and with such force, the tip of Billy's truncheon was sliced off. The clown then sprinted up Grenville

Street, where it again faded away into the fog, but just before it did, Billy saw Funnybone turn left into Cornwallis Street.

Fred suddenly slowed down after giving chase for a few yards, and seemed out of breath. He told Billy the fog had kicked his chest off and urged him to go after Funnybone to see where he was going to ground. Billy chased the weird sword-wielding figure to Duke Street, where something very unexpected took place. A Ford Zodiac travelling up Duke Street towards Berry Street hit Funnybone as he was crossing the road, and the impact threw the clown into the air. He landed on the pavement with a thump – and yet, despite the sickening collision, the clown immediately picked itself up off the pavement and ran off – turning left at the corner onto Berry Street.

'I didn't see him 'cos of the fog, officer!' the young panic-stricken driver told a panting Billy through his rolled-down window.

'Hang on, what's that?' Billy noticed something sticking out of the front grille of the vehicle. It was Funnybone's sword. Billy took out a handkerchief and then he carefully removed the antique-looking sword from the grille. As the driver asked if he'd be charged for knocking down the man, Billy ran to the corner and saw Funnybone dart into the doorway of a certain second hand shop. He realised it was the very shop Fred had mentioned in his theory! A few minutes later, Billy saw his colleague's torchbeam raking the fog, and he shouted to him. 'Fred, you're right!'

Once PC Cartwright had caught up with his young partner, he was told about the clown going into the second hand shop on Berry Street – the shop owned by Martin Smarte, and Billy showed him the sword the clown had lost in the collision with the Zodiac.

'I knew it was that tappy bastard,' Fred gasped, and after a cough into his hankie, he proceeded with Billy to the shop in question – and found it locked.

Fred hammered on the door of the shop with the truncheon and shouted: 'Police! Open up!'

Less than a minute after this a light went on in the room above the shop.

'Come on Mr Smarte! Open up! Police!' Fred continued, and he smiled and looked at the sword Billy was holding with the handkerchief wrapped around its grip. 'Good move Billy, but he had gloves on didn't he?' said Fred.

'Yeah, but he might have got his dabs on it before he put the gloves on,' Billy reasoned.

A light went on in the shop, and a man in spectacles came to the window of the door. His hair was a mess. 'What is it?' Mr Smarte asked.

'We want a word with *you* mate,' said Fred, and he could hear a key rattling about in the lock followed by the sound of a bolt being drawn back.

The door opened – and the policemen saw that Smarte had on a dressing gown which showed them that one leg was bare – and the other one was encased in a plaster cast. Smarte stood there leaning on a walking stick. 'What is it?' he asked the policemen.

Just as PC Cartwright was about to explain why he and his colleague had called at such an unearthly hour, Billy swore and said: 'Fred, look!'

About ten feet behind Martin Smarte was the figure of Funnybone, sitting in the corner with his head craned back, as if he was looking at the ceiling. In the faint light filtering into the shop from a streetlamp, the clown looked very sinister as it sat in the corner.

'We've come about him!' Fred pointed to the seated clown with his truncheon. He's been terrorizing people in the city centre!'

Mr Smarte switched on the light in the shop and two neon tubes – one on the ceiling and the other in the shop window, flickered into life, pulsated, then lit up the interior of the shop with a bright steady luminance.

'What are you doing with that? That's mine.' Mr Smarte pointed to the sword Billy was carrying, and the young policeman was so fixated with the clown he and Fred had been trying to apprehend for so long, he didn't answer.

Fred walked ever so gingerly over to Funnybone. 'Get up! Come on! Up!'

The clown didn't respond. It didn't even move.

'That's a dummy,' said a baffled Mr Smarte. 'It's full of sawdust. What *is* going on here? I'm going to put in a complaint about this first thing in the morning believe me!'

'A dummy?' Fred asked, and he prodded the chest of Funnybone with the truncheon.

The head of the clown flopped forward and swung side to side.

Fred prodded it again, and the lifeless trunk of the effigy toppled sideways.

'Look!' Smarte hit the clown's body hard with his walking stick twice. 'It's a dummy! What did you think it was? We found it in a condemned house in Norris Green last year. What's all this about?'

Fred knelt down and felt the stuffed life-size figure of the clown and once he was satisfied that no one was inside of the thing, he turned to face Billy and said, 'It's a bit uncanny this, isn't it?'

'Where did you find this?' Martin Smarte took the sword from Billy, who reflexively withdrew the sword from Smarte's reaching hand for a moment, until he realised – as Fred had also realised – that there was simply no case to prosecute here. This wouldn't stand up in court, and if superiors of the policemen heard about this back at the nick, they'd assume Fred and Billy had been drinking on duty – or had been at the purple hearts.

'You wanna burn that thing,' Fred sincerely advised Mr Smarte as he backed away from the bizarre 'doll'.

'Whatever for?' Mr Smarte asked with a perplexed expression.

'May I ask who your doctor is, sir?' Billy Greenleaf suddenly said to the second hand store owner.

'Mr Tombuk – why?' was Smarte's reply.

'How long have you had that cast on your leg?' Billy asked.

'For a fortnight – I fell down a flight of stairs – what about it?' Smarte told him, and he looked as if he'd reached the end of his tether with the strange behaviour of the policemen.

'We'll check that out, sir,' Billy assured the shop proprietor.

Smarte's face turned red with rage. 'The doctors at the Royal Infirmary treated me for the broken leg, not my doctor! What in God's name is all this questioning about, eh? Getting me out of bed all hours in the morning for what?'

'It's alright sir,' Fred headed for the door and grabbed Billy by the sleeve of his uniform and guided him in the same direction. 'We just had a report of a break-in, that's all,' lied Fred, 'so now that we've established that everything's in order we'll be on our way. Bye sir. Come along Billy.'

Outside on the foggy street, Fred shook his head and told Billy: 'Don't breathe a friggin' word of this to any of the lads back at the station or we'll be a bleedin' laughing stock, *and* they'll have us sent to a psychiatrist.'

'I reckon that cast on his leg is fake, Fred, and I think *he's* Funnybone, I do – and we'll prove it.' Billy then looked at his truncheon with its missing tip.

He checked with the doctors at the Royal Infirmary – and they told Billy that a Martin Smarte had indeed had a cast put on his leg two weeks back after he'd broken it because of a drunken fall down stairs.

A few months after this, there was a fire at the second hand shop on Berry Street. Mr Smarte had fallen asleep in an armchair with a lighted cigarette. Most of the stock downstairs was destroyed in the blaze – but that stuffed clown was nowhere to be seen – and not a trace of it could be found among the charred stock. Billy and Fred later heard strange rumours about Funnybone; that he had been seen looking through the ground floor windows of houses in the south of Liverpool, but there were no reliable sightings of the unearthly clown with the sword after that blaze. What is Funnybone? I simply do not know, and I have a very unsettling feeling that whatever he is, he may still be around somewhere; and if it's night out there, he could even be looking through your window right now...

THE LITTLE TRUMPETER

The following paranormal story unfolded one infernally hot August afternoon in 2010, just a few days before the Summer Bank Holiday, when Maurice Walker, a 60-year-old Woolton divorcé, returned from the funeral of a close friend, foregoing the chance of a boozing session at the usual after-funeral knees-up at the nearest pub because his eyes stung with hay fever. His eyes were so red and the August sun was so fierce, he wore gold-tinted sunglasses as he left the private cab. He paid and tipped the driver and then headed for the Woolton branch of Sainsbury's with designs for a bottle of Pink Moscato, a 500ml pot of Haagen-Dasz ice cream and a box of Loratadine hay fever tablets. And then it would be home to his semi on Menlove Avenue to watch *Diagnosis Murder* and *Cash in the Celebrity Attic* to mellow out with the plonk. That was his straightforward intentions, anyway, but life had different plans for Maurice that blistering afternoon.

As Maurice came down the supermarket's wine aisle he thought he heard a distant trumpet playing a piece of music – and this faint melody immediately brought back a very strange memory from his childhood. When he was seven years of age he had been plagued by a certain tune which sounded as if it was being played on a flute, and only the young Maurice could hear it. He had asked his best friend Phillip Fairbanks if he could hear it, and Phillip had said he could hear nothing. A worrying Maurice then asked everyone in his family if they could hear the flute music and no one could. Maurice was therefore sent to ear specialists and even a psychiatrist because the interminable tune rendered him unable to concentrate at school and disturbed his sleep. His music teacher Miss Clarke asked Maurice to whistle the tune and she even transcribed it onto the staves of her manuscript paper and played it on the piano, but she could not identify the piece. Miss Clarke had asked other musicians if they could identify the piece but none of them could, although a university professor of music said he believed the piece sounded as if it belonged to the Tudor period (1485-1603). After being plagued by the phantom flautist for months, Maurice happened to identify the tune one day as it came on the radio as he sat in the barber's chair. The BBC Radio light music programme presenter said that the tune was *Pastime with Good Company* – written by none other than Henry VIII around 1509. When the song on the radio ended, the accursed unseen flute player stopped too. Young Maurice asked the barber to stop snipping away around his ears to determine whether the maddening melody had ceased, and when he realised it had, the lad had cheered, jumped out of the chair and bolted home to tell his parents the great news.

So why on earth had the mystifying music returned to haunt him? Maurice looked about in case one of the supermarket shelf-stackers had a transistor radio playing somewhere but there wasn't a single member of staff about, and there was only one customer on the wine aisle, and she was a middle-aged handsome woman standing in front of him about fifteen feet away, and the trumpet melody seemed to be *coming from her direction.* When Maurice ascertained that the sinister strains of the trumpet music were not from his mind, he felt so utterly relieved, but he was still curious as to why the tormenting trumpeter was in the vicinity of the female shopper. Then Maurice *saw* it. On the right shoulder of the woman was a tiny glowing figure of a man about six inches in height. The miniature figure was playing a tiny silvery trumpet – and he was aiming it into the lady's ear. 'Oh – my – God,' Maurice paused between each gasped word and lifted his sunglasses off his nose for a moment to get a clearer view of the radiant being. He crept in a bit closer to the woman, who bent down to pick up a one-litre bottle of Smirnoff vodka from a shelf, and Maurice noted that when the lady crouched slightly to grab the bottle, the trumpeter did not lose balance and sway as she tilted forward. The woman put the vodka into her trolley and moved along the aisle.

Maurice was so fascinated by the luminous little trumpeter he followed the woman to the next aisle, and he pretended to look for items as he made numerous glances at the lady's shoulder. A young woman of about twenty-five came down the aisle with her young son sitting in a special seat attached to the shopping trolley. The child looked as if he was about two or three years of age, and he pointed to the shining fairy-like musician on the woman's shoulder as his mum pushed him along – so the child could obviously see the weird little apparition, but his mother took no notice when her boy laughed and pointed at the trumpeter.

Maurice had an idea. He delved into his front-left trouser pocket and took out his Apple iPhone. He almost made an audible grumble as he keyed in the security passcode – something he hated doing because his nephew had recently changed the code for him. Maurice then pressed his thumb on the phone's camera icon, lifted it, got the little glowing man in the centre of the wireframe square – and took a snap. The shutter sound effect was obviously heard by the woman and she turned around sharply as Maurice hid the iPhone in his pocket. She looked away again, and he checked the camera roll. There was nothing on the woman's shoulder in the photograph he had taken – which worried Maurice. He wondered if he was seeing things; was this the beginning of the senile dementia he was forever dreading? He was sorry he'd attempted the picture now. Still, he continued to follow the woman about, and at one point she stopped and looked at him with an annoyed expression, and Maurice decided to have an imaginary conversation with someone on his mobile in an effort to throw off the woman's suspicion, but she came over to him, leaving her trolley behind, and she confronted Maurice.

'Are you a store detective?' she asked.

Maurice hung up from his make-believe phone conversation and replied: 'Sorry?'

'You've been following me all around the aisles,' the woman told him, 'and you even tried to take a picture of me before – I heard you – I'm not daft!'

'I am certainly not a store detective madam,' Maurice assured her, and his face turned a shade of pink. 'Why on earth would I be following you?'

'You might be one of those perverts,' said the woman, 'taking pictures of women on the sly. I've seen them – taking pictures up women's skirts and that.'

'How *dare* you suggest that!' Maurice retorted, lost for words, and then he was distracted by the beaming little imp with the trumpet on the woman's shoulder. Maurice was now close enough to see the detail in the little man's attire. He wore a pointed pale-green cap, a white tunic of some sort, and the type of tights and pointed shoes he associated with Robin Hood. His face was black, as were his hands, and he was still playing that trumpet.

The woman noticed that the possible store-detective was looking at her right shoulder and she followed the line of his gaze to see what he was focussing on. 'What are you looking at?' she asked.

'Oh, I suppose I have nothing to lose by telling you this,' Maurice replied in a resigned voice, 'but – well – do you know you have a little man on your shoulder – and that he's playing a trumpet?'

'What?' the woman looked very surprised, yet not at all doubtful.

'Yes, I know,' Maurice sighed, 'the men in the white coats will be here at any moment.'

'I can't see him but I *hear* him; can you?' the woman asked, her eyes bulging with surprise.

Maurice was completely flabbergasted by the woman's reply. 'So I'm not imagining the little blighter?' he asked.

'No, you're not,' the woman told him, and she sniffled, and searched her handbag for a tissue, but Maurice pulled his silk handkerchief from the top pocket of his blazer and offered it to the lady.

'They said I was going mad,' the woman sobbed into the handkerchief.

Two passing shoppers slowed down nearby but Maurice smiled and said, 'It's alright – she's okay.'

The woman looked up at Maurice, her eyes full of tears, and she asked: 'Please tell me you really can hear it.'

'Not only can I hear the music, I can *see* the little devil with his trumpet playing away – and that's why I was following you, and that's why I tried to take a photograph of him with my phone.'

'Oh thank God! I really did believe I was going insane,' said the woman, and another shopper, an elderly lady, appeared behind Maurice and said: 'Is everything alright Mrs Parr?'

Mrs Parr nodded and tried to smile, and told the concerned old lady: 'Yes, I'm alright thanks, Mrs Wilson.'

Mrs Wilson looked Maurice up and down, smiled at him and walked away, carrying her wire basket.

'Mrs Parr – is that your name?' Maurice asked, and when the persecuted woman nodded, he continued: 'Well, I had the same problem as you when I was a boy of seven, and I heard the very same piece of music.'

'Really? I wonder what it is?' Mrs Parr asked, and she looked at her right shoulder. She could see nothing, but that was the side she always heard the damned buzzing and sometimes screaming trumpeter all hours of the day and night. She'd heard him for over six months now playing that never-ending tune. 'The doctor said it was tinnitus, and he put me on antidepressants, and when they didn't work they thought I was imagining it. They gave me more pills, but none of them worked, so I tried vodka and got so drunk I used to join in and accompany the trumpeter.

What's he doing now? The little man.'

Maurice told her. 'He's just standing there, head back, blowing that trumpet up to your ear. He's a black man, and he's that clear I can see his cheeks puffing as he blows, and he looks quite medieval – his clothes are like something from the Middle Ages.'

'Try and knock him off my shoulder,' Mrs Parr suggested, and gave a faint smile.

'What?' Maurice asked with some reluctance in his face and body posture. He stepped back.

'*I'll* try then,' said Mrs Parr and she looked as if she was brushing dandruff off her shoulder.

'Your hand went right through him – amazing,' said Maurice, narrowing his eyes.

'Damn. I wish I could get him in my fist and crush his little guts out,' Mrs Parr fumed through gritted teeth. 'I'd wrap that trumpet round his little neck!'

'That tune he's playing was written by Henry VIII – it drove me spare too,' said Maurice. 'I'll play a recording of the song to you and it might stop – it did for me.'

'Henry VIII eh?' Mrs Parr said, and then she grinned with a far-away look in her tear-reddened eyes as if she was gloating on some distant private joke. 'My name's Catherine – Catherine Parr; wasn't she a wife of his?'

'A wife of who?' Maurice asked, still watching the glowing tormentor on her shoulder.

'Henry,' Catherine told him.

'Oh yes, I see what you mean – weird coincidence that,' he replied.

Maurice entered the Safari browser on his iPhone and went to YouTube, where he keyed in the song title *Pastime with Good Company* into the search box. A recording of this song came up immediately, and there, in the middle of the supermarket aisle, Maurice played the video of the recording.

'Yes – that's it!' Catherine Parr told him, and for a minute and a half she listened to the melody which had blighted her life for six months – a torment she would not wish on her worst enemy.

And when the recording ended, the little trumpeter vanished in an instant, and the tune he had played without a break for half a year came to an abrupt end. The absence of the tune seemed like a concrete presence to Catherine, and she started to breathe heavily and seemed on the verge of bursting into tears. 'I've got to get outside! I've got to go out!' she said, and sounded as if she was hyperventilating. Maurice took her outside and in the car park he embraced her and said, 'It's okay Catherine, its okay – it's gone now and it will never come back. Calm down.'

That night, Catherine awoke with a start in bed, for she had a dream that the trumpeter was back, but when she awoke she heard nothing but her own gasps. It was just a nightmare.

Maurice ended up dating Catherine, and she subsequently moved into his house on Menlove Avenue. The couple, brought together in such a strange way, are still together, and each has no idea why they were persecuted by the Tudor "earworm" at different times in their lives. I did a modicum of research into this intriguing case and discovered that the first wife of Henry VIII – Catherine of Aragon – brought a cultured African attendant named John Blanke to England in 1501. Blanke was a gifted trumpet player and a very mysterious individual who was rumoured to dabble in some sort of sorcery. Henry VIII liked him so much, he even gave John Blanke a wage rise because of his musical ability – and Henry was a renowned penny-pincher. Almost no mention is made of the black trumpeter in the history books but there are depictions of Blanke on the Westminster Tournament Roll – a 60-foot-long sheet of vellum which depicts a joust called by Henry VIII in 1511 to celebrate the birth of his new son – who would sadly later die aged only 52 days.

I do find it curious that Catherine shares the same name as Henry VIII's last wife, and suspect there *is* some arcane connection there, but why would a 7-year-old boy named George Walker also be haunted by the diminutive ghost of a Tudor trumpeter? We will probably never know the answer to this baffling case.

LADY SORROW

The following strange story took place in the early hours of Friday, 24 June 1994 – Midsummer Day. An attractive 18-year-old named Samantha Aitken of Lancaster Avenue, Sefton Park, was minding the house while her parents spent their wedding anniversary in Torquay, where they had first met twenty years ago. Samantha had invited David - an 18-year-old Wavertree lad who attended her college – to spend the night with her as she was a bit nervous staying at the place on her own because Toxteth Park cemetery lay close to the house. Samantha's amateur boxer boyfriend Gus didn't know about this arrangement, and he was working as a security guard that night – or so Samantha thought. Someone evidently told Gus about his cheating girlfriend and he called at her house at twenty-past four that morning and hammered on the door. Samantha told a panic-stricken David to hide under the bed in her parents' room and she hid the lad's clothes and underwear in her wardrobe. She answered the door and told Gus she was ill and on her period and wanted to be alone, but he just let out a loud grunt, pushed past her and went in search of his rival – with a baseball bat. Samantha ran up the stairs and tried to drag Gus back, but the amateur pugilist let out a string of profanities and growled: 'Who is he? I'll do him in! He's good as dead already!'

And then, entering the bedroom where Samantha and David had made love, Gus spotted a packet of condoms, and he went berserk. 'I'll smash the bastard's skull in! I'll beat him to pulp! Where's he hiding?'

David heard the threats from Samantha's enraged boyfriend, and he was so scared, he climbed out the window of the Aitkens master bedroom in his birthday suit and descended to the backyard wall via a drainpipe. He walked along the wall and dropped into an alleyway leading to the old turnstile gates of Toxteth Park Cemetery. His home on Alderson Road, Wavertree, was on the other side of the cemetery, and being Midsummer morning, it was already getting light, so he wasn't nervous of anything supernatural being about; he was more afraid of the living – and Gus in particular. He ran off down the path listening to the distant voices of Samantha and her crazed boyfriend arguing. As David padded along the tarmac path in his bare feet, the sounds of the uproar became fainter and he realised he'd have to be on his guard now in case Gus came calling round – if Samantha told on him. David only had to cover around six-hundred yards and he'd be out the cemetery and home and dry. Then he'd have to throw a stone up at his brother's bedroom window to wake him. David wondered who had tipped Gus off as he made his way through the cemetery.

And then, out the left corner of his eye, David saw something moving – and he turned to see a pale figure about 200 feet away. It was a woman, and by the looks of her she wasn't that old – possibly in her late teens or early twenties, and like him she was unclothed. She seemed to be looking in his direction. Her skin looked as white as chalk and a slight breeze was stirring her long hair. She lifted her left arm and waved, and straight away he just had the unsettling feeling that she was a ghost. He looked away and ran north, in the direction of the cemetery's Smithdown Road gates – the direction of his home – but she ran at an incredible speed, weaving between obelisks, tombs and gravestones – and by taking this diagonal path towards the north-east, she cut off his escape route. He turned around, and ran off with goosepimples covering his body, heading back towards the turnstile, and he heard a female voice shouting: 'Please don't leave me!' She sounded as if she was well-to-do, and there was no accent in her voice. David wanted to believe she was just a student who was stoned – anything but a ghost – and yet his intuition told him she was something paranormal.

She ran in a curve and he ended up running towards her, so once again he turned around and headed north, and by now, terror had gripped the teenager. He swore at his chilling pursuer and he heard her shout something but he couldn't make out what it was.

She chased him as far as the lodge, and he ran out of the place of the dead and just missed being hit by a car. The female driver pulled over and shouted out the window of the vehicle: 'Arsehole!'

David looked back towards Toxteth Park Cemetery and saw the naked female ghost holding her hands to her face, as if she was crying. He felt sad at leaving her somehow; his fear had been replaced by sympathy, but he had to get off the streets being naked. He gathered a few small stones and hurled them at his brother's bedroom window. He shouted his name and waited and threw more stones, but his brother was fast asleep. David went to the front door of his house and shouted his brother, but his father came down the stairs and opened the door. When he saw his naked son standing there he was naturally shocked.

'What the bloody hell are you playing at?' he asked, and stood aside.

David told the truth, and his father called him an idiot and a coward. 'That Samantha will think you're a right yellow belly!' said David's father. 'You should have given that Gus a hiding! Streaking through a cemetery to get away from that bully? You don't take after me lad.'

David telephoned Samantha on the following day and she told him that she'd dumped Gus, and what's more, she had pushed him down the stairs of the house during his rampage and he had sprained his wrist. She also told David that he had been amazing in bed, and that she wanted to go steady with him.

David was naturally nervous when he visited Samantha the next day, and when he came into the house she said a strange thing. 'When you went home, Gus went looking for you, and he said there was a girl with no clothes on walking around the graveyard. He asked her if she'd seen you, and she didn't answer. Isn't that weird? Did you see her?'

David had told no one about the naked ghostly girl, and he could hardly get his words out. And then he told Samantha how the girl had chased him through the cemetery, and Samantha seemed to be terrified. She said that the girl had just been a real person who had been drunk or on drugs, but David said he'd had the strong feeling that she had been a ghost by the way she had moved as she ran like the wind through the cemetery. 'Okay, let's drop the subject David, you're freaking me out,' Samantha said.

A few weeks after this, Samantha looked out her bedroom window one evening, just as it was getting dark, and there, in the middle of the road in Lancaster Avenue was a naked girl with long dark hair. Her skin was abnormally pale, and she was looking up at Samantha's window. Samantha went downstairs to her mother and told her about the weird nude girl. Mother and daughter looked through the nets of the downstairs bay window and saw the naked girl walk silently away – in the direction of the alley that leads to the cemetery's turnstiles.

The apparition of the naked girl is known by some of the locals as Lady Sorrow, and she has been seen since the mid-1960s, but no one has identified her. A female medium who tried to investigate the haunting in 1971 said the ghost was that of a young woman who had died from a heart condition weeks before she was due to marry. The girl later started to haunt the man she would have married when he started seeing someone else who lived on Sydenham Avenue – which lies close to the cemetery where the tragic young woman had been buried. Scores of people living in the vicinity of Toxteth Park Cemetery have seen the ghost wandering the cemetery, and just as many have heard her sobbing in the lonely watches of the night. Is she crying for the man who would have been her husband, now with someone else (if he is still alive)? We may never know.

THE WARDROBE MAN

There's a tree-lined street in the affluent Cressington area of Liverpool where two neighbouring houses share an intriguing secret, and this secret was discovered in a most unexpected way in the summer of 1977.

One muggy afternoon around 4.50pm in late August 1977, Sydney Hartford, a chartered surveyor in his forties, popped into a pub on Bryanston Road, Aigburth for a swift half of icy lager on his way home, and in doing so he bumped into an old friend he hadn't seen for ten years – Brett Crowther, a sales executive for Rolls Royce.

'Well, well well, it's Mr Crowther!' Sydney patted his friend - who was perched on a stool in the bar - on the back, giving him quite a start.

'Sydney!' Brett recognised the voice, even after all these years. He turned on the stool and pointed to his friend's gunslinger moustache with a beaming smile. 'What's all this?'

'Oh, I'm going for the mature and sophisticated man-of-the-world look,' said Sydney, sounding as if he was somehow apologising for the moustache.

'Well, it's not working,' joked Brett. 'What are you having?'

'Just half a lager,' said Sydney, and his smiling eyes scanned Brett's centre-parted long hair. 'I thought you were a girl from the back, mate. Starve the barber.'

'I'm on shandy by the way,' Brett told him, attracting the barmaid's attention with a wave. 'Driving you see.'

'That roller outside isn't yours is it?' Sydney asked, all tongue in cheek. He couldn't help but notice the Rolls Royce Silver Shadow convertible parked outside the pub on the way in.

'Yeah, it is, actually,' Brett told him, his raised eyebrows vanishing into his centre-parted fringe.

'Pull the other one!' Sydney pulled a stool nearer and sat on it.

Brett leaned in close to his face. 'No, honestly, I work for Rolls Royce now – I'm a senior sales exec.'

'Seriously?'

'Seriously,' Brett nodded. 'I got the Rolls at a knockdown price – nine grand - because of my great record of sales. That's why I'm on the shandy; don't want to crash that baby.'

'Well wonders never cease,' said Sydney, and he took the half of lager from the barmaid and clinked it against Brett's glass of shandy. 'Cheers, moneybags. Hey, but what's a playboy of the Western world doing supping in here? Surely you should be drinking at the Devonshire Club down in London – '

'It's closed old boy,' Brett poked in.

'Or the Cercle de Lorraine over in er, whatchamacallit – '

'Belgium; no thanks,' said Brett, 'they don't have girls like Georgina in here.'

The barmaid smiled at Brett's mention of her friend's name.

'Georgina?' Sydney was curious.

'A beautiful barmaid who works in here,' Brett explained, 'but unfortunately I've come on the wrong day; she's off today.'

'Haven't you settled down yet?' sighed Sydney, gently shaking his head, and his friend looked at the barmaid – who was now heading for a beckoning customer at the other end of the bar. Brett pulled at Sydney's elbow and in a gruff whispering voice he said: 'I'm married, but they don't know – Georgina and her friend there, Jenny.'

Sydney loved his wife and had a strong dislike of married and engaged people who cheated, so this admission from Brett pained him a little. 'How long have you been, you know?' Sydney asked Brett, then whispered the word: 'Married.'

'Three years,' Brett told him (out the side of his mouth), and then he got up from the stool and nodded to a corner of the pub. Sydney picked up his drink and followed him. Once the two old friends were seated, Brett told him something odd in the way of an explanation for his infidelity.

'There's an old saying isn't there: what's good for the goose is good for the gander?' was Brett's cryptic remark, and from inside his jacket he took out an impressive silver cheroot case that was rather ostentatiously engraved with arabesque swirls and featured the coat-of-arms of the Crowther family. Its interior was gold-plated and it was loaded with little Burmese cigars. It was thrust at Sydney, and he noticed the uncharacteristic bitter look on his friend's face.

'Thanks,' Sydney took a cheroot. 'And what *is* good for the goose, Brett? What are you trying to say?'

'She's been seeing someone behind my back – Prue that is. She's a vicar's daughter, and she looks and acts as if butter wouldn't melt in her mouth, but I noticed this smell in the bedroom one night – a sort of old-fashioned cologne – a man's cologne – my Uncle Billy used to wear it when I was a kid. Anyway, I asked her if anybody had been in the bedroom and she said no one had been in there.'

'Scents can travel quite a distance you know?' Sydney speculated. 'Especially in the summer, I mean, was the window open?'

'This wasn't drifting in on a breeze mate,' Brett told him with a dismissive shake of his head, 'this was hanging in the air and it was strong. Anyway, that to me sounded the first alarm bell, right?'

Sydney coughed after inhaling the potent sweet aroma of the cheroot and nodded.

'Now, have you ever seen that fellah who plays the butler in the Robinson Barley Water adverts on the telly?' Brett asked. It seemed a bizarre question given the serious context of the conversation. 'He's round-faced, smarmy-looking and has his hair slicked back real neat.'

'Yes, I think I remember him; the butler in the hammer-tail coat who serves the cordial on the tray when they play tennis?' said Sydney, trying to picture the actor. 'Anyway, what's he got to do with this?'

'Just hear me out,' Brett's voice faltered a little, and he exhaled smoke from his nostrils. 'I woke up one morning last month, just before dawn, and the sun wasn't up yet, but there was some light coming into the bedroom - shining into the room from a lamp post outside. Anyway, as I was lying there in bed, I thought I heard a squeak, and then there was a sound – it came from the wardrobe. I thought the cat had got into the room at first but then remembered Prue had let him out the night before. I thought I was seeing things. The door of the wardrobe opened a few inches, and then it opened a little more, and this obviously gave me a start. I sat up in the bed, trying to take it in, and a man's head popped out – from the wardrobe – and he looked out at me.'

'What? Out the wardrobe?' Sydney asked, thinning his eyes with scepticism.

Brett nodded, and replied: 'Yes, I swear on my mother's life Sydney. I saw his face pretty clearly because the light from the lamp post in the street shone on him, and he looked exactly like that fellah who plays the butler in the Robinson's barley water advert.'

'What did you do?' Sydney asked, and he was halfway between intrigue and disbelief.

'Before I could move, his head went back into the wardrobe real fast, and then I heard a click. I got up, turned the main light on, and looked for something to hit him with because I was certain it was a burglar. I play golf and I used to keep a long iron in the corner to use as a weapon in case we were ever broken into but Prue must have tidied up and put the thing away because I couldn't find it. I woke Prue up, then told her to call the police, and then I banged my fist on the wardrobe. There was no noise inside of it. I was so annoyed by anyone trespassing into my house I yanked the door of the wardrobe open – and there was no one there, just all of our shirts and jackets and stuff.'

'Are you sure it wasn't a dream?' Sydney asked, worried a little about his friend's mental wellbeing.

'No, I am one-hundred per cent sure it was not a dream, Sydney. Prue said I'd dreamed it as well, and I could tell she was scared because I'd found her out,' said Brett. 'Now listen to the next part. I checked the wardrobe – and the back's hollow; it's as if there's a secret passage in the back of the wardrobe which leads to the bedroom in the house next door. I know it sounds nuts. It's a fitted wardrobe and it was there when we bought the house. I never liked it; it's dead old.'

'And who lives next door?' Sydney asked. Brett said a widowed man of fifty and two young daughters in their twenties lived there.

'And does the man next door look like the butler in the Robinson's Barley Water advert?' Sydney asked. It was an obvious question to pose.

'No,' replied Brett, 'the man next door's bald as a coot.'

'And he has no relatives or friends visiting who look like the man you saw peeping out of the wardrobe?' asked Sydney.

Brett shrugged. 'I haven't seen anyone like him visiting next door, no.'

'It's a strange one,' said Sydney, and then he sat there as silent as the Sphinx. He suddenly looked as if he felt awkward being there.

'You don't believe me, do you?' Brett asked his old mate, and his voice sounded broken.

'I believe that you *think* you saw a man peeping out your wardrobe in the wee small hours but I'm trying to work out why anyone would go to the trouble of installing a door in the back of a wardrobe. It's like something out of that kid's story – *The Lion, the Witch and the Wardrobe*. No offence Brett, but it *does* seem like something that'd happen in a dream.'

'No, this is reality, Sydney,' said Brett, 'Someone went to the trouble of putting a door in the back of the wardrobe because they want to have an affair with Prue without anyone seeing them enter or leave the house.'

'There must be easier ways of having an affair,' reasoned Sydney, and he saw the look of anger swelling in his friend's face. 'I'm not being facetious about this Brett, but – I mean – come on!'

'Okay Sydney, here's the deal mate. Come back to my place now. Prue is visiting her aunt till seven. I want you to come and have a look at the back of the wardrobe. If I'm wrong I'll give you a hundred quid!'

'It's ridiculous Brett – '

'Please, you're an old friend – just have a look – and if you think there's nothing in it and I'm imagining things I'll never mention it again – scout's honour.'

The two men left the pub and Brett glided the Rolls Royce to his palatial semi in Cressington, where Sydney realised the friend he hadn't seen for a decade lived less than half a mile from him. They went upstairs to the master bedroom and there was the large fitted wardrobe. Brett opened it and parted the clothes hanging up in the deep interior. 'Have a look for yourself,' he said, and tapped gently on the backing of the armoire. Sydney gingerly entered the wardrobe and tapped the backing, and then he came out and asked his friend if he had a torch.

'Ha! So you're intrigued now eh?' Brett remarked, and he went downstairs to a drawer in the kitchen and returned with a long chromium torch. Sydney examined the back of the wardrobe for a minute or so, and then he came out and gave a wry smile. 'It *is* hollow. Have you got a toolbox?'

Brett brought up his toolbox from the garage and placed it at Sydney's feet.

'So, Sydney, you agree there *is* something very odd about the back of that wardrobe eh?' Brett's eyes were full of childish glee now.

'Well, being a chartered surveyor,' said Sydney, 'I know a little about the layout and structure of these houses, and if there *is* a door at the back of the wardrobe, someone has gone to an awful lot of trouble to chisel through a party wall; that's eleven or twelve inches of bricks and mortar. Whoever did it has broken the law.'

'Have they now?' Brett asked with a lopsided smile. He took out the silver case and offered Sydney another cheroot.

'Ta,' said Sydney. 'Yes, mate it's a serious crime. It contravenes the Law of Property Act 1925. You don't have to report him – you can just tell your neighbour and you and he can get the brickies in – unless your neighbour's the culprit of course.'

'Oh no, I'd have to obey the letter of the law and get him nicked,' said Brett, lighting Sydney's cheroot. 'Hey, Syd, are you in a hurry to get home? I've got an old bottle of malt whiskey that I've been keeping for a nice day like this.'

Brett looked at his watch. 'Just a finger; she gets home around half-five.'

Three whiskies later, a tipsy Sydney wrenched the panel of chipboard from the back of the wardrobe and there was a black varnished door – with a brass keyhole.

'So, this is how that bastard got into the bedroom,'

said Brett in a slurred voice, and the torch swayed side to side as he tried to train its beam on the mysterious door.

'No one's been through this in recent times Brett,' Sydney told him, wiping away dust and abandoned spider webs from the door.

'How are we going to open that lock, Sydney?' Brett peered into the keyhole but saw nothing.

'It's a basic mortice lock. Has your wife got any hair clips knocking about?' said Sydney, gently pushing Brett's head out the way. He stooped to look at the keyhole of the mortice lock by the torchlight.

Brett went to Prue's dresser and went through the drawers.

'It'll have five pins,' Sydney's voice emanated from the wardrobe. 'I need two hair clips.'

There was a heavy ran-tan-tan at the door downstairs.

'Who's that? Prue's got the key,' Brett walked to the window and pulled back the curtain a few inches. He could see that the caller had on a cap. 'It's the window cleaner,' Brett hissed. 'What's he calling early for? Piss off.'

He knocked again downstairs, then walked away after fifteen long seconds had elapsed.

Sydney came out the wardrobe. 'You got the hairclips yet?' he asked.

'I've looked in the drawers,' muttered Brett, opening the top drawer of the dresser to begin another search. 'Where the hell are they? I have seen her using them.'

'Try that pink tin on top of the dresser,' Sydney suggested.

Brett prised the said tin open. 'Yes! Nice one Syd.'

Sydney took two hair pins and recalling an old trick his grandfather had taught him, he used his teeth to remove the rubber blobs at the end of the clips and bent one into a P-shape. This was inserted into the keyhole to exert pressure on the five pins of the lock, and the other clip (which he bent into an L-shape) was used to manipulate the pins. Because Sydney was slightly under the influence, and because he was working by the light of a torch held by a swaying Brett, it took him a little longer than normal to pick the lock, but pick it he did, but the door wouldn't open, no matter how hard he pushed.

'Try pulling it instead,' Brett suggested.

'It's hard to – there's no handle to pull on,' complained Sydney, but he managed to pull at the protruding cylindrical part of the lock surrounding the keyhole – and the door opened a few inches. There was only darkness visible beyond it.

'Let's have a look,' said Brett, and he pulled the door open – and the headstock of an acoustic guitar fell towards him and hit him in his left eyebrow. Brett's eyes slowly adapted to the dark, and he realised he was in the back of someone's wardrobe. It smelt of sweet female scents and there were soft silky dresses, blouses and tee shirts suspended from coat hangers of wire and plastic.

'What can you see?' Sydney asked, and he shone the torch through the gap in the partially opened door – and he saw a single bed, and the face of Marc Bolan on a poster above the headboard of the bed.

'We're in next door's bedroom,' gasped Brett, and he chortled. 'Must be the room of one of his daughters.'

'Come on Brett, let's close the door and seal it up,'

urged Sydney. The realisation that he and Brett were now trespassers – intruders into the room of a young woman – seemed to sober him up.

'No, hang on, let's just make sure it *is* next door, ' said Brett, opening the door wider. 'It might be an extra room in my house.'

'You know very well it's the bedroom of one of those girls next door!' snapped Sydney. 'I'm going!' he threatened, but Brett took no notice and he stumbled over the shoes in the wardrobe and fell forward, landing on the bed.

'Sydney, come and have a look! Don't be a big Jessie,' said Brett, and he seemed to think the whole thing was a joke.

From the doorway at the back of the young woman's wardrobe came the huffish voice of his nervous friend. 'Get back in here! Do you realise what's at stake? Your job, your marriage – '

'Frig the marriage,' murmured Brett, and he came back into the wardrobe holding a black bra to his chest with an inane grin on his face.

'That's it! I'm going! Bye!' Sydney turned and headed for the door of Brett's bedroom.

'Alright you party pooper! Hang on!' Brett turned and lurched across the shoes at the bottom of the girl's wardrobe and threw the bra onto the bed. He then returned to his own wardrobe, and he and Sydney closed the door that connected the two houses. They carefully replaced the board at the back of Brett's wardrobe and Sydney made his friend promise that he'd never open that door again.

'Cross my heart and hope you die!' Brett joked, and then seeing that Sydney didn't find the quip at all funny, he exhaled a groan and added: 'But seriously, I promise you I'll never open that door again.'

That should have been the end of the matter.

Three days later, Brett was sitting up in bed, tapping his bottom lip with a Parker pen as he tackled a puzzle in a *Times* crossword book, and next to him, Prue was laying on her right side, facing away from him, when she suddenly let out a sigh and sat up.

'Brett, I think I saw that man you saw,' she said with a very solemn look.

'What?' Brett took off his reading glasses and turned to face her.

'You know – that man you saw in the wardrobe? Remember?'

'Of course I remember – it's not something you're likely to forget is it? You saw him?'

She nodded and adjusted a shoulder strap on her ruffle trim nightie. 'I wasn't going to tell you at first in case you thought I was imagining it, but I saw him this morning around seven or maybe around ten to.'

'You should have woken me, love.' said Brett, laying down the book and pen. 'What did he do?'

'I woke up because I heard a noise, and then I looked up, trying to see the alarm clock because I'd left it on the dresser, and I saw the wardrobe door open a bit, and then it opened some more, and then I saw this man look out. His head just popped out. Really gave me a start.'

'Did he have a sort of fattish face and an old-fashioned sort of short back and sides haircut?' Brett asked.

'Yes, that's exactly how he looked, and there was this old pongy type of smell, like an old man's aftershave –

or maybe Brylcreem. Anyway he just smiled – he knew I was looking at him over the edge of the blankets, and then his head went back into the wardrobe and the door closed over. I lay there for ages, and I was going to tell you but I didn't want to ruin your sleep and I thought you'd shout and say I was dreaming.'

'No, you should have given me a nudge,' said Brett, and he thought about the door at the back of the wardrobe, and then he realised how he'd been silly enough to think some man was coming into his room to carry on with his wife – or had he known deep down that it was a stupid notion that he'd merely used to justify his own infidelity?

'Why is he haunting here?' Prue wondered. 'Why a wardrobe?'

'Maybe we should get the place blessed,' mooted Brett, and then, seeing fear in the eyes of his wife at the extreme suggestion, he backpedalled: 'Although I don't think he's a bad ghost – more of a nuisance.'

A few days after this, Brett came down with a terrible bout of flu, and he was forced to take a few days off. Eventually the condition improved after two days and left him with a sore throat, and in the afternoon while Prue was at work, he suddenly had the urge to go through that door in the back of the wardrobe. A strange lustful mood came over him, and he swished the clothes apart hanging on the wardrobe rail and reached out to prise the chipboard backing away. He halted for a moment and asked himself what the hell he thought he was doing, and he recalled Sydney's warning about him losing his job if he was caught snooping about in the bedroom of the young lady next door. He couldn't control himself – he had never had a sexual urge like this – not since he was about eighteen. He removed the backing and took it out of the wardrobe and rested it against the wall. He looked at the mortice lock. How had Sydney picked it? He couldn't do what he did with the hairclips – but there had to be another way. He'd seen a film once where someone had destroyed the lock with an electric drill, so he went down to the garage and located his drill and put a masonry bit into it. Again, he tried a bit of introspection. He told himself he was not some pervert who was a notch up from a Peeping Tom; that he should put the panel back over that tempting black door and think about his wife rather than a girl who was half his age. 'Grow up, Brett,' he whispered to his libido.

But he couldn't help himself, and he rushed back into the house with the drill and went to his bedroom.

That door in the back of the wardrobe was slightly open – which was impossible – it had been closed minutes ago. Brett gently opened the door a little more, and peeped in, and he heard a girl's voice. She was singing. He ventured much more carefully into the girl's wardrobe than on the last occasion, because now he was sober as a judge. He felt sweat trickle from his forehead as he placed his hands on the door of the wardrobe, and he pushed as lightly as he could. At first the door wouldn't budge, but then it clicked, and his heart felt as if it had bounced like a medicine ball in his chest. He could hear the girl singing quite loudly now. She was singing Donna Summer's *I Feel Love* - a hit of that time – and the singer had a decent voice. Brett actually found himself shaking as he peeped out of the wardrobe, and he felt as if he could sense the primary sex hormone testosterone gushing through his brain, and it frightened him a little. His mind was a torrent of sexual impulses mingled with fear, and yet he felt as if he was a virgin teenager again.

When Brett peeped out of the wardrobe he felt his face burn as the strange fever took a hold. There was one of the daughters of the man next door, laying on her back on the bed in only her knickers and a bra, and she had on a huge pair of headphones connected to a hi-fi system, and she was singing with her eyes closed and waving her arms about. A seductive sweet perfume hung in the air, and Brett found himself on a knife edge of indecision – one half of him was saying 'Get the hell out of there!' and a strange animalistic urge he had never experienced before was saying: 'You're a man - and she wants you!'

'Get stuck in.'

The low, well-spoken voice came from behind Brett, and he turned, and there, silhouetted against the pale rectangle of daylight – the doorway at the back of the wardrobe – was the figure of that man. Brett swore at him and somehow got past him as he ran back into his bedroom. He ran to his bedroom door and looked back, and the man came out – and now he could see without a doubt that it was the very same man who had peeped out of the wardrobe at him that morning. His skin looked pale, and his eyes seemed bloodshot. He wore a suit and a maroon tie with dark green stripes. He angled his head sideways, motioning towards the wardrobe, and with a smile he said: 'She'll love it – go on.'

'You're dead you bastard! Beat it!' Brett cried, and he ran down the stairs. He waited in the hallway and stood there, looking up the stairs, and he saw the black shiny shoes and black lower trousers of the ghost pad silently to the top step. Brett felt butterflies in his stomach and the sexual fever had cooled to a shiver. The feet walked back the way they had come. Enough was enough. Brett went next door and knocked on the door of his neighbour. A bald man answered and seemed surprised to see Brett, who had hardly acknowledged him in the couple of years he'd lived next door.

'I'm sorry to bother you,' said Brett, struggling how to phrase his lie, 'but I was clearing out the wardrobe in my room and I noticed this panel at the back of it. I er, pulled this panel off and there was this door – an unlocked door, and I opened it, and it appears that the door leads into the back of a wardrobe in one of your rooms.'

'Yeah, that's right,' said the neighbour, 'I've been meaning to get it bricked up for years. It leads into Melanie's wardrobe; Melanie's my daughter. You'd better come in.'

Brett went into the house and the neighbour said: 'My name's Frank by the way.'

'I'm Brett.'

'What it is, is this – er, it's a barmy one this,' said Frank, gently keeping his cat at bay with his right slip-on as it tried to run to Brett. 'The man who lived here years ago made a bloody doorway at the back of the wardrobe upstairs. It's a fitted wardrobe - solid oak and Edwardian, and a friend of mine in the antiques business valued it at around two grand. Anyway, the fellah who lived here – he's dead now – a Mr Stroud – he was a randy sod I believe, and he made the doorway in the back of the wardrobe and it went into the wardrobe next door, and at the time a woman in her thirties lived there named Mrs Stanbury, and she was married, but her fellah was always away in the Merchant Navy like, and this Stroud chappie was carrying on with her. He also got Mrs Stanbury's daughter up the spout and she was only sixteen. I think he was even carrying on with someone else on this road as well, and this fellah was married like.'

'And his wife didn't know?' asked Brett.

'Oh yes - she encouraged him, I believe – she was as eccentric as him, like.' Frank walked to the stairs. 'So, when you opened the door could you see into Melanie's wardrobe? Come up – I think she's in.'

'No, I'll wait here, you have a look – Frank.' Brett didn't want to go into the bedroom where Frank's daughter was laying half naked with those headphones on. He crouched down and stroked his neighbour's cat.

'Nah, come on Brett, she won't mind,' Frank insisted, and continued up the stairs.

Brett reluctantly went up to Melanie's bedroom with her father.

'Mel? You in, love?' Frank asked, and knocked. He and Brett stood there, listening.

Frank turned the handle and walked into the room and Melanie was sitting cross-legged on her bed – now dressed in denim shorts and a yellow smiley tee shirt as she read a magazine called *Music Star*.

'Mel, this is Brett, our neighbour, he was clearing his wardrobe out and found that door I told you about; you know the one at the back of your wardrobe?'

Melanie just nodded and looked Brett up and down.

Frank went into the wardrobe and said, 'Oh, I can see right into your bedroom, Brett. He made a neat job of that doorway didn't he?'

'Yeah,' said Brett, 'so er, what I'll do is get a bricklayer in, and get it filled in and then plastered. I'll pay for it.'

'Nah, I'll go half, mate,' said Frank.

'No, it's okay Frank. I'll let you know when I get it sorted anyway,' he said, and went to walk out the bedroom, but Frank smiled and said: 'You don't have to go that way, go this way,' Frank nodded to the back of Melanie's wardrobe.

Brett smiled and walked into the wardrobe and Melanie shouted: 'Oi! Watch my shoes and stuff will you?'

Brett closed the black inter-house door behind him in his wardrobe and put the chipboard panel back into place. He could not get Melanie's face and body out of his mind. He also had the uncanny feeling that the ghost of Mr Stroud was watching him, so he went downstairs and made himself a hot toddy with whiskey and honey to soothe his throat. On the following morning at four, Brett awoke, and immediately found himself longing for Melanie. He tried to picture Georgina the barmaid to drive the burning temptation of Melanie out of his mind but it wouldn't work. He got out of the bed wearing only his y-fronts, and he looked at Prue sleeping serenely in the strand of moonlight shining through the gap in the curtains. He carefully opened the wardrobe, stumbled over his wife's shoes, and set about removing that panel of chipboard with his head full of the strangest venereal thoughts and sadistic carnal urges. He had this inexplicable desire to have sex with Melanie and to make her suffer in the process, and he found himself gritting his teeth as he came out of the wardrobe with the backing board to rest it against the wall. He heard a click in the wardrobe and he knew it had been opened again. He was about to step back into the wardrobe when he heard his wife call him from the bed.

'Brett? What are you doing?'

He turned to face her.

'Who are you?' Prue asked in a trembling voice, and she reached out to the bedside lamp and switched it on. The face she saw on her husband's body was the very same one she had seen peeping out of the wardrobe on that morning. Prue screamed and crawled over the bed to get to the door. She ran in a hysterical state down the stairs.

'Prue! What's wrong?' Brett went after her. He halted on the landing because she screamed and asked: 'What's wrong with your face?'

Brett walked into the bathroom and looked in the mirror above the sink. He saw to his horror that he now had the face of that ghost from the wardrobe – the fat-faced man who reminded him of the actor who played the butler in the Robinsons Barley Water advert. 'Oh my God! No!' Brett backed away from the mirror. He looked once more at his reflection and his face had returned to normal. Later that day he visited the local church and tried to see a priest about this terrifying matter but a secretary said he was not available and asked Brett for a contact number. Brett gave his home number and the secretary asked him what he wanted to discuss with the priest. 'We have a ghost,' Brett told her, 'a really bad ghost, and it's making our lives hell.'

'Well, I'll pass it on to him and he should get in touch by tomorrow afternoon,' the secretary told him, but she was looking condescendingly at Brett as if he was mentally unbalanced. The priest never called. Brett tried the local vicar, and he told Brett he should go and see a doctor – and Brett swore at him and called the Church "Just a money-making business!"

Brett met up with Sydney, who believed his friend's account. 'Sounds like possession. Maybe we should try a spiritualist church; they take these things more serious than the normal churches.'

Sydney managed to get a member of a spiritualist church group to visit Brett's house. His name was Robin and he was younger than Sydney imagined him to be from the telephone conversation they'd had. Robin had a look at the doorway in the back of the wardrobe, then said to Brett and Sydney, 'Alright, first things first; this bedroom needs to be vacated.'

'What do you mean?' asked Brett.

'You and your wife need to sleep in another room for now, ideally for three days – more if possible,' said Robin, 'and I'll cleanse the place. And then you need to get that doorway to next door bricked up for good, and I'll leave a cross there and bless it.'

'Look, would it be better if we just left?' Brett asked. His sorrowful eyes were red and glistened. 'I've got the money – I could get another place like that,' he said, snapping his fingers. 'I've gone off this place now.'

'That's entirely up to you, Mr Crowther,' Robin told him, 'but of course, whoever moves in here will still have to deal with this.' Robin nodded at the wardrobe.

'That's their lookout,' said Brett, 'I've had enough,

and more importantly, my wife has had enough. She's on edge in bed all the time – we can't sleep because of *him*.'

'As I say, that's up to you, sir.' Robin looked to the floor, as if he was disappointed because his services might no longer be required.

'Yeah, I'm out of here – thanks anyway Robin,' said Brett, and he shook hands with the sincere young man, and then he and Sydney went to the front door with him.

On the last night at the house in Cressington, Brett and Prue went to bed, and they left their bedside lamps on. Prue smiled with her left hand entwined in Brett's right hand, and she said, 'This is lovely. We used to be like this when we first met.'

Brett looked at the ceiling and laughed. 'You'd think we'd been married for twenty-five years.' And then he turned to his wife and kissed her. 'I know what you mean though. Well, we'll be moving into the house in Aigburth soon.'

'Green Elms,' said Prue. That was the name she had chosen to call the new place.

They dozed off, and Brett awoke to his right shoulder being shaken.

'Turn on your side,' said an annoyed Prue, 'you're snoring the roof off!'

'Sorry love,' he said, and turned left. He quickly drifted off into the sanctuary of dreamless sleep.

Then came a scream which brought him sharply back to the conscious world. It was Prue screaming, and she was shaking him violently.

'What? What?' Brett sat upright, and standing there at the end of the bed was a female with long hair – a naked female – and she was holding a huge knife aloft, ready to strike! Brett's eyes were partially blurred by dried-our tear secretions, but by the lights of the bedside lamps he could see that the girl with the long-bladed knife was Melanie, and the door of the wardrobe was wide open. Brett threw his legs out his side of the double bed, and then he instinctively gripped the top of the thin duvet and threw it over Melanie as she made a violent thrust downwards with the knife. Brett threw himself at the struggling body in the duvet and knocked her against the wardrobe with a thud. He heard muffled screams.

'She dropped the knife!' yelled Prue, pointing to the twelve inch carving knife on the carpet.

'Get it then!' Brett cried out, and wrestled with the girl on the floor.

Prue picked up the knife and she lifted the mattress on her side of the bed and hid it under it.

Brett pulled the duvet off Melanie and he saw that the girl had the most disturbing grin on her face, and yet her eyes were white because they had rolled back, as if she had suffered a seizure. She was saying something nonsensical. 'Wah wah wah, wah wah wah!'

'Melanie, wake up! Wake up!' Brett gently shook her but she kept making the strange vocalisations, but then they stopped shortly afterwards and Brett and Prue heard the sound of the girl urinating with some force on the bedroom carpet.

Melanie opened her eyes, and when she saw Brett and Prue leaning over her, she asked, 'Where am I? What happened?' She got up and looked about. She pushed Prue away when she tried to guide her to the bed. She eventually calmed down and Brett took her back to her bedroom and went in search for the girl's father. When Frank heard what had happened, he seemed very frightened. 'She has never walked in her sleep before,' he told Brett and his wife, and Melanie burst into tears and sobbed, 'What's wrong with me?'

Brett and Prue were only too glad to get out of that house in Cressington. I hear that the fitted wardrobe was left intact but the passageway created by Mr Stroud was eventually bricked up. In 2011, the father of a family of three emailed me and asked if I had heard of a ghost haunting the very address where Brett and Prue once lived, because he and his family lived there now, and the man's teenage daughter Clodagh had reported seeing a man standing by the wardrobe in her room all hours in the morning. I emailed the man back and told him the strange history of the house, and I received no word of reply. In 2012 I noticed a For Sale sign at the house in Cressington. I'll bet Mr Stroud is still there, just waiting to play havoc with the next people who move into his old abode...

THE MANY WIVES
OF STEPHEN

One of the strangest cases I ever looked into concerned a 71-year-old Huytonian man named Stephen – a dead-ringer for Vincent Price with his debonair looks, pencil moustache, and a unique accentless diction, due to intensive elocution lessons he had received as a boy to treat a speech impediment. Stephen was also a confirmed bachelor who had reached the autumn of his life utterly contented to be single. Most of his friends were either widowed or divorced, and Stephen had a close friend named Calvin Shepard who had just celebrated the Ruby anniversary of his divorce. Calvin was due round this Saturday afternoon in 2002 for a game of chess and a few glasses of Muscadet, so imagine the face on Stephen when he answered the door to find a young woman he'd never seen before in his life. 'I forgot my key Stevie,' she said, and lunged forward to kiss him. Her shiny black hair hung straight as a laser and she wore some thigh-high black and white mini dress from the Mary Quant era.

'Who on earth are – ' Stephen gasped as she hurtled past him, through the hallway and into the kitchen with a carrier bag. He went after her and asked her who she was and she seemed to think he was joking. At last she said: 'Cathy, your wife, Stevie – you okay babe?' And Stephen shook his head.

'Look what I got ya!' she pulled a lollipop out the bag and unwrapped its yellow cellophane. Stephen started to believe he was suffering from dementia; it seemed as if he had forgotten that he was married – and yet he knew he was single – so where did this Cathy come from? He was confused, and for a while he wondered if he was dreaming. The flat TV screen on the lounge wall was gone, and he now had an old bulbous black and white cathode-ray tube sitting on a small table in the corner. The place had changed within the last minute; gone were the painted walls and vertical blinds – replaced by dated floral-patterned wallpaper and dark green nylon curtains. To himself, Stephen muttered: 'If this is a dream, then I'm aware that I'm dreaming, so it's a lucid dream, and that means I should wake up now that I have cottoned on that it's all a dream.'

'What was that, babe?' Cathy asked from the kitchen.

'Wake up, come on,' Stephen pinched his forearm, and it hurt, but he did not wake up, and so he panicked. He took long deep breaths and reasoned he'd fight the anxiety by going along with this unearthly situation. It all started coming back now – he *was* her husband. He walked to the mirror over the mantelpiece and saw that he was now young – in his late twenties from the look of it. His hairline was just three inches above his eyebrows and his skin was tight, firm and peachy in colour. 'What's happened to you?' he solemnly whispered to his reflection.

The couple went to bed early and he made love to Cathy, and she kept chewing gum in her mouth throughout the act. Afterwards, he slumped beside her and began to recall his *other* life in the Huyton of the

21st Century. Cathy snuggled up to him, kissed him on the lips and played with his hair, and then she said, 'Come on – again, again!'

'I don't think I have the energy, my dear,' Stephen told her.

'Oh come on, tiger, anyone would think you were old,' said Cathy, and she began to kiss his hairy chest. The hairs on that chest were usually crooked and white, but now they were straight and black.

'Old? I'm positively Palaeolithic,' Stephen assured her as he gazed abjectly at the ceiling.

'Thirty isn't old, babe,' Cathy told him, her lips close to his ear now. She climbed on him and issued her order: 'Come on, stand to attention!'

'This might just kill me,' Stephen said, with blithe unconcern. 'I suppose this could be termed "voluntary euthanasia"'

Three times he made love to Cathy and by 11pm the couple were sound asleep.

Stephen awoke to the diffused light of a miserable grey morning – and turned in the bed to catch a glimpse of another strange woman with a huge head of blonde hair lying next to him. She turned out to be another wife – 24-year-old Amanda.

Don't You (Forget About Me) by Simple Minds was oozing from the alarm clock radio. Stephen looked at the bedroom. The 1960s wallpaper, curtains and fittings were all gone, and in their place there were matching Laura Ashley Floral patterns in the wallpaper, duvet, pillows and carpet. The door and skirting boards were neon yellow. Stephen now knew he was going insane. He ran to the toilet in an effort to escape the mind-boggling incongruity of it tall, but

342

decided again to go along with this bizarre illusion; he felt as if someone – some higher intelligence - was playing a metaphysical prank on him. He told himself it was 2002, not the 1980s. He went down to breakfast and Amanda handed him a copy of the *Today* newspaper – a publication he had not seen for well over a decade. Stephen watched the colour television set in the corner and saw Frank Bough and Debbie Greenwood presenting Breakfast Time. He looked at the newspaper and saw that today's date was Wednesday, September 10, 1986. He read about the SDP party, British Coal, the mysterious disappearance of Suzy Lamplugh, Desmond Tutu, and the American Star Wars space defence research programme – all people and things that Stephen vaguely recalled from the 1980s. That day in 1986, Stephen also discovered that he owned a Vauxhall Nova and he was a very able driver – and yet in his 'real' life in 2002, he never owned a vehicle and had never learned to drive. He drove Amanda to a former warehouse in the city centre where she was the manager of a sex chatline company, and then he drove to a second-hand science fiction bookshop he ran on Rodney Street called Fahrenheit 451 – named after the famous Ray Bradbury dystopian novella. This bookshop was located at 16 Rodney Street – and being something of a gourmet in 2002, Stephen knew that the upmarket Puschka bistro should have existed at this address. He sat in an easy chair behind the counter, and reflected upon this strange life which could not be explained by logic. He wondered if he was in fact dead, and that these lives with different women were just the imaginings of a brain decaying as he lay in his coffin, buried under the six feet of soil in Allerton Cemetery – in the burial plot he had bought for himself twenty-five years ago. He pinched his forearms – and finding that it hurt, he decided that this present life *was* real after all, but simply couldn't be explained. He pondered on the possibility that some psychology teacher in a future age might be messing with his mind to demonstrate to his class how humans eventually accept any metaphysical stimulus if they are subjected to it for a long enough period. Or was this rampant paranoia? He philosophised till he felt nauseous. He sold six books that day, and then he drove to the sex chatline company off Victoria Street, picked up Amanda, and took her home. That evening she cooked Stephen a fine dinner and at 10pm the couple went to bed, where Amanda tried to get her husband to take a sleeping tablet. He refused and in the end she took one and was soon in the arms of Morpheus. Stephen lay awake beside her till two, ruminating on his uncanny, disoriented life. When he awoke the next morning he found himself in the arms of his 1950s wife Tina. She was looking into his eyes and he was startled by the unfamiliar face. He was about to ask her who she was but soon realised that the trickster from beyond was playing another prank on him. 'I think we should have three children, Stephen,' Tina told him, and pressed her index finger on his lips. She then told him she was looking forward to the street party – for the 1951 Festival of Britain. She also patted her abdomen and told Stephen she was pregnant and wanted to call the child Winston – but before Stephen had a chance to contemplate the gravity of being a parent, he was back with 20-year-old wife Cathy in the 1960s when he awoke the next morning. Then, a few days after this, all three wives appeared in the same house, which changed its decor to suit the time periods they were from, and Stephen became so dizzy on this extraordinary marital carousel, he ran into his back garden and hyperventilated as he hid behind the old beech tree. 'Please make it stop, make it stop! You're driving me insane! Stop it, please!' he said, eyes closed, and shook. He was terrified of the three wives meeting one another as they moved around the different rooms in the house, and although he knew he was a bachelor in the life he'd led before all of this, he felt like a three-timing cheat. There was a roll of thunder and a heavy downpour.

'Stephen!' came a *male* voice nearby.

'Calvin!' Stephen ventured out from behind the silver-grey trunk of the beech with a tincture of a smile on his lips.

'Stephen! Where on earth have you been?' Calvin came running towards him. 'The front door wasn't locked,' said Calvin Shepard, 'and I have told you repeatedly about the rogues knocking about nowadays.'

'Did you see anyone in there?' Stephen asked his friend, and his eyes turned towards the house.

'No, why?' Calvin asked.

'Calvin, how long have I been away? Something happened to me – something you will never believe.'

It transpired that Stephen had only been missing for a few hours. It was *still* that Saturday when he had answered the door to the first of the three wives. But how? Yet another mystery to confound the card-carrying lifelong bachelor.

He told Calvin what had happened, and Calvin, who had been his friend since they met in the same nursery 65 years ago, had never known Stephen to tell a lie – not even a little white one. Calvin knew something which could not be explained by the science of this world had taken place. Stephen kept thinking he might have hallucinated the wives for some unknown reason, and he visited his doctor. 'One of the common key symptoms of dementia is memory loss,' the doctor told Stephen, 'but your memory seems sharper than mine, and I'm only forty. The confusion you have reported *will* have to be investigated though, so I'll send you for a number of tests and assessments to see if you have some other condition.'

'Yes, please do, doctor.' Said Stephen enthusiastically, 'I'd like to get to the bottom of this strange experience too, believe me.'

Stephen was subjected to a battery of thorough tests and it soon became clear that he was not suffering from dementia, Alzheimer 's disease, nor any of the related brain disorders – and so, the blame was put on that good old scapegoat – stress. But Stephen said he had not been under any stress whatsoever. The specialists then started suggesting that he was some time-wasting attention-seeker. I talked to Stephen and told him about the concept of the "Multiverse" – the countless universes of which our one is just one of a countless series, and in each of these universes we differ slightly by degrees. This is not science fiction, but a concept rooted in quantum physics. In July 1952, Nobel Prize-winning physicist Erwin Schrödinger gave a lecture at the Royal Irish Academy in Dublin in which he made an intriguing comment that confused and amused some of the twenty people attending his seminar. Some believed Professor Schrödinger had suffered a nervous breakdown. The physicist said: 'Nearly every result the quantum theorist pronounces is about the probability of this or that happening with a great many alternatives." To illustrate this part of Schrödinger's statement, we could visualise a person flipping a coin to see if it comes up heads or tails, and the probability of getting a head or tail is of course 50% - we have a 50% chance of getting either – but Schrödinger then told the audience that in fact we get both results at once. 'The idea that they may not be alternatives but all really happen simultaneously seems lunatic [to the quantum theorist] - just impossible.'

Schrödinger then went on to claim that when we toss a coin we get a head and a tail at once, and that even the histories and outcomes of the way subatomic particles behave are the same – they all happen at the same time – and he explained – by way of baffling mind-stretching mathematical descriptions - that this was because of the multiple universes existing alongside one another. The audience fell silent. Schrödinger was one of the few people in existence who understood the complexities of quantum physics and it took a while before other minds caught up with his strange findings. This 'Many Worlds Interpretation' of reality means that in other universes, JFK survived an assassination attempt in 1963, whilst in another universe, *your* life has turned out quite different from the way it has progressed in this universe – and in that other universe you may be single, or you might have a partner quite different from the one you're with now – and in some of them you will be dead – or unborn.

This is not some fanciful 'what might have been' pipe dream, but a fact, according to quantum physics, which has now superseded classical physics. I think Stephen's three wives in different time periods might have been the result of his mind crossing over into different timelines in other universes – or perhaps, as Stephen felt, that someone or a something was drawing his mind to those three women. But why? Stephen found himself feeling very lonely once the 'phantom wives' had vanished, and he felt as if he had missed out on being a husband. Because of his loneliness he started to go out to socialise, and he ended up dating a neighbour named Fiona, and he married her in the following year – with Calvin as the best man. Did something beyond our dimension – some metaphysical Cupid - steer the certified bachelor into a relationship? That's the feeling I get, but of course, we may never know.

SOME WALK BY DAY

A very old myth persists that ghosts cannot walk by day, and yet a majority of the reports I receive about hauntings concern daytime visitants. Here are just a few accounts of these ghosts who walk in the daylight hours.

On a remarkably sunny Saturday afternoon in October 1977, West Derby housewife Sally Wilson took advantage of the out-of-season weather and sat in a deckchair in her well-kept back garden. She began to read a Harold Robbins novel and her thoughtful husband Sid brought out an old card table, spread with gingham, and plonked a cup of tea and a saucer of custard cream biscuits upon it. He then said he was going to the shop (the betting shop, that is) and Sally asked him to get her a pair of dark tights – and not the American tan ones like he did last time. The couple were going out tonight to celebrate their 25th wedding anniversary.

Later, while Sid was gone, four stocky men appeared at the garden fence, and looked over it at Sally, giving her quite a shock. 'Is Sid in?' asked the oldest of the four strangers, a debonair man in a tweed coat.

'Who wants to know?' Sally asked, full of suspicion. Sid suddenly came into the garden, and the four huge men almost destroyed the fence as they climbed over it. 'Oh no!' Sid cried, and tried to run inside but the four cumbersome brutes trampled flower beds and knocked over gnomes as they ran after Sid. They caught him, as Sally screamed, and they held him aloft, lengthwise, like pallbearers holding a coffin. Sid laughed and swore and demanded to be put down. To his wife, he then shouted: 'It's the gang I used to work with love! Dafyd, Mike, Bob and Tim!'

The gang of builders carried Sid out of the garden – to the pub, as Sally began to cry. 'What about our anniversary?' she yelled, as the heavyweights carried Sid off, singing like a Welsh choir as they went.

A palatic Sid returned at two in the morning from a marathon pub crawl, and Sally wouldn't let him in, so he slept in the garden shed. Sally eventually forgave him. In June 1978, Sally was sunbathing in the back garden when she heard her cat hiss. She looked up. 'Oh, not again!' she cried. Those four men who had abducted Sid for the pub crawl were gawping at her over the fence. 'Sid in?' one of them asked, and Sally got up and screamed: 'He's not well! Beat it!'

Sid was in bed, shivering with flu, but the four giants came through some gap in the fence, and despite Sally's loud protestations – they crossed the lawn, went into the house – and carried Sid (still in his pyjamas) out on their shoulders. This time, Sid shouted 'Sally! Help me! They're *dead!*'

Only then did she notice that the pallor of each man was very pale. They walked off and passed through the fence, and Sid was later found outside West Derby Cemetery, where one of the builders had been buried. Three had died in a car smash a month back in

Germany and one had suffered a fatal heart attack a week ago – marking the end of a life of chronic alcoholism. The four old friends had told Sid "You're coming with us, matey!' – meaning to the afterlife. Sid almost died that week from pneumonia, and kept seeing his old workmates around his hospital bed. Sally even swears that the gang came for him again one day in 1989 – the day Sid died. She heard heavy footfalls in the hospital ward where Sid was lying in bed, ready to breathe his last breath. He smiled, passed away, and then Sally heard the sound of men marching out of the ward.

In 2009, Sophie and Ellie – two students in their early twenties – moved into a ground floor flat at the Smithdown Road end of Claremont Road. The flat was unfurnished – there wasn't a stick of furniture in the place and the living room wasn't even carpeted. The girls went hunting for furniture in the various charity shops, and on this sunny morning, Sophie and her mother Sue went to the Oxfam shop on Smithdown Road to buy a few chairs and various nicknacks, and then they went to the Claremont Road flat – and got the shock of their lives. The front room was completely furnished with old fashioned chairs and a small chaise longue in front of the bay window, where lace net curtains and heavy velvet Tyrian purple drapes were hanging. There was also an upright piano situated against the wall the doorway was set in, and a cabinet full of porcelain ornaments to the left of the doorway. The floral-patterned art deco wallpaper looked as dated as the rest of the decor, and Sophie said to her mother: 'Have we come into the wrong house?' The mother and daughter checked the number on the front door and saw that they had most definitely not gone into someone else's flat – but who had furnished the living room in the forty minutes they had been away shopping?

The bedroom, kitchen and toilet were still bare – but the front room resembled a museum; the quaint furniture and decor gave the impression the place belonged to the 1920s. Ellie has misplaced her key to the Claremont Road flat, and when she called that morning just before noon, Sophie and her mother rushed to the front door, as both of them were eager to tell her about the weird goings-on. An Oxfam delivery man pulled up in his van outside and told Sophie he had come to unload the chairs and a table, but the student told him he'd have to put the furniture in the bedroom for now because someone had furnished the place. However, when Ellie went into the living room she found it completely empty. Sophie and her mother could not believe it, and it slowly dawned on them that the house had to be haunted. Days after this, when Sophie and Ellie had moved in most of their stuff and furnished the living room to their liking, they both heard a piano being played somewhere. It seemed to be coming from the living room itself, because when Sophie put her ear to the wall she established that the music was *not* coming from next door. As the flat above was unoccupied, the music was obviously not coming from there either. Sophie thought of the ghostly piano she and her mother had seen a few days ago when the room had become ethereally furnished for a while. The piano music would play for a few minutes then fade away, and Sophie and Ellie could not identify the piece that someone, somewhere was playing, but it sounded sombre and classical. Ellie was very nervous at all this supernatural activity, and suggested finding another place to live, but Sophie – who had a penchant for things paranormal – hugged her friend and assured her she'd be alright and that the activity would die down soon. A couple of days after this, Ellie was writing a text message to her mother as she sat on a sofa in the living room of the Claremont Road flat when she suddenly noticed an old man looking in at her through the bay window. She was incensed at the way he just stood there gazing at her, and she went to draw the curtains. The man knocked on the window after Ellie had closed the curtains and so she opened the top window and asked him what he wanted. He asked a strange question which chilled the student to the bone. 'Have you seen the ghost yet?'

'What are you talking about?' Ellie glared at him through the pane.

'A red-haired woman haunts this house – she has done for years. She's barmy as well,' the man told Ellie, and grinned.

Ellie closed the window and ignored him, and the man went away. She told Sophie about him, and on the following afternoon, when the man came to the window again, Sophie went out and asked him to come in for a cup of tea and some biscuits. The old man, who said his name was Bob, and that he lived on nearby Kenmare Road, seemed delighted at the offer and over tea and a Kit Kat, he explained that he was eighty-one and had lived in the Wavertree area all of his life. When Bob was 10 years old in 1938, his older sister Marie married a man named Brian and they moved into the house next door to the one Sophie and Ellie lived in. The newly-married couple began to hear a woman screaming next door, but when they called around to see what the matter was, they never received an answer and they were told by neighbours that the house was empty. No one would live in it because it was haunted by the noisy ghost of a woman who would scream and slam doors, and make a dreadful racket on the piano. No one seemed to know the identity of the ghost, but there were rumours that a woman had committed suicide at the house in Edwardian times. In the end, Marie and Brian left their house because of the noisy antics of the ghost. Bob's story really put the wind up Ellie and she warned Sophie that she'd leave if she heard or saw anything spooky again at the house.

A fortnight after this, the two students were in the kitchen at 4pm, preparing a meal as they listened to YouTube music videos on a laptop. During a pause between videos, the girls heard the piano playing clearly in the living room and looked at one another. Sophie went into the living room first, and as she did the music stopped dead. As soon as she walked back into the hallway with Ellie, the piano started to play again. The two students stood in the hallway, listened to the vaguely familiar melody.

'I know that tune,' said Ellie. She was now getting somewhat used to the resident ghost.

'Yes,' Sophie answered, looking at the floor of the hallway as she listened intently, 'ah yes, that's it - it's that old song from years ago: *Just Be Good To Me*'

'Yes!' Ellie nodded enthusiastically, and then she gave a puzzled look. 'That's a bit modern for our ghost though isn't it?'

'That's from the Eighties,' said Sophie, 'can't remember who did the song but it's definitely the Eighties.'

The music faded away. The girls went back into the kitchen and kept listening for the phantom pianist to play again, but they heard no more music. That night, Sophie and Ellie clung on to one another in bed, jumping at every sound they heard and listening to the eerie cacophony of two tomcats as they confronted one another in harmony in the alleyway, but the piano-playing ghost remained silent.

On the following Sunday in the afternoon, Sophie went to her house in Gateacre to fetch some more belongings, and Ellie decided to paint the hallway fuchsia. She poured the paint into the tray, ran the sponge roller back and forth through it, and was about to tackle the wall inside the vestibule area when she heard the sounds of hysterical female laughter coming from the bedroom. Ellie put the roller down in the tray and backed away down the hallway. She opened the front door and went outside. She could still hear the screeching laughter, and she conjured up enough bravery to peep through the bedroom window. In the bedroom, just to the right of the double bed, a red-haired woman with a very pale face and two black spots for eyes, was swinging a boy of about three years of age around by his ankles. The woman was screaming with laughter as she swung the boy around and around, and then suddenly she let go of the child and he flew head-first into the wall, and Ellie cried out because it looked as if the boy's neck had been broken as his head struck the wall. Ellie found herself walking down the street in a daze towards Smithdown Road. She stood there on the corner of Claremont Road for some time in the denim bib and brace she'd donned to do the painting of the hall. She heard a loud beep and jumped. It was Sophie's mother beeping the horn of her car after the vehicle had swung into the terraced street from Smithdown Road. Sophie got out the car and asked Ellie why she was standing there on the corner. When Ellie told her friend the reason, Sophie went back to the car and told her mother what her friend had said. They all went to the house and found that someone had emptied the can of fuchsia paint all over the floor and walls of the hallway. There were also handprints of a child in paint on the vestibule door. That was the last straw as far as Ellie was concerned, and she moved out the flat that day. Sophie also left the flat, and she and Ellie found smaller accommodation at a house on Penny Lane. I have researched the history of the house on Claremont Road and so far, I cannot find any report of a child murder on the premises. I believe that the woman still haunts the flat – which never seems to be occupied for long.

Our next daytime haunting takes place four miles north of Claremont Road at a house on Carisbrooke Road in the Walton district of Liverpool in 2012. In March of that year, some very strange occurrences took place at the 3-bedroom house, the home of a young couple named Izzy and Zak – and their two-month-old baby girl Jacinta. Izzy adapted well to the new routine of getting up at an unearthly hour to feed Jacinta, and Zak also adjusted well to being a parent, but then one day when he came home from his job (a sales advisor at a certain popular fashion store on Church Street) to find Izzy in tears in the bedroom with the baby asleep in her arms.

'What's the matter, love?' Zak asked, rushing to his wife and child.

Izzy was so upset she could hardly get her words out. 'This house is haunted,' she told Zak, and she tried to say more but her words became unintelligible as she began to sob.

'Haunted?' Zak pondered the word as he curled his arm around Izzy. 'It's alright, love – what do you mean, haunted?'

'Zak, we've got to get out of here,' Izzy told him with great urgency in her uneven, quivering voice, 'we've got to. They were standing over Jacinta's cot – bent over her – horrible shadows!'

'Calm down love,' Zak told her and tried to smile. He rubbed her back and said, 'Take a deep breath; I'm here now, you're okay. What was standing over the baby?'

'They were like angels with wings, only they were shadows, and they were bent over – arched – silhouettes, and they were both looking down at the baby, and I heard them whispering her name – it was horrible.'

'When was this?' Zak asked, and already he was wondering if his wife had been seeing things because of some postnatal condition.

'Three o'clock this afternoon. She was fast asleep, and I went the toilet for about a minute, then came back, and they were standing over her – one on each side of the cot. They were taller than you Zak, about 6 foot six I'd say, and they had no legs, just a long robe that went to the floor. I couldn't see their feet.'

'Strange,' was all that Zak could muster.

'I was *not* seeing things Zak.'

'I know – I never said you were, love.'

'The way you looked at me then – you think I imagined them don't you?' Izzy seemed angry and disgusted with what she perceived to be a sceptical attitude.

'I am not doubting you, please drop the attitude Izzy!' Zak told her, and his raised voice woke up Jacinta. 'What happened? Did they vanish?'

Izzy nodded. 'I picked the baby up and as I leaned over the cot they vanished.'

'So, they had wings?' Zak asked.

Izzy nodded. 'The wings were tucked behind them. They weren't angels though, they looked very sinister, and they kept whispering '*Jacinta*'. They had no depth either – they were like cardboard cut-outs.

'Two dimensional?' Zak queried.

'Yes, and I just had the feeling they were evil. I think they're going to take the baby. We should move out or sleep in another room Zak.' Izzy then started to sniffle and her eyes poured with tears.

Zak told his older sister Hollie about Izzy's story, and Hollie told her brother that Izzy might be suffering from postpartum psychosis. Hollie always had her nose in a family health encyclopaedia and Zak always consulted her when he had any symptoms – real or imagined.

'Post what?' Zak asked his sister.

'Postpartum psychosis,' she replied, and she explained that the condition was sometimes experienced by women a few weeks after they had given birth. 'The symptoms include hallucinations, paranoia, depression,' said Hollie, 'all the symptoms Izzy seems to be exhibiting.'

'What should I do then?' asked a distressed Zak.

'You'll have to get her to go to the doctor,' replied Hollie, and her voice sounded calm but she conveyed the graveness of the situation. 'Go with her, Zak, and tell him what she said about the weird angels trying to take the baby.'

'They might put her away or something – ' Zak worried.

'Don't be daft,' said Hollie, shaking her head,' they'll probably take her into hospital – '

'What!'

'Zak, calm down,' Hollie rolled here eyes. 'You love Izzy don't you? They'll take her in and probably give her lithium or some other mood stabilizer, and then she'll be out after a few months, maybe sooner.'

'Hollie, it mightn't even be what you say it is; it could all be down to sleep deprivation and maternity blues. I think I should let Izzy decide. I don't want her getting hospitalised; I couldn't live without her.'

'Zak, some people with postpartum psychosis have committed suicide,' Hollie told him.

'Suicide?' Zak felt his stomach drop and go into freefall.

Hollie nodded. 'So please, make sure she gets treatment – before it's too late.'

Zak tried to be tactful when he mentioned the possibility to Izzy that she might be suffering from postpartum psychosis, but his wife was furious at Hollie's diagnosis and told Zak he shouldn't have told his 'meddling sister' what she had told him in confidence. Zak assured Izzy that he did not believe she was suffering from postpartum psychosis and said they should forget the whole thing. He apologised for talking about Izzy behind her back with Hollie, and eventually the couple made up. However, on the following day, the two sinister looking silhouetted entities returned, and again they stood on each side of Jacinta's cot, whispering unintelligible words. Izzy screamed at the apparitions and as she scooped the baby out of her cot the tall shadowy beings vanished with a hissing sound. Izzy put Jacinta on the sofa in the living room and sat with her till 5.30pm, when Zak came home. He had bought Izzy a box of chocolates, a bouquet of flowers and a bottle of wine. When he saw Izzy cradling the baby on the sofa and the redness of her eyes, he experienced a feeling of dread in his stomach. 'Did you see them again?' he asked.

Izzy said nothing. She looked at the baby and closed her eyes as she started to sniffle.

'Izzy, did you see them again?' Zak asked again and he sat beside her and saw a tear escape from his wife's closed eye.

'It doesn't matter,' she sobbed, 'you won't believe me anyway.'

'I do believe you – what did you see?' he said.

She gave a brief account of the strange visitors and then Zak became quiet. 'What would they want Jacinta for? It's bizarre,' he said, looking at his baby.

'I don't know, but I am not imagining them Zak,' said Izzy. 'I think it's the house,' she told him, her glistening eyes darting about as she spoke, 'I think we should find another place.'

The twist in this strange affair came on the following

Sunday. Zak was off that day, and in the afternoon he heard a cry from the bedroom. Izzy was shouting him. He ran out of the living room and bounded up the stairs two at a time. He burst into the nursery – and there they were – the creepy silhouetted forms his wife had reported to him twice before. They were exactly as Izzy had described them: well over six feet in height, with prominent arched backs and what looked like wings of some sort tucked behind those curved backs. They stood on each side of the cot, and the profiles of their faces were pointed down at Jacinta, who was fast asleep.

'Do you believe me now?' Izzy asked her husband, 'You can see them can't you? Please say you can.'

'Yeah, I can – get the baby!' shouted Zak, staring in horror at the unearthly figures, and Izzy casually walked to the cot, leaned over it and picked up Jacinta, and as the baby, startled out of its sleep, began to cry, the two weird attendant phantasms of shadow made that hissing sound, straightened up a little, looked at one another, and faded away.

Zak dismantled the cot and brought it down into the living room. He talked incessantly about the ghosts and agreed with his wife now – the best thing to do was to find another place to live, as far away as Carisbrooke Road as possible. He started to browse flats and houses to rent on several websites and talked about borrowing money from his father to pay the deposit should he find suitable accommodation. By 5pm, Izzy was making the tea, when there was a knock at the door. Zak went to answer it and received the shock of his life.

A little old woman dressed in black with a strange

black bonnet on her head stood there on the doorstep. The brim of the bonnet stuck out quite a bit beyond the face (which sounds to me like a poke bonnet – a popular item of fashion in the Victorian age), and the face of the elderly lady was very pale - *deathly* pale in fact, Zak thought, and the eyes of the quaintly-dressed visitor were of a striking sky blue; they almost seemed to be glowing.

'Listen carefully sir,' said the woman, and it was not a local accent. 'Your baby is ill and the two spirits visiting it have been trying to heal it. Let them heal the child and do not interfere!'

'Who are you?' Zak asked the diminutive woman in black, and he stepped back a little, sensing she was a ghost.

The woman turned, walked down the four steps and walked straight through the closed gate, before fading away into nothingness on the pavement of Carisbrooke Road.

As Zak slowly closed the door, Izzy's head popped over his shoulder, giving him quiet a start.

'Who was it?' she asked, a spatula in her hand.

'A ghost,' he managed to say, quite shook up by the visit from beyond, and then he wondered how to phrase the old woman's disturbing message.

'What do you mean?' Izzy asked, her eyes turned now towards the closed door. 'Did one of those things call here?'

Zak felt his heart palpitate as he gathered his thoughts for a reply. 'No, an old woman with a funny hat on – and she said Jacinta's ill and that those things hanging round over the cot are trying to heal her.'

There was a pause as Izzy took in the information. She panicked when she processed the part about something being wrong with the baby. 'What did she mean – something wrong with the baby?'

'I don't know, but that's what she said, and then she walked away and vanished,' Zak recalled the uncanny dematerialisation.

'Are you sure it wasn't just someone messing about, Zak,' Izzy asked, and she started to breathe heavy because she felt as if she couldn't get enough air into her lungs.

'It wasn't anyone messing about – she disappeared in front of my eyes,' Zak assured his wife.

'Oh my God, is there something wrong with Jacinta?' Izzy asked, and she walked back to the kitchen and turned off the cooker. She had lost her appetite. She went into the living room to look at the baby and Zak joined her and hugged her and the infant. 'We've got to get out of here, love,' he said. 'Maybe we could stay in my your mum's house – she's got a spare room.'

'I could ask her,' said Izzy, gently rocking the baby in her arms, 'she'll say yes, but she'll want to know why, obviously.'

'Just tell her the truth,' said Zak.

Izzy's mother Joanne believed that the so-called silhouetted figures were just the products of her daughter's mind, and she seemed to agree with the diagnosis of Zak's sister Hollie – that perhaps Izzy was suffering from some form of postpartum psychosis. Izzy was livid at her mother's take on the situation and left her house immediately with Zak and the baby. Izzy made an appointment to see the doctor about her child, and when she saw him she said she believed that there was something wrong with Jacinta. The doctor said the child seemed fine but Izzy insisted that there was something wrong with her daughter, although she couldn't say exactly what it was. She obviously couldn't say that she was worried about Jacinta's health because of the say-so of a ghost, so she had to pretend that her concern was borne out of a mother's intuition. The doctor finally gave in and agreed to send the baby for a scan. Jacinta was found to have a congenital diaphragmatic hernia – a dangerous condition that would require surgery. Izzy almost fainted when she received this news. Jacinta however, underwent the operation, and the surgery was carried out through a tiny incision in her abdomen. The baby was then put into intensive care for a week as a precaution and made a very rapid and successful recovery. After that, no more supernatural beings visited the house on Carisbrooke Road, and the couple left their home in 2013 and moved to Crosby. The nature of the silhouetted figures which haunted the cot of the baby Jacinta are hard to fathom; were they angels or were they something demonic? It really is hard to say.

The Grade II-listed Anglican parish church of St Mary's in West Derby was the unusual backdrop to a number of very strange daylight manifestations of the supernatural in the 1940s, 1950s and the 1990s. In 1946, a 10-year-old child named Len Archer reached his home off West Derby's Meadow Lane in a terrible state. The boy claimed that he had been chased by a vampire disguised as the local reverend of St Mary's Church. Len's parents and older sisters put the lad's seemingly far-fetched story down to an overactive imagination, but Len's best friend Georgie Rowntree assured the Archer family that Len was telling the truth. Georgie said that he and Len had been playing cricket in the front garden of his house on Almond's Green when a gang of children had run past the house screaming. Georgie and Len went to see what all the excitement was about and one of the gang said a man in black with long sharp teeth had chased them outside of St Mary's Church, and at one point he had jumped clean over a six-foot-high wall. Georgie and Len went to the church to see if this bogeyman existed and saw a man in a white collar who shouted 'Come here you two!'

The boys walked towards him, thinking he was the reverend of the church, but when they got within six feet of the man his face turned into something horrible, his eyes seemed to glow, and then he opened his mouth to reveal long sharp teeth. The boys ran off in terror and the thing pretending to be a man of the cloth gave chase and almost caught up with them until he vanished half way up Meadow Lane. Not much was known about vampires in the 1940s and most people thought such freakish beings were like Bella Lugosi's depiction of the eponymous bloodsucker in the film *Dracula* (1931). Len's father said to his son, 'If you tell the truth, I'll give you a banana.' Banana's were a luxury hard to come by during the post-war years, and yet Len still maintained that he *was* telling the truth, and this made his parents realise that he and Georgie *had* encountered someone very strange. A few more people – adults and children – claimed to have seen the West Derby vampire, but the alleged sightings and encounters of the fiend dressed as a clergyman died down and he was not reported until 10 years later in 1956. By then, Georgie and Len were 20-year-old Teddy Boys but they went cold when they heard the strange rumours of a vampire knocking about near St Mary's Church. Within days though, the reports dwindled and ceased. Then, in 1996, at the age of sixty, Len Archer (who now lived in Chester) attended a meet-up with his old friends in the Sefton Arms, and they talked about the old days in the "Village" and eventually the subject of the supernatural came up and a few at the reunion talked of the so-called local vampire, but treated it as a mere urban legend that had spiralled out of control. A few hours later, Len had to leave the group at the pub to catch the train back to Chester, but before he left West Derby he walked over to St Mary's Church to reminisce on his younger days – and there, standing inside the gates of the church, was a man Len took to be the reverend, as he was wearing a white collar, but he had his back to Len. Len said "Excuse me Reverend," and the man slowly turned – and Len saw it was him – the thing that had chased him when he was 10. He wore glasses on this occasion, and the look of evil on the entity's face chilled Len to his marrow. He backed away in terror as the thing masquerading as a holy man bore its fangs – then charged at him. Len tried to run but he'd only covered about thirty feet when he felt agonizing pains in his chest and a sense of pressure not unlike a bloated stomach. Len felt his legs give way under him and he collapsed and lost consciousness. He had suffered a mild heart attack. He awoke in Broadgreen Hospital, and the first thing he asked a nurse was: 'Did he get me? Did he bite me?'

The nurse was baffled by the questions and told Len to relax, but he looked about the ward, convinced that the vampiric being was about. A doctor was summoned by the nurse and he believed that Len was in what is medically termed "an acute confusional state" because he was suffering from a delirium as he recovered from the heart attack and he had him sedated. Eventually the nurse convinced Len he was safe in the ward and she assured him there were no vampires about.

Till the day Len died in 2001, he never returned to West Derby again. I gave a brief mention of this case on BBC Radio Merseyside and received some amazing feedback from listeners – many of whom recalled the vampire scare. Some thought the West Derby vampire was nothing more than the product of weird rumours and embellishments of accounts of an eccentric local, but I also received accounts from people from all walks of life who said they had actually encountered the vampire. One woman in her seventies named Joan Williams said that on one sunny Sunday afternoon in September 1953, when she was twenty, she was being escorted home to her house on Muirhead Avenue East by her boyfriend David Rimmer after a visit to Joan's Aunt Margaret in Kensington. It was a warm and pleasant late-summer's day, and as the couple walked up Meadow Lane holding hands, an old man coming from the opposite direction warned Joan and David that there was a 'nutcase' further up the lane dressed all in black, and he was jumping over garden hedges and acting very strange. Joan and David smiled and dismissed the warning, thinking that the old man was just describing someone engaged in a bit of alcohol-fuelled high-jinks, but a few minutes later, the couple were confronted by a 6ft-tall man in a black suit, white shirt and maroon tie who had a ghastly pale face with red bloodshot eyes. His hair was black, slicked back, almost shoulder length (unusual for the 1950s) and he had a striking widow's peak. This sinister figure lunged at David Rimmer with lightning agility, grabbed his neck with both hands and started to shake him violently. As the stranger throttled David, Joan's piercing screams brought some of the residents of Meadow Lane to their windows, and two men who saw what was happening ran out to David's aid. By then, David had lost consciousness and the assailant with the sickly pallid face said something unintelligible to Joan before running south down Meadow Lane at an incredible speed. When the weird strangler reached the junction where Parkside Drive exists today, he jumped clean over a 5-foot-high stone wall, landing on a grassy area which is now part of Croxteth County Park. David recovered consciousness but the throttling left him unable to speak for about twenty minutes. He later said that the man's hands felt ice cold as they gripped his throat. Around this time, a neighbour of Joan Williams, a man named Robert Jones, said that he had almost run over a man in black who had jumped into the path of his car as he drove down Meadow Lane one morning at eight. Seconds before the car would have hit him, the man had made an incredible leap from the middle of the road onto the sandstone wall which runs along half the length of the lane. I received many more similar accounts from the denizens of West Derby telling me how a man in black had approached them disguised as a policeman and a priest, only to give chase once he was rumbled. A myth has endured for years regarding vampires – namely that they cannot tolerate sunlight or even the feeblest daylight – yet there is no evidence to support this belief in the original descriptions of vampires. It would seem to date back to *Nosferatu* - the German Expressionist horror film written by Henrik Galeen and directed by F. W. Murnau. In this take on Bram Stoker's Dracula tale, the vampire is said to fear daylight. Almost every filmmaker and writer since then has portrayed vampires as photophobic beings who burn in shafts of sunlight and even turn to dust when exposed to ultraviolet light. The only exception to this is seen in the *Twilight* books of Stephenie Meyer (and the highly successful films based on those books); her vampires sparkle in sunlight! Whatever the fanged being was which prowled West Derby, it was rarely seen at night, but went about its sinister business during the hours of daylight, albeit on leafy secluded lanes. The way the being impersonated policemen and even a priest reminds me of the antics of Spring-Heeled Jack decades before, except that Jack was mostly seen at night-time.

For well over twenty years, the ghost of a nun has been seen – always of a morning in the summer months – sitting on the wall of the graveyard of St Peter's Church, Woolton. The surreal but eerie apparition of the smiling nun sits with her legs hanging over the Church Road side of the cemetery – not far from the grave of one Eleanor Rigby (possibly the inspiration for the Beatles' song, as John Lennon and Paul McCartney met at a garden fete in the field behind this church in 1957). Why the ghost of a nun would sit on the graveyard wall is unknown, for I have not yet been able to discover any nuns buried in St Peter's Churchyard. She has been seen by early risers going to work, milkmen, a policeman, a postman, and on one occasion a priest is said to have seen the figure sitting there on the wall. The man of the cloth noticed that the ghost did not have a rosary, and asked her where it was, and immediately the nun ceased smiling and vanished – so some believe that the ghost is a Satanic projection. The phantom has been seen since 1997, and seems to prefer the months from June to August to put in an appearance and always between the hours of 7.30am and 9am. The identity of this bizarre daylight ghost remains a mystery.

THE COAT OF
NARCISSUS MESSINGER

The page before me lies blank, as bare as that stage built in the middle of a warehouse in cratered post-war Liverpool, and now, as I commit the strange story to print, I see the figures assemble and take their places in the first scene of this eldritch drama...

Across the moonscape of a city almost blitzed to destruction by the Luftwaffe's Angels of Death stumbled two seasoned thespians of the English stage - and a young man of 21 who hoped to become an actor. The thespians would later become seduced by the syrupy maw of Hollywood, rise to starry heights and become household names in some of the greatest films of the 20th Century, but I will not give you their names as I was given this story on the understanding they would not be identified, for the early days of their careers were marred by drugs, drink and sexual scandals. Let us call the first theatrical performer Alastair Krookshank – a forty-something force of nature on the stage – and off it; a man who struck emotional chords in the hearts of audiences on every level of society with the sheer genius of his vocal delivery alone; a player who could bring the hoary old words of Shakespeare to Technicolor life like no other actor of his generation. Krookshank was nothing short of a verbal terrorist when he delivered lines, instilling feelings of sheer horror, choking grief, as well as uproarious laughter among even the most dispassionate theatregoer. This juggernaut of drama was also large in stature, a Buddha in a Burton suit, and the wisps of his greying hair fluttered in the Mersey breeze under the brim of his black felt fedora. He complained and swore in his trademark rich voice as he tried to cross an acre of rubble where a row of shops had stood before the war. Krookshank's walking cane – once owned by James Joyce – prodded the bricks and powdered mortar as he called the Germans 'Bastard krauts!'

The second role-player extraordinaire walking behind Alastair Krookshank was a 30-year-old man we shall assign the nom de guerre of Richard Le Queux – the very epitome of the archetypal romantic hero, a handsome slim Adonis with olive green eyes, raven black hair, an aquiline nose and perpetually pouting lips. He was the very antithesis of the corpulent Krookshank.

The bronzed ganger of a band of sweltering labourers clearing up the aftermath of an air-raid spotted Krookshank and Le Queux lurching across the uneven stretch of debris and excitedly told his men: 'Hey lads, look who it is! It's Alastair Krookshank! Over there! Look!'

One of the men stopped his pneumatic drill. He was no cultured theatregoer but he had heard Krookshank on the wireless over the years and his mum loved him.

'Mr Krookshank!' shouted a Scotsman on the gang,

waving his pickaxe aloft. Another workman let out an ear-piercing whistle.

Krookshank halted, turned unsteadily, and looked at the twelve workmen, most of of them stripped to the waist in the burning sun. He took off his hat and saluted them, and was about to walk on, but he saw them clap, and so he went over to them, but out of professional jealousy, Richard Le Queux stayed put and he sighed loudly with impatience. Hadrian Atkinson, the 21-year-old carrying the cases belonging to Le Queux and Krookshank went with the latter to the workmen.

'I think you were marvellous in *Alice and Wonderland*, Mr Krookshank sir!' said the ganger, removing his cloth cap, and then he added, 'And that other one at the Playhouse with the black fellah, er – *Othello*. Wait till I tell our Ethel I saw you – she's your biggest fan.'

'Thankyou sir, you are most kind!' Krookshank's voice boomed, and he turned to Hadrian Atkinson and said, 'Hadrian, in my portmanteau you will find my photograph; bring it here, lad.'

Hadrian came over, tripped over a thick rusted cable protruding from the detritus but managed to stay upright, and he opened the travelling bag and handed it to Krookshank, who rummaged about in it and produced a small monochrome photograph of himself, the size of a playing card. Krookshank handed the portmanteau back to Atkinson and thrust his walking cane into the earth between the bricks. He took a Waterman fountain pen out of his inside coat pocket, uncapped it, and began to write upon the card as the ganger and his men watched. 'This is my carte de visite. To Ethel! Regards, Alastair Krookshank,' he said as he wrote the words. He waved the card in the noon day heat to dry the ink and handed it to a very grateful ganger.

'Ah, you're a hero Mr Krookshank, and in my opinion, the greatest actor I've ever seen. You can do anything sir; I wish you'd do more plays at the Playhouse.'

'Can we get a move on?' came the distant voice of Mr Le Queux through the dusty air.

Krookshank ignored him and sombrely said, 'I'm afraid the Playhouse does not recognise my abilities, and they have treated me like a leper. I intend to found my own theatre soon.'

'Oh,' said the ganger, glancing at the little signed photograph with glee in his eyes.

'Thank God we have men like you!' Krookshank told the gang of workmen, and he put on his hat. 'Look at you all! Anglo-Saxon thoroughbreds every one of you. Direct descendants of the lads who fought at Agincourt! The blood of Robin Hood's loyal men runs in your veins!' he announced, and then slowly pulling the tip of the walking cane out of the ground he told the diggers: 'King Arthur would have been proud to have this company seated at his table. Truly lads, I say this unto you: that you are of the very same flesh and blood of the men at Waterloo who routed that French dictator, and no doubt you also showed that Austrian upstart that no one messes with John Bull! No one!'

All of the workmen clapped and nodded in agreement, and some looked as if they were close to tears by the patriotic speech.

A deep-sounding horn of a ship echoed on the River

Mersey, and as it faded, Krookshank told the workmen: 'Three hundred years ago, an Englishman named William Shakespeare wrote about lads like you and this beautiful country of ours.'

Krookshank gave a little cough, and then, holding the cane under his arm as if it was a sergeant's swagger stick, he let loose one of Shakespeare's most famous speeches, taken from *Richard II*:

This royal throne of kings, this sceptred isle,
This earth of majesty, this seat of Mars,
This other Eden, demi-paradise,
This fortress built by Nature for herself
Against infection and the hand of war,
This happy breed of men, this little world,
This precious stone set in the silver sea,
Which serves it in the office of a wall
Or as a moat defensive to a house,
Against the envy of less happier lands,
This blessed plot, this earth, this realm, this England!

'Jesus Christ Krookshank!' Le Queux bellowed fifty yards away and walked on, away from him and Atkinson in a huff.

All of the workmen cheered and clapped at the performance on the wasteland, and Krookshank could see the tears of some of the men glistening in the sun. He bowed with a very earnest expression, and turned and walked away as the begrimed men hurled plaudits after him.

When Krookshank and Atkinson rejoined Richard Le Queux he was livid. 'It's a pity they blew up most of the piers in the war Krookshank,' said Le Queux through a barely-open mouth, 'you could have done that patriotic pantomime speech in between the comedian's spot and a juggling act.'

'Envy eats nothing but its own heart, Le Queux,' said Krookshank, without even looking at his colleague.

In the distance, the pneumatic drill began to clatter again and the gang of workers resumed attacking the hard ground with their tools under the cruel noon sun.

The two actors and the apprentice reached the condemned warehouse. Before the war, the cracks had been appearing in its walls and yet it had survived the aerial onslaught of Nazi bombs and stronger warehouses had been reduced to dust. The asking price of the agent for King & Cardinal Engineering was £5,000. The two thespians had between them £72 and ten shillings, and Hadrian Atkinson had contributed his savings, which amounted to £15. Krookshank was optimistic that the asking price could be raised over six months, and the agent was currently discussing this irregular arrangement with the executives of the engineering company. In the meantime, a criminal friend of Richard Le Queux had picked the padlock on the doors and switched on the electricity in the warehouse. Across the green doors of the warehouse, Krookshank had painted the words: 'Krookshank Playhouse' in white two-foot tall letters. All that needed to be done next was build a stage, and Hadrian Atkinson, who collected glasses and mopped the floors at his father's pub, had been entrusted with finding some reputable carpenters and builders to erect the stage. So far, Le Queux had painted the border of the unbuilt stage in whitewash. He saw it as a start. Other actors in the profession thought the whole thing was a scream. 'People who build castles in the air are being far more realistic,' said one well-known local actor at the Old Vic who had heard of the unworkable scheme. Had Krookshank and Le Queux not been blacklisted by most of the theatres for being drunk and disorderly on stage, they could have approached a bank for a loan, but they were veritable lepers. Le Queux had also made some *very* serious allegations regarding the managers of one local theatre.

Alastair Krookshank stood in the centre of the two-dimensional makeshift stage and yelled: 'Welcome to the Krookshank Playhouse! Once more unto the breach, dear friends, once more; or close the wall up with our English dead!'

'The acoustics are fine, Alastair, but your voice sounds somewhat gravelly,' Le Queux observed.

'Yes, my throat is rather dry,' Krookshank replied, and to the apprentice he said: 'Hadrian! Drink, drink!'

The young man nodded, and stammered: 'Y – Y – Yes, M – Mr Krookshank, sir.' He opened a suitcase which was little more than a mobile bar and he knew the thespian would require a glass of neat whiskey. He poured out the large measure and brought it on stage. Krookshank gulped away, emptied the glass, regained his breath, then took off his coat and dropped it onto the ground. 'Now, Hadrian, let us resume our elocution lessons. Put the case down.'

Le Queux smiled across his eyes, for he knew that Atkinson would never be an actor; not because of his stammer – that could be treated and corrected. The boy did not possess an atom of talent and seemed to have difficulty reading. Le Queux knew that Krookshank was just using the lad; leaching off his meagre wages and using him as a dogsbody.

'Stand up straight Atkinson!' Krookshank roared like a sergeant major.

The boy did as he was told and his face turned red.

'Now, Atkinson, say after me: the ragged rascal ran around the rugged rocks.'

'The r – r- rugged rascal – ' the boy attempted, and closed his eyes.

'Ragged rascal – not rugged! Concentrate boy!' thundered Krookshank's voice.

'The r – r – r – r. The r – r – ragged rascal runs about – '

'No! No! No!' Krookshank hollered, swinging the walking cane perilously close to Atkinson's head. 'You're adding your own words now! To the letter! To the blasted letter!'

'You're making him more nervous, Krook!' Le Queux protested and walked to the suitcase to grab the whiskey bottle.

'Spare the rod and spoil the child!' Krookshank swiped the cane towards Le Queux and he seemed to be foaming at the corners of his mouth.

'I can't do it!' Hadrian Atkinson threw his hands up to his face and walked 'off' the stage.

'You didn't stutter then, did you?' cried Krookshank, 'All in your mind that stutter! A little bit of pressure and you're off!'

Atkinson ran towards the door of the warehouse sobbing.

'There is no royal road to becoming an actor!' Krookshank shouted after the youth, then grabbed the bottle of whiskey from Le Queux.

Atkinson swung open the large heavy door of the

warehouse and found his exit blocked by a smiling man with a handcart.

'Is this the Krookshank Theatre?' the stranger asked Hadrian, who wiped his tears and nodded.

'Krookshank Playhouse – not theatre!' shouted Krookshank, and then he saw the bundles of clothes in the cart and exclaimed: 'Ah! The wardrobe department arrives! Splendid!'

'Ten bob for the lot Mr Krookshank,' said the man, and Krookshank said he was embarrassed because he seemed to have mislaid his purse, and so Hadrian gave the carter a ten-bob note and he left, smiling at the painted sign on the door as he went.

Krookshank and Le Queux rummaged through the coats and garments. Not all of the clothes were someone's shabby cast-offs; some of the outfits were in pristine condition – so why hadn't the carter sold them for a much higher price? Krookshank never met the carter after that day and thought there was something odd about him.

'A soldier!' Krookshank held up an old redcoat and Le Queux said, 'King's Regiment, quite old; I'd say the 1890s. You'll never get into that unless you can shed ten stones.'

'A tuxedo!' Krookshank picked up the jacket and located the matching trousers. 'Now this might fit me!' He examined the waist and grunted. 'No! You'd need a bloody schoolgirl's figure to wear that. And what's this? A top hat!' Krookshank tried on the top hat but his head was simply too big, so he handed the topper to Atkinson as a sort of peace offering, and the young man gave a slight smile and took it from him.

'Look at this! Father Le Queux!' Richard Le Queux

had found the vestments of a priest.

By one that afternoon, Krookshank suggested a trip to the palatial house of a friend named Rodney Harvey, an 80-year-old retired impresario who also happened to have a well-stocked wine cellar. 'Rodney will have some spiffing ideas for raising money for our theatre and his wife has recently passed away so he'll certainly appreciate our company,' said Krookshank. Mr Harvey was an out-and-out snob and someone as unrefined and low-bred as pub-worker Hadrian Atkinson would simply not be admitted to Harvey's home – so the youth was left behind to lock up the theatre. However, at 1pm on the following day, when Krookshank and Le Queux called at the dock road pub run by Atkinson's father Arthur, they were told that Hadrian had not been seen since noon yesterday. Arthur Atkinson said he was ready to notify the police about his son because his wife – who was "psychy" – had a feeling something had happened to him. 'He's never done this before,' he told the actors, 'never stayed out, not once. My missus has second sight and she has bad feelings about Hadrian. There's a bond between him and his mother, because he's a bit psychy too.'

'Hadrian has the keys to the warehouse, so we must find him, or we'll have to break the padlock, ' said Krookshank, looking red-eyed and in need of a shave after an all-night drinking session with Rodney Harvey.

'Let me give you and Mr Le Queux the hair of the dog,' Arthur said to the players, and he took them into the bar of the pub, which had not yet opened, and began mixing beer with something he called a tincture of persimmon fruit, brought to Liverpool from Japan many years ago by a merchant seaman.

'Get that into your bloodstreams,' Arthur gave the half pint glasses of hangover cure to the thespians.

The door of the pub burst open, and an elegantly-dressed man in a top hat – perceived by Arthur Atkinson to be a toff – entered.

'Oi! We're closed!' he shouted – and then with heart-stopping astonishment he saw that it was his son – Hadrian!

'Father, dear Father! Don't you recognise your own son?' Hadrian asked in a faultless accent heavily reminiscent of Noel Coward. He wore white gloves, carried a black shiny walking cane with a large chrome-plated knob at the end. He looked like Fred Astaire in his silky topper, close-fitting tailcoat, narrow black trousers and shiny shoes with spats.

'What the devil are you wearing?' Arthur asked with a crooked grin.

Krookshank almost spat out the hair of the dog concoction and Le Queux stood there lost for words.

'Clothes maketh the man, pater,' said the dandified Hadrian, adjusting his white bow tie, and it was plain to those present that he had overcome his speech impediment. He pursed his lips as he looked at his reflection in the mirror behind the bar which was emblazoned with the words: Guinness Extra Stout. 'By Jove, I'm as handsome as my sister,' he told his reflection, 'so why have I been lacking in confidence all these years? Silly boy!'

'Hadrian, are you ill?' Krookshank asked, slowly moving in on the transformed young man as he looked him up and down.

'I have never felt better Krookshank!' Hadrian

replied in a sharp loud retort. 'I've just noticed something quite striking about your bulky frame Mr Krookshank, and that round pudding face of yours and those walled eyes; you really should try and join the Marx Brothers – you'd make a great stooge!'

'How dare you – ' Krookshank gasped as Le Queux giggled behind him.

'Drink! Come on!' Hadrian bashed the counter with the silver knob of the cane.

'How dare you insult Mr Krookshank!' Arthur Atkinson roared and he lifted the counter-top door, ready to apprehend his son, but Hadrian placed his white gloved hand on the counter and merely smiled. He then threw his legs over the counter and shouted "Whoopee!" His coat tails flew into the air behind him.

He landed behind the bar counter and ran down to the till, which he opened and ransacked, and when his father charged at him, he once again leaped with amazing agility over the bar counter and ran out of the pub.

'He – he's gone raving mad!' said a confused Arthur Atkinson, clutching his chest, 'Someone must have slipped him a Mickey Finn!'

'No, it's much stranger than that sir,' said Le Queux, walking towards the open door of the pub. 'He's like a completely different person – how strange. Did you notice his nose?'

'His nose? What about it?' Mr Atkinson asked.

'Well, ' Queux looked through the doorway of the pub at the bustle of life on the hot dusty street, and he ran his index fingertip down his own nose, 'it was straight, and seemed thinner and longer, whereas

Hadrian's nose turns up slightly and it's quite wide.'

'I don't understand what you're getting at,' confessed Arthur Atkinson.

'I don't either – what on earth is going on?' Le Queux replied.

'I'll give him the bloody Marx Brothers when I catch up with him!' snarled Krookshank, and then he held his forehead because the hangover headache had increased with all of the excitement.

That evening, a man in a top hat and morning coat tapped his walking cane on the scarlet door of an upmarket male brothel on Huskisson Street, the haunt of some famous local people who led double lives. The night caller was the transfigured Hadrian Atkinson, now barely recognisable because his face had turned as white as the moon and his eyes had taken on a very sinister aspect; they looked dark and narrow, whereas Hadrian had possessed large expressive blue eyes.

'Who is it?' asked the keeper of the brothel, a man in his thirties named Mr Somerset. The caller should have uttered a password, but Somerset was accustomed to clients – especially the drunken kind who would call at such a late hour – who forgot the watchword. And so he opened the door a few inches, and seeing that the caller was dressed so elegantly, he made the mistake of opening the door fully and to Hadrian he said: 'Yes sir?'

'I'm mad about the boy!' Hadrian replied, attempting to sing the opening sentence of the Noel Coward song.

For a moment in the moonlight, Hadrian's features reminded the keeper of a young prostitute who had worked at the brothel before his tragic death a few years ago – a beautiful actor and dancer named Narcissus Messinger. 'Who sent you?' asked Somerset, thinking the distinguished caller was intoxicated. 'Didn't they give you a password?'

'Yes, Somerset,' said Hadrian, nodding, and he leaned forward and whispered 'Hi Ho Kafoozalum.'

Somerset smiled and said, 'No sir, that used to be the password years ago.'

'Oh in that case, Somerset,' said Hadrian, and in a flash with a full-force overhand motion he struck the keeper with the great silver knob at the end of the walking cane, bringing it down with sickening ferocity on the top of the custodian's head.

The keeper crumpled to his knees in the vestibule area of the hall, and seemed dazed. Hadrian kicked him aside, and he began to sing the bawdy old song *Kafoozalum* as he closed the door behind him. He stepped over a groaning Mr Somerset and ran up the stairs like a man possessed, singing in an almost operatic voice. Somerset got unsteadily to his feet and saw the ascending assailant's coat tails swish around the newel post at the top of the first flight of stairs. There had been something almost balletic in the way the fancy felon had floated up those stairs, the groggy keeper thought. Somerset wasn't sure what to do next, and his pounding headache was impeding the workings of his mind. He couldn't go outside and call for the assistance of a copper on his beat because this was a house of ill-repute, a den of vice in the eyes of the law. A curious realisation popped into Somerset's mind: how had the well-attired thug known his name?

Upstairs, Hadrian Atkinson wreaked havoc, bursting into one room after the other, gate-crashing orgies and disturbing all sorts of sexual acts. He began to shout: 'Where are you Colonel Daffodil?' And he danced, pirouetted and cavorted about the place like a man high on Wake-amine, a combination of Nijinsky and a crazed policeman bludgeoning everyone with the cane-cum-baton. Pirouettes and smashed teeth, virtuoso ballerino performing gravity-defying leaps one moment, and then in a heartbeat Atkinson was breaking noses. Clients and prostitutes charged at him from both sides, but it was like trying to catch a shadow. He moved like Fred Astaire, brandishing the walking cane as an Akido staff, running up walls, back-flipping and singing to the chorus of agonized cries and the beat of wood against flesh and bone. The choreographed blood-letting continued till everyone had either fled, fallen or gone into hiding, and then an uneasy silence permeated the bagnio, and Hadrian heard a click behind him. He spun to face the brothel doorman Somerset. He was standing on the top step and he had a pistol aimed at him.

'Who – what,' the words came with difficulty from Somerset's mouth, and then he asked: 'Who in God's name are you?'

Hadrian smiled as his eyes travelled down towards the barrel of the gun. 'My name is Narcissus Messinger, and I am out for revenge Mr Somserset, so put that pistol away before I smash your skull in. The last blow to your head was just a kiss.'

'You can't be – Mr Messinger died seven years ago. Are you his brother?' Somerset said, staring hard at the handsome features of the young man; his face seemed to be slowly turning into the visage of the deceased prostitute. Somerset's hand trembled.

'What's the devil's going on?' said a husky voice behind Hadrian. He turned to see a man of about seventy standing in the doorway of a room lit by a red lamp. The man wore only a pair of briefs. He had a head of wild iron-grey hair, and a chest of thick hair of the same shade. When this man saw Hadrian's face he stepped back and his striking pale-blue eyes widened.

'It's a man claiming to be Narcissus Messinger, Colonel!' Somerset shouted to the elderly man.

A naked young man of about eighteen appeared in the doorway of the bedroom behind the old man and softly asked, 'What's going on Daddy?'

'Well, well, if it isn't Colonel Daffodil,' said Hadrian, addressing the senior citizen, 'and who is that floozie hiding behind you?'

'You're dead,' Colonel Daffodil muttered, and the rest was babble cut short by Hadrian's stentorian interruption.

'And yet I am here! You know more than anyone how I dabbled in the Black Arts Colonel, and although a man can leave this life through the countless gates of death, it is nigh on impossible to find a way back from the grave, but I was six foot under – in that damned suffocating blackness for seven long years – and still the spark of consciousness remained in that decaying brain. I discovered that was the First Hell, Colonel – the slow rotting of the body while the mind remains intact. I struck a deal with a demon in that grave and now I am using another man's body to carry out my sweet revenge!'

'Revenge? On me? What did I do to you?' Colonel Daffodil asked, and seemed genuinely puzzled.

'You tied me up, Colonel, and you had your way and then you fell into an opium-induced sleep. And I suffered a severe attack of asthma while I was still bound up. Remember it? I slowly died from choking – anaphylaxis they call it.'

'That wasn't my fault – I didn't do it on purpose!' the Colonel had guilt written all over his face despite his protestation, and he glanced at Somerset and nodded, and Hadrian knew what that meant, so he swung around and before Somerset could pull the trigger, the bulbous chrome handle impacted into his forehead and the doorman fired the gun once before falling backwards down the flight of stairs. Hadrian then advanced slowly towards Colonel Daffodil as he tapped the cane on the palm of his white gloved hand, but the old man suddenly clutched his grey hairy chest, and he fell down, knocking his forehead on the floor with a ghastly thud as he collapsed. The colonel's 'boy' knelt beside him and shook him by the shoulder and turned him onto his back but there was no reaction. The Colonel's blue eyes were lifeless and they gazed at the ceiling.

'He's dead,' the boy murmured, and he laid his head on the chest of his old lover and listened for a heartbeat. He heard nothing.

'An eye for an eye, and a tooth for a tooth,' laughed Hadrian, 'much better than turning the other cheek.'

The front door of the brothel had not been locked after Hadrian's violent entrance and a policeman on his beat who had heard the loud report of Somerset's pistol came in and saw the unconscious body of the brothel's doorman lying with the limbs in unnatural positions at the bottom of the stairs. 'What's going on here?' the copper shouted up the stairs to Hadrian. He then spotted Somerset's pistol still in his grasp and carefully retrieved it.

'This place is a den of iniquity constable!' was Hadrian's reply, 'It is a male brothel, and some maniac has caused havoc up here! Bodies everywhere!'

'Oh aye?' said the constable, and he came up the stairs and advised Hadrian: 'Just stay put sir, I'll have to interview you, see?'

Hadrian let out a manic roar of laughter and he ran up a flight of stairs and eventually found the garret of the house. He smashed in the skylight window and calmly climbed out onto the slated roof. He then slid down the other side of the roof and hung from the guttering. He slung the walking cane into the street below and grabbed the drainpipe. He shinned down fifty feet of the pipe and eventually came to earth in a backyard. He climbed the wall of that yard and headed north up Hampton Street. Just before he ventured out onto Princes Road, Hadrian took off his top hat and the hammer-tail coat and threw them into an alleyway – and immediately, a strange partial amnesia clouded the young man's brain. Now Narcissus Messinger had gone, as if he had just evaporated from the pub worker's brain. Hadrian Atkinson walked with a bowed head through the moonlit streets, all the way to the warehouse, where he found Alastair Krookshank and Richard Le Queux rehearsing – with slurred voices – a cut-down version of Goldsmith's *She Stoops to Conquer*. Le Queux was dressed as a woman for his part in the play. When Krookshank saw the warehouse door open, followed by the entrance of Hadrian, he let slip a barrage of profanities and threats, then asked:

'Where have you been? And who gave you those awful elocution lessons?'

'I – I – I d-don't kn – know what you mean Mr Krookshank,' replied the apprehensive youth.

'Hadrian?' Le Queux took off his wig of long hair and approached the young man. 'Is that blood on your shirt?'

'It'll be *his* bastard blood on his shirt when I get my hands on him!' cried Krookshank, leaving the rectangle of the demarcated stage. His face was a shade of carnation pink, and as he closed in on the trembling Hadrian Atkinson, his voice boomed away like a railway gun, and when he was within twelve feet of the young man, Le Queux shouted "Leave him alone Krookshank!'

'He said I have a pudding face and that I should work as a stooge for the Marx Brothers!' Krookshank bellowed, when suddenly, a loud crack echoed throughout the cavernous interior of the warehouse, and the corner of the walls started to buckle inwards. Anticipating the collapse of the Krookshank Playhouse, Hadrian turned and ran to the warehouse door and yanked it open, but by then, the place was full of crumbling brick and mortar dust and there was an almighty rumble which deafened the three men – followed by blackness as the lights went out. The dust cleared and moonlight bathed the half-buried and bruised thespians, and Hadrian lay under one of the doors of the warehouse with a sprained wrist.

'Ha! Looks like the final curtain for your theatre, Krookshank!' said Le Queux, his face covered in greyish green dust.

'Out brief candle,' lamented Krookshank, his voice

sounding gravelly because of the dust in his throat.

'Looks like you've brought the house down again Mr Krookshank,' quipped Hadrian, getting to his feet, and Le Queux and Krookshank burst into laughter. The young man's speech impediment had mysteriously vanished, perhaps from the trauma of the warehouse falling on top of him.

'I think we should piss off over to Hollywood Krookshank,' sighed Le Queux, on his feet now, brushing the dust from his dress.

'I agree,' chortled Krookshank, sitting up, 'but they *do* have earthquakes over there you know?'

The two thespians borrowed the money from the impresario Rodney Harvey, and they boarded a ship to the United States within the week. Hadrian chose to remain in England, where he eventually gave up his acting ambitions and married a girl he had loved since infant school. Krookshank and Le Queux hit the big time in the optical fairyland of celluloid dreams, and probably fondly reminisced about their struggling days as blacklisted actors in England.

Hadrian Atkinson had strange recurring dreams about that mysterious alter ego Narcissus Messinger for years, and to his dying day he had a strange phobia of top hats.

SLINKY'S TWIN

On a foggy morning in November 1965, PC "Booty" Boothwaite was walking up School Lane, near the Bluecoat Chambers, when someone in the doorway of a nearby café attracted his attention with a "Pssst!" It was Mr Stratford, a man who ran a shop on Church Street. Booty went to see what he wanted, and Stratford beckoned him into the café where he told him: 'Slinky Edwards has been seen round here, eyeing up a tobacconist and that musical instruments shop around the corner. Has he been released already?'

'As far as I'm aware, Slinky is still incarcerated in Walton Prison,' the policeman told him. 'Are you sure it was him? He's got a twin brother named Alf.'

'Well, I was getting to that,' said Stratford. 'The word on the street is that Alf is doing time for his brother and that he'll get a big pay-out when he's released.'

PC Booty's eyebrows rose at this intriguing tittle tattle. 'That *has* happened before with criminal twins – one has done time in the nick for the twin brother, but Slinky has a small scar on his left cheek where Bernie the Blade slashed him ten years back. Did you actually see him around here yourself?'

Stratford nodded, 'Yes, on this very lane, and the funny thing is that Slinky's girlfriend Val works at the tobacconist up the road, in that little kiosk, so maybe he's been visiting her.'

Later that day, Booty asked a detective about Slinky's whereabouts and was told that, beyond a shadow of a doubt, he was still in Walton Prison, and that Alf his twin brother was now married and living a respectable life in Ince Blundell. Booty therefore believed Stratford had obviously mistaken someone else for Slinky – but on the following morning, as another autumn fog cloaked the city, PC Booty spotted Slinky on Hanover Street. It was him alright, because Booty could see that knife-blade scar on his cheek. The rumours had to be true; Alf had swapped places with Slinky before the trial and was doing bird for him! But that didn't make sense, because the detective Booty had talked to had assured him that Alf was living in Ince Blundell. There was only one way to get to the bottom of the enigma. Booty crept like a cat after Slinky as he walked up School Lane in that fog, which seemed to be getting thicker by the minute, and the policemen had his handcuffs at the ready for what would be a spectacular arrest. He smiled to himself as he shadowed Slinky – or his twin - up the lane. Slinky halted at the gates of the Bluecoat Chambers to look at the canvases exhibited by the shivering local artists, and Booty hid behind the large oak there, watching him like a hawk. He then followed the criminal to the tobacconists' kiosk where he spoke to a young lady who seemed to know him. He addressed her as Val – so Booty realised that she was the crook's girlfriend. Booty pounced at this point and shouted: 'Games up, Slinky!' he yelled, and suddenly, the copper had Slinky's hands behind his back and the handcuffs went on them. The criminal at large seemed stunned, but then he grinned.

'So, Slinky, your brother is doing time for you, eh?' Booty said with a smug expression. 'I've got you taped lad; come on, let's take a little walk to the station.'

'I will always love you Val, please remember me,' Slinky said to Val at the window of the kiosk – and then his face seemed to go quite pale, and his eyes glistened as if they were brimming with tears. He then vanished into thin air. The handcuff's hit the pavement with a jangling sound. Val and the policeman looked at one another in shock. Booty slowly bent down and picked the handcuffs up, and then in shock he asked Val: 'Where did he go?'

At that moment, Slinky Edwards died from a heart condition in hospital. He'd taken ill the week before in his cell and had been transferred to Walton Hospital, where his condition deteriorated. The detective who had assured Booty that Slinky was in the nick was not aware of the prisoner's transferral to hospital. Sometimes ill and dying people can project a ghostly twin of themselves – or a *doppelganger* as we call such unearthly doubles in the world of the occult, and I believe that Slinky Edwards had loved Val so much, he had visited her in spirit as he hovered between this world and the next.

THINGS UNKNOWN

In my study I have a large purple folder marked "Things Unknown" and it is crammed with some of the strangest reports of supernatural phenomena I've ever come across. There are currently some seventy-odd cases in the folder detailing bizarre incidents of a paranormal nature that have remained inexplicable to me; they have defied every explanation offered by myself and others, and this chapter touches on just a small selection of these insoluble cases.

The strange incident which was to cause so many nightmares took place in the July of 2011, on a Sunday morning around 5.15am. Two university students in their early twenties – Kelsea and Liv – had been to a party on Gambier Terrace which had started at 8pm on Saturday night and had ended at 5am the next morning. The girls decided to walk the mile to their tiny flat on Benson Street (off Renshaw Street, not far from the casino), and they were feeling groggy but not intoxicated. Neither of the girls used drugs and neither of them even smoked. Liv was looking forward to doing a big fry-up for breakfast, and Kelsea was texting her Polish boyfriend Kaspar on her iPhone. It was a quiet sunny Sunday morning and the girls were certainly not thinking of anything remotely supernatural. As the students turned right into Pilgrim Street from Upper Duke Street, Liv thought she saw someone very tall in some type of long black robe at the Mount Street junction a hundred yards away flit from right to left at an alarmingly fast speed, but when Kelsea looked up from her mobile to see what her friend was referring to the figure had gone. Liv was nearsighted – objects within three or four feet were crystal clear, but anything beyond that was a bit fuzzy and out of focus, and Kelsea told her friend she had probably seen an urban fox.

'Foxes aren't black,' Liv replied, irritated at the ridiculous suggestion, 'and they aren't over six feet tall either.'

'This predictive text is doing my head in!' Kelsea growled at her phone as she composed the text message.

The couple walked on along Pilgrim Street through the morning stillness and when they were some 30 yards from Hardman Street, something terrifying took place. Near number 2 Pilgrim Street, the weird apparition of a very strange-looking being came out of a wall. It was roughly cone shaped, black, about seven feet in height, and it had a terrifying grotesque pale face at the end of a neck that curved like the handle of a walking stick. The long arms of the unearthly entity reached out for Liv, and she screamed, turned and ran. Kelsea backed away in utter shock, and for a moment she could not move her legs. The weird thing did not to seem to have any legs, and it slid along the cobbled road towards her, and Kelsea thought she heard it emit a hissing sound. Liv looked back and saw two tentacles protruding from the back of the unknown creature in addition to its outstretched arms. Kelsea suddenly managed to move her legs and ran off screaming with the thing in close pursuit. The students fled up Hope Place, and when they reached Hope Street they waved their arms and whistled at a Hackney cab which had pulled up outside the London Carriage Works Hotel. The girls got into the cab, out of breath, and before one of them could speak to the driver, he said: 'What in God's name is that?' as he looked out the nearside window. The uncanny black funnel-shaped entity was coming up Hope Place with a sliding motion. Kelsea begged the cabby to drive off, and he seemed to be spooked by the thing and after swearing, he drove away. The traffic lights outside the Philharmonic Hall on Hope Street were on red, but when the driver saw the conical monstrosity in his rear view mirror as it emerged from Hope Place, he jumped the lights without an iota of hesitation. The girls looked back through the rear window of the Hackney cab and they lost sight of the nightmarish being as it got as far as the Philharmonic public house. The Hackney swerved left as it passed the Everyman Theatre and continued down Mount Pleasant, and the driver talked incessantly about the surreal but scary conoid, and although he repeatedly asked the girls what it was, neither of the students could finish a sentence of explanation because the cabby kept talking over them and he constantly glanced out his kerbside window as if he thought it might come out of one of the side streets. After dropping the students off, the taxi driver refused to take any money from them, and he said he was going to get as far away as he could from the area. He seemed more shaken than the girls.

Liv emailed me on the following day with her version of the strange incident, and I visited the students and quizzed them separately. I interviewed Liv at the flat and Kelsea was interviewed at a local café. Their stories matched perfectly, and I asked both students to try and sketch the thing that had attacked and chased them during the interviews. The sketches were almost identical. I contacted a certain taxi firm and explained who I was and what had happened, and within a few days the very taxi driver who had rescued the girls that morning – a very down to earth man in his twenties – got in touch. His story backed up the testimony of the girls and his sketch only differed slightly from the ones made by Liv and Kelsea; they had drawn the entity with an arched neck that was almost like an upside-down U, but the cabby had only seen the being from the front, so the neck to him looked normal. I recognised the being as soon as it was described to me. That same entity – or something belonging to the same species of that unknown creature - was seen back in 1968 in a fog on Canning Street, where it chased a group of children from Toxteth when they came out of a nearby sweetshop. One of the children was so scared by the thing as it tried to grab him, he suffered a fit and fainted. The child was later found to be epileptic, and his mother said her lad had never suffered a seizure before that encounter, but students dressing up to stage some hoax were predictably blamed – but no one ever owned up to staging such a weird prank, and the children all swore that the thing had come out of a solid wall at Number 2 Canning Street and had seemed to float a few inches off the ground as it closed in on them. A car travelling along the street slowed to avoid running into the freakish being. The children were chased as far as the corner of Blackburne Place, where the thing vanished into thin air, and the boy who had actually fallen under the base of the cone-shaped entity was found unconscious on Hope Street when some of the children dared to retrace their steps.

What is the nature of the creature and where does it come from? Modern physicists tell us that there are many other dimensions in this universe beyond the one we live in, and heaven knows what inhabits those dimensions. We have child molesters and killers on our plane of existence, and perhaps the intelligences that reside in higher dimensions have similar miscreants who have the advantage of being able to appear (to our limited senses anyway) out of thin air when they attack. These things also go to ground awfully fast, perhaps by returning from whence they came through some type of portal. They would be able to prey on us as an angler preys on fishes, simply removing them from their everyday world of water to the unknown region above the waterline. To us, the higher dimension of the predator is the equivalent to the world above the fish's waterline. Hopefully the beings of these other neighbouring regions of time and space have some sort of police force to deal with these ethereal malefactors. I believe the next two cases are probably the work of someone or something unknown which preys on the most vulnerable form of the human – the child.

Many have passed the unremarkable cul de sac which exists between two elegant Georgian houses on Woolton's Vale Road without giving it a second glance. It is a blind alley some 35 feet in length where local residents park their cars, but this quotidian impasse has something of a sinister supernatural history. In the summer of 1982, a 10-year-old boy named Robin Fairhurst left his home on Menlove Avenue with his beloved brand new leather Olympic Match football tucked under his arm. He was heading to his friend Barry's house on Quarry Street, and as he walked up Vale Road, he saw something that delighted him – that cul-de-sac I mentioned earlier was now the entrance to a sprawling fairground. Robin could see the red and white helter-skelter, the Ferris wheel, a merry-go-round, and what looked like a big top tent in the distance. Waltz music jangled away, mingled with children's excited voices, and the sweet smell of freshly-spun candy floss hung in the air. At the end of the cul-de-sac was the turnstile to this funfair extraordinaire and standing in front of it was a very tall and sparely-built woman in a pink knee-length dress and a matching pink shark tooth-pattern jacket. On her head she wore a strange round carnation-pink hat, and upon her rather big feet, this rummy individual wore pale pink loafers. She was pushing a rather vintage pram with a hood towards spellbound Robin and she stopped, turned the pram so the boy could see that a monkey with a weird, almost human-like face was sitting in the perambulator, wearing a flower petal bonnet. At closer quarters, Robin noticed that the odd woman had a prominent pointed nose, and with excitement in her voice she said to him, 'Come to the fair! Come on!'

Robin stepped back – there was something quite not right about the tall lady, but she sprang forward with lightning agility and before the lad could turn to flee, she dragged him by his collar backwards, and he dropped the ball and screamed. She carried him by his ankles so he was suspended upside down, and as she walked along, Robin felt the abductor's bony knees knock against the back of his head. Robin cried out for his mum and shrieked, 'Help! She's taking me away!' All of a sudden, a huge fat man in what looked like a purple boiler suit came out of nowhere and grappled with the weird woman. There was a scuffle, and the abductor lost her grip and Robin fell, spraining his arm. He got up, and before he ran for his life, he saw that a clown in a purple suit with a massive pot belly was fighting with the woman and the language he was hurling at her was very rude. That clown had been the obese man Robin had seen upside down as the outlandish woman dangled him. The boy started to cry as he ran home, and he bumped into his parents as they returned from a shopping trip on Menlove Avenue. Robin told his parents what had happened, and when his dad went to the cul-de-sac, he found his son's burst football. It had been punctured more than a dozen times with a knife. There was no sign of any fairground, but Mr Fairhurst thought he could detect the sweet aroma of candyfloss, as described by his son. This is just one of a myriad of strange happenings that have taken place in that dead-end alley. A smiling clown in a yellow outfit, described as resembling the fast food firm McDonalds mascot Ronald McDonald, was seen juggling multicoloured balls at the end of the Vale Road cul-de-sac in 2010, and when two young children went to walk down the alleyway to him, their mother, sensing the clown was sinister, dragged her children back. The woman's husband investigated the alleyway minutes later and saw no one. What was undoubtedly the weird pink lady was last seen as recently as 2013, dancing in the alleyway with an unknown man in a dark blue suit. When a local man tried to take a picture of the bizarre-looking couple, they vanished into thin air. About an hour after this, the walls in the dead end alley were found to be covered with chalked eerie-looking smiley type faces. I am currently investigating claims that the pink lady has been seen in other parts of Woolton. Who she is I do not know, but she seems to come and go as she pleases – but what does she want? I feel there is an eerie similarity to the phantom fairground of Woolton in the following strange account.

On the Saturday evening of July 14 1973, at around 7.10pm, a 30-year-old man named Brian Jones was watching a film, *The Great St. Trinian's Train Robbery*, on TV at his aunt's flat on the 20th floor of Entwistle Heights, a hi-rise tower block in Toxteth. Brian's aunt asked him to bring a bottle of cider and a few glasses in from the kitchen, and when Brian happened to glance out the kitchen window, he noticed an illuminated merry-go-round revolving in the middle of one of the acres of rubble where whole rows of streets had been bulldozed to make room for new housing projects. Brian thought it was odd how a merry-go-round was there but no other rides, and he assumed that the other attractions of a fairground would turn up tomorrow, but when he looked out the window half an hour later, the whirling carousel had vanished without a trace. People on the ground who saw the mysterious merry-go-round that evening from closer quarters had stranger tales to tell about the out-of-place amusement ride. Kevin and Julie – a brother and sister aged 12 and 15 respectively, had left the nearby Myrtle House tenements that evening and were on their way to their cousin's home off Lodge Lane, when they saw the merry-go-round in the middle of the bleak wasteground off Upper Parliament Street, and they noticed a few other bizarre things as well. First, no one was on any of the carousel's horses, and there were two real white horses close to the rotating structure, and they were standing on their hind legs and seemed to be dancing to the jangling waltz music issuing from the whirling merry-go-round. Then Julie pointed to two stray mongrel dogs about thirty yards away; the canines, like the horses, were standing on their back legs and moving in a surreal dreamlike manner as if they were dancing. Julie thought the dancing animals were amusing but Kevin was spooked by the spectacle and he urged his sister to go around the barren wasteground rather than cross it and pass close to the eerie merry-go-round; instead, Julie marched off towards the lonely fairground ride – and all of a sudden, the waltz music issuing from it turned into a loud metallic sound – and then the merry-go-round and the dancing animals disappeared in an instant, leaving nothing but the echo of the strange cacophony to prove it had been there.

I mentioned the incident on the *Billy Butler Show* and I received other reports of the phantom carousel and more dancing animals, including cats which seemed to do the quickstep. One listener named Steve – who was aged 10 at the time of the ghostly carousel incident - said he actually touched the pole of the merry-go-round, but had the intense unsettling sensation that someone inside the fairground machine was watching him, ready to pounce, and so Steve ran off, overcome with a feeling of impending doom.

When he looked back from a safe distance, the merry-go-round was nowhere to be seen. The whole sinister incident remains a mystery. Sometimes the *thing unknown* does not hide itself, as it did with the ethereal merry-go-round case; sometimes these denizens from elsewhere come out of the woodwork and openly stalk their prey. This happened on Gateacre's Cuckoo Lane in the winter of 2010, when a 13-year-old girl named Izzy was on her way home through heavy snowfall after spending most of Sunday at the home of her friend Libby. The time was around 9pm, and as Izzy was trudging through a blanket of snow near Siskin Green, she saw a very strange-looking man coming towards her up Cuckoo Lane. He had on a tall hat, similar to a topper, except that it tapered in a bit at the top. This hat and the coat – which had hammer tails – and the thin trousers the man wore, were all dark green. The face of the man – who was about six feet in height - was very unsettling, for he had a very sharp long nose, a pointed chin, and his eyes seemed to have a faint red glow to them. Izzy couldn't see another soul on Cuckoo Lane on this inclement night, and she was quite a distance from her home on Rockbourne Avenue – about 600 yards away in fact. Izzy was wearing a black fleeced hoodie with two teddy bear ears attached to it, and she pulled this hood around her face as she noticed the creepy stranger looking at her. He passed by, his feet crunching the snowy mantle on the pavement, but then Izzy heard this crunching halt; the man had stopped, and then, in a stony monotone voice, the stranger said: 'Izzy. Is that you?'

The girl froze, and her hand in her right coat pocket

felt for her mobile.

The snow-mashing foot falls came her way. 'Izzy, it's me, Griffin – don't you remember me?'

His long nose and those red glowing eyes swung into view as he poked his face into her hood, and he had a ghastly twisted smile. 'It's me! Griffin!' he said.

It all came back in that one stomach-spinning moment; Griffin, the terrifying man who came into her bedroom each night and told her bizarre stories which scared her so much, she wet the bed and screamed her lungs out for her parents. Izzy felt a weakness in her lower legs, and she swore at the unearthly man in green and ran off up Cuckoo Lane, heading north for her home. By the time Izzy reached Gateacre Park Drive, which was much better lit, she had her inhaler in her mouth, and her heart was kicking away in her chest like a frightened horse. She looked back and was relieved to see that Griffin was not there. When Izzy got home, she told her mother Jacqui what had happened. 'You haven't been taking drugs have you, Izzy?' her concerned mother asked.

Izzy was furious at the question and yelled that she hadn't and she swore on her baby brother's life that she was telling the truth, and her grandmother told her off for swearing on an infant's life. Jacqui eventually realised that her daughter apparently *had* met someone strange and she tried to remember the childhood bogeyman Izzy had lived in mortal fear of all those years ago. 'Oh yes, I remember – Mr Griffin – dressed all in green.'

'Yes, him,' said Izzy, 'and he used to tell me horrible stories, and then he'd vanish just before you and dad came into my room.'

'I don't know what to say, Izzy,' the teenager's mother confessed, 'he was just a figment of your imagination – so how can he be real?' Izzy's eyes widened. 'Mum, I swear I met him tonight as I was coming home, and he said "Remember me?" and he knew my name.'

'You've just got a very vivid imagination Isabel,' said the girl's grandmother, seated in the armchair close to the telly. 'You take after your Uncle Len. He used to see a big yellow cat sitting on his bed at night. We couldn't see a thing, though.'

That night, Izzy got into bed and sent a tantalizing text to Libby which said that she'd tell her about something amazing which happened to her earlier on. 'Wot happened?' Libby asked, via a text message. Izzy said she'd tell her friend what happened in the morning. At some point after that she began to doze off when she heard his voice – the voice that was unmistakably Mr Griffin's – and it came from under the bed.

'Izzy, is it okay if I come out?' said the paranormal pest below the terrified teen. The girl got out the bed, intending to run for the door, and she distinctly felt a clammy hand grab her ankle. She screamed, the hand released its grip, and Izzy ran downstairs, to her mother, who was in the kitchen doing the washing up. Her husband was in bed. 'You and these spiders – ' Jacqui was saying, when Izzy ran into her and cried out. 'It's not a spider! He's in my room! Griffin!'

Jacqui went to her husband, roused him from his slumbers, and together they went into Izzy's room – but the green-attired Mr Griffin was nowhere to be seen. Jacqui slept in her daughter's bed that night, and

Izzy clung on to her mum in the bed, but suddenly became more angry than scared at the return of her childhood bogeyman, and said she wanted him dead. At 4 in the morning, Jacqui's mobile rang, and she answered the 'unknown caller'. A man's voice said: 'So, she wants me dead does she? Well, tell your daughter I will not be bothering her anymore! I will find someone else to be friends with! Good bye and good riddance!'

Jacqui told Izzy it was just someone who had called the wrong number, but she told her the truth in the morning, and since then, Izzy has not seen Mr Griffin – whoever he is – but I wonder if he has found someone else 'to be friends with' now?

I have touched on vampires many times in my books, including this one, under the chapter 'Some Walk By Day', and what appears to have been a vampiric being of some sort features in the following story, which is in turn rooted in a bit of obscure vampire history concerning a ghastly murder in Stockholm in 1932.

On a cold but sunny morning in February 1995, the comprehensive school's heating system failed and the pupils were sent home. Three 15-year-old girls from the school, Kerry, Michelle and Siobhan, caught the bus to town, and on Lord Street, Kerry and Michelle compared the contents of their "bum bags" (waist pouches worn at the front) – a bottle of Tippex, pens, tubes of lip balm, dinner and bus fare money and a bottle of that ubiquitous perfume – Dewberry oil – purchased from The Body Shop. The girls went into Stationery Box to get one of those new pens that contained a roll of paper you tore out to make notes on, and while the trio were in there, Siobhan noticed *that* man again. He was tall with short white hair, a long dark blue coat, and he possessed a pair of the most sinister eyes she'd ever seen behind yellow-tinted spectacles. She had seen him five times now in different places ranging from Huyton to Bold Street, and he always seemed to be fixated by Kerry, yet he looked old enough to be her father. He stood in the shop, and he angled his head back, closed his eyes, and sniffed the air near Kerry, when she noticed him too. When the girls left Stationery Box they soon realised the creepy man was following them. Siobhan stopped a policeman and went to point out the stalker – but he suddenly wasn't there.

The schoolgirls visited Quiggins – a hub of alternative shopping in the city - on School Lane, and here, Michelle and Siobhan discovered that Kerry was missing. Kerry had always said that her friend Michelle and she had some weird telepathic bond of the kind that is said to exist between identical twins, and sure enough Michelle said she felt as if Kerry was in grave danger and she had a strong impression of Derby Square at the end of Lord Street. The girls went to this location, and there was Kerry, walking hand in hand with the tall wiry stalker! The two girls shouted to their friend but Kerry seemed oblivious to their cries, and she walked on with the creepy man towards James Street railway station. A black transit van came tearing up Castle Street and braked hard in front of the girls, blocking their way. Two men, both of them aged about thirty, got out of this van and bundled the girls into the vehicle, and Michelle and Siobhan screamed, thinking they were being kidnapped. Inside the van, one of the men said to the scared girls, 'Don't worry, we're part of the police. The man who has taken your friend is a real-life vampire. It sounds far-fetched, I know, but it's the truth. We've been watching him since he arrived in Liverpool. It's safer if we tackle him – he'd kill you two like that,' he warned, and snapped his fingers. 'We'll get your friend back, but first we'll have to get you two out of harm's way.'

Siobhan and Michelle were dropped off on Dale Street. They went home to tell their parents what had happened and Kerry turned up at her home in the afternoon at around 4pm. She looked and sounded as if she was sedated, and she said a type of "Vampire Police" had taken that man who had stalked her into custody, but then he had escaped again. Kerry had been kept at an underground room where doctors in white coats had examined her and quizzed her about the man who had taken her away, but she had not been able to recall anything about the man. The doctors said the man – who was an actual vampire - had used hypnosis on her and that he had killed women and children in the past to obtain type AB blood – which was Kerry's type – and one of the "policemen" mentioned a 1932 murder case involving the alleged vampire. Kerry then burst into tears and fainted into her father's arms. When she came to, a doctor was called out to look at her and he said he could find nothing wrong with her (and there were certainly no bite-marks on the girl's neck or any other part of her body). Kerry suffered recurring nightmares about the man who had tried to abduct her for many years, and sometimes she would see what looked like a tattoo on the man's left wrist in these disturbing dreams. The tattoo was of a circle with an unknown symbol at its centre with a cross mounted on the top of the circle. It reminded Kerry of the old trademark for Harris Tweed, but the significance of this symbol is unknown, and just who the abductor was, is unknown. Equally mysterious are the Vampire Police. As far as I'm aware, the police forces of the United Kingdom have never had a specialist unit to deal with the supernatural, and vampires in particular. The mention of a 1932 case involving the purported vampire may be a reference to the baffling Lilly Lindeström case. On 4 May 1932, the naked body of Lilly Lindeström, a 32-year-old prostitute, was found in her apartment in the Atlas area of Stockholm, Sweden. She was lying face down on the bed and her head had been bashed in. It was believed that a sexual act had been carried out between Lilly and her murderer, and a condom was protruding from the woman's anus. The body of Lilly had been drained of blood, and traces of the prostitute's blood were found on a ladle. Police deduced that the killer had murdered Lilly Lindeström some 2-3 days before, and had consumed every drop of her blood after the murder, using the ladle. The killer was calm and composed enough to fold the prostitute's clothes on a chair after the murder, and he had left the apartment so quietly after his awful deed, Lilly's next door neighbour Minnie had not heard a sound. The hardboiled streetwise police investigating the case thought that there was something almost supernatural about the seemingly vampiric killer – who was never found.

The Augustus John Pub, situated on the campus of Liverpool University (who also own the establishment) has been mentioned in my books a few times over the years because of some spooky things that have taken place on its premises, but I only recently received a number of reports from past regulars of yet another strange supernatural incident which took place at the pub. Today, Rob Clive is a retired Architect, but in the 1970s he attended Liverpool University, studying architecture, and he was a regular at the Augustus John pub, which had opened three years before in 1967. On the Friday evening of 18 September 1970, Rob bumped into his brother-in-law, James Durham - a senior management accountant at a well-known public company – at the pub, and the two men started to chat when all of a sudden, a flash of yellowish green light lit up the bar to Rob's right. He turned, and in full view of the student architect, his brother-in-law, and the dozen or so drinkers, a very strange figure resembling a doll of a clown ran across the counter of the bar for about five feet, and then vanished. The clown had on a small white hat – possibly cone shaped – a frilly white ruffled collar, a baggy pink one-piece outfit (not all that unlike a modern-day "onesie"), a pair of red gloves, and a pair of over-sized black shoes. The face of the clown was white, with small dots for eyes, but the mouth was black and smiling. Rob said that the clown had lifted its arms before it vanished and kicked its right leg into the air. As the entity ran along the length of the bar it had faced its startled audience of students and lecturers. When Rob and James told people about the strange incident the predictable explanations of drinks spiked with LSD and seeing pink elephants were offered. An electrician named Raymond Worth who was present in the pub that day also emailed me in September 2017 and said that he had seen the clown close up, and it had seemed lifelike and not at all like a doll – only in its small stature. 'It was about three feet tall, maybe a bit smaller,' recalled Raymond, 'and it came out of nowhere. My girlfriend was standing by me and she said there was a flash of light before the thing appeared. She thought it was a puppet at first but realised it would be impossible for someone to pull strings and operate it in a bar – and how did it appear then disappear in front of so many witnesses?'

Just why a miniature clown should haunt a bar is unknown, and we'll probably never know just what the entity was.

And finally, I must close this chapter with an account of one of the most touching *things unknown* in my folder, and this is the childish oddity who befriended a boy in Liverpool in the 1970s. Here's the strange story.

'Mam, I love someone and he's not a girl,' said 11-year-old Tony O'Hare as he spooned down Ambrosia rice pudding one teatime in August 1976. His mum Julie was stuck for words. 'His name's Zee and he's not from Earth,' Tony explained, and his mother rolled her eyes and watched the *Magic Roundabout* on the telly. Her husband Mick was in his y-fronts in a deckchair in the backyard of the terraced Everton house soaking up the sun. Like millions of other Brits, Mick was enjoying the hottest summer since records began. Julie's eyes turned from the television to a rarity in Britain – the blue sky. Her eyes dwelt on the almost spiritual blueness behind the net curtains.

'Mam! Mam!' Tony tapped his mother's arm, breaking the cobweb reverie. 'Mam, will you listen?

Zee is only able to come here because of the hot weather. His world has come into ours a bit. Mam!'

'Tony, will you stop talking daft!' Mrs O'Hare snapped. 'And go and play in the park instead of playing on that wasteground! Your pumps are destroyed playing there!'

'Mam, why won't you ever listen?' Tony asked in a musical, groaning voice.

'Stop mithering me Tony!' his mother snapped, picked up the broadsheet *Liverpool Echo* and not having her reading spectacles at hand, she looked at the print close up, her nose almost touching the paper.

In a huff, Tony left the table and crossed the road onto the "oller" – ancient Scouse slang for "the hollow" – a rectangle of rubble where the other side of the street had stood, now covered in dandelions, bricks and rotten timber. But when Tony stepped onto this ground, he entered a land of wonder, as far as the eye could see. There was Camelot, shimmering in the north, and straight ahead stood a sleek rocket-ship, glinting in the sun. The men in green and brown in the distance were Robin Hood and his Merry Men, and there were cowboys here too, and dragons, and there, sitting cross-legged on the big red and black polka-dot toadstool was Zee, the greatest friend Tony ever had! He ran to his peculiar little companion, and hugged him. Zee asked why all the houses in Tony's street looked the same. Tony shrugged. An ice cream motor came down the street to the glockenspiel melody of *Greensleeves*, and Zee seemed mesmerised by it. He wanted to try an ice cream, and Tony willingly spent the last of his pocket money on a Ninety-niner for him. When he came back onto the oller, Zee excitedly took the ice cream, tasted it, and then, after a quiet pause of stock-still time, he burst into tears. 'Cold!' he wailed, and handed it back to Tony. He wiped the chilling cream from his wide thick lips and said, 'We have warm ones.'

'How can you have warm ice cream?' Tony laughed, and immediately started to eat the vanilla.

'Oh!' Zee exclaimed, and becoming annoyed at the question he did a strange dance, hopping on his black boots as he turned around.

Tony bit off the handle end of the cornet and sucked the ice cream through it with immense satisfaction on his face as Zee exclaimed, 'Yokker!'

A ladybird landed on Tony's fringe, and Zee let out a ghastly scream upon seeing the red bug, and he turned and ran at a phenomenal speed across meadows, vanishing into the distance. When he returned much later, Zee explained that the ladybugs had caused some disaster in his world a long time ago and were much feared.

The two friends from different worlds walked miles into the Secret Land and enjoyed many adventures together. Time moved ever so slowly on that hidden world on the 'oller. But eventually it was time to go, signalled by the echoing yodel of Tony's mother calling her son home. Zee was always so sad when he heard this call, and he'd always walk with Tony to the grey edge of the make-believe world where the earthboy's dreary home stood. Zee's childhood would last another fifty of our years, Tony recalled as he went home. Day after day in those summer school holidays, Tony would rush breakfast and head for the oller, and sometimes his dog Patch went there with him, and when the dog did enter the Secret Land, Zee was somehow able to communicate with the canine by some odd-sounding language. Patch loved the fantastical boy as much as Tony, and Zee said he himself had a pet called Omlic but he was bigger than an elephant and too dangerous to 'bring over'.

Tony knew the extraordinary friendship wouldn't last forever, but he always kept this dark thought at the back of his mind. Then one day Zee burst into tears and said his world was drifting apart from Tony's one. 'The temperatures will fall soon,' Zee predicted, 'and it'll be bye-bye. Please don't be friends with anyone else Tony.'

'I won't,' Tony promised, feeling so choked up, 'cross my heart and hope to die.'

A drizzle fell upon Liverpool on the Saturday afternoon of August 28 that year in 1976, and Tony ran onto the 'oller, where no one even noticed him talking to what they assumed to be a make-believe friend. Zee was shaking as he clung onto Tony, and he looked in horror at the fine droplets of water appearing on him and his friend. Fortunately, the shower ended and the drought and the cruel blowtorch heat of the sun continued to bake the land. The two worlds of the boys became stable again.

Two days later, Tony's dad came home from work, stripped down to a pair of khaki Army and Navy shorts, and began slapping olive oil on his arms legs and chest as his wife took the deckchairs into the back "garden" - which was actually three square feet of lawn in the back yard.

'They said there'll be showers today, love,' he told Julie, looking at the reflection of his pot belly in the glass of the kitchen door. 'They always get it wrong, the weathermen.'

'You're gonna cook yourself alive putting olive oil on, you daft thing,' Julie warned him, and went to fetch the cans of lager.

'Showers?' said Tony, sitting on the sofa in the living room, sketching Zee from memory with a felt-tip pen.

'Yeah,' said his father in a dismissive downward tone, 'and pigs might fly. It's getting warmer in my opinion. There'll be palm trees growing in this garden soon, I'm telling you.'

Tony was relieved to hear this, but on the telly teatime news, there were reports of flooding from heavy rains down in Exeter. The weathermen, however, warned the public that the end of the drought was still some way off and that water rationing was still in force. It seemed as if the summer demon was determined to scorch the UK till November at least, but then for Tony and Zee, the end came without warning. Tony awoke on a September morning in his bed to the sound of rain pattering against his window, and he quickly put on his sky-blue tee shirt, navy shorts and black scuffed pumps, and he ran downstairs. His mother was singing *September in the Rain* as she stood in the doorway of her kitchen, looking out at the rain soaking the deckchairs. 'Well, that was a summer we'll talk about for years,' she said to Tony without turning to face him, and he said nothing. He was out the front door in seconds. He ran across the road to the expanses coloured by brown crumbled brick, sun-faded grass and dandelions that were being sniped by the heavy rain. Down the street, a gaggle of girls were screaming and laughing as the rain soaked them, but people came out of their houses and started cheering at the cool downpour.

And at Summer's end, the rains fell, and the bronzed people of the street chanted "Hooray!", and Tony stood in the centre of the 'oller in tears. 'Zee!' he cried, the rainwater running in rivulets down his face, joining the tear tracks. 'Zee! Where are you?'

The Secret Land was nowhere to be seen – just a desolate Marscape. No Camelot, no Sherwood Forest, just bleakness.

'A faint reply reached Tony's ears from somewhere that was getting more and more distant. *Tony! Tony!*'

'Zee! Where are you?'

There was no reply, and Tony waited until his tee shirt and shorts clung to him like wet tissue, and then he started to sob. He felt something touch the back of his rain-slicked calf, and he turned with glowing expectation – but it was a drenched Patch with a pair of sorrowful eyes looking up at him. The dog seemed to be missing Zee too.

There came a faint nursery chorus from the girls on the street behind him which razored his heart. *'It's raining, it's pouring, the old man is snoring, he went to bed and he bumped his head and he couldn't get up in the morning!'*

Tony and his dog went home, and his mother immediately threw a towel over his dripping head and declared: 'You're going to catch your death of pneumonia! What did you go out in that for?'

In shock, the boy replied, 'Mam, I'll never see Zee ever again,' but she didn't hear a word he said.

September and October were the wettest months on record, and yet Patch would run out of the house almost every day and go to the place where Zee had talked to him. Tony would be heartbroken as he yanked a whining Patch away from the 'oller, and as the years went by, the memory of the remarkable friend remained in his memory. He dared to tell a few people about Zee, and they all said the same thing – that he was an imaginary friend – a mere figment, but Tony says he had no imagination as a child and could not have dreamed up any imaginary playmate. What was Zee? Some being from a dimension which temporarily overlapped our one because of freak weather conditions? Someone from outer space? Tony hasn't a clue, and although he is now an adult and the father of three children, he still often travels back in his mind to those far-off sunny days of 1976 when he met, then lost, the greatest friend he ever had.

THE MAN AT THE SIDE OF THE BED

In January 2012 I received an email from Laura, a 26-year-old woman living at a certain semi-detached house on Walton's Graylands Road, just a stone's throw from Walton Hall Park. Laura told me how, one morning at around 3.10am in December 2011, she awoke in her double bed to see a man leaning at the side of her as he looked at her face from about 10-12 inches away. He was Caucasian, appeared to have no clothes on and had black curly centre-parted hair, very dark beady eyes, and prominent eyebrows which almost met in the middle. Laura recoiled in shock at the sight of the naked stranger leaning on the bed so close to her, and she turned to her left to tell her boyfriend Jay, but the bed was empty. Jay was in the toilet and had left the bed just a few minutes ago. When Laura turned to look back at the bedroom intruder she saw he had vanished. She got out of the bed as fast as she could and ran to the toilet. She burst into the toilet and startled Jay, who was washing his hands in the basin. She told him she'd seen a man leaning over her in bed and Jay immediately hurried to the bedroom and saw it was empty. 'You've had a nightmare, Loz [his nickname for Laura],' he said, but Laura insisted she had been awake when she had seen the weird man at the side of the bed. Jay told her the man must have been 'super thin' because he would have had to fit in the small gap of about four inches between the right side of the bed and the wall. Laura was so scared of seeing the sinister entity again, she swapped places with Jay and he slept on her side of the bed. On the second night after the frightening incident, Laura had decided the bedroom 'ghost' must have been a product of some nightmare which had overlapped into her waking mind, and she slept on the right side of the bed again. At around four in the morning she awoke because Jay was snoring loudly as he lay on his back, and Laura was about to tell him to turn onto his side when she saw that eerie man again – and he was in the exact same position as before; he was leaning on the edge of the bed and staring intently at Laura's face.

'Go away!' she cried out, 'Leave me alone!' and she ducked under the blankets and shook her boyfriend hard, startling him out of his slumbers. As Jay woke up, he thought he saw a man run from that narrow gap (between the right side of the bed and the wall) to the wall facing the end of the bed. The figure fled into the wall and vanished, and in the brief time Jay had seen the fleeing figure, it had appeared to him to be naked.

Laura crawled over Jay and almost fell out the bed to get to the light-switch, and then, after turning the bedroom light on, she gazed with a look of horror to the spot where she'd seen the man gazing closely at her, and she screamed and ran out of the bedroom. Jay ran after her, partly because he was concerned about his partner but also because he felt a little unnerved in the bedroom after seeing that figure run into a solid wall. Now he knew that Laura had indeed seen some ghost a few nights ago and it had not been a psychological after-effect from a nightmare. Down in the kitchen, Jay hugged Laura and calmed her down.

He told her that he too had seen the man, and that they should sleep in the living room for the rest of the morning, which they did. Laura slept on the sofa and Jay slept in an armchair with his feet propped up on a dining chair. The couple saw nothing more of the paranormal bedroom invader for the next few weeks. Christmas came and went, and Jay and Laura thought that perhaps the ghost had stopped visiting for some unknown reason, but they slept in the bedroom with a nightlight on all the same.

On the evening of Monday 31 December 2012, Jay and Laura went to town to celebrate the New Year. The couple arrived home, slightly intoxicated, and they went to bed at around two in the morning. Jay was soon snoring, but Laura only managed a few snatches of sleep because she kept getting up to go to the toilet because of the drink; Laura always had interrupted sleep when she'd had alcohol. She returned to bed around 3:10am and soon drifted off into the realms of sleep. She had a strange dream which started with the sound of music being played backwards. It sounded like violins and the arrangement really filled her dreaming mind with fear. This 'backwards music' has been reported to me so many times over the years, and occultists sometimes refer to it as the Devil's Signature Tune, as it seems to be heard just before the dreamer experiences a terrifying nightmare. Laura can only recall parts of the nightmare she had that morning. That man - the one who had appeared at her bedside – featured in it. His head emerged from the solid wall at the far end of the bedroom, and she screamed for jay in the dream but she was alone in bed for some reason. The creepy naked man then ran over to the bed and jumped onto it before he pinned her down. His face came close to Laura's and she found herself unable to move. The eyes of the fiend were bloodshot and the irises were jet black. In a cold monotone voice he told Laura. 'Three women don't like you and they have sent me to tell you that you are going to have the worst luck in the world!'

Laura let out a scream, and she woke up – and *he* was on top of her – the supernatural visitor. Unlike the nightmare, Laura couldn't see his eyes in the darkness, but she felt the weight of the man pressing down on her. She screamed, and suddenly, the figure was gone, and she felt the immense weight of the entity lift off her. Laura's scream awakened Jay but he didn't see the ghost this time, and the room was spinning from the onset of a hangover. Laura went downstairs in a dreadful state, and waited for her boyfriend to follow, but instead she heard his snores echoing in the bedroom upstairs. She had to call Jay on his mobile to wake him up because Laura could not bring herself to step into the bedroom until it was light. When I received the email from Laura, I realised that she and Jay were being visited by a type of incubus which had been encountered at the very same address on Graylands Road back in 1994. I wasn't sure if I should tell Laura and Jay about that case because the couple were frightened enough as it was, but shortly after meeting Laura at the house, she asked me if I'd heard of any similar ghosts haunting her home in the past. My face must have said it all because she asked, 'You know something don't you?'

I admitted that I did, but what I did know was minimal, and I told her and Jay the details of the 1994 case. In October 1994, a couple in their thirties – Carmen and Nathan – rented the house. Carmen taught English at a comprehensive school in Liverpool and Nathan – Carmen's boyfriend of six months – was a commercial artist and visualiser for an advertising firm. Carmen had divorced the year before and had no children, and Nathan had split up with his partner Karen the year before and had a 3-year-old daughter named Molly. Carmen and Nathan both hailed from the Walton area and had decided to live on Graylands Road because the rent was very reasonable, but Carmen had ambitions to move into a house in an affluent south Liverpool suburb in a year or so. In the very same bedroom where Laura and Jay slept in 2012, Carmen and Nathan had slept in a double bed in a slightly different position. Not long after the move to Graylands Road, Carmen began to have a series of terrible nightmares about people in her family dying, and she blamed stress at first for the frightening and very graphic dreams. She also began to experience palpitations at work, and then Nathan began to suffer from hair loss. Nathan shaved his head to tackle what a doctor diagnosed as alopecia, and then the couple's 3-year-old cat died. Bad luck dogged the couple almost every day, and Carmen was diagnosed with a heart murmur and she also began to experience strange stabbing pains behind her ears, in her jaw and in both feet. By late November, Carmen was also experiencing recurrent sore throats, swollen lymph nodes, joint pain, weak muscles, blinding migraines and then, on top of all this, her mother had a heart attack and her younger brother was seriously injured in a car crash. Carmen self-diagnosed her symptoms and believed she had chronic fatigue – a condition that was not even recognised till 1988 – but her doctor said her symptoms sounded more like fibromyalgia – and he sent her to a specialist who tried to tackle Carmen's condition with magnets and electro acupuncture – all to no avail. In early December, Nathan's father died in his sleep from natural causes and then a gifted pupil at Carmen's school was diagnosed with leukaemia. The pupil, a 13-year-old girl had excelled at English and Carmen really admired her because she came from a broken home in an impoverished area of the city and had still managed to write incredible essays.

All of the bad luck piled up, and on Christmas Eve, Carmen finally burst into tears at her home, and she screamed, 'Someone's doing something to me! Some evil bastard!'

'There there, love,' Nathan hugged his partner and then he went to the kitchen, tore off a few feet of the kitchen roll tissue, and hurried back to her. She dabbed her tears and rambled on about her suspicions about something wicked inflicting all of the bad luck upon her. Nathan thought it was all down to paranoia, and he had never seen this side of Carmen before. She usually took the rough and the smooth in her stride and nothing fazed her. 'Everyone has a run of bad luck at some time,' he told Carmen, but she smiled in the midst of her tears and looked at him with a puzzled expression. 'Run of bad luck? This isn't just bad things happening at random,' she said, her eyes reddened with the tears, '*someone* is doing all this to me, and to you as well – your father passing away, our cat dying, my brother nearly dying in a car crash, the girl in my school getting leukaemia – '

'Alright, alright, Carmen, I admit we have had an inordinate amount of bad luck,' Nathan stroked her head. 'But it's just the way life is sometimes – it's just life.'

Carmen shook her head with a dismissive expression. 'This is not "just life" Nathan, I'm telling you, someone's doing something to us, and the bastards are winning.'

'You mean like a curse?' Nathan asked with a painful-looking smile, 'Come on, it's just the law of averages – we all have runs of good and bad luck.'

Carmen disagreed. 'No, it's not. It's something to do with this house, Nathan, I can feel it, ever since we moved in here, things have gone wrong.'

Carmen eventually calmed down, and that night, she slept in Nathan's arms, but at around 3.40 am, she awoke – and saw a man kneeling at her side of the bed, and by the lamp post light shining into the room she saw that the man appeared to be naked, and he had long black hair and a pair of piercing dark eyes like two black buttons. He was staring intently at Carmen as if he was fascinated by her.

'Oh, Nathan!' Carmen screamed at her boyfriend, and he awoke and he too saw the man kneeling on Carmen's side of the bed.

'What the – ' Nathan swore and he jumped out the bed and switched on the light, but there was no one there but Carmen, and she was lying on the bed as she clutched her bosom. Nathan thought she'd suffered a heart attack, especially with her having a murmur, but she was alright – just in shock.

Enough was enough. Carmen and Nathan decided to leave the house and they moved into a one-bedroom flat in the city centre until they could find accommodation elsewhere. Once the couple had moved out of that house on Graylands Road, their troubles seemed to evaporate. The fibromyalgia literally ceased – something the condition could never do – and the pupil in Carmen's class made a slow but sure recovery from leukaemia. The couple never returned to Walton, and a family that moved into their former home on Graylands Road left after a few weeks and told the landlord that the place was haunted but did not specify what had caused them to vacate the house. The landlord visited the family and tried to convince them that the place had no ghost, but as he talked to the family in the living room, something in the bedroom above knocked heavily on the floor three times – and yet the family and the landlord knew that there was no one upstairs. When the landlord went upstairs, he saw a very strange sight. A glowing 60-watt bulb was suspended in mid-air, about seven inches below its socket. There was no way electricity could make that bulb light up because it was not in contact with any wires. As the landlord tried to comprehend what he was seeing, the bulb fell, and went out before it smashed on the linoleum floor.

When Laura and Jay heard my account of the eerie history of the house, they decided to get a place elsewhere. Laura asked me about the strange dream in which the ghostly visitor had told her that three women had sent him; who were these three women? I told her it was easy to surmise that the women were occultists or witches practising Black Magic, but this was just supposition. They might have been three people known to Laura, out to wreck her life for reasons known only to them, or they might have been three dead women operating from the spirit world. It was fruitless to speculate, but it did seem that whoever or whatever was responsible, the object of the entire exercise was to get the couple out of that house on Graylands Road. I get reports of incubi and succubi (female demon-like entities) every now and then, and many of them start by appearing at the side of the victim's bed, where they peer intently at their prey. Some people experience terrible 'out-of-character' nightmares – bad dreams that stand out because they are truly terrifying and particularly horrific – when the incubus is visiting. I recall a case in Bootle where a 22-year-old woman awoke from her sleep one night because she had somehow sensed someone was in her room as she was asleep. She opened her eyes and there was a naked man leaning over her on the right side of her bed. His eyes were like two huge grey disks and his mouth was wide open as if he was in awe of her. The woman screamed and the figure stood up and vanished, but he came back on many occasions, sometimes night after night, and on some occasions the entity clawed at the woman's back as she lay in bed, leaving long red scratch-marks. The final straw came when the woman awoke one morning and felt as if she had been sexually violated by the sinister night visitant as she had slept. The woman explained what had happened to her priest and he let her sleep in a spare room at his house next to the local church. I have a feeling that the incubus of Graylands Road will be active again at some time in the near future...

THE MINIKINS ARE COMING

Inexplicable nocturnal sounds are doing the rounds again in the North West, including Knowsley, Liverpool and parts of Wirral. I have received numerous reports of an annoying low-pitched hum which sometimes sounds like a swarm of hyperactive bees behind the walls of the dwelling when it's heard indoors and at other times the unidentified sound is reminiscent of a diesel engine idling in the distance. This sound has been heard all over the country and even beyond our shores, and not only in the 21st century either; it was heard in the 1970s, 1960s, 1950s and there is even a report in the now-defunct *Manchester City News*, dated 8 May, 1878, which calls the enigmatic humming sound plaguing North England "the hummadruz". In recent years, the ubiquitous hum has been followed by some very strange phenomena – people have been awakened by it in the dead of night to find themselves completely paralyzed, and whilst they are in this state of immobility, some bizarre and frightening things have happened to some victims which defy our logic. At a house on Kingsway, Huyton, on the Thursday night of 17 September 2009 at 11.40pm, a 27-year-old hairdresser named Bethany Aries was watching *Dragon's Den*, the TV series about entrepreneurs presenting their products, when she dozed off on the sofa. She awoke around midnight, and set the burglar alarm, turned every light out except the one on the landing, then went up to her bedroom carrying her young housecat Rio. The cat usually curled up on the duvet, but tonight for some reason, he opted to sleep in his basket in the corner of the bedroom. Bethany became aware of a low-frequency sound in the bedroom, and so she checked the plug-points, thinking she had left one of the power-chargers of her mobile or iPad on. The transformers in these chargers often emitted a barely audible buzz, but they were all switched off. Bethany decided the hum was coming from somewhere outside, and she relaxed back into the bed, and was soon sleeping soundly. She awoke at around 4:20am and immediately noticed that the bed was bathed in a soft green light – and she also became aware of the humming sound she had heard earlier and it was now much louder. Bethany tried to yawn – but she could not move a muscle – only her eyes, and moving them took some effort. Panic gripped the hairdresser as she wondered if she had suffered a stroke, but then she saw something which made her think she was still dreaming. A bizarre little figure which resembled a doll with a disproportionately large bald head stepped into her field of vision on her left, and its little feet trod on her shoulder as it walked over the bed. The weird miniature humanoid was about fifteen inches in height, and of an olive green colour. Bethany had the natural urge to get out of that bed and run, but she couldn't move. She suddenly regained the ability to move her head slightly, and she looked to the right, and saw another little green entity sitting on the right side of her chest. The eyes of the doll-size being were black with golden specks in the middle, and to Bethany, there was something feminine about the face of the unearthly entity, which was touching her hands (which were resting on her chest). A third figure, out of sight because it was behind Bethany's head, was running its tiny hand over her nose and lips. Bethany opened her mouth slightly, trying to scream out for help, but found she could not make a sound, and the little green hand gripped her lips and her front teeth. The hand felt warm. The dwarfish green figure who she had noticed first suddenly turned around and he was holding a rod with a ball at one end, and he was prodding Bethany's upper arm with this sphere at the end of the rod. This figure had masculine features and smiled at her in an unnatural way that made her flesh creep. The face seemed artificial and plastic in appearance. This diminutive intruder suddenly started speaking in some unintelligible language to the feminine being seated on Bethany's chest. The babble sounded similar to Welsh to Bethany, but it was spoken at a fast rate and was very monotonic. The three toy-sized beings explored Bethany's face, hands and arms for what seemed like an hour, and then they walked to the edge of the bed and jumped off. About a minute after this, Rio the cat leaped onto the bed, startling Bethany – who discovered that she had regained the ability to move.

Bethany Aries got out of that bed, turned on the main ceiling light, and looked at the floor, expecting to see the little pygmy-like trio, but they were nowhere to be seen. Bethany was so shaken by the strange incident, she tried to sleep on the sofa down in the lounge but her nerves remained on edge and she was unable to get a wink of shut eye. Later that day, she told Amanda, a close friend at the hairdressing and beauty salon about the weird figures and the paralysis, but she assured Bethany she had been overtired and had been dreaming she was awake – having a very realistic lucid dream which she had mistaken for a real incident. Bethany was absolutely sure the invasion of her bed by the three little people had not been a dream, although she could not explain what they were, and she hoped she'd never see them again. Amanda advised Bethany to get a man in her life again, and somehow suggested that the alleged dream had been caused by Bethany being nervous about sleeping on her own. Months later, on Christmas Eve 2009, Bethany went to bed at precisely midnight, and at this time she was seeing a man named Scott, who worked as a nurse at a residential care home in Liverpool. He was working through the night till eight in the morning, and Bethany texted him a long romantic message, then turned the bedside lamp off and fell fast asleep.

She awoke at 3:20 am. Not only did the hairdresser feel cold – she also felt a sharp pulsating pain in the big toe of her left foot. As she opened her eyes, Bethany saw that same greenish light she had seen four months back when she had encountered those little people, and she heard that distinctive humming sound again. The duvet was not on her, and when she looked towards the bottom of the bed, she saw two of those diddy green people kneeling at her left foot, and one of them was hitting her big toe with what looked like a tiny ice pick. This time, Bethany was not frozen with that frightening paralysis and she kicked at the little figures, knocking them clean off the bed. She heard them making high-pitched noises on the floor.

Bethany sprung out of the bed and ran down to the lounge, where she sat, wondering what to do. She didn't fancy telephoning Scott because she thought he'd think she was nuts, so she sat it out till daybreak. Since that yuletide encounter with the little people, Bethany has not seen them, and hopes it stays that way. I told Bethany that I had received many reports of these undersized humanoid pests over the years, but was at a loss to explain just what they were. Bethany was naturally relieved to hear that other people had encountered the creepy little green people.

In August 2017, two night nurses in a Liverpool hospital saw little green-skinned men in orange suits walking about on a patient's bed in a darkened ward, and when one of the nurses tried to take a picture of the beings with her iPhone, the entities vanished. They were described as being about a foot to 14 inches in height, and had large bald heads with skin of a pale green colour. They seemed to have been looking at a female patient on the bed who actually woke up after feeling a tingling sensation in her jaw similar to mild electric shock. The nurses and a security guard waited for the tiny beings to put in an appearance at the hospital on the following night but they didn't show up.

We next move up to Pinehurst Avenue, Brighton Le Sands, in the borough of Sefton, quite close to Crosby, where a teenaged girl was visited by crowd of little green-skinned men of similar height to the ones previously mentioned in this chapter. The incident happened in 2011 on the Tuesday evening of the 25 January – Burns Night, a date when people of mostly Scottish descent commemorate the life of the celebrated Ayrshire poet Robert Burns. The father of the family living on Pinehurst Road was Scottish, and without fail every year he observed Burns Night with a traditional Caledonian dish of Haggis, plenty of whisky, the mandatory reciting of the Burns poem *To A Mouse*, followed by dancing and singing with his wife. On this night, at around 9.30pm, the man's 13-year-old daughter Ava wanted no part in the Burnsian celebrations and she picked up her old cat Pablo and retired to her bedroom where she drowned out the sounds of her father's singing with her vintage record player. The LP on the turntable was the Blur album *Modern Life is Rubbish* 'borrowed' from her mother's vinyl collection, and the track she played was her current favourite: *For Tomorrow*. She texted her best friend Ayesha as she listened to the music, and, not receiving a reply straight away, Ava lay on her bed, propped up with an extra pillow, and decided to whistle to Pablo, but the cat suddenly ran around the room, then scratched at the door to get out. Ava couldn't be bothered getting up to the let the feline out, but then she saw it was ripping up the carpet from the gripper beneath the door, so she swore and went over to open the door. Pablo, despite being twelve years of age, flew out of the room and hurled himself down the stairs. He sometimes went mad like this for no apparent reason, but tonight he seemed scared of something.

Ava went back into the bedroom, slamming the door behind her after being deserted by her cat, and she lay on the bed again and looked at her phone. Still no reply from Ayesha. Then Ava saw something moving out the corner of her left eye, and for a split second she thought it was a small animal. She turned reflexively towards the object, and recoiled in shock. From out of the eight-inch gap between her wardrobe and the wall, a line of little men with green shiny hairless heads and round black button-like eyes came running, and they wore purplish one-piece garments like boiler suits. Ava thinks there might have been about a dozen of the bizarre figures, and they momentarily vanished behind the bottom of the bed, then emerged from the other side and came running towards her making high-pitched sounds of laughter, and now she could gauge their size more clearly. They looked the size of the old Tinky Winky Tellytubby doll she had bought from Oxfam — about fifteen inches in height. Ava jumped onto the bed as the surreal visitors ran towards her, and then she leapt off it and almost ran into the bedroom door. She opened the door and ran down the landing, and she could hear the manic laughter of the little people as they chased her. Ava ran down the stairs, and looked over her shoulder to see the pint-sized pursuers slowing down as they reached the top step. As Ava hurried down the second flight of stairs, she looked up and saw some of the weird dinky beings slowly descending the steps, while the other halted, as if the stairs presented some insurmountable obstacle. Ava burst into the living room, where her father was doing the Highland Fling in an intoxicated state. She ran past him and told her mother what had happened, but her mum couldn't hear her over the CD of an old Scottish reel that was blaring through the speakers. Ava pulled her mother out of the living room and pushed her towards the stairs, and she and the teenager saw the little men on the fourth step down,

But as the mother and daughter looked on, the beings turned and quickly climbed back up the steps and ran in the direction of Ava's bedroom.

Ava went to run up the stairs after them, but her mother became hysterical and her mother grabbed her by the arm and pulled her back. Ava broke free and ran up the stairs and then gingerly entered her bedroom – but there was no sign of the dozen little oddities. Ava noticed that the plug to the record player had been pulled out of the wall socket. Ava heard the music downstairs cease, followed by the sound of her mum and dad having a row. Her mother was trying to give an account of what she had seen but Ava's father said she'd had too much to drink. He eventually came up to Ava's bedroom and she told him what had happened but he was too drunk to take it all in and simply smirked and shook his head.

Ava hardly got any sleep that night because she naturally thought the little people would make another appearance, but they never did, and the family moved out of the house on Pinehurst Avenue in 2016. It will be interesting to see if there are any more reports of these fantastic yet menacing entities in that house.

I feel these 'Minikins' as I label them (for want of a better name), are just curious explorers from another dimension, and perhaps they have been coming here for quite some time. They may even be responsible for the many reports of the Little People that are found in every culture on this planet. Furthermore, it would seem from the frequency of these reports of the Minikins that their visits seem to be on the increase; perhaps they'll pay *you* a visit in the near future...

THE GAMBIER TERRACE TERROR

At twenty minutes past midnight on a warm September night in the early 1980s, two guards at a warehouse overlooking the Brunswick and Coburg Docks giggled as they listened to the DJ on Radio City reading out a bogus request on the popular Peaceful Hour programme. The guards, Terry Chance, a thirty-year-old Gateacre man, and 25-year-old Duncan O'Leary, who hailed from Belle Vale, fought the boredom of the long watches of the night with such practical jokes. Sometimes Terry would dial some random number and say to the person who answered it: 'How are you?'

The recipient of the call would invariably ask: 'Who's that?'

Terry would tell the person: 'It's me you soft thing – don't tell me you've forgotten me, have you?'

And Terry and Duncan were always surprised at how many times the stranger would think they were talking to a family member, partner or a close friend before eventually tumbling the prank. On this night, the poor unsuspecting Radio City DJ was reading out a romantic letter from an Alf Davis of Walton (in reality Duncan O'Leary) who had fallen head over heels in love with a Jo Grimly of Fazakerley and the letter ended with Alf asking: Jo, will you marry me?'

Of course, this Alf Davis and Joe Grimly were two security guards with a rival security firm, and Terry and Duncan knew they'd be listening in to the radio station. There was no way to differentiate a Jo from a Joe when the name was spoken on the radio, which meant the hoax worked like a dream.

'Well, it looks like another white wedding might be in the offing,' said the naive radio presenter, 'so, Jo, what will your answer be? Will you make Alf Davis a decent man at last? Give us a call, because we're all waiting here with baited breath for your answer.'

Terry and Duncan were literally rolling about in their corner of the vast dark warehouse as the DJ invited the imaginary Jo to give her answer. Duncan was the best at doing female voices in the pranks, so he telephoned the radio station, claiming to be Jo Grimly, and the DJ put her on the air after playing *Going to the Chapel of Love* by the Dixie Cups. 'Well, Jo, what's your answer to Alf in Walton?' the DJ asked Duncan, 'I'm sure Alf's heart must be beating pretty fast at this moment.'

'Alf, piss off,' said Duncan, 'I'd never marry a security guard!'

There was a sound – like a sharp intake of breath – from the DJ, and Duncan slammed down the telephone and he and Terry screeched with laughter.

The guards listened to the annoyed DJ on the radio apologising to his listeners, and then the little transistor radio was switched off and the guards did their rounds. Terry went to patrol the loading yard outside on the Caryl Street side of the warehouse, and Duncan inspected the upper floors of the building where the rooms were stacked to the ceiling with boxes of goods. After carrying out these duties the guards played cards and discussed other possible practical jokes. At 3.15am Duncan and Terry went up onto the roof of the warehouse and had a smoke. On this morning, Duncan had an old telescope he'd found whilst clearing out his loft. He looked at the moon – which was in its last quarter phase, and then he scanned the River Mersey, where the red lights of warning buoys flashed.

'Giz a look,' Terry asked, and he flicked the stub of his cigarette over the low wall and it arched in a red incandescent curve onto Parliament Street about a hundred feet below. Duncan handed the telescope to his friend. Terry looked at the bright star in the southern part of the sky and asked, 'What's that? Bit bright to be a star, isn't it?'

'It's Sirius, the brightest star in the sky, mate,' answered Duncan, who had a smattering of astronomical knowledge. 'It's not a UFO, Terry,' he added, knowing how Terry was always looking out for flying saucers.

Terry had a look at Sirius, and remarked on its scintillating colours, and then he turned to his left and looked in the direction of the black hulk of the Anglican Cathedral. He was silent for a moment, and then Terry said, 'There's a fellah standing in the window over there – where is that?'

'What?' Duncan flicked his cigarette over the wall into the night street below and looked in the direction the telescope was pointing to.

Terry lowered the telescope from his eyes and looked at the cathedral. 'What are those rooftops to the right there, Dunc?'

'Where do you mean?'

Terry pointed. 'See the trees to the right of the cathedral? The treetops?'

437

'Yeah, they're the trees in the cemetery,' Duncan estimated.

'Well, see that light in the window? Must be an attic light? To the right of the trees?' Terry asked, and impatiently waited for Duncan to see what he was seeing. 'You *have* got twenty-twenty vision haven't you, Dunc?'

'Yes, I have! It's your bleedin' directions Terry,' retorted a squinting Duncan, 'that's er, Gambier Terrace that. Where's the man in the window?'

'Have a look,' Terry handed him the telescope, 'he's standing either inside the window on the ledge or he's outside the window – as if he's gonna jump or something.'

Duncan peered through the telescope's eyepiece and sighed. 'Your eyes must be knackered mate, it's out of focus.'

'Well focus it and you'll see him,' replied Terry.

'Oh yeah, I can see him; he's just a silhouette. Hey you're right, he is standing on the window ledge outside the window. Hey maybe we should call the police – he might be suicidal.'

'Nah, don't get involved, mate,' said Terry, 'light plays some funny tricks this time of night. That could be one of those manikins in the window. Students live in those old houses on Gambier Terrace. Maybe some student studying fashion lives there.'

'Well, this manikin just moved its arms,' said Duncan, 'and - he's just gone back into the attic. The light's gone off.'

'Probably a student on drugs; LSD or something; they're into all that,' Terry reasoned.

Duncan looked at his watch, then out of habit he

looked over at the ghostly dial of the Liver Building to see that the time was 3.30am. 'Better get back to the grindstone,' he said, and he and Terry left the roof and went back to their little illuminated corner of the warehouse for a coffee before doing the rounds again.

On the following night at the warehouse, just after he'd turned up, Terry took out a huge pair of binoculars from his backpack. 'Got these at that army surplus shop – Callan Military,' Terry told a smiling Duncan. 'You can see the mountains on the Moon with these. They're forty times seventy magnifications – is that powerful?'

'Yes! You'll be able to see the rings of Saturn and Jupiter's moons with these, our kid,' said an hyper-excited Duncan, and he made a grabbing gesture at the binoculars.

'Wait till later on, Dunc, you're like a big soft kid,' said Terry, and he put the binoculars back in the bag and took out tonight's carrying-out. 'Me Mam made these for us, Dunc, and you know what? All she had for herself was an Ocean Pie in the freezer and a packet of Tuc crackers in the larder. I felt terrible. I'll do a big shop for her when I knock off in the morning.'

'What did she make for us?' Duncan asked, his eyes aglow as he watched his colleague take the plastic boxes and a Thermos flask out the backpack.

Terry tapped his palm on one plastic box and said, 'In here, we've got top-notch scoff, lad; smoked salmon sausages, and in this other box my old Ma has made us bacon and banana kebabs.'

Duncan seemed deflated and stuck for words – it was usually roast beef sandwiches and even salmon spread sarnies when Terry's mum was hard up, but these concoctions left him cold.

'What's in the Thermos?' Duncan queried, and dreaded the answer.

'In here,' Terry held up the tartan-patterned flask, 'is lentil and cashew nut soup, and I know it sounds like shit but I tasted it earlier and it's dead creamy and heart-warming – tastes like the essence of autumn.'

'Have you swallowed a dictionary?' sneered Duncan, 'essence of autumn – you never came up with that, you're too thick.'

Duncan sampled the salmon sausages. They were a mixture of chopped smoked salmon, prawns and curd cheese rolled up into passable sausage shapes, and were surprisingly tasty. 'Not bad,' Duncan conceded with a nod.

'See?' said Terry, 'There's more to life than the Dairy Lea cheeses and Ritz crackers you bring in. Try the kebabs and educate your chops mate.'

The guards turned on the radio, and could not believe their ears. The same DJ they'd hoaxed from the night before was reading out what was obviously another bogus request on the Peaceful Hour – and this one was aimed at Duncan and Terry. The presenter said: 'So, Terri Chance, Duncan O'Leary wants to know if you'll have him back. He says he's sorry for all he has put you through, and he wants to know if you'll marry him. I do hope this is a genuine letter, because, if you cast your mind back to last night, some idiot sent in a fake marriage proposal. Yes, there are some sad people out there who get kicks out of pulling silly stunts like that. Terri Chance, will you have Duncan O'Leary back in your life - and will you marry him?

Maybe Terri could give us a call now...'

'Bastards!' Terry switched off the radio. The two rival guards had got them back for last night's prank.

'I need to go for a smoke – you coming?' Duncan asked, sick because of the retaliatory prank.

'Yeah,' said Terry, getting up, 'I don't feel like eating any scran either.' He recalled the high-powered binoculars and took them from the backpack. All the way up the stairs to the roof, Duncan kept badgering him for 'first look'.

The air was a little cooler tonight, and Terry uncapped the binoculars and scanned the city centre. He saw constellations of sodium streetlights, car headlamps crawling about and then he spotted the waning crescent of the moon low on the eastern horizon. 'Wow, looks close enough to touch,' he said with a smiling mouth.

'Let's have a gander, come on,' Duncan's grabbing hand gripped the binoculars.

'Hang on a mo – haven't even had a chance to look myself yet!' said a narky Terry.

He looked for that man in the window over on Gambier Terrace, but the light in that window was out.

Terry handed the high-magnification binoculars to Duncan, and he scanned the panorama until he saw a cluster of luminous squares of yellow, blue and pale red swim into his field of view. These were the windows of Mill View, a high-rise block where Toxteth overlaps the Dingle. 'Cor, you should see this bird undressing for bed, Tel,' said Duncan, but Terry could tell from his inane grin that he was just pulling his leg.

The guards went back down to carry out their duties, but at 3.15am sharp, Terry and Duncan were back on the roof for their smoke break, and the moon was much better positioned now, being a little higher in the sky, so Duncan had a good look at it with the binoculars.

Then Terry tapped him on the shoulder.

'What?' Duncan lowered the binoculars and looked at his friend.

'The light's on in that window again,' he said, reaching out for the binoculars, but Duncan had a quick look at the window concerned before he handed the binoculars to his workmate.

'He's there again.' Duncan adjusted the focusing wheel of the powerful field glasses.

'They're my binoculars – can I have a look - please?' said an agitated Terry.

'Wonder what he's playing at?' Duncan asked, handing the binoculars to his friend. 'That stupid get must have a death wish. If he slips he's had it.'

'There he is,' Terry brought the distant silhouette into focus. 'That's an attic window he's stepped out of. He's lifting his arms. I can see his hair flowing in the breeze. He's got real long hair.'

'Sure it's not a woman?' Duncan asked, looking at the distant point of yellow light with his unaided eye.

'No, it's a fellah this, Dunc.' Terry replied, 'what's he doing. Oh my God!'

'What?' Duncan jumped and turned to face his friend.

'He's just stepped off the ledge and he's just hovering there!'

'What do you mean, hovering? It must be an optical illusion – ' Duncan was saying as his hand touched the binoculars.

Terry batted his hand away without even moving his wide eyes from the eyepieces of the binoculars. 'It's not an optical illusion – he's hovering in mid air, and he's lowering his arms now. He looks as if he's getting nearer – he's coming towards us.'

'Terry, let me have a look – I've got better eyes than you! You're seeing things!' Duncan tried to wrest the binoculars from him but his friend swore and shouted: 'Gerroff!'

'He's flying in this direction – he's getting bigger!' Terry moved the binoculars away and downwards from his eyes and looked over them at the light of that window in the distance.

'Hey, I can see him now – he *is* coming this way!' observed Duncan.

'Here, impatient hole, have a look,' Terry handed the binoculars to his colleague, and Duncan grabbed them and trained them on the weird silhouette.

'Terry, I can see his face now, it's dead pale,' gasped Duncan, 'and he is coming towards us, pretty fast too. What in God's name is he?'

'I'm not hanging around to find out!' was Terry's reply, and he ran to the stair bulkhead, which looked like a little hut with a door in it. Terry opened the door and ran down the metal steps, shouting, 'Come on!'

'He can't see us, Terry, he's over half a mile away at least – he'd have to have Bionic eyesight,' said Duncan, peering through the binoculars. 'You're not half a flapper, mate.'

Terry ran back up the steps, swearing to himself, then popped his head out the doorway of the stair bulkhead. 'Duncan! Will you get in here? I've got a bad feeling about that *thing* - just trust me!'

'I will now.' Duncan gazed through the binoculars at the airborne shadow for a moment, and then he said, 'Shit – I think he *might* have seen us!'

That weird hovering man was now just 250 yards away, passing over the junction of Parliament Street and Beaufort Street – and he looked – in Duncan's estimation – as if he was travelling at a speed of about fifty miles per hour. Duncan turned and ran across the bitumen roof, and Terry, who was facing him in the doorway of the stairwell bulkhead, saw the levitating figure closing in. Both of the guards also heard the creepy flying entity shout out something, but they could not make head or tail of the words. Duncan thought it sounded like something in Spanish.

Duncan bolted past Terry, and the latter closed the door with a slam and locked it. He heard the sound of heavy running on the other side of that door, and he quickly descended the stairs, and when Duncan slowed down and asked him what he thought the thing was, Terry almost pushed him down the steps.

There were three heavy thumps on the door up on the roof, and the knocks echoed down the stairs. The guards hurried down to the ground floor and Terry locked the door leading to the stairwell as an extra precaution.

Duncan turned the air blue with swear-words and suggested that they should desert their posts and do a runner, but Terry said it was safer staying indoors with that thing outside. Just *what* was that thing, anyway? The guards were in shock and they just couldn't take in what had happened. Terry checked the loading bay doors were secured, and Duncan examined the padlock on the door leading to the Grafton Street side of the warehouse. There were no windows in the warehouse, thank God, Terry realised, because he imagined that thing outside peeping in.

'Maybe we *should* call the police, Tel,' said Duncan, off the top of his head.

Terry had never seen him like this; he looked petrified. 'And say what, Duncan? A fellah who can fly through the air is trying to get in? The two of us would be carted off to the loony bin – our feet wouldn't touch the floor, mate!'

'How did he do it? Fly like that?' Duncan recalled the silhouette, flying across the streets towards him. 'Is it a ghost?'

'I don't know, that Gambier Terrace is ancient – it's Victorian isn't it?' Terry answered, and he began to pace. 'We'll just have to sit tight till it gets light and we'll have to forget doing any rounds outside.'

'How did it know we were watching it?' Duncan wondered. 'Gambier Terrace is about half a mile off.'

'Listen!' Terry stopped pacing and froze, as stock-still as a statue. His eyes swivelled up.

Thud! Thud! Thud!

'It's on the roof!' Duncan's voice sounded broken, and his face twitched.

There was an almighty crash beyond that door which gave access to the steps leading to the roof. The guards knew that something had just smashed that door off its hinges up in the stair bulk head on the roof. They heard the door slide down the first flight of steps up there. Then came the descending footfalls. It was coming down the steps and soon, the only thing that stood between the guards and that powerful entity would be that wooden door six feet away.

'Let's cut!' said Duncan, pointing to the keys to the street door on Terry's belt.

Terry and Duncan ran to the street door, and as Terry fumbled with the key in the padlock, they heard a loud thump on the door to the stairs.

'Hurry up you dozy bastard!' Duncan yelled at Terry.

There was a splintering sound now as the door bulged forward.

Duncan looked at the fire extinguisher twelve feet away and thought about hitting the thing with it, but Terry yanked off the padlock, and then he and Duncan seized the crash bar and threw their weight behind it. The cool night hair wheezed in and the guards ran to the nearest car, which happened to be Terry's Ford Escort. Ever since Terry had started his job at the warehouse he'd complained to the boss because he was not allowed to park in the yard, but now he was so glad this was the case because he would not have to unlock any gates to get away. He and Duncan were in the car in seconds, and then, as Terry started the vehicle, Duncan shouted, 'There it is!'

A head with a very pale face and prominent black penetrating eyes peeped out of the doorway of the warehouse, and this person must have been quite tall in the estimation of the guards, perhaps about six and a half feet in height. It did not come out of the warehouse, but it watched the Escort as it screeched away from the place.

'Finnegan [the boss of the warehouse] will have our balls for garters for abandoning our posts and leaving the door wide open,' said Terry, looking in the rear view mirror, expecting that thing to come running after the car.

'I don't give a shit what he says, I'm handing my cards in,' Duncan replied, 'because I am not spending another night in there.'

'We'll have to go back, Dunc, even if it means going back with the police,' Terry said.

'Terry, you said it yourself – as if the police are going to believe all that about a man flying through the night from Gambier Terrace. We wouldn't believe it ourselves if it hadn't happened to us.'

'I hope we didn't hallucinate all this,' Terry muttered, 'those salmon sausages me 'arl lady made might have been off.'

'I don't think so – ' Duncan was replying when something came down upon that Ford Escort like the wrath of God. It pounded the roof and shook the guards and Terry almost lost control of the vehicle as it mounted the pavement on Chaloner Street, some 200 yards from the warehouse. The giant in black jumped off the roof of the vehicle and stumbled, fell forward, and landed on one hand. He got up, turned to face the guards with a grin. There is a survival mechanism in all mammals – including us humans - known as the 'fight or flight reaction' – and this mechanism swings into gear when we are under attack or seriously threatened; the heart rate increases dramatically, pumping blood to the muscles, and in a split second we decide whether we are going to run or go in for the kill. Even the most mild-mannered person can become a raging killer because of the fight or flight reaction, and the most violent individual might turn and run. In the case of Terry, he instantly decided that this monstrosity – whatever it was – was not going to make him lose his job – and so, he screamed at a startled Duncan to put his seatbelt on, and swore at him when he questioned the order. Duncan's trembling hand clicked the belt on, and Terry did the same – and then he rammed the car into the thing, and the Ford Escort ended up on top of the strange goliath. The car rocked about as the creature under it roared and tried to shift the 767 kilogram vehicle off. Terry continually swore as he put the car into reverse in the hope of the tyres would take its skin off like a sander to a piece of wood, and sure enough, unholy screams erupted from under the Escort as Terry pressed down hard on the accelerator pedal. The sinister colossus then somehow lifted the front of the car and freed itself, and it ran down the road. As soon as the thing had lowered the car back down the Escort had zoomed backwards onto the road, and Terry brought it under control. The guards caught a fleeting glimpse of the tall figure darting around a corner into Bridgewater Street, and then Terry drove back to the warehouse with his colleague, who could hardly speak because he was in shock. The guards barricaded themselves into the warehouse and with chains and padlocks they secured the broken door in the stair bulkhead on the roof. They expected the thing to return but it didn't. The guards had to tell their boss Mr Finnegan that the broken door downstairs had been wrecked by thieves with crowbars who had gained entry from the roof, and Finnegan seemed to doubt the story, and he interviewed the guards separately and told them their stories didn't match or add up. Terry said he'd had enough and threatened to leave but the boss told him to calm down and the doors were replaced. The suspension on Terry's Ford

Escort had to be repaired after the encounter with the nocturnal entity, and the nervous systems of Terry and Duncan took a little longer to recover. A week later, the guards ventured up onto the roof for the 3.15am smoke break and this time Duncan had a break-barrel air rifle loaded with a .22 pellet, and Terry brandished a hatchet with a broad blade which had been in the cellar of his house since he was a kid. Terry held his high-powered binoculars in his other hand. The guards looked towards the distant rooftops of Gambier Terrace and again saw that solitary light burning away in the attic that menacing figure emerged from. With great trepidation, Terry put the hatchet down and took a look at the light. He couldn't see anyone in the attic this time. He handed the binoculars to Duncan and he placed the air rifle on the floor, refocused the binoculars for his eyes and said, 'Can't see anyone.'

'I should have sharpened the blade on this thing,' Terry said, lightly running the fleshy pad of his thumb along the edge of the hatchet's rusty blade.

Duncan swore. 'He's there again!'

'If you're having me on I'll throw you off this roof!' Terry told him, and he felt his heart kicking.

'I'm serious – he's climbing out the window. He's on the ledge!'

'Let's cut! Come on!' Terry was so eager to flee from the roof he stumbled and fell, and quickly got up, then ran to the bulkhead stairs.

'He's just jumped!' Duncan reported.

Terry's bulging eyes gazed towards that light in the distance. 'Come on – or I swear to God I'll lock that door once I'm on the other side of it!' 'Just calm down a sec, Tel!' Duncan urged. 'He's not coming this way –

he's going up at an angle.'

Terry ran to the door in the little shed-like structure and yanked it open. 'Get off this roof now! I won't ask you a second time!'

Duncan picked up his air rifle, ran to the doorway and looked back as Terry quickly descended the steps. Duncan took another look through the binoculars. 'Where's he gone?'

'Get down here now you stupid bastard!' came Terry's echoing voice from downstairs.

'Ah, there he is!' Duncan could just make out the silhouetted figure as it floated up towards the Vestey Tower of the Anglican Cathedral. He could even see the pale face of the eerie man as he came to rest on one of the pinnacles of the tower.

'Duncan!' Terry roared below, and Duncan closed the door, padlocked it, and went downstairs.

'It flew up onto the roof of the Proddy cathedral,' he told Terry, who locked the ground floor door with two stainless steel padlocks.

'Smoke breaks are down here from now on,' Terry told his colleague, and he went to the corner of the warehouse lit by an anglepoise lamp and sat looking at the locked door leading to the roof with the hatchet in his hands.

The tension dissipated as the morning wore on without any incident, and on the next morning at the warehouse, the guards again went up onto the roof at a quarter-past three to have a smoke – and to see if that thing was knocking about. The light was on again in that attic room over on Gambier Terrace, but the frightening figure was nowhere to be seen. Duncan and Terry took turns scanning the rooftops and skyline of chimneys for the levitating giant but he was nowhere to be seen. Then, around 3.25am, just before the guards were about to leave the rooftop and go back downstairs to commence their rounds, Duncan got the shock of his life. He happened to take one last scan of the roofs with the binoculars when he noticed the telltale silhouette of a head and shoulders peeping over the tower of Cain's Brewery plant – less than 200 yards away. Duncan lowered the binoculars slowly and pretended he hadn't see the thing, and he turned to Terry, and said, 'Don't look, but it's on the tower of that brewery behind me.'

Terry naturally looked in the direction he wasn't supposed to look, and asked, 'What?'

'I said don't look,' said Duncan, walking rather eagerly towards the doorway in the stair bulkhead – and of all nights he had left the air rifle downstairs on the ground floor.

'Where?' Terry asked, and looked at the only nearby tower he could see – and there it was, lifting off as if it was a man-shaped helium balloon. The silhouette rose steadily and moved towards the warehouse, its flight path running parallel with Fisher Street below. Terry found himself running to the doorway, and he pushed past Duncan, and the latter closed the door behind himself and put on the two padlocks.

The guards waited downstairs, expecting the thing to smash its way into the warehouse again, but everything remained as silent as the grave. When dawn broke, Duncan suggested going up onto the roof to see if the thing was still around but Terry told him to stay put.

That morning at 11am, Terry was fast asleep at his Gateacre home when his mother came up to his room and woke him. She said his boss was on the telephone and wanted to talk to him. Terry went down to see what the matter was and Mr Finnegan informed the guard that the body of an Alsatian dog had been found on the roof of the warehouse. Its throat had been ripped out and yet there was no blood on the roof.

'How did a dog end up on the roof?' Terry asked, rubbing his bleary eyes.

'I was hoping you or Duncan would be able to tell me that,' said Finnegan, 'no one saw anyone throwing a dog on the roof today and I can't even see how anyone could throw an animal that high into the air.'

'Is it a guard dog?' Terry asked.

'It didn't have a collar or any tags – I don't know,' said Finnegan, 'there are some sick people about. Anyway, I just thought you might have been able to throw some light on the matter. Bye.'

Terry went back to bed and had difficulty sleeping, because he suspected that thing of killing the Alsatian and dumping the body on the warehouse roof as some sort of veiled threat. He told Duncan about the incident by phone before he went to work, and Duncan thought the same; that the supernatural entity was threatening them. Over the next three days, mutilated seagulls and pigeons were found on the warehouse roof, as well as smears of blood on the rooftop door. Terry told his mother about the weird figure and did not expect her to believe him, but she seemed scared and told her son to pack the job in. Terry telephoned Duncan and said he'd had enough and was going to hand his cards in. 'I'm spewing it,' he told his friend in a broken voice.

'Well, if you are, so am I mate,' Duncan replied. 'The

pay's abysmal and the hours are unsociable. I was thinking of getting a job on the cruise ships or going to uni.'

The two guards handed in their cards, and then they drove to a nearby pub – the Baltic Fleet - where they discussed their futures. Terry said he'd try for a job as a guard at ICI and Duncan said he was thinking of being a private detective, which seemed to amuse Terry. Just before the men parted, Duncan said he was going to 'stake out' the houses on Gambier Terrace tonight by parking outside a friend's house on Hope Street. Duncan said he had an SLR camera with a telephoto lens and fast film and that he was determined to capture that *thing* on film because no one believed his story about it.

Terry urged his friend not to go anywhere near Gambier Terrace after dark because he believed that entity was something that should be left well alone. Duncan could not be talked out of his madcap idea, and at one in the morning he drove to Hope Street from Belle Vale in his brother's Volkswagen Camper Van. He parked it near to the corner of Hope Street and Huskisson Street, and this gave him an excellent view of the attic window the weird humanoid had been seen to emerge from. At 2.15am a prostitute noticed Duncan peering out the back windows of the van and kept tapping on the vehicle, asking him if he wanted any business. Duncan finally told her to get lost and she stormed off. At 3am, Duncan was feeling quite tired, and yet he felt on edge because he knew that this was around the time the entity was usually active. At 3.25am, a silence fell over the area, and Duncan poured himself a black coffee from his

Thermos flask. He happened to move the curtain aside and look out towards Gambier Terrace – and there it was floating through the air, moving away from the illuminated attic window. Duncan put down the coffee cup and fumbled about for the SLR. He tried to get the thing focused in the viewfinder but the figure was moving too fast as it headed towards the cathedral. Then he lost sight of it as it passed the blinding element of a sodium street lamp. He looked out again and could not find the enigmatic airborne humanoid. He cursed it under his breath and kept saying, 'Where are you?'

A hackney cab came down Hope Street from the Upper Duke Street end with its headlamp on full beam, dazzling Duncan. 'Dip them you arsehole!' said Duncan, shielding his eyes and drawing the curtain on the window. The cab passed the camper van, and Duncan peeped out again. That thing was still nowhere to be seen. He looked out the side windows of the van and saw a weary yellowed waxing gibbous moon hanging low over the treetops of St James's Cemetery to the south of the cathedral. He then returned to the rear window, pulled the curtain aside – and what Duncan saw chilled him to the bone. That thing was floating back towards the attic window of Gambier Terrace, and it was holding what looked like either a girl or a very petite woman by her ankle, and she was dangling upside down, her arms flopping about, but she seemed to be unconscious or dead. The female's long blonde hair was swinging about, and as the unearthly figure was within about twelve feet of the attic, the light from the window showed something red on the body that was being carried. In an instant the thing had stepped onto the ledge of the window and had vanished into the attic. The light in that window then went out.

Duncan knew he would now have to go to the police. The nearest police station was just 500 yards away up by the Philharmonic Hall. As Duncan looked up at the dark attic window, he felt cold inside. What on earth was that thing? Had it just killed a child? A car parked about a hundred feet away outside Gambier Terrace on Hope Street flashed its lights and dazzled him. 'Don't these people know how to dip their headlamps?' growled Duncan, and he made his way to the driver's seat and wondered how he could convince a policeman that some giant flying being was abducting or even killing people. A huge grotesque head with long greasy strands of black hair partially obscuring large bulging pink eyes with pinpoint irises suddenly peeped into the nearside window of the camper van. It swum into view from above and was almost upside down, and in a heart-stopping instant, Duncan realised it was that sinister entity. He started the vehicle and a screech of tyres echoed along Hope Street as the Volkswagen peeled rubber. Duncan covered the 400 feet between the corner of Huskisson Street and Hope Street and the junction of Upper Parliament Street, and a car overtook him on the left and beeped its horn.

It was Terry in his Ford Escort.

The caper van and the Escort turned left onto Upper Parliament Street and accelerated until they reached the junction of Grove Street and Mulgrave Street. The lights were on green but there was hardly any traffic on the roads at this unearthly hour, and Terry leaned over to the left front window of his car and shouted, 'Are you blind? I flashed the lamps at you on Hope Street! He was hovering over you!'

'Let's get as far away from here as we can!' Duncan shouted to his friend and they both tore off up Upper Parliament Street. The men kept taking glances up at the sky, thinking the thing would swoop down on them, and they didn't pull up till they were at a safe distance along Smithdown Road, near to Sefton General Hospital. Here, Terry got out his car and got into the camper van.

'What were you doing down there?' Duncan asked.

'I didn't like the idea of you on your stupid stake-out by yourself, so I thought I'd go and see if you were okay,' Terry explained, 'I recognised your brother's camper van.'

'Did you see what that thing was carrying?' Duncan asked his friend, and he felt a chill in his bowels as he recalled the inverted young woman.

'Yes, I did, but what can we do, mate?' said Terry, looking at his car through the windscreen. 'No one is going to believe us. We're better just forgetting -'

Duncan shook his head and interrupted him. 'I'm going to make an anonymous call to the police in a minute – I know the number of the house on Gambier Terrace now.'

'That's up to you mate, but I'm going home now, and I am not going anywhere near Gambier Terrace again, so if you start playing Scooby Doo down there you're on your own and that's a promise.' Terry told him and he left the vehicle and went back to his Escort.

Duncan dialled 999 at a call box further down

Smithdown Road and asked to be put through to the police. A man answered and Duncan told him the body of a girl would be found at the attic of a certain house on Gambier Terrace. The police operator asked him his name but Duncan became irritated by the question and told him, 'You don't need my name, I'm just reporting the crime,' and hung up.

He scanned the local newspapers for days and saw nothing about any missing women or girls and no mention of Gambier Terrace, and he told Terry that they should go on another stake-out but his friend told him to forget the whole strange matter, and eventually Duncan did. Terry's mum became seriously ill not long after this and he was unable to work because he opted to look after her. Duncan met a woman who worked at a job centre around this time and they married in the following year and moved to Southport. The two guards often met up over the years and talked about that terrifying flying figure from the attic on Gambier Terrace. Duncan eventually emailed me with his account of the story, and I told him that there had been rumours of vampires at Gambier Terrace for decades – dating back to the 1930s at least. I had a look at the electoral register for the early 1980s to see who lived at the address where the thing came out of the attic at Gambier Terrace and saw that a Hungarian man lived there during the time the guards saw that entity. That Hungarian man later vanishes from the electoral register and I have been unable to find any further records of him. I also introduced Duncan to a retired night watchman named Alf, who used to work at a warehouse near to Brunswick Dock in the 1960s.

Alf was sitting at a brazier of glowing coals in the

yard outside the warehouse one morning in 1964 at around 3.45am, and upon this night there was a full moon hanging over the city. Alf happened to look up at the moon on this morning and he saw the silhouettes of three people crossing the lunar disk. These figures seemed to be about two hundred feet up and they were going towards the east – in the direction of Gambier Terrace. Alf told a colleague named Jimmy, another watchman who had been watching road works nearby, and he was very sceptical, but a few days later, he came running over to Alf and told him he too had just seen the three figures passing overhead – and he believed that they had landed somewhere by Gambier Terrace. Around this time in the 1960s, there was an occult revival going on everywhere, and there were many strange stories in circulation about grave robberies in St James's Cemetery and vampires living on Gambier Terrace. The origin of the grave-robbing stories was traceable to actual acts of desecration at St James's Cemetery that were even reported in the newspapers, but the origin of the vampires of Gambier Terrace were never traced. I have so many reports about all sorts of supernatural goings-on at Gambier Terrace, and I am convinced that some very real paranormal incidents are behind the tales, and I also feel that there is *still* something very unsavoury hanging in the air in that part of Hope Street...

THE SATANIC ARCHBISHOP
OF LARK LANE

On the surprisingly sunny afternoon of Friday 5 December, 2003, a gaggle of girls, all in their late twenties were drinking on Lark Lane. Two of these young ladies – Jessica and Casey – should have known better, because they were supposed to be at a church in an hour for a wedding rehearsal. Jessica was getting married in just over a week's time and had a morbid fear of fluffing her lines and letting her nerves get the better of her. The vicar suggested rehearsing the wedding so he could take her through the service so she'd know what to expect, where to stand, what to say, and so on. Casey eventually realised what time it was and pulled Jessica out of a wine bar. Jessica ran up the road, trying to flag a hackney cab, and as Casey passed the shaded opening of Hadassah Grove, a pleasant L-shaped cul-de-sac, she was accosted by an archbishop – well, that's what he appeared to be.

'Casey!' shouted the man in the long black and grey ministerial robes. He wore a black velvet mitre and held a crook which had a snake's head at the end of its hook. Casey turned to face him, looked him up and down, and immediately sensed this man was something unearthly. His smiling pale face looked insincere. 'I think your money troubles are over at last!' he told her. His voice sounded refined and he enunciated the words perfectly.

'I'm not interested,' Casey said, 'I have to attend a

wedding rehearsal. I've got to be going.'

'She'll *never* marry,' said the 'Archbishop', glancing up the lane at Jessica.

Casey thought this was such a cold offhand remark to make and she was about to condescendingly ask the oddly-dressed stranger who the hell he was but he spoke before she got a chance to pose the pointed query.

'So, listen, Casey, I'll give you tomorrow's Lottery numbers and you can start to live.'

Casey suddenly felt a mild hypnotic pull from the stranger's dark eyes, and she saw a small purplish billowing cloud form to his right – and luminous gold numbers started to appear in this cloud.

'And here are the numbers,' said the weird figure. '1 for the month you were born in, 7 is your house number, 9 for the day you were born on, 28 is your age, 33 is your brother's age, and 39 is the house number of your boyfriend.'

'And what do I have to do in return for all this?' a light-headed Casey asked, and the man said, 'Well, I know what you're thinking – no, we don't want your soul, just a few favours from you.'

'Casey!' Jessica's distant voice broke the spell. She beckoned her to the taxi she'd flagged down at last, and Casey reluctantly turned away from the bizarrely dressed man and went to Jessica as the peculiar personage shouted: 'All that money! It will change your life, Casey! Come back!'

But Casey walked on, despite the welling up of a tremendous appetite for wealth within her. She almost broke out in a sweat as she tried to resist the temptation, and by the time she reached Jessica, her friend noted her flushed expression and asked her if she felt okay.

Inside the hackney cab, the taxi driver asked: 'Where to love?' and when Jessica told him the name of the church, the cabby joked: 'Have you seen the light then?'

'Going to a wedding rehearsal actually,' Jessica told him, and the taxi driver started telling anti-marriage jokes - and Casey suddenly swore at him and shouted, 'Just drive will you? You're not Peter Kay!'

'Casey, what's gotten into you?' Jessica asked in a whispered voice.

The cabby's face went red and he gritted his teeth and glared at Casey in the rear view mirror.

'Jessica, did you see that weird man I was talking to before?' Casey asked.

'God, which one? You mean that fellah with the plucked eyebrows?' said Jessica.

'No, I mean the man I was talking to when you shouted me – where that street comes out onto Lark Lane,' she replied, and the street she meant was Hadassah Grove.

Jessica gave a puzzled look and told Casey: 'You were just standing there on your tod when I shouted you – I couldn't see anyone.'

'Jessica you're scaring me,' said Casey with a worried look, 'there was this weird man all in black with a bishop's hat on, and he knew my name – and he gave me tomorrow's Lottery numbers.'

'Casey,' Jessica said in a barely audible voice close to her friend's ears, 'have you been taking ecstasy or something?'

Casey shook her head. 'Jessica, I swear on my Nan's

life – a man dressed like a bishop or an archbishop – you know, with those big hats they wear and that – and a staff – came out of that street and there was something creepy about him.'

'I didn't see a soul when I shouted you,' said Jessica, and then she looked out the side window in the hackney and smiled. 'Oh, look who it is!' she said, and pointed to the hackney cab travelling alongside the taxi. Three of the other girls who had been drinking with Jessica and Casey were in the cab, and they were laughing and waving at Jessica.

Casey didn't even look out the window, and Jessica could see that something must have happened to her friend to make her look so anxious.

Casey told Jessica about the Lottery numbers the unknown man had given her, and on the following evening – a Saturday night, those very numbers came up. Jessica almost wept when those numbers came up on the Lottery programme on BBC1, because it would have provided her with immense financial security for her forthcoming marriage. She hadn't put the numbers on because she really did think someone had spiked Casey's drink and that she had hallucinated the 'archbishop' character. Casey had not put the numbers on because she thought she'd lose her soul in return for winning. Casey recalled that the figure had told her that Jessica would never marry, and she didn't dare tell her friend this, as she knew it'd upset her, but, as predicted, Jessica was stood up by her boyfriend at the church on the big day and she never did marry. In 2015, Jessica tragically died from a rare form of cancer.

Hadassah Grove is said to be haunted by that mysterious 'benefactor', for I have many other accounts concerning him, and he seems to date back to the 1960s at least – but who is he? The Devil, or one of the fabled 'Archbishops of Hell'? Was the ecclesiastical attire he wore some sort of mockery of the Christian Church? I'm not sure who he is, but curiously, Hadassah Grove is named after an alleged mystical myrtle bush that flourished on the site in the 18th century. People allegedly addressed the bush with questions in the middle of the night and a voice within it was said to issue accurate predictions – till a priest uprooted it. I get the feeling that the myrtle bush was some parody of the Burning Bush mentioned in the Bible's Book of Exodus – which might hint at a Satanic joke.

A VAMPIRE IN GATEACRE

Some of the names in this story have been changed to avoid unwanted publicity towards the people concerned, but, as far as I can ascertain, the rest is fact; something very strange and terrifying seems to have taken place at a house in Gateacre in 1977. In October of that year, Helen, the 19-year-old daughter of Terence and Patricia Glover, returned to her semi-detached home on Lee Park Avenue and told her mother that she was now engaged to Dominic Martin, a 20-year-old man from Childwall. Helen had only been seeing him for two months, and tonight, after leaving the Abbey Cinema in Wavertree, Dominic had got down on bended knee and proposed with an engagement ring in his hand. Helen had said, 'Yes,' and all of the people pouring out of the picture house had cheered. After the romantic proposal by moonlight, the engaged couple had a celebratory drink at the Coffee House, where Dominic worked, collecting glasses and occasionally serving.

Being an occasional drinker at the Coffee House because a close friend lived in Wavertree Green, Helen's father Terence Glover knew of Dominic and his felonious family, and thought the young man was far below his daughter. 'No, Helen, you are not getting married to the Missing Link, and you're too young anyway. I've told you before, that chartered accountant chap you dated last year – Norman – has a tremendous future, unlike this good-for-nothing layabout Dominic

Martin – '

Helen interrupted her father's sermon with a scream, threw her hands melodramatically up to her face and yelled, 'I am marrying Dominic and that's that, or I'm leaving home!' And she ran up to her room.

Mrs Glover told her interfering husband off and went after her sobbing daughter.

On the following evening whilst returning home late from the office, Mr Glover drove to the Coffee House pub and confronted Dominic, who had been chatting to a young woman. Mr Glover noticed the tattooed words "Love" and "Hate" on the four fingers of each hand of the betrothed and said, 'Listen here, you tattooed lout, Helen is not marrying you! She's too young and quite frankly she's too good for the likes of you!'

The cross words sparked a heated argument and Mr Glover even chased Dominic Martin around the pub before the landlord barred Helen's dad from the premises. When Dominic told Helen about her father's bullying behaviour she threatened to leave home, and so Mr Glover reluctantly accepted the engagement, and to make matters worse, Helen and her mother decided to throw a party to mark the betrothal. The Glovers lived in a four-bedroom semi, and on the evening of the engagement party – which took place on Wednesday 26 October - every relative came out of the woodwork to attend and there was hardly standing room at the Glover household. Camping tents were put up in the back garden and six cousins even got into sleeping bags in the garden shed and greenhouse. Dominic's two brothers, Jimmy and Davy – and their girlfriends – slept in the loft, and of course, a number of gatecrashers turned up as well. Mr Glover drank large measures of vodka to get through the "bacchanalian orgy" as he called it, with young couples openly kissing and 'carrying on' on the stairs, landings, hallway, the bath, and even the front garden of the house as a stereo blasted out all of the pop hits of the day. The party went on until just after four that morning, and although the music had stopped by then, there were still people in the living room, hallway and kitchen drinking and eating. About 4:20am, a female scream echoed throughout the house, startling Mr and Mrs Glover from their much-needed slumbers. It sounded like Helen screaming, and it was coming from her bedroom. Thinking that someone might be assaulting his daughter, Mr Glover barged into the room in his pyjamas and fell over a drunken teenage girl who'd been stretched out on the carpet. He got up and saw Helen covered in blood that was issuing from a wound on Dominic's neck.

'What happened?' asked Mr Glover, and Helen said she had been asleep on the bed, and had been awakened by two men fighting. It had been Dominic and some tall red-haired man all in black with a very pale face who had bit Dominic's neck.

'Where did he go?' Mr Glover asked, and Helen pointed to the curtains fluttering in front of the open bedroom window.

'He just jumped out, and when I looked out he was gone!' Helen told her father, and she tried to stem the bleeding wound on her fiancé's neck with her fingers, pinching the skin, but the blood continued to spurt everywhere. Mr Glover called an ambulance – which arrived at the house on Lee Park Avenue within five minutes. An ambulance man who took a close look at the ghastly wound in Dominic's neck asked, 'Where's the dog?'

Mr Glover and his daughter returned a blank look.

'This is a dog bite – you can see the fang marks,' the ambulance man said with a slight grin, 'probably an Alsatian.' He then insinuated that the family had hidden the dog to protect it in case the police decided it would have to be put down.

'We have no dog in this house,' seethed Mr Glover, 'now, what are you going to do about this man's serious wound?'

'We'll have to take him in, get a few stitches in that wound after we clean it up, give him a tetanus jab in his backside and then he can go home,' the ambulance man replied.

Dominic was taken away with a sterile bandage coiled around his neck and Helen followed him in tears into the ambulance with her mother.

Doctors at the Royal Infirmary discovered that whatever had bitten Dominic's neck had punctured his carotid artery, and furthermore, the pattern and radius of the bite was not that of a canine, but apparently of a human with long fangs. Dominic claimed that a man had come into Helen's bedroom via a half-open window. He had been dressed in some sort of black robe and must have been about 6ft 5 in height, with red hair and a weird pale complexion. He had attacked Dominic immediately and had forced him onto the bed, where he overpowered the 20-year-old man and bit his neck. Dominic pulled at the bloodsucker's hair, then butted him, and Helen let out a scream which awakened a female guest who had been sleeping on the floor of the bedroom. The vampire-like intruder had then fled by climbing out the window and jumping onto the moonlit drive below.

The medical men at the hospital were having none of this, and said that someone with unusually long canine teeth had bit Dominic, perhaps as a prank that had gone dangerously wrong.

Days after this, Dominic told Helen a strange thing. On that Wednesday night when he had been on his way to her house with his brothers Jimmy and Davy, they had taken a short cut through the cemetery of All Saints Church, Childwall, where Dominic had decided to relieve himself on a certain tomb. He thought it'd be a laugh, but he and his brothers saw the heavy stone lid on the tomb move slightly, and they all ran out of that cemetery as fast as their legs could carry them. Dominic had a sneaking suspicion that the tomb he had defiled had contained a real-life vampire. Dominic became very depressed and lethargic after sustaining that bite to his neck, and ended up becoming seriously ill with a condition that was diagnosed as glandular fever. He lost his job at the pub because of his illness and had so little energy, he became a recluse who would only venture out of his house in Childwall after dark. His eyes also became very sensitive to daylight and he had to wear shades when he went into his back garden – the only place he'd visit outdoors during the daytime. Helen broke off the engagement with Dominic and started dating the chartered accountant Norman – the man she eventually married. I had a look at the tomb where the suspected vampire is said to lie and discovered through long weeks of research that there had been an actual vampire scare at the cemetery in Victorian times – all centred on the very tomb Dominic had desecrated. The body within that tomb belongs to a well-known family who were said to dabble in the occult – and almost every member of this family had red hair. The family were so persecuted by the rumours of one of their kin being a vampire, they later moved down to the Highgate district of London – and there, they became the cynosure of another vampire scare in Edwardian times. There are even later reports – from the 1980s and 1990s – of a vampire being at large in Childwall, Gateacre, Woolton and Tarbock – and many of these latter-day reports mention the bloodsucker as having striking red hair. It may be a coincidence – or maybe not – but I am currently investigating an incident in which a woman living on Woolton's Chartmount Way awoke at 5am with an intense pain in her neck and bloodstains on her pillow. She discovered she had two tiny holes – one of which had punctured her Trapezius muscle and grazed the external jugular vein. The woman's doctor said he had never seen a wound like it and noted bruising on other parts of the neck which indicated that a hand had held the neck with some force as it was bitten. The woman now sleeps with a rosary around her neck and a copy of the Bible at her bedside.

I have a sixth sense regarding the vampiric undead and I have the unsettling feeling that the Gateacre Vampire might be going in search of blood again quite soon...

BARNABY BRIGHT

One misty September afternoon in 1971, Erica and Pauline – both aged forty – were passing Joybringer Antiques off Rodney Street when Erica gasped and pointed to the red polka-dot dress hanging in the window. It was the replica of the one she had worn when she was twenty, and her mind travelled back to that night in 1951 when she had met her husband Robert at a dancehall on Smithdown Road. Within seconds the bell above the door was jangling as Erica barged into the shop. There sat Barnaby Bright, the smiling old proprietor of the shop, eating cherries as he listened to a gramophone record of *Jupiter – Bringer of Jollity* – the fourth movement of Holst's Planets suite. Erica asked to see the dress and Mr Bright nodded and brought it from the window. 'Size ten,' said Pauline, smirking at the dress, 'those days are long gone, Erica, and never shall they return.'

Erica had a tear in her eye as she held the dress to her body and glanced in a full length mirror. Bright swooped on her and almost shoved her into a little curtained booth. 'Try it on!' he urged, and Erica shook her head vigorously and Pauline yodelled a forced laugh – but Mr Bright swished the curtain aside and gently pushed Erica into the changing booth. 'I promise you it *will* fit – be positive for once, child – just once – it won't hurt!'

For some reason, Erica did as he said, and Pauline

brushed past Mr Bright to go into the booth, but the old man barred her way and said, 'You're a negative influence on her. Stay there.'

An insulted Pauline went to the other side of the shop, where she called a cabinet labelled "Genuine Chippendale" 'as bent as a fourpenny bit'.

Three minutes later the booth curtain swished aside and out came Erica – in that size 10 dress, and the tinsel strands of grey had gone from her hair. 'Pauline, it fits!' she beamed with glistening eyes.

Pauline looked stunned, and then she seemed discomfited. A crooked, counterfeit smile formed on her thin lips, and she said, 'Can't be a ten then; no way could you fit into a ten. And Erica, what's happened to your hair?'

'It *is* a size ten! Look at my waist!' Erica said to the long mirror, and Mr Bright chuckled. Pauline scowled. 'It does make you look thin but you're not a ten, you're a size fourteen Erica.'

'I'm closing in five minutes,' announced Mr Bright, and then he turned to Erica and softly asked, 'Are you taking it?'

'Yes, how much?' Erica rushed to her handbag in the booth to get her purse, but Bright protested with a dramatic wave of his hands towards her. He cried, 'No, Erica, what do you take me for, girl? The dress is free; that expression in your eyes when you saw how it fitted you just then was more precious than jewels.' Then he added, 'Erica, listen to a bit of wisdom from an old man. Surround yourself with positive people and remember this: you can do *anything* if you believe in yourself – any bloody thing!'

Erica felt there was something *saintly* about the shop

owner; it was in his eyes – they radiated compassion and sincere love. 'Thank you Mr – '

'Bright, Barnaby Bright,' he replied, and he held Pauline's hand with both of his warm hands and winked at her.

'Oh, he's a conman that one,' Pauline suddenly remarked, eyeing the way he was holding Erica's hand – and she left the shop and walked off.

'I'm sorry about the way my friend just called you – ' Erica said, glancing at the back of Pauline through the window as she crossed the road in a huff, but Mr Bright just closed his eyes, shook his head, and said, 'She's just hurt because she doesn't look as nice as you.'

Erica left the shop wearing the polka dot dress, and she caught up with Pauline, and passing men smiled at Erica and cast amorous – and even lustful – glances at her – just as they used to do when she was twenty. Pauline pretended not to notice, but Erica could see that all of the attention she was getting was making her friend jealous, and she sympathetically said, 'Pauline, you could easily knock ten years off your age if you cut down on - '

'Oh Erica stop it for God's sake!' Pauline suddenly exploded. 'You're the age you are and that's that!'

When Erica got home, she was scared to take off the polka dot dress because she thought she'd go back to being a fourteen, but she stayed at size ten. She knew it was impossible to be that size, and she suspected Barnaby Bright of being some male witch or some wizard. Everyone asked Erica what diet she had used to get into shape, and she'd say, 'Just positive thinking.' She returned to Joybringer Antiques with chocolates for Mr Bright a week later, and found the premises empty. A passing policeman told her the shop had been like that for years.

TIMESLIPS GALORE

I have spent many years investigating what are known as timeslips – incidents where a person somehow finds himself or herself in a future time or at some point in the past. Sometimes a group of people may enter a timeslip, and even animals may be 'transplaced' in time; for example, I have a 2012 report of a farmer who looked up and saw a vast cloud of migrating swallows flying through the late-September skies of Lancashire bound for South Africa, when the birds all vanished in mid air. One second they were there, and then the beautiful murmurations of the birds ceased abruptly and they were nowhere to be seen. On the following day in the late afternoon, the farmer happened to glance up into a clear sky and see the sudden materialisation of a flight of swallows, and suddenly the heavens was alive with their excited chirps and tweets. It was as if the swallows that had vanished in the sky on the previous day had reappeared twenty four hours later – but if that was the case, *where* had these creatures been in the intervening period of time? I believe the swallows somehow flew into a hole in time and seconds later, found themselves exiting the hole twenty-four hours into the future. To the birds, the passage through the hole – or portal, as some physicists call such openings – would have seemed smooth and lasting only seconds, but to the farmer on the ground, the passerine songbirds would appear to vanish in mid air as they entered the portal – and this is exactly what he witnessed. Locally, in Sefton Park in 2005, another time-displaced creature was apparently at large, and from descriptions of this animal, it seems to have been a prehistoric beast called an Estemmenosuchus – which lived during the geological period known as the Middle Permian – some 267 million years ago. As far back as 2001 I had been contacted by quite a number of people by snail mail and email who had informed me of sightings of a strange and rather frightening animal in Sefton Park near Mossley Hill Drive. Then, in the summer of 2005, I was on a Liverpool radio show talking about local mysteries when I received a flurry of on-air telephone calls about the 'Monster in Sefton Park'. A nurse and a postman provided me with the best accounts of the creature, which I believe to be a time-displaced specimen of Estemmenosuchus – a prehistoric mammal which roamed our world in the remote past when all of today's continents were still joined up as one super-continent called Pangaea. The first encounter occurred on the sunny Saturday morning of 2 July 2005 at around 9.40am when a 22-year-old off-duty nurse named Claire took the 'scenic route' on her bicycle through Sefton Park from her home off Aigburth Road to do a bit of shopping on Smithdown Road. A neighbour, Mike Allen, was cycling about ten yards ahead of Claire along the leafy curved drive that morning when a surreal nightmare walked out of the parkland just to the left of the nurse. At first, Claire thought it was an elephant that had perhaps escaped from a circus in the park, but then the thing turned its head towards her, and Claire became so numb with fear, her legs turned to jelly and she could hardly move the pedals of her bike. The face of the huge unknown animal had some sort of antlers, and also strange rounded horns protruding from each side of its head. Its huge mouth was like that of the hippopotamus, only it had prominent teeth, and the thing's eyes were wide and fixed upon the terror-stricken nurse. With failing legs, Claire tried to pedal her way out of this waking nightmare but the bulky 12-foot-long animal galumphed forward on elephant-like feet and intercepted her path. At last, Claire managed to let out a scream which pierced the morning air and her neighbour Mike Allen slowed on his bike and took a look back at her over his shoulder. At this point that animal let out a cry which sounded like a trumpet blast, and Claire believes its head nudged the back wheel of the bike. Claire suddenly managed to regain the power to move the muscles in her legs, and she sped off out of the park, and when she later met her neighbour, he said he had watched the weird unidentified animal walk in a very clumsy manner back into the park, where it seemed to vanish among the trees. Claire avoided the park for years after this traumatic incident. About a month after Claire's encounter, a postman saw the exact same type of animal walking out of Sefton Park's car park on Aigburth Drive, where an oncoming car stopped, then reversed when the driver saw the huge beast. The postman bravely went looking for this beast, which had roamed the earth in a time before Genesis, because he hoped to get a picture and some video footage of it on his phone but it had apparently vanished into thin air. Other people have seen this unidentified animal since, and I believe some occasional timeslip is allowing the creature to enter our era from aeons back. Keep your eyes peeled if you visit

Sefton Park – you might find yourself in Jurassic Park. There have been other similar reports of local timeslips where actual dinosaurs seem to have strayed into our era. Take the following astounding story from the 1950s.

If ever there was an ideal time for the Martians to invade, it would be 1 April, for no one believes any strange news on that date, and on Tuesday 1 April, 1958, two bizarre news items were suspected of being April Fool jokes. John Pritchard, conductor of the Royal Liverpool Philharmonic Orchestra, was being driven to distraction by an unusual six-second echo in the cavernous Anglican Cathedral as he rehearsed Bach's *St Matthew Passion* for Good Friday. Acoustic advisers told Pritchard nothing could dampen the echo, so the Philharmonic choir had to perform with their backs to the audience on the day. That same April Fool's Day, another 'echo' was causing problems – and this was apparently an echo of something that had lived aeons ago. It all started when a gang of Teddy boys over in Wirral accosted a middle-aged policeman on his bike near the Wishing Gate, Red Hill, and told him they'd seen a 'big monster' that looked like Godzilla stomping towards nearby Brackenwood Park.

'Get out of here, idiots!' the bobby told the dapper youths but they seemed genuinely shaken. The policeman later saw huge three-toed prints in the sand of a local golf course. It had to be an April Fool prank, the copper decided. Then, on the Friday afternoon of 22 August that year, the entire country was visited by some of the worst summer thunderstorms in living memory, with many fatalities from lightning strikes, and Wirral did not escape lightly. The Wallasey Fire Brigade tackled blazes caused by lightning igniting houses, and that afternoon, a fork of lightning struck something in the woods north of Redhill Road. That something crashed to earth with a sound that was initially mistaken for a roll of thunder. Two schoolboys came upon the unearthly casualty – a dinosaur – possibly a Tyrannosaurus Rex – lay crumpled in a clearing with a smoking wound on its head where the lightning had struck it. It was breathing when the schoolchildren found it but when they returned with two policemen, the flesh-eating reptile from the Cretaceous Period (85 to 65 million years ago) seemed to be dead and its eyes were closed. As chance would have it, two of the Teddy boys who had told the bobby about the monster back in April came on the scene and said they had seen the thing before. A man holding his child dared to touch the snout of the fallen giant and a nervous policeman yelled at him to keep away from the animal. I later spoke to this man (when he was 70) and he told me that the 'monster' had feather-covered patches of skin on some parts of its head. It is now known that some species of Tyrannosaurus Rex *do* have such feathers on parts of their bodies, but this fact was unknown back in 1958. A schoolboy told the other policeman that there was an old man in the monster's mouth. People looked into the dark hollow of the carnivore's gigantic mouth, through the bars of its massive deadly-looking teeth, and there was the body of an inert man identified by some as an elderly local tramp known only as "Old Hughes".

'We'll have to get him out,' the Teddy boy told the

gathering crowd, but the police told everyone to get away from the nightmare lizard. 'You should contact the RSPCA,' an old man surreally suggested, and then there were screams. The eyes of the thing opened. Everyone ran off, but when they looked back, the dinosaur had vanished. The old tramp in its mouth was never heard from again. Had such a timeslip concerning a prehistoric monster happened at sea, we would have tales of sea serpents, and if a timeslipped Plesiosaur (a marine reptile from 200 million years ago) had appeared in one of the United Kingdom's lakes or lochs, we'd have people swearing they had seen the Loch Ness Monster.

Some 300 yards west of the spot where the dinosaur was allegedly felled by a bolt of lightning in 1958, there is a timeslip hotspot where some spectacular incidents have taken place over the years.

'The distinction between past, present and future is an illusion,' said Albert Einstein, 'although a very persistent one.' Einstein was always decades ahead of the scientists of his day, and nowadays we know that what he said is perfectly true – that the past, present and future all exist simultaneously, and what we perceive as the course of history is like the groove on an old vinyl record; the 'present' is merely the stylus needle playing a certain part of the groove. All of the songs on the record can be likened to the periods of our history, and to travel in time you have to 'lift the stylus' - detach yourself from the present - and move up or down the 'groove' to the desired period in the past or future, and sometimes nature uproots people from the here and now in what we label – for want of a better name - as timeslips, and some of these slippages in the space-time continuum can be truly terrifying. In September 1998, two Liverpool schoolboys, both aged 15, named Nigel West and Gareth Watson, played truant one afternoon, and took the ferry over to Wirral. They wandered about without any clear idea of just where they were going, and ended up on Bebington Heath, where something very frightening and unexplained took place. The truants approached Brackenwood Golf Club (which dates back to 1935), with mischief on their minds, but then the thwack of golfballs in the autumn stillness was steadily replaced by a roar of voices, like a crowd at a football match only much louder, and this din became so loud, Nigel and Gareth pressed their palms to their ears. Coming from the fairway of the golf club the boys saw what could only be described as a sea of people stretching back as far as the horizon – and this vast mass of thousands of people came swarming towards the skivers. 'They've got swords and spears!' shouted Gareth, who had much superior eyesight than Nigel.

'What?' Nigel could hardly hear his friend's words because of the awful cacophony.

'They've got swords and spears and shields, look!' Gareth had to shout close to his friend's ear, and he pointed at the approaching hordes. Nigel saw his friend was right and so the boys turned to flee – and found themselves confronted with another oncoming crowd of immense proportions – and these people were dressed in what was obviously the attire of ancient soldiers. They wore helmets, held huge round shields, and were thrusting swords and spears as they thundered towards the petrified schoolboys. The lads heard whizzing sounds that seemed to be coming from over their heads, and then they realised with horror that these sounds were of arrows being fired from both crowds – and the schoolboys were slap in the middle of what looked like some archaic war. The boys had to get away from the ground where two mighty armies were about to clash – or they would be pulverised or hacked to death by the swords. Gareth literally froze with fear, but Nigel somehow dragged him onto Bracken Lane, where the teenagers hid behind the garden wall of a private upper class residence.

'What's going on?' Gareth kept asking, and Nigel saw his classmate start to shake.

'Just be quiet and don't pop your head over that wall, whatever you do!' Nigel told his friend.

'Maybe they're shooting a historical film, Nigel,' Gareth stammered, as his nerves got the better of him. 'Do you think that's what it is, Nigel?'

Nigel's vexed eyes said it all. He shook his head and advised: 'Stay behind this wall and don't move or say a word.'

The ground was shaking, quaking with what sounded like hundreds of thousands of pounding feet – and the boys could also hear the steady rumble of distant horse's hooves. There were screams and unintelligible cries and the sounds of swords clashing – and then the sounds of the titanic battle rose to such intensity, the very bones of the truants vibrated. Gareth started to cry, and he hid his face in his hands, expecting to be killed by the enigmatic troops. Nigel suddenly let his curiosity get the better of him, and he got up to look over the garden wall, and Gareth shrieked, 'No!'

At this point, all of the sounds of the converging troops came to a complete halt.

A strange silence fell on the area. To Nigel it was like the psychological silence you detect when a clock you have not been listening to ceases to tick. Nigel scanned the leafy road, and saw no one. The unknown battalions had vanished. Nigel told his father about the strange incident when he got home.

'So you admit you bunked off school!' His father roared.

Nigel shook his head and looked up at his towering, stern father. 'Yes, but dad, that is of no importance! Gareth and I must have somehow travelled back in time!'

Nigel's father just couldn't take in what his son was saying regarding the apparent time slip, and he said, 'If you were just a few years younger you'd feel the back of my hand across your face!'

Nigel stormed out of the living room and decided to try and find out if there had been any battles near that golf course that could account for the things he and Gareth had witnessed. He had a word with his history teacher – who told him something which blew the teenager away. On the very site of the Brackenwood golf course, in the year 937, King Athelstan of England, with his united Saxon tribes, defeated a vast invasion force of Scottish, Welsh and Norwegian Vikings that sailed to Wirral from Dublin. This bloodbath, known as the Battle of Brunanburh (Bromborough) is regarded by historians as a far more important battle than the ones at Hastings, Bannockburn and Waterloo, for it was the first time all the tribes of England united as one - and fought under one king. And yet, most history teachers hardly mention this highly important battle which shaped the destiny of the English. Before the battle, England was breaking up into various factions and petty warring tribes, but when the threat came from abroad, they all rallied together under King Athelstan and English nationalism was born. Casualties on both sides were very heavy, and wolves and ravens picked the rotting flesh off the bones of the dead on that vast bloodsoaked battlefield. The battle was recorded in the *Anglo Saxon Chronicle* and in the parchment of the 13th century *Egil's Saga*, but the site was eventually forgotten, and as far as I know, even today there are no markers or memorials to the most decisive battle in the genesis of the English nation. The *Anglo Saxon Chronicle* said of the battle: 'Never yet on this island has there been a greater slaughter.' It is possible that combat on such a gargantuan scale would generate a vortex of emotions ranging from sheer fear to intense hatred, and these energies might have scarred the very fabric of space-time, making the area susceptible to timeslips – or perhaps I am wrong in my reasoning and there is a geological basis for the timewarp. Footprints of dinosaurs have been found quite close to the site of the cataclysmic battle at a sandstone quarry in Storeton – and in my experience, where there are sandstone and quartz deposits or sandstone buildings, you will often find timeslips, and locally, the capital of timeslip occurrences is Liverpool's Bold Street, which has an immense block of sandstone called the Lyceum situated on its thoroughfare. However, I have been widening the search for timeslips in Liverpool, and have uncovered another intriguing locus where people have found themselves walking into the past and future. You've probably passed Mitchell Place many times without giving it a second glance. It is an opening on Great Charlotte Street to the left of McDonalds, and to the right of Pizza Hut (which has since moved, and a new "Irish Pub" now stands on the spot), which gives access to Back Lime Street, an L-shaped alleyway 143 yards in length which comes out onto Elliot Street between a Wetherspoons pub and the neglected hulk of the old ABC Cinema building. One foggy morning in November 2007, at around 1.40am, a 21-year-old Knotty Ash girl named Olivia stormed out of a nightclub on Lime Street after an argument with her best friend, and she decided to try and get a Hackney cab at the taxi rank on Great Charlotte Street. As Olivia walked down Elliot Street, she had the urge to have a wee, and the only suitable place she could see was the alleyway to her left – Back Lime Street, which was very poorly lit, and on this foggy night, the narrow street looked like a tunnel of darkness stretching into the whirling night vapours, but the young lady *had* to go and powder her nose. There was a gang of rowdy men singing and shouting just thirty yards away, and Olivia was scared of these rowdies seeing her crouched with her knickers around her ankles, just ten yards down that alleyway. Olivia had a wee, and almost fell over because she felt so tipsy. She got up and then she tried to get her bearings. She didn't know that the alleyway led to an opening which would bring her onto Great Charlotte Street (where the taxi rank was), and even if she had known, she wouldn't have risked walking down Back Lime Street because it was too dark and the fog only added to the spooky atmosphere there. Olivia walked towards the well-lit Elliot Street, but all of a sudden, she felt pins and needles all over her body, and a peculiar hissing sound suddenly surrounded Olivia. The laughter and banter of the young men round the corner died away, and a hand grabbed the girl's right arm, just above the elbow, and before she could turn around to see who the hand belonged to, another one grabbed her left arm, and Olivia was dragged backwards with such force, she fell onto her back and found herself being dragged down that dark foggy alleyway by two very strange-looking men. One was taller than the other, and the taller one wore what looked like the type of hat Olivia associated with highwaymen like Dick Turpin – in other words, the abductor in question was wearing a tricorn hat – an item of fashion that had long gone out of vogue centuries ago, and he also wore a long black cloak and a pair of leather boots. The smaller man dragging Olivia along a dark green coat with large cuffs which went into his waist then came down to his knees. He wore what looked like pale stockings of some sort below this coat and black boots. The hat on this man's head was like a boater, only it seemed to be black and made of leather. This was possibly an old Jack Tar Hat of the type worn by sailors in old Liverpool. Olivia managed to pull her right hand from this smaller man, and she twisted about and screamed, then got to her feet, and when the taller man in the tricorn hat turned to face her, Olivia saw that the bottom half of his face was covered by a black cloth, possibly a scarf. His eyes were dark and penetrating, and in his right hand he brandished a small club or cosh. When Olivia struggled to get free of this sinister man, he simply tugged her hard with his hand around her wrist and she impacted into the front of his coat. The other man laughed, uttered the C-word, and said something that sounded like "Miss Horner puddin' puss, Jack,' and the taller man laughed deeply and then he pushed Olivia towards a wall, but that wall seemed to dissolve, and instead, Olivia found herself on a wide open space. It looked like a heath, and the men took her to a huge tree, and there, against the trunk of this tree, the man in the tricorn hat tore off Olivia's top. Realising that the men looked ready to rape her, the young lady let out a scream, but the smaller man struck her face with the back of his hand, and Olivia felt a sharp pain in her cheek. She recalled that the smaller man had looked at the ring on his hand after that hand had struck her, and she felt blood run from her cheek, down her face and neck as the man in the three-pointed hat threw down the club, then fumbled with the buttons on the front of his trousers. He was undoing his flies. For a moment, Olivia felt like a statue. She was unable to move and she saw the pockmarked face of the man in the Jack Tar Hat as he smiled, revealing discoloured teeth. The next thing Olivia knew, she was running away, back the way she came, and yet she could not see any alleyway – just a field and cottages in the distance, barely visible through the mists. She heard the men chasing after her and she heard them swear and cry, 'Come back!'

Back Lime Street suddenly reappeared on both sides of the running girl, and she started to cry as she ran along. She realised she was wearing only her bra because that rapist had torn off her top. All the same,

Olivia ran onto Elliot Street, and she saw the gang of young men she had dreaded meeting just minutes ago, and they all stopped talking when they saw her running towards them with her hands covering her bra and breasts. 'Men tried to rape me!' she screamed to the gang, and the lads ran to her, and when they heard Olivia's account, most of them ran down the alleyway of Back Lime Street. Franky, the lad who stayed with her and asked her if she was alright gallantly took off his shirt and told her to put it on. He then produced a hankie and dabbed the blood on her cheek trickling from the wound inflicted by that man's ring as he truck her. Olivia burst into tears because she just knew that the men who had tried to violate her would not be found, and people would think she was seeing things or on drugs – but minutes later, some of the lads returned from Back Lime Street and one of them – a man named Robbie - said to Franky, who was holding Olivia's hand, 'Franky! We chased two fellahs, and one had a cloak on and a hat shaped like a triangle – you know, like the ones you see in the old films about highwaymen and that!'

'Shut up!' said Franky, thinking his friend was larking about.

'Franky, he's telling the truth,' said another one of the young men, out of breath from running, 'he looked like something out the days of Dick Turpin, and you should have seen him run.'

'Well where did he go?' Franky asked.

Robbie coughed and told him. 'He came out onto Great Charlotte Street with some other fellah, and this is on our kid's life; he legged it across the road – you know where the Blob Shop is?'

Franky nodded, intrigued.

Robbie continued his account of what had happened. 'The two of them just ran round the side of the Blob, and there's like two big gates there – they couldn't possibly have climbed them, and we even looked behind the wheelie bins there. It's as if they just vanished into thin air.'

'Not a trace, lad,' said another of the men to Franky.

Stripped to the waist, Franky walked with Olivia to the taxi rank on Great Charlotte Street and asked if he could see again after he had escorted her to a hackney cab. The driver of the taxi saw the blood on Olivia's face and the way she was holding the handkerchief to her cheek, and he got the wrong end of the stick. 'Hey Tarzan, have you been hitting her?' the cabby asked bare-chested Franky.

'No I haven't!' Franky roared at the driver.

'This man saved my life tonight,' Olivia told the driver of the hackney, 'I was nearly raped by two men.'

'Raped?' recoiled the cab driver, 'You should go to the police and make a report.'

'They'd never believe me,' Olivia sighed, and she looked at the blood on the hankie, then she asked Franky where he was from.

'Tocky – Toxteth,' he told her, 'the south end.'

'Thanks Franky,' Olivia told him and tears welled in her huge eyes.

He gave her his mobile number and he even paid the cabby to take the girl to her home on Knotty Ash. A few days after this, Olivia rang Franky to thank him again for his help after the unearthly ordeal, and she ended up seeing him not long after that. Today they are still together. Were the two oddly-dressed men who tried to rape Olivia sex-offenders who had donned period costumes for some bizarre reason (a fetish even), or were they ghosts, and very solid ones at that? It's hard to tell, but Olivia said that the alleyway she was abducted in had faded away to reveal a wide open space like heath land with a large solitary tree – and to me, this sounds more like a timeslip; it could be a description of early 18th century Liverpool. I wonder if the would-be rapists (who might have even murdered Olivia after they'd had their way) were familiar with the timeslip and had been laying in wait or even watching the passing females of 2007, or whether the perverts were just opportunistic criminals making the most of a very unusual phenomenon? The Mitchell Place/Back Lime Street alleyway has been the backdrop to some other intriguing timeslips over the years. A man named Ronald Stephens called me at BBC Radio Merseyside one afternoon in December 2010 after I had been discussing timeslips on the *Billy Butler Show*. Mr Stephens said that in the late 1970s he had lived off Brownlow Hill, close to St Andrew's tenements – more widely known by their nickname, the "Bullring". On the Friday afternoon of September 12 1980 at around 1.20pm, Stephens left a pub on Hanover Street, where he had been to see his brother and headed for home through gale force winds and lashing rain. He had only consumed half a pint of stout and did not feel intoxicated. Mr Stephens turned into Great Charlotte Street and immediately saw a man named Williams coming down the street. Stephens owed Williams thirty pounds (used to finance a gambling addiction) and before Williams could notice him, Stephens took a sharp right into the archway of

Mitchell Place and hurried along the L-shaped alleyway of Back Lime Street – an obscure passageway that was the very antithesis of its well known counterpart Lime Street, the most famous thoroughfare in the city. As Ronald Stephens hotfooted it along the alleyway, he became aware of two things – the gale force winds and rain were now absent, and a strange electronic humming sound was coming from above. The hum rose in volume, then quickly died away. When Stephens emerged from Back Lime Street, he looked above at something incredible. A gigantic black rail, as wide as Lime Street, was running across the sky from north to south, at a height of about a hundred feet, and along the underside of this rail, futuristic trains in shiny yellow and green livery were moving. As they passed overhead, Stephens heard a humming sound come from the trains, and he realised that this was the sound he had heard a minute ago. He knew very well that there was no elevated rail running across the city. There had been an overhead railway once which had run through Liverpool's dockland, but that had been closed in 1956. This was some sort of futuristic monorail with gigantic trains that looked like something out of a science fiction film. That rail had not been there earlier in the day, and as Ronald Stephens was trying to make sense of what he was seeing, a voice behind him said, 'Trying to avoid me eh?'

Stephens turned to see Williams, the man he owed thirty pounds to.

'If you don't pay up this week, I'll have you done in!' Williams threatened.

In an effort to deflect and diffuse the dire threat,

Stephens said: 'Hey, have you seen this?' and he looked up – and saw that the mysterious giant monorail had gone. The winds buffeted the face of Stephens and blew his hair into a mess, and the torrential rain pummelled the pavement. Williams looked heavenwards, wondering what Stephens was referring to, and then he reiterated his threat and left the way he had come, via Back Lime Street. Stephens is certain he did not hallucinate the ultramodern monorail, and has never seen anything like it since. The only plausible explanation is that Ronald Stephens somehow had a glimpse of some future monorail system which will one day be in use in Liverpool.

In early September 2016, a 39-year-old American tourist from Texas named Mike Gracecouer left the Crown Hotel pub on Lime Street at around 10.45pm and set out for a friend's flat on Slater Street, not far from the old Jacaranda club. Mike passed the narrow opening of Back Lime Street as he walked down Elliot Street, when he distinctly heard a woman scream. It came from somewhere down the alleyway, and Mike hesitated in his steps, walked a few feet back, and looked down Back Lime Street. This time he heard a woman cry out: 'Oh God! No! Help!'

Mike went down the poorly-lit narrow lane to a point where the street led to a type of long courtyard on the right (possibly a loading bay), where the fire exits and back doors to the Richard John Blackler pub are situated. The concerned American looked behind the large Biffa wheelie bins, but saw no woman in distress. Then he heard a woman crying further down the bleak, dismally lit back street, and so he walked towards the source of the sobbing, but could not see anyone about. The American reasoned that if he continued to walk down the narrow passageway and turned right at the corner he could already see about thirty feet ahead, he'd come out onto Great Charlotte Street. He noticed a wooden pallet leaning against a wall to his left, and thought he saw someone standing beside it, but it was his own shadow, projected by a wall lamp somewhere to his right.

Then everything in Mike's field of vision went fuzzy and grey. Mike likened it to what you'd see if you had goggles on and they steamed up. All points of illumination on Back Lime Street suddenly went out, and the Texan found himself walking in a grey void with no reference points. Beneath his shoes, the ground felt like a cobbled road, but he could see no road below him, just greyness. He took out his smartphone – a new Samsung Galaxy S7 – yet he could not get a signal. He dialled the number of his Liverpool girlfriend Emily, but the call failed. Mike looked for the walls of Back Lime Street, but they were nowhere to be seen – just an all-enveloping fog, and through it he could see no landmarks. He walked for what felt like miles, hoping to find another living soul, but he saw no one and he could hear nothing but his own rhythmic breathing and the footfalls of his shoes on the invisible cobbled ground. Mike strained his ears, hoping to hear distant traffic, a passing plane overheard, or the voices of late-night revellers, but he felt as if he was the only man on earth. He halted, tried to call Emily on his mobile phone again, but there just wasn't a signal.

Then he heard a sound which startled him. It was that woman – the one whose cries had caused him to take this accursed short-cut into limbo. She was sobbing, but Mike could not tell what direction the sobbing was coming from. The lamentations of the unseen woman started to echo, and they sounded quite sinister. The crying turned to laughter, and this really unnerved Mike. He had been raised by an auntie after his parents had died in an air crash when he was a child, and his aunt had been a Southern Baptist with immense faith. The faith had rubbed off onto young Mike, although in recent years he had lapsed somewhat and had even considered atheism, but he just felt that there was a higher intelligence in nature which was a source of good. He thought of his pious aunt, and how she had told him to always call upon God if he should ever find himself in trouble. 'Lord, get me out of this mess, please,' Mike whispered, and the thing obscured by the thick grey mist shrieked with laughter. Out of the depth of his memory, Mike Gracecouer grasped a hymn his beloved aunt used to sing - *What a Friend We Have in Jesus*. Mike did not have a singing voice by any stretch of the imagination, and yet this hymn came out beautifully, and the eerie laughter faded into shrieks.

All of a sudden, Mike was blinded by a bright light and a horn, and for a moment he thought it was some religious manifestation, but it was the headlights and horn of an oncoming car coming down Great Charlotte Street. He hopped out of the way in shock and felt the wind from the vehicle as it missed him by inches and screeched to a halt thirty feet down the road. The driver popped his head out the kerbside window and screamed profanities at Mike, but the American smiled, because hearing another human being after the inexplicable ordeal he had been through was music to his ears. He hurried to his friend's flat on Slater Street, and on the way he tried to call Emily on the Samsung and this time he was put through immediately. He told Emily he had just had a very strange experience, and that it had somehow rekindled his faith in God. 'Oh, I've got to hear this,' Emily laughed, but when she did hear of the strange incident on Back Lime Street, she was of the opinion that it had not been some trick of the Devil, but some sort of timeslip. Considering the reputation of the back street, it's possible that Emily is right, but how does one explain that strange crying woman who seems to have lured Mike into that disorienting and terrifying limbo? At the time of writing I am interviewing Richie, an air-conditioning engineer who worked on the roof of one of the shops that gives a perfect aerial view of Mitchell Place/Back Lime Street, and Richie told me how, in August 2009, he and his colleague Steve were having a lunch break on the roof when they happened to look down to see two very creepy men in skin-tight black suits and black balaclavas. These men were running up and down Back Lime Street at an incredible speed, moving about in a way that was reminiscent of the rapid jerky way the people used to walk in the early silent films. The figures crouched with bent backs as they darted about between wheelie bins, and when a car or a pedestrian came down the narrow street, the figures would run away and quickly take cover behind the bins. At one point, Richie's friend, Steve, coughed, and the faces of the bizarre-looking figures in black looked up at the engineers. Their faces were very pale and their eyes looked like black spots. The engineers were very unnerved by the weird strangely-attired men and were only too glad when they had fixed a faulty air conditioning unit so they could leave the roof. Until I can get more information on the uncanny duo in their black skin-tight costumes, it's probably pointless to speculate on their nature, origin and agenda, but the report of their peculiar activity on the paradoxically secluded backstreet in the heart of the bustling city centre seems to underline the alleyway's high incidence of strangeness.

Of course, Bold Street – which has been nicknamed Timeslip Central by some Forteans and researchers into the paranormal – remains the premier location for time disturbances in Liverpool, and I have looked at every conceivable angle as to why this should be the case. Earlier in this chapter I mentioned the Lyceum, a neoclassical Grade II listed building located at the foot of Bold Street. It was built in 1802, and the building was originally a gentlemen's club but later became Europe's first lending library. I have mooted whether the quartz elements in the material the Lyceum is made from could be acting like a giant electronic component (as quartz and many of the other elements in the makeup of the building are used in the fields of electronics), but recently, a reader of my books named Terry Long offered me a very novel suggestion regarding the possible source of the timeslips on Bold Street, and that is the presence of an underground stream that travels the length of the street. This stream used to be tapped by several wells on Bold Street, including the only extant one in Jeff's, a clothes shop at Number 80. The well was discovered beneath the shop when the owner of the premises, Jeff Pierce, was refurbishing his store. First he came across an old wartime air-raid shelter, and then he discovered a well that had been in use since the 17th century at least. The well has now been reconstructed and is used as a charity wishing well in Jeff's store. The stream that feeds the well travels the length of Bold Street and Church Street, and empties itself into the original "Pool" from which the city derived its name. The stream was once visible in some parts of the city centre until it was covered over by the authorities in 1725. Terry Long reminded me of the Bold Street stream and suggested that it could be some source of energy related to the unusual concentration of timeslips on the street. It would be interesting to see if dowsers can detect any energy flows on Bold Street. Some think that the Biblical passage about God asking Moses to 'smite the rock' to obtain water might have been an early reference to dowsing for water, and dowsing even predates the Bible, for the ancient Celts and Druids were said to use the divining rod, an implement that was probably the origin of the magician's wand. Later dowsers used a Y-shaped twig – holding the two ends with each hand – to detect water. The rod supposedly dips down or rises when the dowser walks over ground where this subterranean water is present. The most popular woods for dowsing rods are witch-hazel, hazel, peach and willow, but in modern times, dowsers have even used L-shaped lengths of wire cut from wire coat hangers with their shorter length inserted into empty ballpoint pen casings. Two of these L-shaped wire detectors are used by dowsers - one held in each hand - and when water is below, the lengths of wire will swing inwards towards one another and form a cross. No one knows how dowsing works, and some think it's all pseudoscientific nonsense, but even the military have dabbled in dowsing, and dowsers were even used in the Vietnam war to detect Vietcong tunnels. I would be very intrigued if dowsers picked up any energy flows from the underground stream on Bold Street and other places where timeslips seem to frequently occur.

As I was writing this book, a man named John Crawford emailed me to tell me of a very strange experience he and his family had on Bold Street on the afternoon of Wednesday 6 September 2017. John and his wife Jessica and their three children went shopping in the city centre, and Jessica noticed a new shop called Greenland, situated on the corner of Bold Street and Ropewalks Square. This would make the premises 110 Bold Street. The shop sign was a long rectangle of white plastic emblazoned with the word Greenland in dark green, and beneath this, Jessica Crawford thinks it said something along the lines of: 'Everything Natural for You and the Environment'. Jessica walked into Greenland, followed by her husband and children and noted the aroma of something akin to newly-mown grass. The floor was wooden and highly polished, and the counter to the left was of a matching wood. Behind this sat a man and a woman, both in their mid to late twenties. The store was large, about 900 square feet, according to Jessica's husband, and the walls were covered in shelves stocking all sorts of health products and on tables in the middle of the shop there were things like folding solar cells mounted on a type of garden parasol, and even some sort of small wind turbine which could be fitted to the roof of a house or onto a pole in a garden. John Craford and his two young male children went to look at all the ecological hardware, while Jessica and her 13-year-old daughter had a look at the health products and a counter called Organo Make Up. All Jessica bought was a 75.5g bottle of 100 curcumin capsules with bioprene and vitamins, and her daughter purchased a 7ml certified-organic volumising mascara. The curcumin capsules were produced by a company in Hamburg and the organic mascara was manufactured in West Grinstead, West Sussex. There was a sticker on the bottle of curcumin capsules that said "Greenland, 110 Bold St". The Crawford family had entered the store at about 1.50pm that afternoon, and left after about ten minutes and carried on shopping until they went to a café, and then returned to their home in Halewood. On the following day, John Crawford accompanied his neighbour Jake to town to get a few books for Jake's wife, as it was her birthday. The men called in at various bookshops, and then ended up on Bold Street, where John Crawford noticed something very strange indeed. The shop he and his wife and children had visited only yesterday had gone. In its place there was another shop which sold vintage clothes, and its interior bore no resemblance whatsoever to the shop called Greenland with all the organic health products, make up and ecological hardware. Jake told his neighbour the shop was probably further down Bold Street, and John became determined to find the place because he thought he was going mad. He went to the end of Bold Street, down by the Lyceum, and could not find any store that looked remotely like Greenland.

Jake asked him if it had perhaps been on the other side of the street, but John was adamant that it had been on the left side as he had gone down Bold Street. He telephoned his wife to tell her that the shop where she had bought the curcumin capsules had vanished into thin air, and Jessica said, 'Don't be daft, you've probably walked past it. It's on a corner, facing Minskys and that Italian Club café place.'

'I'm standing on that corner you're talking about now, and it is not there!' John shouted, and then apologised to his wife for raising his voice. 'Jake and I have been traipsing up and down Bold Street looking for the place,' John told her.

'Ask someone in one of the shops,' Jessica suggested, 'it might have closed down.'

'What?' asked her bemused husband, 'within twenty-four hours?'

'These are hard times John, businesses go to the wall fast nowadays,' Jessica told him.

So John asked in six different shops about the Greenland store. He asked someone in Rennies – they'd never heard of the place. He asked in a boutique – and got the same answer and a blank look. He visited two newsagents and a café, and he asked at the East Avenue Bakehouse – but no one had heard of a place named Greenland. John and Jake went to a pub on Renshaw Street, and John even mentioned the strange case of the vanishing shop to the barman, and he told John and his friend: 'Some strange things have happened like that before on that street,' and he then told the men about some of the many timeslips on that street over the years. John thought the barman was trying to say that Greenland had once existed on Bold Street, but Jake got the gist of what the barman was really hinting at – that Greenland *would* exist on that spot – at 110 Bold Street – at some future date. When Jake spelled this out to John Crawford, his friend returned a puzzled look and said: 'But the future hasn't happened yet, has it?'

Jake shrugged and said, 'I'm just a plumber, John; I'm not Stephen Hawking. I don't know anything about time.' John and his neighbour took another look at the place where Greenland had existed the day before, and then they returned home. Jessica drove to Bold Street on the following Saturday to clear the mystery up – and discovered that John had been right – the store was nowhere to be seen. She contacted me and I told her about the many timeslips on Bold Street, and I asked her if she had retained a receipt for the purchases made at the shop, but she couldn't find the slip or the plain brown paper bag the items had been placed in after the sale. Furthermore, the products had been purchased with cash. Had a credit card been used, I could have analysed the transaction on a bank statement. I did look at the products and I saw the label on the bottle of curcumin capsules that bore the name and address of the store, but beyond that, I could not prove that the products had been made in the future. They had been made by firms that were currently in existence.

If you should ever find yourself in a suspected timeslip on Bold Street, and if you have your mobile phone at hand, please take a photograph of the timeslipped location. John and Jessica Crawford wish they had taken snaps of the Greenland store, because the mystery continues to tantalize them, but of course, they never expected the place to vanish after they had visited it that September afternoon.

Some timeslips are, without a doubt, a warning from the future. We are led to believe that if something is going to happen, then there's nothing that can be done to prevent it from taking place, but I don't think this nihilistic view is valid. A case in point is the timeslip account related to me by a Liverpool woman named Maude, who is now in her eighties. In 1952, Maude was a beautiful 20-year-old girl who worked at a tobacconist shop in West Derby. One day at the shop, Brian, a 25-year-old customer came in to buy cigars for his uncle's birthday, and cheekily asked Maude out. She said no, but he kept coming into the shop to see her, and eventually she went out on a date with him. Months later the couple became engaged and in the summer they went camping in Wales at the Snowdon Forest caravan campsite, a mile north of Beddgelert. Maude and Brian's romance really blossomed in the Welsh tranquillity of such a beautiful picture postcard setting with breathtaking mountain views, clean healthy air, and a sweeping forest to explore. The campsite manager warned the lovebirds as they set out for the forest on a sunny August morning that they should make sure they knew their way back, as some people had become lost in the denser areas of the forest. Brian laughed at the warning. He said he had a good sense of direction, and he set out with Maude, and sure enough, the couple lost their bearings. 'There should be a path up here to Snowdon,' Brian said, squinting at the harsh midday sunlight filtering through the trees.

'Didn't he call it the Rhyd Ddu Path?' Maude asked, recalling the campsite manager's directions from earlier in the morning.

'Yeah, but where is it?' Brian pondered, and he walked on with Maude, holding her hand as they made their way from the forest into a clearing of knee-deep ferns. Maude noticed the strange castle first; three of its turrets and its keep were visible above the treetops about 500 feet away.

'What castle's that?' she asked Brian, who shrugged.

'Can you see that flag?' he asked, pointing to the black flag rippling in the breeze above one of the turrets. It looked as if it had a white cross on it.

'Love old castles,' said Maude, and she swung the hand that held Brian's hand as they walked through the ferns. 'They're so romantic, castles,' she told him, 'all damsels in distress and knights in shining armour and all that.'

The young couple eventually left the clearing and came to a road where they had a much clearer view of the castle. The flag they had seen earlier looked very odd, and Maude thought there was something ominous about it. It was black with a white cross – in the same design as St George's Cross – only this black flag's white cross had a red inner cross. Something about the design - the red white and black - made Brian think of the Nazi Party. The couple then saw that the turrets of grey blocks of stone had black domes at the top, and protruding from these domes were huge gun barrels. Maude gasped, stumbled backwards, and pointed to a yellow sign fixed to the wall of the castle with studs about twenty feet away. This sign warned: 'LOITERERS WILL BE SHOT'.

'What type of castle is this?' Brian asked, 'Is it a prison?'

'I don't know – let's get out of here!' Maude pulled

her boyfriend's hand and walked back to the wood, but Brian stopped after a few feet and turned around to take another look at the strange grim fortress.

'Brian! Look!' Maude pointed to something above.

A dark red globe with lights and a barrel protruding from it came slowly hovering down from the top of the curtain wall of the fort, and a harsh amplified voice from it blared: 'Stay where you are! Do not run or you will be shot!'

Maude screamed as Brian ran off, pulling her with him, and she fell over. Maude heard a rapid succession of cracks and three white holes appeared in the tree trunk to her right as the outer bark was blown away to reveal splintered sapwood.

Maude and Brian let go of one another and crawled through the ferns as more bullets flew around them, and Maude expected to be shot dead at any moment, but she somehow made it across the field of ferns, and her bare knees were scratched and bleeding from rubbing against the stones in the field. When she reached the cover of the trees, she cried out in agony as she touched her bloody kneecap. The couple looked back – and saw that the castle and that terrifying floating globe had vanished. Brian and Maude became lost, and eventually asked an elderly sheep farmer for directions to the camp site. Brian told the farmer what had happened and the old man seemed to know something by the way he reacted, and he told the couple to keep well away from that field – but he did not specify why they should avoid it.

When Maude and Brian returned to the campsite, they told the manager about the castle with guns on its towers and the deadly flying red sphere which had fired at them and he said there was no castle in the area. The older assistant of the manager, a man named Mr Thomas, then said a strange thing. He remarked, rather enigmatically, 'I've heard about that ghost castle – that's what they call it, but I don't think it's a ghost of the past.'

'What are you talking about?' the manager asked him in a condescending manner, and smiled at the young couple, but Brian and Maude did not find the assistant's remarks funny. They were intrigued by them.

'Ghost castle?' said Brian, looking at the assistant.

The manager's assistant nodded. 'There's a concentration camp about twenty miles east of here at Frongoch. You won't find that in the tourist guides, though.'

'That was an internment camp, not a concentration camp,' the campsite manager cut in sharply.

'All the same thing chief,' said the adjunct, and then he told Brian and Maude: 'They kept German prisoners of war in there in the first lot – World War One like, and then they put eighteen hundred Irishmen in there because of the Easter Rising. Some horror stories in that place, there was.'

'What has all this got to do with the castle these people think they saw?' the manager asked with a lopsided smile and raised eyebrows.

The assistant manager lit a cigarette. He looked down at the ground as he gave his reply. 'They say history repeats itself, and a lot of people have seen that castle the young 'uns speak of. Things come around again, 'specially bad things. What has been, may be.'

'You think they'll build concentration camps again –

but for whom?' Maude asked, catching the man's drift.

'Anyway, let's forget all this nonsense,' said the campsite manager. 'We're having a singalong tonight at supper.'

Just what did Maude and Brian see that summer's day in 1952? Was it a futuristic prison glimpsed via some shift in time – or, as the assistant campsite manager suggested, was it a future concentration camp? Was the globular 'sentry which fired upon Brian and Maude some type of armed drone? Another thing: was the black flag flying over that castle with its white and red cross some future symbol of a fascist England? Across Europe there has been a steady rise of Neo-Nazism, possibly fuelled by recessions and the unprecedented amount of immigrants coming into Europe because of the various tragic civil wars going on. Every now and then the politicians ask the peoples of the countries who make up the United Kingdom if they would like to leave the Union, the most notable case being the politicians asking the people of Scotland if they would like to leave the UK and become an independent sovereign state. If Scotland and Wales leave the Union, the UK will be no more, and the familiar Union Jack would be consigned to the dustbin of history, with the simple St George's Cross taking its place for the English. Could the strange flag seen by Brian and Maude in the 1952 timeslip be a future glimpse of England's political fate? If so, why was the white in that flag replaced with the colour black? Is it merely a new design, or could it have associations with some sinister dominant political party of the future – perhaps even a totalitarian dictatorship. These are politically unstable times and I have the unsettling feeling we'll be seeing more of this flag in our lifetimes, and I also believe we will soon see the dawn of a dynasty of technocratic dictators who will indoctrinate and enslave the people of Britain.

In 1969, an apparent timeslip seems to have revealed a future religious movement to three humble men in Liverpool. I interviewed the men concerned separately several times and all of their versions of the strange incident which follows were in complete agreement. Let me start this strange story by telling you that there was an Englishman, a Scotsman and an Irishman, but this is no retro joke. The Englishman was a respected 65-year-old bricklayer from Old Swan named Jack Bullington, the Scotsman was 44-year-old plasterer Doug McCray (who was then living in Huyton) and the Irishman was 60-year-old painter Liam Murphy, born in Cork but raised in the Kensington area of Liverpool from the age of five. The three men left a building site on the campus of Liverpool University that cold spring day in 1969 and went in search of a pie and a pint for lunch. Murphy noticed the strange building first and remarked, 'Will you look at that? They're bleedin' throwin' them up! That wasn't there yesterday!'

Jack pulled on his rolled-up ciggy, narrowed his eyes, and he agreed that the tall tapering ivory building had not been there yesterday. He pointed at the Metropolitan Cathedral (which had opened two years back) to the right of the mystery obelisk and calculated: 'That building must be at the back of the convent on Mount Pleasant.'

'Nah, it's down by the Adelphi that,' was Murphy's opinion.

'No, you're way out Murphy,' said Jack, exhaling smoke, 'it's behind the convent, that!'

Doug McCray had a constructive suggestion; 'Let's go and have a decko, then go to the Beehive for a bevy. If Murphy's right, you have to buy him a pint, but if you're right, Jack, he has to get you a pint.'

'Haven't you got an opinion, McCray?' asked Murphy, 'Or are you scared you'll have to get someone a drink if you're wrong?'

The workmen walked in the direction of the new building, and upon reaching Mount Pleasant, they were intrigued to see a huge archway in the buildings facing the Irish Centre, and this gave access to the unknown structure.

'I *told* you it was behind the convent, Murphy, you owe me a pint,' said a gleeful Jack.

'Don't talk about the demon drink so near to the convent, Jack,' said Murphy with one raised eyebrow, 'you'll have no luck.'

'Hey, listen,' said Doug McCray, angling his head and looking down at the roadway leading into the new building. The trio heard strange chanting. They entered a massive hall which had the huge image of a circular labyrinth laid out in the polished stones of the floor, and at the centre of the maze there stood a giant oak tree, which caused Jack to swear and say: 'I've seen everything now!'

Liam Murphy suggested leaving the place, saying, 'There's somethin' heathen about this – somethin' odd; let's cut, lads.'

'Oh be quiet Murphy you superstitious fool!' said McCray, walking on as the other two slowed down.

The air was heavy with sweet-smelling incense, and

the domed ceiling had constellations of blue and white lights set into it like a planetarium depicting constellations. The three men walked under the indoor tree and passed into a chamber of rainbow light from some amazing stained glass windows featuring nature scenes, flowers, mushrooms, and the sun and moon – and also something Doug McCray - the intellectual of the trio - quickly recognised: the double helix of DNA.

'What does all this mean?' the Scotsman asked, his eyes full of wonder and multicoloured light.

Then the three curious workers saw them at the other end of the chamber – rows of men and women in long white hooded robes, their eyes closed as they said unfamiliar prayers about Mother Nature. A childlike voice boomed behind the trinity, and they got the shocks of their lives. A figure with a sinister wooden mask depicting intricately carved leaves stood in a pulpit inscribed with runic symbols and adorned with carvings of squirrels, acorns and birds. The masked sermoniser spoke of "The Church of Mother Earth" and communion with a "Fountain of Eternal Life" as well as reincarnation and sacred trees. The three workmen stood transfixed by the unusual sermon – and then the person in the pulpit removed the wooden mask to reveal she was a beautiful young elfin-faced woman.

At this point, the Scotsman Doug McCray experienced a state of intense ecstasy – what some psychologists describe as a 'plateau experience' or peak experience. He had never felt so intensely happy in his life, and this state of euphoria made McCray feel as if he had somehow transcended himself. It was pure rapture, an ecstatic sense of immense enlightenment, and he felt as if he belonged with the people of this unusual cathedral as he stood there bathed in an ethereal spectrum of light. McCray felt as if he was about to cry tears of happiness.

'What is this damned place?' Jack asked, 'Where's the cross? This is not the house of *my* God!' he yelled - and then suddenly everything started to slowly fade away, and Doug McCray screamed 'No!' and he attacked Jack, bringing his large sledgehammer fists down on his workmate's head and shoulders and arms, and Murphy threw himself into the affray as the rainbow lights of the beautifully stained windows died to a sombre greyness. The unearthly cathedral of some unknown religion was gone; the walls, the stained glass, the robed figures and the beautifully carved pulpit – all gone now.

The three fighting men found themselves surrounded by the nuns of the Notre Dame Convent on Hope Street.

'Break it up!' Murphy hollered at his fighting friends, and he turned to the bemused Mother Superior and said, 'Forgive them, please!'

McCray fell onto his knees, his nose bloodied, and he was whimpering like a child now. Jack, with his hair in disarray, crouched down and shook the Scot gently by his shoulders and asked, 'What got into you, you stupid Scotch git?'

'Jack! Will you mind your language?' Murphy reprimanded him and tutted as he looked at the nuns.

'They were my people,' sobbed Doug McCray, 'for once in my life I *belonged* - I actually felt as if I belonged to them.'

'Come on Doug, we're making a show of ourselves,

in front of these holy ladies too,' said Jack, and he helped Doug up and one of the angelic-faced nuns said to Doug, 'Come and have a whiskey, you'll feel better.'

Doug thought it was so funny, a nun offering him a drink, and he laughed and said, 'Ah, thank you sister, I think you've just converted me.' An elderly nun later told the three men that the phantom building had been seen a few times over the years and the builders were very surprised at the open-mindedness of the nun, for she told them: 'That phantom building and its strangely robed figures is, in my humble opinion, not a trick of the Devil. I think it's some future religion based on Mother Nature – a Druid cathedral even.'

Some local timeslips in my files have persisted for hours, and some have lasted for seconds. In 2014 a terminally-ill man named Russell asked a nurse at the hospital he was confined in if she could get in touch with me because he had an incredible story to tell and wanted to communicate it to me before it was too late. The nurse emailed me and I went to see Russell. The basic gist of Russell's story was that in 1997, he was aged fifty and was suffering from severe depression. He'd run up gambling debts of thousands of pounds and had even stolen from friends and family members to finance his gambling addiction. Now he had also started to seek refuge from his problems in drink, and his partner of many years, a very patient and loving man named Robert, had walked out on him after putting up with Russell's deplorable behaviour for years. Russell was a very down-to-earth and practical man who was not given to entertaining fancy thoughts about the paranormal and time travel – he lived on a day to day existence in a nitty-gritty world of trying to find the next few quid to put a bet on. One Saturday, Russell visited a second-hand shop and sold a beautiful semi-acoustic guitar Robert had bought for him, and he had received £25 in return. Fifteen pounds was squandered immediately on several bets at the bookies and the rest went on drink at a pub on Renshaw Street, where Russell even managed to cadge a few drinks off people after coming out with a cock and bull story about a pickpocket on a bus taking his wallet. The barman at the pub finally barred Russell and called him a parasite, and Russell ended up staggering down Renshaw Street in a Biblical downpour. He had never seen rain like it, and he was soaked to the bone in minutes. He bumped into an old friend named Harry whilst sheltering from the rain at the covered entrance to Lewis's – a spot known as Lewis's Corner, where blind dates often agree to meet (below the statue of Dickie Lewis). 'Hey Harry, could you possibly lend me fifty quid till I get paid at the end of this month?' Russell asked his old friend, but Harry swore at him and said, 'Get a job, benefit head! You think the world owes you a living you lazy bastard!'

And as Harry walked on, Russell started to cry, and he slid down the jamb of the doorway and sat there for a while. An old woman asked Russell if he was okay, and he tried to smile and nodded, and somehow he got to his feet and walked up Mount Pleasant on the right side. Russell could hardly see because of the rain and the tears in his eyes, and he ended up going into Roscoe Gardens at the back of the Grand Central building. These gardens were once a Unitarian Churchyard from 1811-1899, and buried there is one

William Roscoe, the slave abolitionist and veritable Renaissance man of art and literature. In the centre of Roscoe Gardens there stands a domed memorial supported by eight Tuscan columns on a base of three steps, and this Grade II-listed monument was where Russell sought refuge from the unrelenting rain. He was not a religious man, but Russell cried out, 'Oh Lord, please turn my life around will you? Please give me another chance! Please!'

A sudden silence greeted the distressed man, and he realised that the rain had stopped, and he felt the wonderful heat and harsh sunlight of a summer's day. He walked out of the sunny gardens and found himself on a Mount Pleasant that had undergone some change. The multi-storey car park was gone. He saw the old Mardi Gras nightclub, and thought that strange because it had long been demolished. With squelching shoes and not a penny in his pocket, Russell walked down Mount Pleasant and saw that it looked as if it was in the 1960s. The buildings looked black with soot and air pollution unlike the modern sandblasted ones of 1997. All of the old shops he had known in his younger days were there. He looked in a jeweller's window and the price tag on an Omega watch was in pre-decimal. Russell went into a newsagent and took a look at the date on the front of the *Daily Mirror*: Wednesday, July 10, 1963.

'It's no good that swimming with your clothes on you know?' quipped the newsagent behind the counter, looking at a drenched Russell.

Russell wore a huge smile, because he realised that he had somehow travelled back in time some thirty-four years. He realised that the Beatles were still going, that President Kennedy was still alive – and, more importantly, Russell realised with immense joy that his mother and father were alive and well – but then he thought: 'What about my younger self?' and after a quick mental calculation he determined that, being born in 1947, he would now be sweet sixteen. What would happen if he met himself?

'How did you get like that?' the newsagent asked with a smile, 'we haven't had a drop of rain for weeks.'

'Oh, you'd never believe me,' replied Russell, 'not in a million years.'

The newsagent was aged about thirty-five and he was named Gerald, and Russell cheekily asked him if he happened to have a towel, as he was soaked to the skin. Gerald smiled, and said, 'Come through here.' He lifted a flap in the counter and Russell said, 'Ah, nice one, whatever your name is.'

'Gerald,' said the newsagent, 'now tell me, how did you get so wet?'

Gerald, like Russell, was also gay, but in 1963 it was an offence to be of that 'sexual persuasion' so Gerald had to be careful about showing his true sexuality off, whereas Russell had come out when he was twenty-five to his mother, who had nonchalantly told him, 'I had an idea love – put the kettle on and we'll have some tea and jammie dodgers.'

Russell moved in with Gerald, who even had a platonic girlfriend named June, and she was not too pleased with the strange new lodger. When Russell got drunk he would find himself slipping up and mentioning future events and even the internet, and eventually June left Gerald and the romance between the newsagent and the compulsive gambler from 1997 blossomed. The only person who knew they were a couple was a (heterosexual) Quaker named Mark, who said that he believed society should be more tolerant towards 'deviants' such as Russell and Gerald. The two men visited the Cavern Club on Mathew Street and enjoyed the Merseybeat scene, and Russell had a morbid fear of waking up one morning back in 1997, but for over a year he stayed in the Liverpool of the early 1960s and had a ball. Gerald never believed his partner was from the future and thought he was hiding his real past from him for some shady reason, and so Russell took him to Brodie Avenue in Allerton to show him the house where his parents – and his younger self – lived, but Russell never had the guts to contact his mother and father or the younger version of himself in case he caused some far-reaching ramifications that would burst this bubble and send him back to dreary 1997. When President Kennedy was assassinated in November of that year, Gerald was shocked, because Russell had told him the assassination would happen for months. Even then, Gerald said that the prediction could still have been just a lucky guess or a coincidence. Russell gave up trying to convince his partner in the end and started to enjoy his new life in another era. He worked in the newsagents and started to control his gambling compulsion. By the spring of 1964, the gambling and drinking were under control. On the Thursday evening of 3 September 1964, at around 11.20pm, Gerald was walking home from a night out at the Philharmonic pub with Russell, and as they reached the corner of Leece Street and Renshaw Street, Russell realised that Gerald was no longer with him. And then he noticed the modern Mitsubishi Shogun Estate car on the road to his left, and he went cold. He looked about, and felt a suffocating sense of fear welling up in his lungs. 'Gerry?' he gasped in a choked-up voice, 'Where are you?' and then he yelled, 'No! No!'

Another car of the 1990s passed with a thumping bass and Russell swore at it. He stood there as bemused passers-by looked on, and he squeezed his eyes shut and tried to will himself back to that beautiful world of 1964 and Gerald, but it was no use – the dream was over.

Russell returned to his home and found it had been boarded up. He had been missing for a year and everyone thought he had either left Liverpool or died somewhere. Russell went to stay with his cousin and told him the incredible story about living in the past, and he even showed him a wallet full of pre-decimal coins and notes, but his cousin just cast a very concerned look at Russell and said he should go and see a doctor.

Russell tried to trace Gerald, knowing very well that he'd been thirty-five 35 years ago – which would make his present age seventy, but he didn't give a damn because he loved him. Russell's cousin promised he'd ask a friend who was into genealogy to trace Gerald, and this friend finally did – and discovered that Gerald had died from a brain haemorrhage in the late 1970s. He'd been cremated, so there wasn't even a grave where Russell could place any flowers.

Shortly after telling me this incredible story, Russell received the Last Rites in his hospital bed and quietly died.

I have no reason to disbelieve Russell's intriguing

story, and I have checked with people who knew him and they have all confirmed that Russell did indeed go missing for a year, from 1997 to September 1998, and during that time no one saw him anywhere in Liverpool. By what mechanism did a depressed and drunken man sheltering under a memorial in Roscoe Gardens in 1997 become transported to the Liverpool of the Swinging Sixties? Was the act of retrograde motion backwards through time fuelled by Russell's desperate longing for a new life perhaps? Or was it something to do with Russell's location? Was time 'weak' in that area – I really am grasping at theoretical straws now. What does seem clear is that a person might be able to break through the time barrier much easier than the test pilots of old who had a hard time breaking through the sound barrier; why, it would seem to be as simple as walking from A to B, as the final story in this chapter hints.

At a prestigious grammar school in Liverpool in 1960, a science teacher, Mr Davenport (a dead ringer for the late actor Patrick McGoohan), battered the blackboard with his cane in an effort to break up the scrum of pupils at the rear of his class. It didn't work and so he went to see what was holding the attention of the boys. It was some sort of cubic puzzle with multicoloured squares. Davenport immediately confiscated it and 14-year-old Clifford Cromwell objected because it was his puzzle. 'Get back to your place and see me at the end of the lesson, Cromwell!' barked Davenport. After the lesson on the Laws of Thermodynamics, the class poured out of the room and headed for the playground, but Clifford went to Davenport, who picked up the strange puzzle and asked him: 'Where did you get this?' Clifford said he'd found it but the teacher, who seemed fascinated by the toy, said 'Don't believe you!'

Clifford stood in silence, and Davenport promised: 'No playtime unless you tell the truth.'

At last the boy said: 'A girl gave it to me.'

'What girl?' the teacher asked.

'A girl named Vicky,' Clifford replied, and blushed.

'And where did Vicky get this from?' Davenport tossed the plastic cube into the air and then swiped it with his other hand.

'I – I don't know, sir,' said Clifford.

Davenport kept the intriguing puzzle and took it to the staffroom, where the other teachers were as transfixed by the toy as him. The math teacher Mr Hall, said that the puzzle would make an excellent educational toy to teach pupils about spatial relationships, and asked Davenport if he could borrow it, but the haughty science teacher said: 'No, get your own educational aids Mr Hall.'

A week later, Davenport was giving a lesson about astronomy when a pupil asked him if humans would ever land on the Moon. 'Perhaps,' answered Davenport, 'but there's six foot of dust on the Moon and as the Astronomer Royal said, all this talk of space travel is utter bilge. It would simply cost too much – it would require an astronomical sum to put a man on the Moon!'

'We won't do it but the Americans will,' said Cromwell, and the class fell silent.

Davenport turned red with rage. 'That's not very patriotic, Cromwell,' Davenport said, and glared at him, adding: 'You should never praise any country but your own. And anyway, what do *you* know about space travel anyway?'

'I know more than you,' Cromwell muttered, and Davenport ran to his desk and dragged him by the collar to the front of the class, where he placed chalk in the frightened boy's hand and announced: 'Lend me your ears! And your eyes! Professor Cromwell will now deliver a lesson on space travel!'

The pupils giggled, but then Cromwell picked up the globe of the earth and the Dunlop tennis ball the teacher had used to represent the Moon, and he talked of escape velocities, orbits, and the Apollo Space Program, and upon the blackboard he drew the huge Saturn Five rocket that was needed to take the astronauts to the Moon, but Davenport told him to sit down. The class groaned and a pupil named Welsh said, 'Sir, please let Clifford continue his lecture, it's jolly well interesting.'

'No!' cried Davenport, and to Welsh he cried, 'Get out! Stand in the corridor you insolent little upstart!'

Clifford Cromwell left the school months later because his family moved to Wales, but in 1990, the 44-year-old Cromwell bumped into Davenport, then aged 70, on holiday in Spain. By then the Moon Landings were history, and that puzzle – the Rubik's Cube – invented in 1974 – was well-known, so how had Cromwell possessed one back in 1960? Cromwell told the retired teacher he used to meet a girl named Vicky, who said she was from 1995. This girl said she had found a way to travel to and from Clifford's time period by using her father's invention, which involved five wire coat hangers, a railway set transformer, a sheet of foil and parts of an electric fire. 'Tell me